Storied Land

Storied Land

*Community and Memory
in Monterey*

John Walton

UNIVERSITY OF CALIFORNIA PRESS
Berkeley   Los Angeles   London

University of California Press
Berkeley and Los Angeles, California

University of California Press, Ltd.
London, England

First paperback printing 2003

Library of Congress Cataloging-in-Publication Data

Walton, John, 1937–.
    Storied land : community and memory in
  Monterey / John Walton.
        p.   cm.
    Includes bibliographical references (p.   ) and
  index.
      ISBN 0-520-22723-9 (pbk : alk. paper)
      1. Monterey (Calif.)—History.   2. Monterey
  (Calif.)—Social conditions.   I. Title.

F869.M7 W35   2001
979.4'76—dc21   00-047519

Manufactured in the United States of America

12   11   10   09   08   07   06   05   04   03
10   9   8   7   6   5   4   3   2   1

The paper used in this publication meets the minimum
requirements of ANSI/NISO Z39.48-1992 (R 1997)
(*Permanence of Paper*). ⊚

For my brothers, Craig and Lar, and in memory of our parents

I will tell you something about stories,
They aren't just entertainment
Don't be fooled
They are all we have, you see,
all we have to fight off
illness and death

You don't have anything
if you don't have the stories

Leslie Marmon Silko, *Ceremony*

Contents

Tables and Figures

TABLES

FIGURES

Preface

In the Falls Road community of West Belfast, one of the many striking political murals that decorate the exterior walls of homes and shops proclaims, "History is written by the winner." For Catholic residents of this beleaguered neighborhood, the message is unambiguous. Although Northern Ireland and its Catholic Republican minority have suffered a long history of injustice under English rule, their story has not been told. On the contrary, the history of their oppression has been silenced, absorbed into a triumphal narrative of efficacious colonial governance. British power controls the historical record while Irish Republican dissent is confined to street slogans.

At first glance, the ability of winners to dominate recorded history seems axiomatic. Significant precolonial achievements and postcolonial contributions of Native Americans to the history of the United States have been excluded from the official transcript, perhaps to conceal a shameful record of mistreatment. African-American history has also been subsumed by the majority's narrative. Thomas Jefferson's illegitimate interracial family life, for example, has been acknowledged only after DNA evidence has offered proof of it. And the Irish Republican Army is still portrayed in the international media as a gang of terrorist bombers despite ample evidence of violence initiated by the police, army, and Protestant paramilitaries.

Yet, when we begin to explore these cases, questions about who writes history, when, and with what effect become complex, nuanced, ambivalent. History is more inclusive than some well-intentioned critics allow. Native Americans left hide paintings recording their annual events cycles and oral testimony about their encounters with invading whites. Architectural and photographic evidence showing the "back of the big house" reveals domestic relations in the adjoining households of plantation slaves and masters.[1] Alternative histories are part of the record or are capable of recovery.

The murals of West Belfast are high political art reproduced around the world in documentary accounts of the political conflict.[2] Visitors to "The Falls" are treated to guided tours of the community along with a provocative history of "the troubles." The oppositional story told in mural art is elaborated in film, drama, fiction, and journalism. Indeed, there is an extensive history of the Irish Republican movement, written when the movement was a loser and rewritten of late as all sides have become winners in the peace process. So history is written from various standpoints in an unfolding process that, at any given moment, may have clear winners and losers but that also changes in ways that rearrange author and actor positions. Not only that. Oppositional narratives may influence the process of historical change. Mural art, and the larger body of cultural production of which it is a part, motivates, energizes, publicizes, and legitimizes political change. The very aphorism "history is written by the winner" has more than one meaning. We read it as irony rather than immutable fact. It says, "our history has been suppressed in the political struggle," but it also says "we protest that fact and mean to redress it."

In fact, of course, history is written by all sorts of people and institutions with wide-ranging results. Who we are, as a community, a nation, a people, is a vigorously debated question—an unfolding negotiation encompassing much of what we know as culture. In this dialogue, "history" has two complementary meanings. We use it to designate both history as a set of events and history as the story of those events. "In vernacular use, history means both the facts of the matter and a narrative of those facts, both 'what happened' and 'that which is said to have happened.'"[3] This distinction helps to clarify the problems of historical interpretation alluded to above (e.g., British vs. Irish versions of events) because it recognizes the relationship, the overlap and the difference, between historical process and narrative. It allows us to compare narratives (e.g., Native American and U.S. colonial stories) with respect to how they square with the historical process, the facts insofar as we know them. Equally important, the distinction allows us to examine the historical conditions in which narratives are produced: how the stories of history are constructed by social groups and institutions; why they differ across social groups and over time; what conditions shape the struggle over history; who has the power to create a dominant narrative or the resourcefulness to challenge traditional interpretations, to make history. These are the inviting questions explored in these pages.

But this is also a history (in the first sense) of California, of the many decisive events shaping California society and culture that took place in Monterey, and of the distinctive local world that grew up on the Monterey Peninsula from its establishment as the Spanish colonial capital in 1770 to its modern florescence as a service economy based on education, marine science, and tourism. The greater part of this book provides a new account of what happened in Monterey over the last two hundred thirty years: what happened to the Ohlone Indians who occupied the region before the arrival of Franciscan missionaries and Spanish soldiers; what happened to the mixed-race Californios who created a distinct society and a small revolution in the early nineteenth century; what happened to their "paisano" descendants who struggled for a place on the land invaded by American soldiers and squatters; what happened to the Chinese immigrant workers who cleared the land and fished the bay; and what happened to their successors, the Sicilian fishermen and cannery women who created an industry and the materials for a legend of Cannery Row.

My purpose is twofold: to recover the experiences of these people from their archival obscurity and to explain how and why their stories were silenced in the more powerful and selective narratives of major institutional actors during successive historical periods, that is, what went into the dominant narratives, what was left out, and how the principles and politics of narrative construction changed over time. We shall recover, for example, the story of Jeronimo, Altarsiano, Proto, and Albana, Indian ranch hands who petitioned government in 1843, claiming that a well-connected landlord abused workers, treating them as servants rather than as Indians with rights guaranteed in law by the reforms introduced by the liberal Mexican state. That Indians understood their rights as citizens and acted collectively to ensure those rights needs to be restored to its proper place in the historical record. But it also needs to be employed as a lens for critical reflection on the dominant narratives of the period that silenced such evidence, the motives behind such omissions, the interests they served, and their influence on subsequent understandings of history.

In the late nineteenth century, the Southern Pacific Railroad built the extravagant Hotel Del Monte in Monterey, billing it as "America's most luxurious seaside resort." Presidents, tycoons, and celebrities visited the Del Monte, adding to its much-publicized reputation and its associated purpose of selling extensive local real estate controlled by the railroad. The hotel's hundreds of rooms and extensive grounds required a large labor force of white managers, bellboys, and chambermaids and Chinese cooks, waiters, and gardeners. Evidently the hotel's public hubris was belied by internal strife. Late one evening in April 1887, an arson fire destroyed all of the Del Monte's physical structure and much of its conceit. The arson was clearly an inside job. Although the crime was never solved, all the clues pointed to a conspiracy of resentful employees. Their story was never told. But today we can reconstruct that story from other aspects of the record. We can document discriminatory treatment of Chinese employees, upper-class arrogance visited on working people, and the tactics of resistance they adopted in related situations. We can begin to tell their story and to explain how it was obscured in the dominant narratives of the time.

Books about California are inevitably also books about the California story (in the second sense of history). Virtually all the classical works on California history have dealt explicitly with the state's vaunted reputation, its manufactured image—with the social construction of California. It is the Golden State, the land of sunshine, new beginnings, innovation, the good life. The name California derives from a sixteenth-century myth. Mythmakers have been at work on the subject ever since. California's best writers have tried to explain this conspicuous penchant for narrative production. Carey McWilliams labeled California "the great exception" among states,[4] a place that grew so rapidly and self-consciously that observers could witness history being produced by commercial interests for purposes of profit. The "cult of the mission," for example, he traced to realtors in search of a romantic past that would help sell land. In his evocatively titled book *Inventing the Dream*, Kevin Starr describes a new population "caught in the throes of a rapidly expanding American present [that] wanted some emotional and imaginative connection to the Southern California past" and the rapid production of stories "which attested to the need in Californians to shore up a sense of present identity by searching out a useable historical myth."[5] Here we have two theories of how and why historical narratives are socially constructed—the McWilliams account based on commercial promotion and the Starr explanation premised on a need for identity. We shall encounter others, consider them in light of evidence from the Monterey case, and in the end develop another explanation that grows out of this inquiry.

California may be extraordinary, but it is far from unique in its capacity to generate distinct social constructions of history. Indeed, the phenomenon is universal, the source of commonplace observations about sanitized history (the founding fathers neither tell lies nor sleep with their servants), commodified history (Disney versions of the Civil War), and revisionist history (a new appreciation of the Native American experience). Generally, we recognize that histories are political in the sense of being formulated and propagated in nations, communities, and schools governed by some negotiated consensus. Memories are social, fashioned and presented to us by groups. A great deal of social theory and research has been devoted to explaining how the collective memory is produced, how history is socially constructed. Some see in this process a controlling role of powerful interests and dominant ideologies, while others see a plurality of group-determined perspectives. These theories have some merit. But this study argues for a very different interpretation. The Monterey case provides a microcosm for developing a new explanation of how public history is constructed in concrete situations.

History is socially constructed in a process of collective action. Action is situated within constraining social structures: populations, economic arrangements, political systems. Collective action is an expression of group purposes; to settle a continent, build a community, worship God or profit, enjoy life, and commemorate these experiences in historical objects (books, buildings, monuments, art). History is not simply a record of these events, it is a justification for them. Public history is created in collective action that takes place in the present and projects the future. Social groups with different agendas and unequal power compete to influence or control the public memory. Monuments are built by those with the resources to build them in order to proclaim, not primarily what happened in the past, but who we are now as a result of how we understand the past and what we propose to be in the future. Historical preservation is typically the result of schemes to redesign the environment for new uses. Architectural fashion re-creates an imagined past for present and future consumption. Academic history, which is but one of a variety of sites for the production of public history, represents the past according to changing intellectual fashion and collegial repute now. None of this invalidates the truthfulness of history. On the contrary, it illuminates the social process in which history is constructed, used, and continuously evaluated.

In *Through the Looking-Glass*, the White Queen says to Alice, "[I]t's a poor sort of memory that works only backwards." Our collective memory has the Queen's "great advantage" of a memory that works both ways. History is simultaneously a process of social production that looks backward at "what happened" and forward at the importance for the future of "what is said to have happened." History in both senses is sometimes a fiercely contested process, in important part because it is about more than just the past. It is social, partisan, imperfectly understood, and yet capable of steady improvement according to evolving standards of consensual truth. In the end, of course, there is no history of "what happened" independent of "what is said to have happened." History can only be understood reflexively through the interplay of process and narrative.

I have arrived at the ideas expressed in these paragraphs and those that follow through an extended period of fieldwork and archival research and with lots of help. The problem of how groups construct their history and how those narratives shape their action arose in the course of research and writing an earlier book, *Western Times and Water Wars: State, Culture, and Rebellion in California*. In my experience, at least, one project's answers lead to the next one's questions. My sense of what constitutes a research question owes much to a (small *c*) catholic upbringing in empirical sociology, subsequent conversion to social and cultural history, and their combination in the resurgent historical sociology of the last twenty-five years. My sensibility and method were shaped foremost by the work of E. P. Thompson. Recently, a number of authors have formulated the problem of collective memory in ways that have advanced my understanding, notably Michel-Rolf Trouillot, Richard Maddox, James Scott, Marshall Sahlins, Richard Price, James Fentress and Chris Wickham, Eric Hobsbawn and Terrance Ranger, Timothy Breen, Yael Zerubavel, James Gregory, Alan Taylor, and Richard White. Fellow sociologists Howard Becker and Charles Ragen have taught me how to think about the relationship between theory and evidence.

A variety of individuals and institutions made this work possible in very concrete ways. I trust the long list will not detract from the debt I owe each one. The following persons and institutions provided access to research materials and protected spaces for work: the Bancroft Library (University of California, Berkeley); Susan Klusmire, Dorothy Sallee, and Colton Hall Museum (Monterey); The Huntington Library (San Marino);

Rosalie Ferrante and the Monterey Fishermen's Historical Association; Joe Johnson, Dennis Copeland, and the staff at the Monterey Public Library; the Monterey History and Art Association; Tim Thomas and the Monterey Maritime Museum; Mona Gudgel and the Monterey County Historical Society (Salinas); Faye Messenger and Mayo Hayes-O'Donnell Library (Monterey); Lisa Miller and the National Archives (San Bruno, California); the National Archives (Silver Springs, Maryland); and the Southwestern Museum (Los Angeles).

Colleagues and friends who helped in the fieldwork, shared their expertise, and provided critical comments on the manuscript include Bob Bettinger, Fred Block, James Brooks, Bill Hagen, Albert Hurtado, Mary Jackman, Skip and Mary Anne Lloyd, Susan Mann, Carol McKibben, Randall Milliken, Andrés Reséndez, Don Price, James Sandos, David Sweet, Tim Thomas, and Linda Yamani. On this manuscript, as on previous ones, I received extremely helpful reviews from Buchanan Sharp and Dale Tomich—fine authors in their own right. Beverly Lozano, my permanent graphic artist, contributed the elegant original illustrations, several of which are redrawn from rough originals. Arnold Bauer provided inimitable advice on the translation of nineteenth-century Spanish-language documents and on poetic questions. Like history in general, books are products of collective action.

John Walton
Carmel Valley, California
May 2000

ONE

Introduction

The one duty we owe history is to rewrite it.
Oscar Wilde, Intentions

PLACE

California began on Monterey Bay. It began in 1602 when the Spanish explorer Sebastián Vizcaíno, in search of a west coast harbor and refitting station for the Manila Galleon, came ashore, held a Catholic mass on the hill overlooking the bay, judged the site ideal, and named it after Condé de Monterey, the viceroy of New Spain. For the next 168 years it returned to a Native American land under decentralized control of local villages. It began again as Alta California in 1770 when the Sacred Expedition from Baja California headed by Captain Gaspar de Portolá and Father Junípero Serra founded the headquarters of Spain's frontier colony and Franciscan mission system at Monterey. And it began anew in 1846 when Commodore John Drake Sloat took possession of the California capital as the prize for U.S. entry into the Mexican-American War. From the initial encounter of Spanish colonials and Native Americans to the present, Monterey has been at the center of California and western U.S. history. If its political importance declined in relation to other growing cities in the late nineteenth century, it continued as a microcosm of western frontier settlement, early-twentieth-century industrialization, and contemporary environmentalism. It bears for western history as much significance as the Massachusetts Bay Colony carries for the east.

Midmorning is the best time for a walking tour of Monterey's historic waterfront. As sunshine dissolves the marine layer fog, the sea turns from dingy gray to dappled cobalt. Here at the southern end of the expansive

1.   Panorama of Monterey Bay from Presidio Hill. On this site Sebastián Vizcaíno landed in 1602, Fr. Junípero Serra said the first mass in 1770, and the monument to Commodore John Drake Sloat (left) commemorates the American conquest of California in 1846. (Photo by the author)

crescent-shaped Monterey Bay, the shoreline curves roundly in an arc from east to west. On the east side, in a grove of imported eucalyptus and coast live oaks, stands the former and fabulous Hotel Del Monte, a late-nineteenth-century luxury resort that was converted in the 1940s for military purposes and currently houses the Naval Post Graduate School. The old Del Monte elegance still shows in the blend of European alpine and California mission architectural styles, the high gloss of tile floors in the main building, the manicured gardens and Roman swimming pool. Across the street and toward the beach, half-buried railroad tracks mark the Southern Pacific line that once brought upper-class guests for the society season. Apropos of today's changing class structure, the city's recreational trail now covers the old tracks, and cyclists and joggers stream past a Salvation Army catering van that feeds the homeless residents of surrounding groves.

Moving westward along Del Monte Avenue toward the harbor, a 1950s auto row gives way to public space in the city's Window on the Bay oceanfront park. Nestled among newer buildings along the beach and marina is the old Southern Pacific train depot, once a symbol of the railroad's control over town land and business. On the city side of the

2.   San Carlos Cathedral in Monterey. California's oldest continuously functioning church, the sanctuary was constructed in 1795, first as the Royal Presidio Chapel, long Monterey's parish center, and currently the seat of the bishop and the Monterey Diocese. Generations of Monterey Catholics have been baptized, confirmed, married, and buried here. (Photo by the author)

avenue, the artfully landscaped El Estero Park and lagoon was once an open sewer until remodeling by the Works Progress Administration in the 1930s. Adjoining El Estero are two of the city's oldest landmarks. San Carlos Catholic Cemetery contains the remains of local families, ranging from prominent Hispanics and American settlers to Asian (Chinese, Japanese, Filipino) immigrants and, in distinctively Old World crypts, working-class Sicilians who dominated the city's fishing and canning industry in the first half of the twentieth century. Across from the cemetery is the site of the original Presidio where Spanish soldiers built a stockade and, slowly, a surrounding town. Today it includes San Carlos Cathedral (the bishop's seat and oldest functioning church in California), San Carlos School, and diocesan headquarters. San Carlos, Saint Charles Borromeo, the great church administrator and cardinal of Milan who died in 1584, was the city's exclusive patron until the 1930s, when, fittingly, the Sicilian woman Santa Rosalia became the benefactor of the fishing community.

Crossing back to the shoreline, two wharves jut out into the bay, the eastside Wharf Number 2 built for the commercial fleet in 1926 and the

3.   Custom House Plaza. This new civic center on the wharf in Monterey
was created by urban renewal begun in the 1960s. Today it preserves historical buildings on the square, including the Pacific Hotel (left) and the Mexican
Custom House (right), in addition to providing a venue for local festivals.
(Photo by the author)

original westside Fisherman's Wharf dating from 1845, when steamships
served the port and coastline from San Francisco. Predating Fisherman's
Wharf and opposite its entrance is the Mexican Custom House, now restored as a state park. The Custom House stands at the epicenter of four
cultures and as many centuries of history. Archaeologists have recently
discovered an ancient Indian fishing village beneath its nineteenth-century
buildings. It was the commercial and administrative center of the Mexican Colony in the 1840s, built with the intention, only partly realized, of
collecting duties on the active hide and tallow trade that passed through
the port. At the Custom House in 1846, Commodore Sloat raised the
colors of the United States. From a symbol of political control in the nineteenth century, the balconied, Monterey colonial–style building has become the contemporary anchor of the Custom House Plaza, the site of
various multicultural festivals and forms of historical commemoration.

Ringed around the plaza are a statue of Santa Rosalia, a brightly col-
ored stone marker recording events in the bay's past, a maritime museum,
headquarters of the Monterey History and Art Association whose Path
of History through the city's adobe structures begins here, a re-created
street of nineteenth-century stores, the 1840s Pacific House Hotel that
is now a state museum, and the bocci ball courts where retired fishermen show their current skills. Like the El Estero–San Carlos complex,

4.   Santa Rosalia statue. The patron saint's statue overlooking the bay was erected in 1970 by the Italian Heritage
Society "in memory of those courageous Sicilian fishermen
whose labors and pioneering spirit at the beginning of the
20th century created and developed a great sardine industry
and whose heritage and culture contributed significantly to
the growth of this city." (Photo by the author)

various histories are jumbled together on the plaza. Historical markers
provide potted summaries of events (first of this, site of that) but little
by way of their connections—how Sicilian fishermen came to inhabit
Spanish churches, North American settlers acquired Mexican property,
or Native Americans sank beneath the surface. What threads connect
these outcroppings of a four-hundred-year history?

5.   Bocci ball. These courts were included in the Custom House Plaza design for the recreation of retired fishermen and other enthusiasts. (Photo by the author)

There is also much the observer will not see, beginning with the absence of memorials to the Indian society that welcomed, supported, and even fed the conquering Spaniards. But Indians are not the only ones whose heritage has been silenced. Today's Custom House Plaza covers a space traditionally occupied by waterfront trades, small ethnic-owned businesses, frame houses of fishermen's families, and the shacks and rooming houses of cannery workers—a "blighted" area in the opinion of real estate developers from the 1890s to their federal urban renewal colleagues in the 1970s. Nearby Washington Street was the heart of Monterey's lively Chinatown and Bad Lands district, devoted to "resorts" for gambling and prostitution before reform interests reclaimed the space. Pacific Street, once the core of a working-class Italian neighborhood running from town to the harbor, now presents a row of hotels and visitor attractions. Yet, on Spaghetti Hill overlooking Pacific Street and the bay, neatly kept homes built originally by prosperous Sicilian fishermen are retained by their close-knit families.

Lighthouse Avenue continues along the shoreline at the foot of Presidio Hill to New Monterey, where the town's legendary canneries were built in a mile-long row beginning in the 1910s and 1920s. Little of that is visible today. At the city's new San Carlos Park on the east end of Cannery Row, the observer glimpses Old and New Monterey mixed together—Old Monterey to the east with its new tourist hotels and service economy, New Monterey to the west with its old industrial under-pinnings, concrete footings that once supported production lines and anchored the off-loading sardine boats. At the park historical markers indicate that this former site of the San Carlos Cannery now overlooks the federal Monterey Bay Sanctuary devoted to environmental protection and marine research—the new rising from the old, according to the hopeful marker. From San Carlos Park, the street renamed Cannery Row in 1957 runs a gamut of hotels, restaurants, souvenir shops, boutiques, and bars before reaching the popular Monterey Bay Aquarium and boundary line with the neighboring town of Pacific Grove.

Today's Cannery Row is a contested zone of commercial hype, beleaguered preservationist effort, educational interest, and the occasional remnant of Monterey's industrial era—foundations of the canneries and reduction plants, loading tanks and disused railroad tracks, restored worker shacks, and, defying commercial growth, a few of the original frame houses that once covered this working-class neighborhood. One block is lined on both sides of the street with a series of murals depicting the halcyon days of Cannery Row—the fish cutters, the women who packed sardines into cans, the boiler men who cooked the cans. Other murals portray the legend of Cannery Row, characters out of John Steinbeck's novel of the same name. Behind these muraled walls, which block the ocean view on one side, lies the unfinished construction of a tourist hotel. Concrete foundations, weeds, and exposed reinforcement bar testify to an ill-conceived, underfinanced development that neither progresses nor liquidates. Meanwhile, projects of the same sort are proposed by new investors and opposed by preservationists endeavoring to retain something of the row's historical character. Up the hill from the commercial street, the old homes have been replaced or extensively remodeled as the whole neighborhood has experienced upward social mobility.

Old and New Monterey are separated by the Presidio, site of the original Spanish El Castillo fort, a U.S. Army post beginning in the Spanish-American War, and today home of the army's renowned Defense Language Institute. The military has always enjoyed an influential presence in Monterey. The reservation extends from the bay several miles up to the forested ridge circling the city. The hillside overlooking Fisherman's Wharf is replete with historical landmarks. This was the site of Vizcaíno's landing and first mass. It was, therefore, the site to which Serra and Portolá returned in 1770 for a mass of thanksgiving on their rediscovery of the bay Vizcaíno called Monterey, which they had chosen as their headquarters. Monuments on the hill commemorate Serra's landing and, re-

cently, Indian graves. By far the dominating symbol on Presidio Hill, however, is the massive white marble monument to Commodore Sloat and
his conquest. Built in the form of a pyramid (with much Masonic symbolism) and topped by a menacing American eagle, the structure seems
to dominate the bay as the eagle glowers over the harbor warning off
any future invasions. The monument's symbolism is blunt, owing no
doubt to its patriotic donors and construction at the turn of the twentieth century and the height of American imperialism. Ironically, however,
from the town and harbor Sloat's monument is hardly dominating,
scarcely visible—a white dot on the hill with little significance for the
multicultural, immigrant, working-class, raucous industrial society
that formed under its nose in the years following its dedication in 1910.
The Sloat Monument is a fitting metaphor for Monterey. It stands for
domination and rectitude but is continuously subverted by diversity and
recusancy.

THE PROBLEM OF HISTORY

Public history, as it is presented to and apprehended by the observer of
commemorative sites and interpreted texts, is a jumble—a puzzling en-
semble of disconnected facts and decontextualized anecdotes. Moments
in the city's past are spread out in space without connecting pathways,
like hypertext on a computer screen with no particular linear arrange-
ment. Of course, the resolute investigator can penetrate this confusion
because, behind the facts, there are stories. Narratives connect the events
of history in an ordered time sequence, embed them in a plot line, and
invest them with a direction, perhaps a moral.

    Monterey's history is rich in stories. Franciscan missionaries, it is said,
arrive in an uncultured wilderness to provide Christian civilization and
productive agriculture through the mission system. The missionary narrative has its critics, to be sure, but it perseveres in changing form at the
behest of its church supporters, romance writers, tourism promoters, and
colonial historians. The widely embraced story of American progress organizes another swatch of local history. Here the origin point is Sloat's
invasion, reconceived as a liberating blessing, which introduces Yankee
ambition and entrepreneurial rationality to a land whose potential lay
undeveloped under the dissolute habits of Mexican governance. New and
reconfigured narratives appear based on contemporary events. Romanticized accounts of Cannery Row draw on the Steinbeck story to the neglect of the real industry and its headlong drive toward destruction of the

fishery—and all for the purpose of high profits in the production of fertilizer rather than food. A new environmental narrative reorganizes the past from the standpoint of the present, incorporating the industrial period as a valuable problem and lesson in a progressive history of ecological awareness.

The problem with these stories, however, is that they simply replicate the previous problem by offering assorted anecdotes, now on the level of unconnected narratives. The stories of Cannery Row and environmentalism, like missionary and American progress narratives, do not engage. If the missions brought civilization, why were things in such a mess when the Americans arrived beneficently to sort it out? If the industrial period was such a grand achievement, why did fishing fall into ecological ruin? On reflection, far from solving the problem of factual coherence, these organizing stories introduce a new problem. Where do the narratives come from, how are they socially constructed, why are they inconsistent, how do they relate to events? In short, public history now presents two problems: how do we explain the events of history *and* the influential stories of those events? The case study of Monterey and the embedded argument to follow shows that the two problems are intertwined, that historical events and narratives shape one another, that one cannot be explained independent of the other, that an explanation of both lies in their interplay.

A small story illustrates the big point. Robert Louis Stevenson, the Scottish novelist and essayist, is closely identified with the history of Monterey. Conventional histories give prominent attention to the poet's three-month stay in fall 1879. Stevenson was there seeking the attentions of Fanny Osbourne, a married woman who shared the writer's affections and was living with her resident sister while she pursued a divorce. Monterey's damp winter climate aggravated Stevenson's chronic pulmonary illness and combined with his penniless estate to make for a doleful period in both their lives. He was unknown to Californians, and few would have predicted his subsequent renown. At this point in his writing career he had published only two collections of stories that appeared in Europe and described his travels in France and Belgium (*An Island Voyage* and *Travels with a Donkey in Cévennes*). The local newspaper editor, perhaps taking pity on his impoverished state, hired RLS to write one or two feature stories, including an interesting piece on the celebration of San Carlos Day at Carmel Mission, which he signed anonymously as "Barbarian." Later he wrote a perceptive description of Monterey titled "The Old Pacific Capital," but the essay did not appear until 1892 (in *Across the Plains*, about his travels in the United States). Judging from contemporary sources, Stevenson had no impact on local life and his presence went practically unnoticed.

Yet Stevenson is celebrated as a key figure in Monterey history. Standard texts devote more attention to RLS than to his fellow Scot, David Jacks, who was the richest person in the county at the time and owned most of the land on which the town was built. The author's rooming house (Madame Girardin's French Hotel) has been preserved as "Stevenson House" and designated a stop on the Path of History by the Monterey History and Art Association. Local fans have begun annual celebrations of Stevenson's birthday at the house. In an endeavor to give some substance to Stevenson's Monterey sojourn, the story is circulated (beginning with Steinbeck in *Cannery Row*) that Point Lobos on Carmel Bay inspired the setting for *Treasure Island*. The story is doubtful. Stevenson had seen plenty of islands more closely resembling his fictional construction by the time he wrote the novel four years later. Why, then, the local obsession with RLS? The answer is commonplace. Stevenson's memory was appropriated many years later, after the achieved fame of his major novels in the 1880s and his death in 1894, and then read backward, reinserted in history—or reinvented as historical myth. The story of Monterey was made more glamorous as a result, more consequential by virtue of its supposed connection to important persons and events. The story made good copy for popular history writers, attracted visitors, provided commercial payoff, gave name recognition to the town and Path of History (by contrast, for example, to the fine house of Prudenciana and José Amestí), and provided an occasion for Stevenson buffs to gather—and it had elements of truth. Generally, the construction of a narrative about Stevenson in Monterey fitted the interests of a set of actors and organizations with diverse motives and no reason to let the meager facts constrain a good story. History is made that way. It is socially constructed in diverse circumstances and processes. It needs to be understood, analyzed in the same way.

In this study Monterey is treated as an exemplary case of western history and of history making. It is a study of events and narratives and how those are linked in the process of collective action. It is reflexive historical sociology, meaning that it focuses on the interrelation of facts, stories, and, like Stevenson's influence on Monterey, stories that become facts.

TWO

Spain's Far Frontier

The struggle of man against power is the struggle of memory
against forgetting.

> Milan Kundera, *The Book of Laughter*
> *and Forgetting*

Seventeen eighty started badly for Father Serra. The Indians grew more
mischievous every day, while the new governor was proving as meddle-
some as his predecessors. California recently had been upgraded to the
status of a province on Spain's North American frontier, and the change
brought Felipe de Neve to Monterey as the first resident military-political
governor. With the political capital now a mere three miles from Serra's
Carmel headquarters, the padre president of the mission system was feeling threatened. Pitched quarrels were nothing new to Junípero Serra, but
his rivals always had been less formidable commanders of the military presidio. Governor Neve personified state power and, worse, a new design
for managing the colony with the support of Mexico City and Madrid.
In one of its most galling aspects, the Neve plan undermined church
authority over mission Indians by requiring that the neophyte Christians
elect their own local leaders (*alcaldes,* or mayors, and *regidores,* or town
council members) who would be exempt from priestly discipline. Although Serra and Neve clashed publicly over the issue before mass at the
presidio on Palm Sunday 1779, the good padre could not defy the king's
representative—at least not directly.

During a sleepless night, Serra asked, "What is the meaning of it all,
O Lord?" Then a "clear voice" counseled, "Be prudent as serpents and
simple as doves." The quotation from Genesis, Serra informed his missionary brethren, when applied to California's Eden meant, "Whatever
the gentleman [governor] wishes to be done should be done, but in such

wise that it should not cause the least change among Indians or disturb the routine Your Reverences have established." The priests would themselves select leaders from the ranks of village chiefs with the governor none the wiser. "Let Francisco, with the same staff of office he uses and his coat, be the first alcalde. All we have to do is change the name. Another alcalde might be the chief from one of the rancherías, of those that visit the mission every fifteen days. As for the regidores, who carry no staff, let one be from that ranchería, and one from another. Whether they are chiefs or not is of little importance, but it is better if they are."[1]

By January 1780 Serra's facile solution had failed. Baltazar, the forty-four-year-old chief of a Rumsen village, had been chosen first alcalde of Carmel Mission. He came from Ichxenta, located on the Carmel River just ten kilometers from the coast and in the heart of the initial recruitment area of Mission San Carlos (Carmel), an area now fully Christianized. Baltazar, to Serra's great surprise, "once in office and aware of his privileges and exemption from correction by the Fathers began to do just as he pleased." Without irony, Serra now complained to Governor Neve about the unruliness of his protégé. "He had a son by one of his relatives, and had a [Baja] California Indian flogged because he carried out an order from the Father. . . . [H]e is living [as a] deserter, adulterer, inciting people here, meeting personally those who leave here with permission, and thereby trying to swell the numbers of his band from the mountains by new desertions of the natives of this mission." Serra omitted any possible explanation for Baltazar's actions. On the contrary, he noted in the same letter to Neve that "spiritual fathers should punish their sons, the Indians, with blows."[2]

Like many Rumsen village chiefs, Baltazar had three wives at the time of his baptism in 1775 (Baltazar, of course, was his Spanish baptismal name). He and his Christian wife had their union reconfirmed by the church a few days later. Four years elapsed before Baltazar became alcalde, during which time he fathered a child by his non-Christian wife, Justina, who was the sister of his first wife. Following his appointment as alcalde, these two wives died within a month of each another, the Christian first and then Justina, who left a newborn. Despite his loss and ritual mourning, Baltazar married in the church again in July 1779. Then something happened during the latter part of the year that caused his disaffection. Perhaps he was punished for polygamy in defiance of Christian marriage (Serra rails about his adultery) or for his independence as alcalde (Serra notes that he urged another Indian to defy the priests). Concerning the status of Indian leaders, Serra conceded to Neve,

"[A]lthough we allowed them the distinction and title of being governors, alcaldes[,] . . . nevertheless, when it appeared to us that punishment was deserved, they were flogged, or put in stocks." Baltazar complained to Neve, which suggests that punishment was at issue. In any case, by the time of Serra's lament in January 1780, Baltazar had fled to the remote area of Sargentaruc in the mountains near Big Sur and was urging others to abandon the mission for his band.[3] Although we must guess at the conditions precipitating Baltazar's repudiation of church and mission life, numerous testimonies from captured fugitives suggest a general pattern of family deaths and corporal punishment as key factors—combined misfortunes Baltazar suffered.[4]

Governor Neve refused Serra's request that troops be sent to hunt down fugitives from the mission and in a variety of ways frustrated the resolute padre for another two years. He found it impossible to deal reasonably with the Franciscans: "There is no mischief these religious will not attempt. . . . [T]hey engage in surreptitious conspiracies against the government and its laws." Serra was equally distrustful of the military governors: "In so far as anything depends on the Captain, we will make very little progress [and have] constant bickering."[5] Neve did not pursue his policy of mission democratization and was happy to leave California two years later with assurances that "kindness, good treatment, and some small gifts" would maintain the peace. In 1782 Serra welcomed the return of Pedro Fages as governor, the very presidio captain whose removal the president had demanded nine years earlier. On his departure Neve instructed Fages: "To maintain this system of wooing these and other heathens, I have left some beads with [the Monterey Presidio commander who] will hand them over to the new governor."[6] Serra believed that the soldiers' gifts were designed to make servants and laborers of the Indians and advised the padres, "[S]tand firm against them. . . . [Y]ou will have plenty of opportunities, in one way or another, to upset their plans."[7] Meanwhile, in resistance and death, Baltazar and his wives withdrew from colonial society. In November 1780 Baltazar died among the heathens of the Santa Lucia Mountains. Serra and Neve joined him in repose four years later, within a week of each another.

The story captures a fundamental truth of Spanish California. Power was fragmented in a triadic, interdependent relationship of state, church, and indigenous groups. Such was their condition that no one group could realize its will without the cooperation of others. Yet such were their respective wills that none could tolerate physical, political, or spiritual subordination to another. While they struggled with the contradiction, none seemed to notice that they were on the fringes of a dying empire, perhaps because frequent and untimely deaths were the grim fact of everyday life. For want of any solution to the dilemma, they blamed one another and trudged onward to their collective demise.

THREE LOCAL WORLDS

NATIVE AMERICANS

The central California coast was settled by Indians moving south and west from the Sacramento–San Joaquin River delta roughly one thousand years before the first Spaniards landed there in the sixteenth and early seventeenth century.[8] California Indians were unique by North American standards. They were numerous, perhaps three hundred thousand before conquest, densely settled in decentralized villages, and diverse. "They were associated with 4 major cultural areas, 60 tribes, and 90 languages and contained both the tallest and shortest native groups in North America."[9] Of the larger population, the Spanish military conquest and missionary campaign launched from Baja California in 1769 affected directly only about a third living along the southern and central coast from San Diego to San Francisco where the interlopers settled. Differences among coastal Indian groups were less dramatic but sometimes telling, as, for example, in the contrast between powerful seagoing Chumash of the Santa Barbara Channel and territorial hunter-gatherer Ohlone spread from San Francisco to Monterey.

Coastal (including delta and near-inland valley) Indians organized themselves in "tribelets" of a few hundred persons that united several extended families in a small network of villages of perhaps ten to fourteen miles in diameter. Two hundred to four hundred people might constitute a tribelet of a half dozen extended family groups living in a (politically and economically) central town, several satellite villages, and seasonal camps associated with different production routines (e.g., seed gathering, hunting). Ceremonial village centers also existed, sometimes at the central place and other times at geographically significant sites. Houses were constructed of reeds and thatched grass in hemispherical shapes and small clusters. Governed by a male secular chief and influential female ceremonial leaders, the tribelet was generally the highest level of political organization. Leadership was a consensual affair. In the gendered division of labor among these complex hunter-gatherers, men harvested protein foods such as game and fish while women collected and prepared acorns, seeds, roots, and berries in intricately woven baskets of their own invention. Developed technologies informed fishing and otter hunting at sea, acorn flour production, stone and obsidian tool making, and preparation of medicinal plants. Although little is known about their sun-worship cosmology, sorcery, and belief in the afterlife, ceremonial activities were central to village life, especially in the form of dancing managed by women. Except for chiefs and wealthy men, who practiced polygamy, marriage was monogamous, divorce simple, and homosexuality commonplace (i.e., the "berdache," or male living and comporting as wife to another male).[10]

Coastal Indians distinguished themselves in trade and commerce. Tribelets were characteristically territorial, most people remaining within roughly a twenty-mile radius of the central village and defending their resources against outsiders. But intergroup exchange was lively, facilitated by a partially monetized economy, regular trade fairs, and customary courting and marriage arrangements. Tribelets, not to mention individuals, differed widely in wealth embodied as shell money, luxuries (e.g., jewelry), and territorial resources (e.g., seashore, forests, mineral deposits). These items were traded actively and across long distances. Wealthy villages, in the Santa Barbara Channel or Sacramento Delta, for example, dominated their neighbors and regional resource bases. Wealth, poverty, and inequality were familiar social conditions. The differences probably gave rise to resentments. California tribelets did not form alliances. On the contrary, they fought with one another frequently, albeit in low-intensity skirmishes. Observing differences between tribelets in the Monterey area, Pedro Fages noted, "[T]he hill Indians of the Sierra de Santa Lucia . . . persecute indiscriminately the new Christians and the unconverted Indians of this region whenever they enter the range to search for acorns, which the hill Indians guard and desire to keep for themselves alone. These unhappy people encounter the same resistance when they go along the beach above Monterey on the same quest, so they are prevented from going far from this district."[11] Resource poaching (of game, seeds, shells) and wife stealing (some of it ritualized) were the most common motives for war. Rival tribelets reportedly engaged in recurrent fights when one made annual gathering visits to the seashore territory of another. But conflict was not the only expression of intergroup contact. People came together for mutual advantage owing to limitations on cross-cousin marriages, complementary resource endowments, and the desire for sociability.

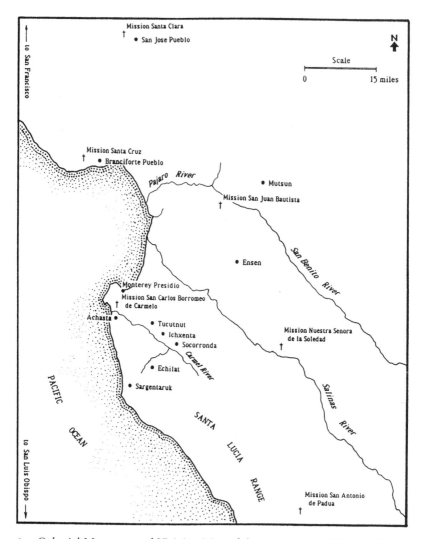

6.   Colonial Monterey and Vicinity. Map of the Monterey and Salinas Valley region in the Spanish colonial period showing missions, pueblos, and Indian villages. (Illustration by Beverly Lozano)

Native American settlements in the area where the Monterey Presidio and San Carlos Borromeo Mission would soon locate fit this description. The Monterey Peninsula lay at an intersection of native cultures. The Ohlone language group occupied the region from Monterey Bay to San Francisco Bay and extending inland to the coastal mountain range. (Some ethnographers refer to the group with the Spanish term "Costanoan" rather than the indigenous word "Ohlone," which identified a village, the arbitrariness stemming from the absence of any self-referential term in the native language.) Ohlones comprised roughly fifty tribelets and two distinct dialects of a mutually intelligible language. It was the largest local group, consisting of roughly 10,000 people before conquest. The Rumsen were a smallish (about 500) Ohlone tribelet with their own dialect living in five villages in the Carmel Valley. At the time of conquest there were no villages on the Monterey seashore, although archaeological evidence, including large shell middens, demonstrates that there were seasonal settlements on the coast. South of the Monterey Peninsula lay Esselen territory. A small but linguistically distinct group, the Esselen numbered between 750 and 1,300 and lived in six tribelets in the upper Carmel Valley, the Santa Lucia Mountains, and along the Big Sur coast. In addition to the fact that all of these boundaries and settlements changed over time, Ohlone (Rumsen) and Esselen territories overlapped in multilingual zones. Although early reports may have exaggerated their mutual enmity, Rumsen and Esselen peoples were certainly rivals and sometimes enemies. To the north and east lay the contiguous lands of Pajaro and Salinas Valley Ohlones (Matsun, Ensen, Chalon), who traded and quarreled with their neighbors.[12]

In 1770, when an advance party of Spanish soldiers and missionaries arrived at Monterey, they stepped into a complex Native American society consisting of three thousand people living in twenty to thirty villages governed by half a dozen tribelets, all embedded in a network of commercial and family ties. Women and men, rich and poor, shaman and trader, governing elites and hunters, members of powerful communities and their rustic neighbors—all played distinctive and interconnected roles. Small local societies commanded their loyalties. If they quarreled with their neighbors, they also prospered in a forgiving physical environment.

SPANIARDS

Spanish colonialism in Alta California began inauspiciously and progressed only slightly during its fifty-year life span. By contrast to the fabled empires conquered in sixteenth-century Mexico and Peru, Upper California was a very different environment and Spain a fading power in the Americas in 1770. Charles III, greatest of the Spanish Bourbons, assumed the crown in 1759 and initiated a set of reforms designed to modernize the politically and financially troubled empire. From 1765 to 1771 José de Gálvez served as the king's visitor general in New Spain and exercised more power than the head of state, the viceroy. Yet Gálvez met enormous resistance to change in Mexico stemming from profitably ensconced colonial bureaucrats, distrustful commercial and mining interests, antimonarchical elements, anticlerical sentiments curiously mixed with resentments over the recent expulsion of Jesuit missionaries and teachers, and a strong undercurrent of Creole independence. Ironically, although Alta California played a minuscule part in the politics of New Spain, or even in the affairs of its northern frontier, stretching from California to Texas, Gálvez's designs on this remote fringe of the empire had revolutionary local effects.[13]

Spain had at least two reasons for extending its colonial purchase on the northern Pacific: first, to give new impetus to settlement and missionization under the Bourbon reforms and, second, to preempt any claims on this coast by interested navigators and intrepid traders from Russia and England. Gálvez established a navy base at San Blas on Mexico's west coast where ships were built to supply Sonora and the (lower and upper) Californias. From Baja California in 1768, Gálvez began to organize a "sacred expedition" composed of soldiers garrisoned at Loreto and Franciscan missionaries who had only just arrived to replace the expelled Jesuits in the chain of nineteen Baja missions. Most of the people Gálvez recruited, including the fifty-five-year-old mission president, Junípero Serra, were new to the frontier, had no knowledge of Alta California, and certainly no inkling that they would soon become its "founders." Captain Gaspar de Portolá had only recently been made governor of Baja, although Captain Fernando Rivera y Moncada had considerable frontier experience. Lieutenant Pedro Fages and his twenty-five Catalan Volunteers were mobilized in Sonora to crew one of the ships. Father Juan Crespi, lifelong companion of Serra, joined the expedition. After gathering a host of mission supplies, food, livestock, munitions, and Baja Indian laborers, the expedition divided into two land parties and two ship's companies of sixty to seventy each. One by one, the four parties of the Sacred Expedition departed from various Baja ports and mission towns headed for Monterey via San Diego de Alcalá, places no European had occupied and names that existed only on faded maps.

Indeed, California above the austere Baja Peninsula was a fantasy projection—its name adopted from a mythical island in the sixteenth-century Spanish romance *Sergas de Esplandian* by Ordoñez de Montalvo. California appeared as a marvelous tabula rasa on which colonial officials and missionaries inscribed their distinct visions. California had been coasted repeatedly in the sixteenth century by Spanish navigators, not to mention Sir Francis Drake and, perhaps, forgotten Asian seafarers. Yet it was the 1602 voyage and nomenclature of Sebastian Vizcaíno that fixed these locales in the minds of subsequent settlers. Sailing three ships north from Acapulco in search of a refueling port for the Manila Galleon, Vizcaíno rounded a shallow bay on November 12, the saint's day observed for Diego of Alcalá, Spain, and hence the site of San Diego. Santa Barbara lent her name to another picturesque harbor encountered on her December 4 birthday. Had Vizcaíno passed along this coast at a different time of year, California cities might bear names like San Antonio or Saint Augustine. Approaching Monterey (named for the viceroy who commissioned the expedition), Vizcaíno's map dedicated a bold mountain range to Santa Lucia and named a quiet river inlet Carmel for the Carmelite friars on board ship; more landmarks along the way became Punto Pinos (Pines Point) and Punto Año Nuevo (New Year's Point). Judging Monterey an excellent harbor, Vizcaíno put his crew ashore, where they found abundant fresh water and wood. A solemn mass was said claiming the land for God and king, a large cross erected above the bay, and a decision reached that this would be the best refitting station for Philippine ships. Curiously, no European seems to have landed at Monterey for the next century and a half until Charles III named it as the destination of the Gálvez expedition and future headquarters of the California colony.

Slowly the four separate companies converged on San Diego in early 1769: one of the ships on April 11, another with a scurvy-ridden and dying crew on April 29, then the bedraggled land parties on May 14 and July 1. Myriad difficulties attended the founding of San Diego, including ill-timed arrivals, ravaging disease, reduced livestock, scarce supplies, rotting rations, broken-down equipment, and a dawning sense of the vast impracticality of the task. Undeterred, the expedition next split into three groups. One ship returned to San Blas with messengers and the sick. A larger group stayed at San Diego to begin constructing the settlement. Portolá headed north by land with a party in search of Vizcaíno's harbor. Inexplicably, they marched right past Monterey Bay without recognizing it from previous descriptions and ended up at San Francisco Bay. On the return trip, they stopped at Carmel Bay, raised a cross, and puzzled again over the elusive harbor. Subsequent speculation about the incident offers varied interpretations, from the geographic (Monterey Bay was so large as to confound their expectations of a compact harbor) to the strategic (they knew where they were all along but needed an excuse to extend the mandated reach of their explorations to San Francisco). In any case, expeditionary disappointments and famine conditions in San Diego convinced Portolá that California would be better abandoned.

The Franciscan missionaries and a game naval ship's captain kept hope alive long enough for one more reconnaissance of the coast below San Francisco Bay. Portolá agreed to retrace his steps by land with Pedro Fages and a company of twenty-eight soldiers while Serra joined fellow Mallorcan and experienced sailor Captain Juan Perez aboard the ship *San Antonio* sailing north in mid-April. On reaching Monterey and Carmel for the third time, Portolá now realized that this spectacular coastline coincided with Vizcaíno's understated description. Within a week the *San Antonio* appeared on the horizon, and the parties were reunited on June 1, 1770, under the same oak tree (they claimed) where Vizcaíno's expedition had said mass 168 years earlier. On June 3 Father Serra celebrated Pentecostal Mass on the spot. "We then raised aloft and blessed a great cross—likewise the Royal Standards. . . . After that the officers performed the official act of taking possession of the country in the name of the King, our lord, whom God keep."[14]

Throughout their travels the Spaniards met and observed groups of indigenous people. Indeed, the Indians were forthcoming with gestures of welcome and gifts of food. Serra noted, "They came out to meet us both along the roads and at our camping places. They displayed the fullest confidence and assurance just as if we had been lifelong friends."[15] Miguel Costansó, an engineer with the land party, observed, "The natives of Monterey live in the sierra. Those nearest the beach are distant from it about a league and a half. They come down at times and go forth to fish on little rafts of cattail rushes. . . . These *serranos* [mountain Indians] are extremely docile and peaceful. They never used to come to visit the Spaniards without bringing them a good treat of game, which was generally composed of two or three deer or antelope, which they offered without demanding nor even asking anything in return."[16]

Indian cosmology clearly attached significance to the European presence, although we lack direct evidence of their interpretation. When Portolá's second party returned to the cross they had erected at Carmel Bay nine months earlier, they saw various offerings left there by the Indians. Father Serra related an account of the incident provided by a young Ohlone who befriended the padres and quickly learned Spanish. "I asked him why it was that the cross, which had been planted by the first expedition on the coast of Monterey, had been decorated by the gentiles [unconverted Indians]—as could be seen on our return there—with strings of sardines, venison meat, and bird feathers tied to the arms, and at the foot had been placed many broken arrows? He replied that they had done so to keep it from doing them harm because they were in deadly fear of it. And, in explanation of their fear, he said that the witch doctors and dancers, who used to prowl about through the night, had noticed, every night, that it rose high in the heavens, not black like a tree trunk, but shining with light, and of a wondrous beauty, and bright as the sun."[17] Although details about shining crosses seem of suspiciously Christian derivation and were rendered through the dual media of Serra and one of his first converts, it is nevertheless reasonable to conclude that Indians understood these events in culturally prescribed meanings and actions. Broken arrows and food, for example, may have symbolized a hope for peace and trade with these strange but clearly powerful intruders.

Construction of colonial Monterey began immediately in summer 1770. Portolá headed south on the *San Antonio* carrying news of the successful occupation to Mexico City, where a mass and grand reception were celebrated. Lieutenant Pedro Fages commanded the settlement with a population of forty-three souls, all men for the moment, including his own twelve Catalan Volunteers, eight leather-jacket soldiers, two muleteers, nine Baja Indians, ten sailors on loan for construction duty, and two Franciscans. Engineer Costansó selected the presidio site one mile from the Vizcaíno oak and facing the beach across a small estuary. A square of 120-yard sides was built, first of saplings and later adobe brick, enclosing rooms and the first Royal Chapel within the interior walls. A circular blockhouse stood at each corner, and the main gate opened to the lagoon. Wooden floors were added later to the commander's house, but accommodations were primitive, with musty windowless rooms, the square usually a quagmire, and fresh water at a distance. At this rustic level frontier life required full-time effort. Mariano Carrillo, a leather jacket from Loreto, wrote, "[W]e soldiers acted as woodsmen and muleteers, without any of us being excused. . . . Within twelve days two warehouses were put up, wherein we stored the supplies that had come with the ship. . . . [W]e started hard at work on the presidio, laboring from sun-up to sun-down. . . . The *Comandante* would never refrain from putting all of us to work on the particular task he had in mind, some of us mixing mud for adobes, others making them, some carrying mud to plaster the huts, others doing the plastering, some sawing boards, and others making lime kilns."[18]

As at San Diego, the settlers faced physical hardships that aggravated social and personal differences. Fages was something of a tyrant, even for a frontier commander. He hounded his troops in long hours of toil, withheld deserved praise, and quixotically issued severe punishments. Carrillo's complaints suggest that construction work was an affront to the leather jackets, who were trained for combat, but the Catalan Volunteer Corporal Miguel Períquez echoed the charges, noting he had been put in irons for remarking that workers needed a lunch break. "Slaves could not have been treated worse." Fages and Serra quarreled bitterly, and Períquez reports that the father president took the unusual initiative of intervening on behalf of the soldiers: "that was when the work in the fields was stopped."[19] If the military declined agricultural work to support the presidio, or simply numbered too small a labor force, workers would have to be found among the indigenous population—an option that set church and state at odds.

Over the next decade, California lived a precarious existence. Supply ships from San Blas were frequently delayed or diverted. Drought and hunger visited the settlements recurrently. Indians sometimes provided famine relief. Soldiers did not receive their wages, and, when in-kind compensation was offered as a solution, they noted that there were few provisions available. "The soldiers could not keep from bartering their goods with the heathen for food, so that several *mangas de pano* (ponchos), pocket knives, daggers, and white handkerchiefs were given away[,] . . . whatever they had with them when they chanced to meet the Indians with something to eat." Reflecting on the combination of hardship and the commander's foul temper, Carrillo concluded, "[P]erhaps that explains why there have been desertions in the ranks."[20] As word traveled south, California service became unpopular, a place for the career-minded official or soldier to avoid. California discouraged civilian colonization for these reasons as well as its physical and cultural distance from population centers in Mexico. Years passed before the first colonization experiments attempted to settle groups of women and families in Alta California. In the meantime, concubinage and abuse of Indian women became a major problem—a practice that endangered necessary Indian support, threatened military discipline and desertion, and added to the large catalog of sins monitored by an understaffed clergy. Serra lamented free unions and the army punished some of the more flagrant incidents of sexual abuse,[21] but like other frontier conflicts, these were inherent consequences of the colonial project.

If California society was rudimentary in the closing decades of the eighteenth century, it was not without political design. Some of the most sophisticated architects of European colonialism had formulated, and then re-formed, the settlement plan carried to Mexico's northern frontier. And some of those who executed the policy were professional civil servants with standards of conduct as clear as clerical vows. Visitor General Gálvez and Viceroy Antonio Bucareli advocated a new kind of expedition to California, one that was equally a spiritual and secular conquest. Indian wars such as experienced in Texas and New Mexico were to be avoided by peaceful conduct and benign intentions. Missions were the principal instrument of colonial policy. The expeditionaries' charge was to reveal the miracle of Christ's grace, teach the ways of the Spanish agrarian pueblo, and then move on—to civilize gently the frontier in order that it prosper in material self-sufficiency. Vaunted statecraft, of course, is easily undone on the ground where priests and soldiers bicker, men abuse women, Indians decline revelation, and nature turns mean. The occupying forces were divided internally between a few Spanish officers (and priests) and a large fraction of mestizo troops and Baja Indians. The frontier was unpredictable, contradictory. It attracted undesirables—or at least lacked attractions for desirables. Colonial policy was fashioned by diplomats for a society of zealots, adventurers, rebels, and aborigines. The gap between colonial design and local practice is precisely where we discover the interpretive keys to California society.

FRANCISCANS

Despite their several branches, the Franciscans are a poverty and missionary order of the Catholic Church devoted to the ministry of Saint Francis of Assisi. They maintained the College of San Fernando in Mexico City (and thus acquired the nickname Fernandinos) where missionaries were trained for work among Mesoamerican Indians in Mexico's central Sierra Gorda. Junípero Serra and his lifelong associates, Juan Crespi and Francisco Palóu, came from the Spanish island of Mallorca to Mexico in the 1750s where they served as Franciscan missionaries in the field and teachers at San Fernando before inheriting the Baja California missions in 1768 from the Society of Jesus. Unlike the popular Jesuits, who were Mexico's prestigious teachers and intellectuals, Franciscans stressed personal humility and theological primitivism.[22] Modesty suited the times. The Jesuits had been expelled from Latin America owing to their accumulated political power and threat to royal prerogative. The Fernandinos could be expected to reject the emoluments of office,

7.   *Reception of La Pérouse at Monterey.* From the original pen and ink drawing by Gaspard Duché de Vancy, 1784. The original, a gift to Father Lasuén, hung in Carmel Mission and was copied by a member of the 1791 Malaspina expedition. The drawing depicts native and European dress as well as the early design of the mission complex. (Courtesy of the Museo Naval, Madrid)

serve the Indians, and stay out of politics. As missionaries they had a lot to prove coming on the heels of the Jesuits, widely recognized as masters of the practice. But Serra and his comrades relished the challenge; this was an opportunity fit to a lifetime of preparation.

Serra's writings are suffused with zeal, joy, industry, and evangelical single-mindedness. In the spirit of the primitive church, Franciscans saw California as Eden, an earthly paradise peopled by innocents but littered with the devil's devices. "Vines grow well and plentiful and in some places they are laden with grapes. . . . [T]here are various kinds of Castilian roses. In short, it is a good country. . . . Gentiles there are in great number. . . . They are very sociable, and all the males—both adults and children— are all naked. The women and girls are decently covered—even the baby girls. . . . All along the road you see hares, rabbits, some deer, and many antelopes."[23] When idyllic encounters turned bad, when Indians resisted their favors or soldiers applied force, Franciscan adepts like Palóu had a ready explanation: "As the joy and the contentment of the friars and the people continued to increase, the greater grew the fury of that great Enemy of souls who was ill content [that the Indians] were putting an end to their pagan customs and surrendering themselves to our true religion." The Devil had many guises. Typically he worked through guileless Indians, such as "two of the converted men" who agitated for rebellion in San Diego, but his powers of evil reached into official ranks such as the "time the Enemy succeeded in stopping the work, not through the instrumentality of the pagans[,] . . . but through the land Commander [Rivera]."[24]

Franciscans saw themselves essentially as teachers, remedial teachers perhaps, because their students were also considered adult children. The missionaries came foremost to teach salvation through faith in Christ. But that concept was embedded in other curricula such that daily religious practice required teaching European comportment, manners, taste, custom, a host of artisanal and agricultural skills, and, implicit in all of this, a common language. They were assisted in this work by the *Manual for Indian Parishes* (9th ed., 1754), which explained, first, that Indians belonged to the legal category *personas miserables* (like orphans, the poor, or the blind) who needed protection and, second, that aborigines existed in a state of "inculpable ignorance," as humans with a redeemable soul who were excused for their sins. Civilizing the pagan or "gentile" required vigorous measures. A school or mission was needed, but it had to be a special "reduction" mission based on total immersion in which Indians lived under the watchful supervision of the fathers and apart from their own benighted world. Effective instruction demanded strict paternal discipline, behavioral models, and a communal society constructed on the plan of a Spanish rural village.[25]

In December 1771 Father Serra moved his headquarters and mission site to a gentle slope overlooking Carmel Bay and began to build a religious community. The new location offered abundant water from the Carmel River, crop- and pastureland, freedom from Fages's oppressive presidio, and, most important, close proximity to Indian villages, which the Spaniards called "rancherías." In the presidio, mission, and village network, colonial society now composed three loci, each with its own culture and internal complexity. From the beginning, the mission was called both San Carlos Borromeo, formally, and Carmel. As it evolved over the next decade, the settlement included a 40-by-70-yard rectangular plaza and palisade or stockadelike wall that enclosed inward-facing buildings accommodating the church, priests' quarters (Serra soon began a library), storerooms, kitchen, and work areas. The *monjerio*, or dormitory, for unmarried Indian women was also within the square and locked at night to encourage chastity. A small detachment of soldiers was assigned as protection to each mission, but their barracks were built apart with a separate palisade. Beyond the fenced, adobe, and whitewashed buildings was the ranchería of small huts built in traditional style by married Indians and their families. By 1775 three soldiers had married Indian women and settled into what Serra proudly called "the beginnings of a town." As Serra described it, "[The newlyweds,] together with the families of the two sailors who were married here, and the blacksmith's and carpenter's families—all live in houses so placed as to form two streets. The storehouse, the house of the Corporal who married one of the blacksmith's daughters that came with me from Mexico [on a return trip he made], and the other buildings belonging to the mission establishment—they all make a square of their own, in front of our little residence and church."[26]

Daily life at the mission was not for the fainthearted. Church bells rang at sunrise to call all adult neophytes (mission residents over nine years of age) to mass followed by instruction in Spanish. Breakfast was a gruel of roasted corn and grains called *atole* prepared in large iron kettles and served in the community kitchen. Work of all sorts followed— tending fields and livestock, artisanal trades for men (carpentry, masonry) and women (weaving, basketry), cooking, hunting, child care, and more. The noon meal was longer and more substantial, two hours to rest and savor *pozole*, a soup of grains, vegetables, and meat when it was available. The afternoon work shift ended at five o'clock when everyone returned to church for catechism instruction, religious exercises, Spanish class, and singing. Supper at six o'clock featured another round of atole. Sundays and religious holidays centered on morning services and instruction followed by afternoons of diversion. Some Indians developed musical skills, while others debauched in animated wagering games.

If this describes the Franciscan ideal of mission routine, actual practices diverged widely. The priests were not farmers, hunters, fishers, or gatherers. Beyond some rudimentary experience with gardening and livestock brought from Mexico, the missionaries had little to offer in subsistence skills. Their advantage, of course, lay in the technology they imported (guns, metal, ships, violins) and the supply ships that brought more livestock and plants. But ships were unpredictable and the settlements lived regularly with hunger, even famine. Mission Indians suffered malnutrition, as skeletal remains now demonstrate.[27] Indeed, at critical times in the early years the Europeans depended on Indian provisions for survival. In August 1772 Serra wrote, "[T]hose who are the *main support-*

ers of our people are the gentiles. Thanks to them we live."[28] Routinely, Indians hunted, fished, and traded food that provided a necessary supplement to mission fare. The irony of instructing native hunters and gatherers on the wonders of European agriculture while depending on them for survival seems not to have struck the ingenuous Fernandinos.

Serra, however, was painfully aware of another paradox. He attributed the slow rate of conversion to "want of a knowledge of their language, a trouble of long standing with me," and hoped that the pagans would assist in their salvation by quickly learning Spanish—as, indeed, the children were already doing.[29] Although several priests later became accomplished linguists and helped to preserve elements of the native languages, a communication chasm separated Franciscans and their presumed audience. According to one estimate for Carmel Mission during the Spanish period, no priest was proficient in the native dialects and no more than 20 percent of the Indians spoke Spanish. Adding to these difficulties, the Esselen and Ohlone Indians congregated at Carmel spoke different languages and shared mutual antipathies.[30]

In some respects, the absence of a common language might have been unimportant. Serra enjoyed visiting villages to uncomprehending salutations of "Love God! Hail Jesus!" voiced by Indians "since they were told to use that expression" and were rewarded for doing so with beads or tobacco.[31] In matters of faith, however, confirmation in the Catholic Church requires that the convert is capable of reason and understands and accepts concepts such as the Holy Trinity and the Resurrection. Serra relied on Indian interpreters to carry his message, typically natives of Baja California with a third language or precocious local youths, but in either case translators only recently introduced to Spanish. The padre president occasionally expressed misgivings about the extent of mutual comprehension: "[T]here are many adults who are catechumens whose Baptisms I am putting off somewhat until I and the interpreters become a little more proficient in the language."[32] Although large numbers of gentiles (children more frequently than adults) were baptized and later confirmed, one might question what sense the Indians made of these exotic sounds and symbols. Years later, when a few parish priests had learned the native dialect, Serra's successor said bluntly, "Do not speak of teaching pagans through the medium of Spanish, or the majority of neophytes either, for it would be a contradiction in terms. How can you teach when the other does not understand? The pagans have not even heard Spanish—how can they understand it?"[33] In light of subsequent events, the language barrier may help to explain why so few adult Indians converted in the first place or remained loyal to the church when the missions eventually declined.

In the end, the great tragedy of the missions was an extraordinarily high rate of mortality and demographic collapse. In defense of the church, epidemics had struck aboriginal California before the Spaniards arrived and subsequent periods of Mexican and American rule witnessed an accelerating, near-complete destruction of native Californians. Nevertheless, missions were unhealthy places owing to overcrowding, poor nutrition, exposure to European pathogens (including syphilis), suppression of traditional medicine (including prenatal care and abortion), drudgery, and restrictions on freedom of movement. Mission mortality was highest among children and women of childbearing age, leading in turn to a reduced birthrate and general demographic collapse. Although no data exist for calculating Indian mortality rates in the native environment or precontact period, the vigorous appearance of Indians reported by arriving Spaniards, their population density, and the inclination of mission residents to return to "the wild" in times of dearth, all suggest that Indians fared better outside than within colonial society. The padres prayed for the sick, anguished over what they recognized as inordinately high mortality, and faithfully marked each passing in the death register. What they could not do was maintain an environment for mission Indians that was as healthy as that of the villages, the presidio, or even their own quarters (occasional reference to "a good dish from the Fathers' table" suggests the padres ate better, just as they enjoyed greater access to the presidio surgeon).[34] "They were baffled, frightened, and dismayed by a social problem they could not solve."[35]

THE UNTENABLE COLONY

Spanish colonial society in California foundered on a set of mortal contradictions. Designed to take root and perpetuate itself, the colony survived only through continuous infusions of material resources and instruments of political domination. Predicated on grateful participation by indigenous peoples, the settlements fostered flight and death. If indigenous cultures were undermined, no sustainable civilization took their place. Frontier actors recognized these dilemmas but lacked the means for their solution. Mutual recrimination diverted much of their energy, and, in any case, they were up against problems beyond their control. Divided rule of church, state, and tribelet limited effective local action. Meanwhile, the colonial state in New Spain was faltering. If the California colony was untenable, however, that fact scarcely discouraged efforts to make it work during the last three decades of the eighteenth century. Presidios were fortified and used as staging areas for extended conquest. The mission system expanded, for a time, as indigenous social organization unraveled. Failing to achieve their intended results, these initiatives nevertheless shaped decisively events to come.

Modern scholarship has emphasized the destructive effects of European encounters with Indians, and with good reason. Analyses of the economic exploitation, political betrayal, and cultural genocide that have characterized (North and South) American history are essential correctives for generations of colonial apologia. Yet it is true that critical scholarship tends to neglect native agency and the reciprocities of group interaction. A good example is the question of mission growth and specifically why some Indians were attracted to the Spanish settlements. When the question is not ignored, it is typically answered with notions of forceful recruitment, enslavement, or kindred ideas that deny Indian choice. Yet it appears that some Indians, under some circumstances, were positively attracted to the embrace of Spanish institutions. Why would that happen? Was it force, the threat of force, material inducements, technological wizardry, spiritual awe, or some other inducement that made sense from the standpoint of indigenous culture? What did the invaders have that at least some Indians wanted?

Indians were obviously impressed by the powers of the Spaniard. Rightfully so, as the invader arrived on tall-masted sailing ships, firing off cannon and muskets, ringing large bells, riding the miraculous horse and towing domestic cattle, swinging tools of metal, sporting elaborate dress, and worshiping all manner of objects (crosses, chalices, books) from which their strength seemed to derive. European accounts of first contact with native Californians include frequent reference to curiosity about these particulars, yet they also report that the indigenous people were not awed or transfixed by the foreign presence. On the contrary, they went out to greet the newcomers in the "fullest confidence" and invited them to their villages. They made gifts of food and ornaments, accepting in return the Spaniards' glass beads. But the Indians knew use and exchange values when they saw them. As Serra noted, "[W]hat they wanted was clothing. And it was only for articles of this type that they would do any business with the soldiers and mule drivers in exchange for fish."[36] In the Yuma region, Palóu observed that "the Indians do not fail to frequent the settlement and there traffic with soldiers and colonists by bringing in their wares for exchange, and also obtaining cloth in ex-

8. *View of the Convent, Church, and Rancherias of the Carmel Mission,* by
José Cardero, 1791. Cardero's drawing provides a picture of mission courtyard activity, Europeans and Indians interacting, work, mission architecture,
and an Indian village in the background. (Courtesy of the Museo Naval,
Madrid)

change for corn."[37] Similar interchanges occurred in the Monterey area,
where aboriginal trade fairs and village exchange networks were well developed. If Spaniards viewed the Indians' arrival at the missions as a good
omen for civilization and conversion, Indians probably saw advantages
to incorporating the new settlements and precious trade articles into local exchange networks. New trade opportunities, in turn, played into village and tribelet competition as the more potent Indian groups had more
resources to barter and thus more to gain over their rivals through expanded commerce.[38]

   If trade was one important attraction that Spanish settlements offered
Indians, conversion to Christianity (or simply to mission life) was another. The central facts of Indian conversion were its differential appeal,
pragmatic character, and limited engagement. Differential susceptibility
to missionary recruitment depended on group and individual attributes.
In 1771 the Carmel Mission set up at a site five to fifteen kilometers distant from three Rumsen villages. (See map p. 16.) "The first converts were
from Carmel Valley and residents of the *rancherias* Tucutnut and Ichxenta.
Apart from the fact that the Carmeleños were the nearest to the new establishment they were the weakest of the Monterey nations and no doubt

realized that the kindly strangers were a good protection."[39] In 1774 Serra noted that the next stage of outreach was to Indians of the same language group but "from *rancherías* very far distant, and lost in the folds of the mountains, [who] arrive every day. At the present time there are some who come from Eselen, called La Soledad, a place about halfway on the road between this mission and that of San Antonio, about twelve leagues distant from both."[40] By the late 1770s most of the adjacent Carmel Valley population had been incorporated into mission routines or residence, although a remnant of the roughly five hundred valley inhabitants never converted. The "Eselen" (or probably Excelen) village Serra mentions is one of a series of settlements in the upper Carmel Valley and Santa Lucia Mountains that spoke the Esselen language and got along badly with their Ohlone neighbors. "Only forty-seven Excelen Indians had been baptized during the first missionary period. These seem to have been reluctant to yield their Christian children for instruction and even the adults may not have been attracted to the idea of dwelling with their despised enemies, the Rumsens."[41] Recruitment moved outward from the nearer and weaker villages of a single language group. This early pattern underwent fundamental changes as mission recruitment reached its peak in the period 1788–95. Villages at a greater distance that maintained their independence during the first twenty years now began to concede. "Most of the catechumens came from the *rancherias* of Excelen but toward the end of the period nearly the whole gentile remnant of the Ensen [Salinas Valley] nation came to the mission. Meanwhile, many people from Kalenda Ruc [Big Sur] were instructed and baptized, and even four or five dozen Mutsuns from the territory later given San Juan Bautista [Mission northeast of San Carlos]."[42]

The pattern of individual recruitment is simpler, although documented with less nuance because baptismal and marriage records noted only sex, age, and place of origin, not such characteristics of persons as occupation or social status. Indians brought their children to the missions for instruction sooner and in greater numbers than they came themselves. Young children were accompanied by Indian women, and when families came together, men were proportionately fewer among permanent residents owing perhaps to their role as hunters, fishers, and gatherers in the sexual division of labor. Inferences about social status are risky. Father Serra recommended village chiefs as alcaldes, and research evidence demonstrates that Indian officials at San Carlos tended to come from the ranks of indigenous authority figures.[43] Conversely, the number of officials was very small, and other reports suggest that the more

powerful persons in village society resisted incorporation more successfully. Perhaps the only conclusion to be drawn is the tentative one recently developed for the northern missions: "The children of some of the
most important families were among the earliest Bay Area neophytes. . . .
For the most part, however, the tribal status of the initial neophyte children and their families cannot be determined from the mission records.
Some of the first neophytes may well have been from marginal families
in the local ranking system."[44]

Recruitment and conversion, in short, followed a pattern. At the village level, initial neophytes came from nearby, weaker, and culturally ho-
mogeneous groups. At the individual level, the order of recruitment was
children, women, men, and last, perhaps, higher-status individuals. The
rise and fall of the mission population (at Carmel and elsewhere) took
place over a limited time, beginning in 1770 and declining gradually after 1795. During this period, the pattern changed from differential to
uniform recruitment. The explanation that best fits this pattern begins
with recognition that initially some Indians were positively attracted to
the missions, if not necessarily for the mysteries of the Christian faith,
then certainly for the pragmatic advantages of trade, individual and village aggrandizement in a competitive society, material reward, protection, and, one is compelled to speculate, insight into the source of the invader's power. And, of course, other Indians—the distant, powerful,
independent—rejected incorporation to the extent that it was an issue at
all. In time, however, Spanish colonial influence spread in ways that
proved overpowering for many, if not all. Much of what follows analyzes the development of colonial society. With respect to the question
of recruitment, the key point is that what began as attraction soon turned
to compulsion. Expanding colonial power undermined Indian society,
its natural environment, health, economy, and polity. By 1790 the choice
was no longer whether to collaborate with the Europeans or pursue the
indigenous way of life but whether to accept subordination or resist. In
fact, they chose both.

For five decades Spanish colonial society grew even if it did not develop into a sustainable civil society. Infusions of personnel and resources
permitted the establishment of new missions (from eight before 1780 to
eighteen by 1800), presidios (at San Francisco and Santa Barbara, bringing the total to four), and three town settlements (the pueblos of Los Angeles, San José, and Branciforte/Santa Cruz). From the arrival of roughly
two hundred Spaniards in 1769, the population of *gente de razon* (literally, "persons of reason" but effectively "whites," meaning Spanish,

mestizos, and any others not regarded socially as Indian) had grown to one thousand by 1790. At the same time, the number of mission Indians reached nine thousand just as the larger indigenous population was beginning to decline. By 1820 Alta California had a population of 3,300 Spanish-mestizos, a historic high of 21,000 mission Indians, yet an endangered majority of nonmission Indians whose numbers had already declined by perhaps 25 percent. Monterey presented a somewhat different pattern. From 1790 to 1820 the presidio housed approximately 200 people: soldiers of various types and ranks, their families, a small contingent of artisans and retired soldiers, servants, and a handful of officials. The neophyte population at Carmel Mission peaked at 876 in 1795 and then went into steady decline to half that number by 1820. Here, too, the death rate was notably high among neophytes and gentiles.[45]

Throughout the Spanish colonial period, Monterey maintained a geographic settlement pattern based on three interdependent but distinct places: presidio, mission, and village. Presidio and mission each grew into small, internally differentiated, villages and expanded into their surroundings with fields and pastures. Land grants were rare under Spanish rule, although a few ranchos were established from the mid-1790s onward (the first California grant, a small plot near Carmel Mission, went to retired soldier Manuel Butrón and his Indian wife). A combination of few settlers and depredations by and against Indians limited the establishment of ranches for several more decades.

As California's capital, the Monterey Presidio was a busy military, civil, and domestic center. A growing number of soldiers took up the professional duties (rather than construction work) that they initially had judged too dangerous. Indian "crimes" increased apace with civilization, and military campaigns were launched to capture mission fugitives and retaliate against raids on crops and livestock. Soldiers also helped to tend the presidio garden and Rancho del Rey (King's Ranch), established in 1794 at Salinas for two thousand to four thousand head of livestock. The presidio housed a variety of artisans (saddle, harness, and carriage makers, carpenters, masons, blacksmiths, weavers, tailors) and storerooms for food and equipment distributed to missions and pueblos throughout the presidial district. Officials (*habilitados*) managed the stores and were counted among the professional class along with doctors (a surgeon and a bleeder) and the military governor.

Families began to populate presidial quarters as a few soldiers married Indians and white women arrived from Mexico (initially four wives and three single women in 1794). By 1813 the number of women had increased to eighty-five, and they contributed to population growth (among Spanish-mestizos) with an average of 5.6 children.[46] Although living conditions at the presidio were overcrowded, muddy, and dull, colonials suffered far less disease and death than did Indians.

Society at the presidio was in motion. Families had a high turnover rate as many returned to Mexico at the end of their military tours. California held little attraction for civilian colonists, government promotional efforts notwithstanding. If Monterey enjoyed any excitement, it centered around the port and international merchant traffic. Distinguished commercial, scientific, and diplomatic expeditions from France, England, and Russia began arriving in the 1780s. The first U.S. commercial vessels would take a growing interest in this coast after 1800. Although responsible for local oversight, the presidio looked over the horizon, to San Blas, the Sandwich Islands, the Russian colony at Fort Ross, the Pacific Northwest, and fundamentally to Mexico City. That was the direction of their life support and, for some, their future after a tour in colonial service.

A few miles over the hill, Mission San Carlos had a different population, attitude, purpose, and culture. Nothing comes across quite so clearly in Junípero Serra's letters, and those of his successor Fermín Francisco de Lasuén, as the great importance attached to establishing new mission settlements. Franciscans were in for the long haul, even if colonial policy envisioned medium-term conversion of missions to agricultural settlements and Spanish towns. At its peak in the 1790s, the mission included more than eight hundred neophytes, a small contingent of artisan-teachers and their wives, as many as six priests, and an equal number of soldiers. Based on the vital contribution of Indian labor, the missions developed into an economic dynamo, even within the political and demographic constraints of colonial society. San Carlos began supplying the presidio with food in 1780 as its livestock population grew from several hundred to more than ten thousand in the early 1800s. Harvests of wheat, barley, corn, and beans doubled over the same period. The missions produced an impressive array of agricultural and manufactured products for their own use and for trade; they made soap, candles, woolens, shoes, saddles, and leather jackets and shipped food to the presidio where they traded for tools, wine, locks, keys, gunpowder, cotton, silk thread, paper, crockery, razors, mescal, and chocolate.[47]

The mission community was also in motion. Father Lasuén's 1788 annual report counted 710 individuals (322 of them married) who "live at the mission within sound of the bell. They take meals three times a

day in common; they live poorly, and in accordance with what the annual stipends of the missionary Fathers and the different products of the
mission allow."[48] Living poorly did not always suit the Indians, who were
accustomed to frequent visits to their villages and provisioning grounds.
Here again the padres faced a dilemma. On the one hand, as Lasuén explains: "If the Christian [mission Indian] is to be given the same liberty
as the pagan, how is he to be civilized? How shall we teach them Christian obedience, and the ways of civil society"—how, that is, if they resist staying put long enough to get it? The solution was to "denatural-
ize" them. On the other hand, an "almost invincible . . . call of the wild"
was so strong among Indians that it would be folly to oppose it: "We
must remember that the majority of our neophytes are so attached to the
mountains that if there were an unqualified prohibition against going
there, there would be danger of a riot."[49] Franciscans managed the contradiction, without great success, by trying to make the missions desirable places of permanent residence while liberally granting permission
for leaves of absence. In some cases, flight resulted in pursuit and punishment, but formal charges of fugitivism were not common[50] and generally occurred in cases in which unauthorized leave was coupled with
another offense such as family abandonment, insubordination, theft, or
working at the presidio without authorization.[51] The mission was a permeable space through which a variety of people and products circulated.

Neither was the mission a total institution in matters of social and spiritual life. Work routines and instructional schedules did not rule out traditional leisure pursuits such as gaming and dancing. Among the achievements of European culture, card playing was the innovation most eagerly
adopted locally. California Indians did not take well to the routine tasks
and work discipline demanded of them. The padres lamented, "[R]arely
and only in few places will one chance to see even half of the people working. . . . They sit down; they recline; they often go away, and come back
when it suits them."[52] For their part, Indians continued to observe traditional ceremonial practices, including shamanistic healing, ritual dancing, rites of passage, mourning, sorcery, and sweathouse purification.[53]
Archaeological evidence shows they also continued to prepare traditional
foods with customary crockery and to appoint their huts with articles
from the villages.[54] This is to suggest neither that Indians lived at liberty
in the mission nor that life was easy. Indeed, for Indians mission life was
hazardous, mysterious, confining, onerous, sometimes profitable, and increasingly the only peaceful option. But the mission was a negotiated
space, a community governed by material contradictions, spiritual syn-

cretism, and working compromises that granted relative autonomy to its interdependent members. The negotiated order worked for a time but steadily devolved as key contradictions played out in the environment, in labor relations, and in matters of gender and social reproduction. Taken together, these three contradictions illustrate the routines of daily life and dynamics of intergroup conflict in colonial society.

ENVIRONMENTAL COMPETITION

Europeans and Indians used their environment in fundamentally incompatible ways. Whereas the Indian economy relied heavily on game, seafood, and native plants, the Spaniards introduced domestic plants and livestock. As mission and presidio herds of cattle, horses, mules, sheep, goats, and pigs multiplied, they spread out over the landscape consuming native grasses and seeds basic to the Indian food supply. In the early 1780s both missionaries and public officials were already commenting on the destruction of the native food supply and recommending various palliative measures.[55] Soldiers and missionaries naturally blamed one another for the worst abuses, and the problem became one of Serra's several briefs against civilian colonization. The Indian reaction was not long in coming. Livestock theft, a depredation that began with the European invasion, accelerated from the occasional mule slaughtered by local villagers to wholesale cattle rustling. Governor Neve launched military retaliation but without success: "Since damages have been suffered not only in the cattle but also in the horse herd of the Christians at Mission San Carlos, caused by the heathen of Sanjones and Soledad in the Monterey area[,] . . . I have ordered that an example be made and reasonable punishment applied [by] seizing the culprits, carrying them to the presidio and shaming them by eight or ten days in the stocks and twenty or twenty-five lashes. . . . Repeated punishments, however, have not succeeded with the Christian Indians of the last-named mission who, it was recently found, had killed as many as ten fillies, mares, and colts of the Monterey herd. It is significant that they do no harm of any kind to the cattle or horses of the mission."[56] Neve's admirable candor supports Serra's more contentious charge that presidio, rather than mission, livestock were a greater threat to the Indian way of life. That interpretation was borne out in the 1790s when the first cattle ranches were established in the Salinas Valley only to be destroyed by Indian attacks.[57]

The environmental conflict set in motion by European conquest took many additional forms. Competition for native grasses and seeds also reduced the food supply of wild game, thereby compounding scarcities experienced by Indians. Grizzly bears were abundant in California's coastal mountains (and, indeed, later became the state symbol) and soon became another predator on the livestock population. Eradication of the bear saved cows but denied the Indians' diet, crafts, and folklore in which bear meat, skins, and symbols played a role. Taken singularly, these environmental changes might have been innocuous, but of course their effects were cumulative, cascading, and summed up in Indian mortality rates that now accelerated. European pathogens were key to the problem, along with dietary changes, living conditions, and, many believe, a mood of apathy and bewilderment that settled over the villages.[58] Colonialism was killing off the Indians it came to save and the labor force on which it depended.

LABOR AND PRODUCTION

In his extraordinary study of the California mission economy, Robert Archibald observes,

> Hispanic California was a monument to the effectiveness and skill of Indian labor. . . . [T]here is no doubt that missions were primarily the creation of Indian neophytes. Indian influence and creativity extended beyond the confines of the mission and it was their labor which constructed presidio buildings and private residences. Without them the economy of Hispanic California would have remained at a bare subsistence level.[59]

At Carmel Mission, Indians performed a variety of tasks: José Antonio and Donato were blacksmiths; Casimiro, a native of Baja California, and Tomás María, from Carmel Valley, were carpenters; unnamed legions worked the fields; and a few were exempted from the prohibition against Indian horsemen to serve as vaqueros and shepherds.[60] Although the military governors feared that mounted Indians might begin to behave like Apaches, the need for livestock-tending labor overrode their revealing fears. Father Lasuén observes, "In these presidios from the very beginning could be found [Indian] cooks, laundrymen, millers, water-carriers, and wood-cutters. And in case of need they have given Indian women to serve as wet nurses. In the nurseries Indian girls are used as 'baby-sitters,' and employed to sweep, and to do the work usually done by maids for no other remuneration than whatever they feel like giving them."[61] Although Lasuén is bitter in this 1801 report, believing that Indians and their proper education were the exclusive province of the missions rather than the presidios, his observation is corroborated by other sources.[62]

9. *Monterey Presidio*, by José Cardero, 1791. This drawing shows the walled military fortress of wooden construction, ships in the bay, and Indians at work in the fields, hauling water, and receiving instruction at the left. (Courtesy of the Bancroft Library)

Rustic mission and presidio settlements enjoyed a transition to productive workshops and ranches in the 1790s. The mission led colonial economic development owing largely to its claim on the indigenous labor force. Mission and Indian workers, in turn, benefited from skilled artisans brought from Mexico to build and educate.

> It was these artisans transported and paid at royal expense who imparted to the missions that style which is now so closely identified with them. Buildings were rebuilt incorporating roof tiles and adobe instead of tule and mud construction typical of frontier California. Fountains, patios, archways, and additional rooms were constructed. Even more significant were new wells, irrigation systems, plows, and tools. Huts of neophytes were gradually converted to adobe. . . . The bulwark of the renovation was done by neophytes with the artisans overseeing the work.[63]

The first contingent of twenty artisans to serve all of California arrived between 1792 and 1795, among them masons, a potter, a mill maker, carpenters, tanners, a shoemaker, tailors, blacksmiths, weavers, a ribbon maker, and two saddlers. Mission San Carlos received five, including Antonio Domingo Henriquez, a master weaver who married an Indian woman; Estevan Ruíz, a master mason who built the new church and taught his trade; and the tailors Tapinto and Joaquin Botella (whom Lasuén judged as possessed of ephemeral skills and unspecified bad habits that were not needed at the mission). The vital role of artisans was to re-produce their skills; at Carmel eight neophytes were trained as carpen-ters, eleven as stonemasons, two as blacksmiths, and others in tanning and leather work. The great success of this program was demonstrated over the next few years as mission productivity escalated and the reli-gious communities became the most potent economic force in colonial development.

If Indian labor was key to development, it was also a fundamental source of conflict between church and state. Labor scarcity sharpened competition for available hands and raised in very practical ways all the nuanced issues of colonial authority. Governors and Franciscans fought one another and maneuvered with Mexico City to command the labor force, routinely charging their rival with mismanagement and physical abuse of Indians. In a marvelously revealing document, Father Lasuén wrote to Governor Fages in September 1787 to report that the Indian Bruno had taken refuge in Mission San Carlos: "Apart from the immu-nity of the holy place and the importance attached to it more than any other place in the world, he comes to us suffering blows received from the soldier Ríos. Neither the military nor the Indians had been able to catch him in the twelve days during which he was wandering in the moun-tains. . . . He has now given himself up. . . . I hope and pray that after punishing him Your Lordship will permit him to go free." In a marginal note on the copy retained in Lasuén's records, the priest added sarcasti-cally, "At [the] present time they are carrying off Indians to the presidio on any pretext of guilt in order to have peons to work for nothing, per-haps in the orchard of His Lordship [i.e., Fages]."[64]

Soldiers and state officials were equally critical of labor practices at the missions. The whole question was aired in a series of reports pre-cipitated, oddly enough, by charges voiced by Father Concepción Horra, a missionary who had been sent back to Mexico after Lasuén judged him insane. Horra protested his exile to the viceroy, claiming, "[T]he treat-ment shown to the Indians is the most cruel I have ever read in history. For the slightest things they receive heavy floggings, are shackled, and put in stocks." Mexico City requested that California governor Diego Borica (1794–1800) investigate the matter. Borica sent a list of "fifteen questions about missionary abuses, 1798," to the four presidio com-manders whose critical responses varied, although none shared the mad priest's intensity. Secular authorities believed that Indians were expected to work excessively long hours, women did heavy lifting even when preg-nant or nursing, children were given lighter labor, and punishment (for neglect of work or religious duties, overstaying leaves of absence, sexual relations, theft, and fighting) was severe, ranging from imprisonment to confinement in stocks and whipping. In a long and informative 1801 "refutation of charges," Lasuén argued that although kindness underpinned all relations with Indians, it was necessary at times to enforce labor and religious discipline. The president acknowledged flogging and confinement, although he qualified charges of extremity by noting that twenty-five lashes were the maximum administered (not fifty as alleged) and only at Santa Barbara were women put in stocks.[65]

Mutual recrimination was rooted in competition for the limited Indian labor force and in contradictory colonial policies. Secular authorities believed themselves the ultimate authority in all matters including Indian welfare, and they understood the objective of colonial policy to be autonomous, self-sufficient Indian pueblos. Franciscans did not challenge state authority directly, but insofar as the king had mandated civilization of the heathen and charged the church exclusively with that responsibility, the fathers saw themselves as independent of secular interference in Indian affairs. The fundamental contradiction expressed itself in labor relations owing to military demands for Indian labor on presidio construction and public works such as roads, drainage, and lumbering. The mission, in effect, owned neophyte Indian labor and "sold" it to the presidio in the form of cash credits owed to the mission. Steven Hackel's detailed study of Mission San Carlos shows that during the years 1787–1817 the Monterey Presidio used anywhere from 500 to 2,900 Indian labor days per year, the result of which (along with food and artisan products) was a strong positive trade balance in favor of the mission that was used to purchase Mexican imports—the high price of which missionaries protested.[66]

The financial benefits of labor contracting, however, were weighed against the demands of mission production and gentile recruitment. Missionaries lamented the lack of sufficient hands to supply firewood or bring in the harvest, especially during seasons when Indians returned to traditional fishing and seed gathering. Meanwhile the demand for labor at the presidio increased, particularly after a devastating fire in 1789. As a result, both mission and presidio sought gentile labor. In his final year as governor, Fages contracted workers for restoration of the presidio and construction of the new Royal Chapel (a sanctuary that stands to this day in Monterey).

> For instructors I made use of three government stone cutters, and for laborers, the various servants left from one year to the next by the supply ships,

together with the pagans of the villages in the vicinity of the pueblo of San
Jose. . . . I first called together their captains and leaders. I proposed that they
send groups of five, ten, fifteen, or twenty according to the number of people
they could do without for the defense of their lands. I promised to reward
them with blankets, shirts, glass beads, and shells. They agreed to the pact,
and in groups of eighty to one hundred they arranged with the commissioner
of the town and the commander of the guard to give them an escort . . . over
the twenty leagues [fifty-four miles] which separates Monterey from the pueblo
of San Jose, in order not to disquiet the pagans they encounter along the road.
They made a specific request to the commissioner regarding the protection of
the villages and the women left behind in those villages, to guard against the
tremendous abuse which they are in the habit of doing to one another whenever they see their spouses left behind.[67]

Fages reports that the Indians were satisfied with their employment and
on completion indicated that they would come again if requested. Such
arrangements were highly unsatisfactory to missionaries, however, and
animate the defensiveness of Lasuén's 1801 report. If the presidio and
the fledgling pueblos could recruit Indian labor directly from the villages,
then a huge threat would be posed to the mission's own profitable labor
contracting system, not to mention its basic monopoly over the incorporation of gentiles into colonial society. In sum, the question of labor
and production pushed colonial policy contradictions to the forefront of
political affairs.

GENDER AND SOCIAL REPRODUCTION

One of the more endearing stories of colonial contact comes from Father Serra's protégé Juan Evangelista, who confided to the padre that Indians believed the first Spaniards were the sons of the mules they rode,
a conclusion informed by the absence of women in their ranks.[68] In a
similar vein, Fages wrote, "[T]he Indians . . . consider that we are exiles
from our own lands who have come here in quest of their women."[69]
Both of these men, so often at odds with one another, heartily believed
that the sooner immigrant women were incorporated into California, the
more effective would be their own reception and recruitment of converts.
Men without women brought problems beyond questions of ancestry.
Sexual abuse of Indian women occurred with some regularity, violating
the trust of potential converts and undermining military discipline. Serra
railed that "the soldiers, without any restraint or shame, have behaved
like brutes towards the Indian women [and] would catch an Indian
woman with their lassos to become prey for their unbridled lust. At times

some Indian men would try to defend their wives, only to be shot down with bullets."[70] Secular authorities also condemned these abuses and imposed heavy penalties on miscreants. In one instance, "a soldier was given stocks, chains, and sweeping for fornication with an Indian woman," and in a more heinous case of abuse of two Indian girls, a private in the Santa Barbara guard was ordered "hanged and the body burned with that of a mule."[71]

Given the frequency of reported sexual abuse, it is doubtful that exploitation of Indian women was vigorously reprimanded, although cases involving children and military discipline were seriously punished offenses. Beyond these observations, the situation gets murky as it begins to involve cross-cultural mores and consensual unions. One of Serra's criticisms of the experiment with Indian self-government, for example, was that alcaldes supplied soldiers with Indian women in exchange for goods, money, or favors. Instances of spousal abuse were also known in Indian society, such as a case of multiple adultery in Monterey that resulted in the wife's murder by the husband. Father James Cullerton describes the colorful marital career of an Indian woman from Monterey. Catalina was married to a neophyte at the mission who became seriously ill, at which time she entered into an adulterous (by clerical standards) affair and became pregnant by a Spanish soldier. When her Indian husband died, Catalina married the soldier with Father Serra's blessing and dispensation for adultery. Within a year the new husband was killed fighting Indians on the Colorado River, and Catalina soon married again, this time to "California's first resident Italian" who was a leather jacket in Spain's army.[72] Sexual abuse of Indian women was a problem not to be minimized, even if it occasionally involved the complicity of Indian men. The more common facts of gender relations, however, were the growing rate of intermarriage, miscegenation, an influx of Spanish mestizo women from Mexico, and an explicit colonial policy to feminize the frontier.[73]

In 1790 the Spanish government conducted a census of New Spain's northern frontier. Generally known as the Revillagigedo Census of 1793 (for the viceroy at the time of its publication), the survey in Alta California focused on the colonial population that had gathered during the first twenty-one years of occupation, excluding for the most part Indians. The bold social fact of the enumeration was the variety of racial mixing that had occurred and the census takers' labored efforts to classify the resulting population. There were clear categories, including "Indios" (the few counted because they were married to settlers or soldiers), "Españoles," and probably some mixed-race persons who were promoted to the social status of Spaniards. But at least half the population of the Spanish settlements, and far more in some towns including Monterey, were of mixed ancestry. Mixed-race categories included "mestizo" (half Indian and half white), "mulato" (half white and half black), persons with smaller black fractions, and other gradations of brown and black in terms such as "color quebrado," "pardo," "moreno," "morizco," and "coyote" (three-fourths Indian, one-fourth white). Collapsing some of these categories, the colony-wide figures show that 50 percent qualified as "Spanish," 18 percent as mestizo, 19 percent as mulato, 8 percent (counted) as Indian, and 5 percent as coyotes. Monterey's population of one hundred adults was more diversified than the aggregate, with fully two-thirds of mixed background (mestizos and mulatos comprising more than half with 22 and 29 percent respectively—the colony's highest concentration of mulatos). The broad social implications of these data underscore a pattern of ethnic diversity set down in the very foundation of California and persisting into the 1820s and 1830s. The population was Spanish (typically of New Spain or Mexican birth) and Indian (Sonoran and Costanoan) and all shades between, including a significant leavening of black (no doubt Caribbean peoples incorporated into New Spain). Given the large number of childbearing unions across categories, the colony's inhabitants were rapidly assimilating as a socially distinct Californio population—*hijos del país,* or children of the country, as they called themselves.[74]

Serra took particular satisfaction in the six marriages (three Indian wives) sanctified at the mission in 1775, several involving people he had brought from Mexico in a party of artisans. Governors Fages and Neve encouraged the influx of women, believing it would persuade the Indians that Spaniards had not come to steal their wives, just as it would advance the pace of pueblo settlements and steadily retire the missions. Monterey's female population grew to eighty-five in 1813 with successive parties of artisan and soldier wives and a few colonists arriving from Sonora and Sinaloa—most of them "castas" or persons of mixed (mestizo, mulatto) ancestry and drawn from the lower classes. Antonia I. Castañeda's study of women at the presidio from 1770 to 1821 reveals that the early and substantial number of marriages involving Indian women (37 percent) declined over time (to 15 percent) as more Spanish mestizo women arrived. After 1798 there were no additions to the total of sixteen mixed marriages. These data recorded at the mission naturally exclude free unions and concubinage and any estimate of their offspring. Castañeda explored the origins of the sixteen Indian women joined in these intermarriages and first California mestizo families. Twelve were Ohlone from the mission and Carmel Valley villages, a few came from as far away as Vancouver Island and the Colorado River, and one, Regina Tespunena, was a medicine woman (then called Toypurina) exiled from Mission San Gabriel near Los Angeles for her part in an Indian uprising against military abuse.[75]

Common aspirations for the settlement of California soon ran afoul of familiar colonial contradictions as missionaries and governors pursued conflicting policies. Neve's governorship (1774–82) was founded on a new Reglamiento calling for reforms in finance, colonization, and mission governance. California should become economically self-sufficient through changes in public accounting, presidio-mission exchange pricing, establishment of new towns (at San José and Los Angeles), and greater state control over missions with the aim of expediting secularization. Even as he passed the office to Fages in 1782, Neve urged, "[T]he continued growth of the towns is very important to the colony. Very soon their harvests and those of the missions will be able to supply the presidios. . . . The fostering of these towns demands very special attention. They will not lack difficulties, and only the vigilance of the government can overcome these."[76] Serra demurred, in letters to the viceroys, for practical and religious reasons:

> [O]n the subject of pueblos of Spaniards, and the way they have begun to establish them, [I have] expressed my opinion that it did not appear the best thing to do; and that even the purpose they claimed . . . [to] fill the royal warehouses with provisions . . . such a purpose would be better obtained by increasing and helping the Missions than by means of such pueblos, and, moreover, by helping them they would also be aiding their spiritual advancement. . . . Missions, my Lord, missions—that is what this country needs. They will not only provide it with what is most important—the light of the Holy Gospel—but also what will be the means of supplying foodstuffs for themselves and the Royal Presidios. Later on, when the gentiles spread throughout all these lands have become Christian, and when they are settled in their various reservations or missions[,] . . . then will be the proper time for introducing towns of Spaniards.[77]

By contrast to his successful opposition to Indian self-government, Serra lost this round in his ongoing fight with Neve. But he never relinquished his resistance to civilian pueblos, or, more precisely, to the timing of their introduction. He claimed that the pueblo at San José was built too close to the Indians' fields at Mission Santa Clara in violation of Spanish law, with the result that settler livestock was destroying crops. In a rare defense of native capabilities, Serra chided the Spaniards' self-designation "gente de razón" for having been applied complacently, "just as if the Indians did not have the use of reason too."

The key point about gender and colonial policy was that women, whether Indians married to soldiers or Spanish mestizo immigrants, were essential actors charged with the responsibility of personifying civilized ways and propagating Christian families. At mission and presidio Indian women were instructed in colonial methods of household production, religious observation, citizenship, and child rearing. Their unique job was to reproduce not only Spanish citizens but also the ideology and institutional forms of Spanish society. As Castañeda notes acutely, California colonization "recognized the centrality of women to Spanish society in the Americas and incorporated sex-gender as a crucial element in politics, policies, and strategies of colonization."[78]

Yet there was a practical flaw in the otherwise coherent plan. Colonization did not work. Few Mexican colonists were attracted to California, and among those who did come, most left again after a short tour. California life was a trial. Monterey settlers still lived within the crowded and fetid presidio in 1795 when the first land grant ranches were attempted in the face of Indian opposition. The northern frontier offered little incentive for migration, as dramatically demonstrated beginning in the 1790s by official recourse to settlement by convict artisans willing to trade imprisonment in Mexico for commuted sentences and permanent residence in California.[79] Agricultural schemes in the presidios and pueblos languished in this period for want of experience, labor, material inputs, and markets. Only the missions succeeded in agricultural and artisanal production, although even that success was threatened by accelerating mortality, native resistance, and competition for labor. "The plan to make the presidios agriculturally productive did not succeed. Neither did the plan for mission-pueblos as racially integrated nuclei of urban centers."[80]

The story of Doña Eulalia de Callis is a parable for Spanish colonization in California. When Pedro Fages returned to California in 1784 as Neve's successor and provincial governor (elevated from his earlier post, military commander), he arranged for his pregnant wife, Eulalia, and son to follow. Coming from a well-placed Catalan family, Eulalia found life in Monterey hardly bearable for herself and the children. Family life was further complicated by Don Pedro's well-known attachment to an Indian girl he had brought from Yuma as a servant. Eulalia was a match for her volatile husband and scandalized the community by publicly accusing the governor of infidelity, leaving his bed, and vowing divorce—unprecedented acts for a woman in this time and place. Denying any infidelity, Fages asked Father Noriega at Mission San Carlos to mediate the dispute and squelch the divorce complaint. Although the facts become clouded at this point, evidently Doña Eulalia spent a month involuntarily secluded at the mission, where pastoral counseling did little to reconcile her with the governor or California living. She petitioned for legal separation, saying that although she was "a woman and helpless," her tormentors "will not close the doors of my own honor and birth."[81] Eventually, a reconciliation was effected, Eulalia bore another child who died after a few days, and ultimately the couple returned to Mexico. Like the Spanish Empire, the gubernatorial couple came to California with conflicting intentions, quarreled during its residence, and eventually returned to a world it understood.

By 1800 the Spanish colony in Alta California had passed its apogee, although it would soldier on for another twenty years. Jerry-built from the start, the edifice was now showing stress fractures at every corner. Extraordinarily high Indian mortality undermined most efforts to foster a self-sustaining society. The combination of a declining indigenous population and unsuccessful colonization from Mexico spelled a precarious colonial purchase on California, sustained mainly through administrative determination—which would soon falter. The contradictions, as we have seen, were pervasive and the colonial response only exacerbated matters. The neophyte population at Mission San Carlos began to decline in the late 1790s, anticipating a trend at other missions. Faced with continuing labor demands, presidio commanders reversed earlier policies of peaceful coexistence and began to pursue fugitives and conscript workers.[82]

Indian resistance grew in these later years, taking a variety of forms. Fugitivism increased, no doubt because the military criminalized the habit of free movement. Traditional ritual and domestic practices were retained in the missions despite repressive discipline. Although Carmel was spared violent uprising, other missions in the Monterey presidial district experienced native retaliation: San Luis Obispo was raided for livestock and partially burned by gentiles in 1776 and threatened with revolt in 1794; mountain villagers attacked the neophyte ranchería at San Juan Bautista in 1798; priests were poisoned at both San Antonio and San Miguel in 1800. The more pervasive brand of resistance, which did plague Monterey, was livestock theft. Indians regularly helped themselves to royal cattle, mules, and horses as a source of food and, later, for commercial exchange. That the actions constituted resistance rather than simply opportunistic poaching is demonstrated by the fact that the early ranches that infringed on native grasslands were raided and then destroyed. Sherburne F. Cook's classic study, *The Conflict between the California Indian and White Civilization,* includes an inventory of Indian actions defined as either "criminal" (e.g., homicide, assault, robbery, incest) or "political" (e.g., fugitivism, conspiracy, armed resistance). Drawing on ninety-four cases of disciplinary action involving 362 persons, Cook shows that political transgressions far outnumbered criminal deeds and that fugitivism and stock stealing (considered "political" when it involved warlike raids) were the most frequent acts, followed at some distance by homicide, robbery, conspiracy, and armed resistance.[83]

If growing resistance may be taken as an expression of Indian agency, it also bespoke cultural collapse. As their numbers and village habitat steadily dwindled, Indians perforce abandoned a culturally embedded way of life in active resistance and a search for survival on the fringes of colonial settlements. Struggling against the forces of imminent change, they came to share the destiny of an equally endangered mission system and colonial realm.

MAKING HISTORY

In *Silencing the Past,* Michel-Rolph Trouillot reminds us of "the inherent ambivalence of the word 'history.' . . . [H]istory means both the facts of the matter and a narrative of those facts, both 'what happened' and 'that which is said to have happened.' The first meaning places the emphasis on the sociohistorical process, the second on our knowledge of that process or on a story about the process."[84] Having explored in some detail the sociohistorical process of Spanish California, I turn to an examination of the first histories of the period. My analytic focus shifts from what happened, as well as that can be determined from a wide variety of sources, to questions of how the story was told in early narratives, by whom, under what conditions, and for what purposes. Equally important are questions about what was silenced, untold, or left out of these narratives and why. I examine the stories that were constructed about Spanish California in the late eighteenth century in light of the sociohistorical process—to combine the twin meanings of history.

Contemporary histories of Spanish California that were recorded, passed on, and incorporated in subsequent interpretations of the period fall into three groups. They were, in order of appearance, histories from the standpoint of civil authorities, the church, and foreign expeditions. Indians left no recorded history, and their rich oral tradition was silenced with the destruction of their lives and culture. Indians appear in the other histories as mise-en-scène, objects about which narrators comment, but never as voices on their own behalf. The Indian understood as a feature of the natural landscape is, of course, a reflection of contemporary European historical mentality and a clue to the selective orientation of these narratives.

The first accounts of Alta California's physical environment and native population were published in Mexico City in the 1770s by Spanish military officers. Miguel Costansó, the engineer who accompanied the Sacred Expedition of 1769 and laid out the presidio site at Monterey, addressed his *Historical Diary* to Viceroy Carlos Francisco de Croix, who became the Marqués de Croix, and Visitor General Gálvez in October 1770 shortly after his return to the capital. In the plain and deferential language of a civil servant, Costansó explained his purpose to inform the Spanish government concerning "the defense of these coasts and what opportunity is offered to whatever foreigners to establish themselves thereon . . . of peopling the discovered part of California with useful inhabitants, capable of cultivating its lands and profiting by the rich products which it offers in minerals, grains, and other fruits." The story centers on events of the Portolá expedition, how its four parties variously reached San Diego, and subsequent misadventures in locating Monterey Bay. A good deal of useful material about native Californians is presented, including their welcoming gestures, physical appearance, dress, village settlement pattern, provisioning practices, family organization, and even the berdache, "a species of men who lived like the women." Costansó noted that the lack of an interpreter prevented investigation of such exotic practices, but his curiosity is demonstrated by his collection of a rudimentary vocabulary of Indian-Spanish terms. "Their language is sonorous and of easy pronounciation," he wrote. His sharp eye noticed that the Indians possessed "pieces of broadsword, iron, and fragments of wrought silver," which sign-language conversation suggested came from trade networks extending to New Mexico. Despite these revelations, Costansó's narrative enjoyed a very limited hearing. The government suppressed the report, perhaps owing to concern that it disclosed state secrets such as navigational data that would assist imperial rivals. An English translation appeared in London in 1790, although no information on its reception survives.[85]

The Costansó narrative informed the longer and more researched work of Pedro Fages, which gives "due credit to the previous accounts which up to now have been published concerning the overland and maritime expeditions to the famous port of Monterey." Addressed to Viceroy Bucareli at Mexico City in 1775, *A Historical, Political, and Natural Description of California by Pedro Fages, Soldier of Spain*, is a classic of the expeditionary genre. Fages writes with modesty and asperity. His tone duplicates Costansó, although his account draws on four years of observation and experience: "nearly all that I note in my narrative occurred in my presence and before my eyes." As a soldier and naturalist, Fages says, "I would have prefered to set forth a purely mathematical cosmography," a goal made impossible by the lack of sufficient information. Nevertheless, the chronicle takes up a description of California divided into seven segments of coastal geography (the first from San Diego to thirty leagues northward and the last on the San Francisco peninsula). Within each area, the missions, the natural and political history, and the indigenous population are examined. In Monterey, Fages discussed Indian territorial and tribelet differences as well as internecine conflict. He probably erred in his conclusion that "they love Spaniards very much and recognize in them a shelter and protection," but the observation shows he was alert to pragmatic motives that encouraged some groups to establish commercial and military ties with the colony. Following Costansó, Fages developed a dictionary of seventy Indian words and inquired into cultural practices ranging from cuisine to cosmology.[86]

Regrettably, as Herbert Ingram Priestly notes in his introduction to the English translation, the *Description of California* "seems never to have been printed in the original." It probably received the attention of an official report and copies were filed in the Mexican and Spanish national archives. It does not appear to have influenced state policy or public opinion in the capital. Fages may have been in bad odor at the time and his views subordinated to those of Father Serra who had just completed a nineteen-month visit to Mexico City, successfully arguing the missionary cause in opposition to provincial government. Much later, French (1884) and English (1919) translations appeared that recognized the unique historical and ethnographic value of the narrative. In its own time, however, the Fages story enjoyed little or no public exposure, resembling in that regard the Costansó report. Whether for reasons of state, politics, or simple disinterest, the Spanish government did not publicize its colonial experience in California, and the result was to minimize interpretations developed by civil authorities for many years until they were resurrected by subsequent historians.

The most celebrated history of early California came from the prolific pen of Father Francisco Palóu, Junípero Serra's lifelong companion, biographer, and fellow missionary. Palóu's important book, titled *Life and Apostolic Labors of the Venerable Father Junípero Serra Founder of the Franciscan Missions of California,* was published in Mexico City in 1787 (frequently referred to with the initial words of the Spanish title, *Relación Historica*). The prologue explains: "[T]his work was not written with the intention of giving it to the public, but simply as an edifying letter, a plain Account which I wished to present to my holy Province of Mallorca. . . . But when the word came to the ears of some of the devoted men of the Order, men who had known and dealt with the Venerable Father, they insisted that I should publish what I had written, offering to defray the expense of printing." Written in hagiographic tones, Palóu's *Life* is nevertheless an engaging academic history of the period, a study of Serra but also a wide-ranging treatment of church, state, and indigenous society as well as an anthology that reprints a variety of letters and public documents.[87]

The story begins in Serra's native Mallorca, treats his early days as priest and professor when Palóu became his student, and describes their enlistment in missionary service, which began their Mexican odyssey in 1749. Twenty years pass before the Sacred Expedition as the Franciscans pursue teaching at the College of San Fernando and missionary work in the Sierra Gorda and Baja California, where Serra attained the presidency of that nineteen-mission system. Palóu's account of the voyages to San Diego and Monterey complements Costansó and Fages, but a wealth of original material follows on founding the first missions, contacts with Indian society, problems of supplying the settlements, famine and Indian assistance, criticism of the soldiers' conduct, financial dealings with the Monterey Presidio, and the disastrous Indian uprising at San Diego in 1775. Palóu's introduction explains, "[A]lmost all I relate has come under my personal observation," and the reader is convinced by detailed accounts of daily life, institutional routine, and Indian custom. At times the author is discerning about grievances suffered by Indians and the potential for rebellion, such as "a feeling of resentment which spread among the Indians as they saw how the pack-animals and the cattle of the soldiers and colonists were constantly eating the grass which was to provide them with seeds and from which they had hitherto supported themselves during the greater part of the year." One is struck, moreover, by the practical occupation of the missionaries, notably Serra's administrative determination to spread the "apostolic net" by expanding the number of converts and new missions.

For all its observational virtue, Palóu's book is still an exercise in veneration of Serra, the Franciscans, and their mission. If the Indians rebel or the soldiers behave badly, the ultimate cause lies with the intervention of Lucifer, "the Arch-Enemy." Policies devised by the provincial governor for peaceful coexistence with the Indians are characterized as "means of which the Enemy availed himself to mortify the fervent Prelate." States of mind are freely imputed to Indians. Christian precepts transcend cultural divides with unalloyed clarity. Serra had only to convey his message through an interpreter, "showing them the way to heaven [and] this they so clearly understood and so heartily accepted that they soon began to ask for baptism." Palóu draws a memorable picture of contrite Indians at San Diego following the violent uprising of 1775 and Serra's celebration (with more relish than commiseration) of California's first martyrs.

> When the Fathers exhibited there another image of our Lady, the Virgin Mary with the Holy Child Jesus in her arms, as soon as it was made known in the surrounding ranches, they all came to see it, and as they were not allowed to enter, being excluded by the stockade, they called to the Fathers and thrusting their full breasts between the poles sought to express in this vivid way their desire to give suck to that beautiful little child of which they had heard from the Fathers.[88]

Palóu never inquired whether the purported "desire to give suck" expressed awe for Jesus and Mary or, perhaps, for the force of arms used to suppress the revolt. Judging from other ritual gestures, such as burying arrowheads in the ground, it is likely that the crowd outside the stockade was petitioning for peace.

Palóu's *Life* quickly established itself as the definitive Spanish-language history of early California—and, indeed, is still a good read more than two hundred years later. Published in Mexico City in 1787 at the expense of the Franciscan college, "it was extensively circulated for a book of that epoch."[89] Copies were distributed in Spain, Mexico, and California. The commissary general of the Indies (or minister of American colonies) at Madrid received a copy and wrote Palóu, "This was a most important project. . . . I myself went to the royal palace of San Lorenzo to deliver copies set aside for the king, the prince and the members of the ministry. The rest have been distributed among the gentlemen of the council and others of first rank and prominence at the court." Other letters of praise came from missionaries in the field in Mexico and California where the book was "causing a stir." Copies were found in the many private libraries of Mexico City and the missions.[90] Mexico City in the late eighteenth century was a vigorous center of cultural life and political debate. Books were published and discussed among the intelligentsia and governing class, making it safe to assume that Palóu's history was read and probably critiqued in the liberal and anticlerical atmosphere of the capital. California became a part of American cultural discourse.

Another irony of early California historiography is that the most influential narratives derived not from the four years of civil service performed by Fages (at the time he wrote) or Palóu's sixteen years of missionary labor but from the brief visits of European expeditions to the Pacific Coast. The first of these came in September 1786 when two ships commanded by Jean François de La Pérouse stopped in Monterey for ten days. In the last years of his reign, Louis XVI launched a major expedition, sending two ships around the world on a four-year voyage of scientific discovery, commercial investigation, and diplomatic reconnaissance. Malcolm Margolin's introduction to the journal notes,

> The lavish outfitting of these ships was, in fact, a huge national effort, comparable in its great expenditure of money and investment of national pride with space exploration programs of modern nations. . . . Well-known engineers, artists, and scientists were recruited[;] . . . a gardener from the king's own garden who would be in charge of collecting useful plants; two astronomers, including one who was a member of the French Academy; a captain of the Corps of Engineers; a geologist; an ornithologist; two physicians and a surgeon; a botanist; and a number of other scientists, artists, and draftsmen.

These distinguished French emissaries doubtless had an imperial agenda concerning trade and potential French outposts in the Pacific, yet their overriding interest was discovery, enlightenment. "La Pérouse viewed himself as a scientist" in pursuit of navigational and technical information, and to ensure a faithful reception for his investigations he makes this request: "If my journal be published before my return, let the editing of it by no means be entrusted to a man of letters [who might corrupt it by] endeavoring to make a pleasing romance."[91]

The journal description of Monterey is a marvelous portrait in words and drawings of the landscape, wildlife, and native population and settlements. Beginning with a notation of time and longitude, La Pérouse moves on to the natural world of coastal fog and birdlife but soon turns to Indians and colonial society. It is clear from the text that he received much of the information from his Spanish hosts, particularly from Governor Fages, but he also visited the mission, with artists who sketched the scene, and he described the Indian village of fifty huts and seven hundred forty persons at firsthand. La Pérouse was a representative of the Enlightenment whose assignment was a public charge. It is not surprising, therefore, that the expedition made diplomatic contact with Spanish officials, relied on their knowledge, and took their side in the three-way conversation about local conditions. The Frenchman praised the earlier work of former Governor Neve, "a man replete with humanity and a Christian philosopher [who] desired a constitution less monastic, affording more civil liberty to the Indians and less despotism." He commended the Franciscans' "pious and prudent conduct" but noted that they were "at open variance with the governor, who appears to me to be a worthy military character." The Indians, in his judgment, looked poorly and seemed to be suffering from corporal punishment, which "brought to our recollection a plantation at Santo Domingo or any other West Indian island. . . . [T]he resemblance is so perfect that we have seen both men and women in irons, and others in stocks." La Pérouse sympathized with the "extreme difficulty" of civilizing primitive peoples, but he also believed that there were better alternatives to the mission system: "A friend to the rights of men rather than to theology, I could have wished, I confess, that there had been joined to the principles of Christianity a legislation which might gradually have made citizens of men."[92]

Two years later, somewhere southeast of New Guinea, La Pérouse and his company were lost at sea. The great navigator's disappearance and the French government's commission of a search made the La Pérouse expedition a cause célèbre. Fortunately, they had passed copies of the journals and drawings to ships they met that were returning more directly to France. In the throes of revolution, the French National Assembly honored the voyage in 1791 and decreed that the journals be published. The richly illustrated text appeared in 1797, followed shortly by several English translations and enthusiastic international attention. The German dramatist Augustus von Kotzebue wrote a popular play in which the shipwrecked French sailor is rescued on a South Sea island by the beautiful daughter of a local chief. An English translation appeared in 1799 and was performed often in England, followed by new versions of the story that moved to stages in the United States for the next several decades. La Pérouse, his expedition, and the journals in many editions and languages passed into popular legend, carrying with them an urbane account of California's new settlements. More than anyone to date,

La Pérouse put California on the world map and into the discourse of enlightenment.

As the nineteenth century beckoned, more expeditions visited California and reported their experiences to a growing international audience. Spanish naval ships called at the Port of Monterey in 1791 and 1792, including the party headed by Alejandro Malaspina that brought artists such as José Cardero to sketch the Indians, settlements, and wildlife. These Spanish observers were aware of La Pérouse's journals and defended the missions against "the ridiculous inventions of many foreign authors," sometimes with more extended observation.[93] Unfortunately for Franciscan and nationalistic histories, however, these accounts were filed with the naval ministry and only later saw limited distribution. Far more consequential was the 1792 voyage of George Vancouver that visited Monterey twice and studied California carefully on a tour of the North Pacific. Vancouver was less a scholar than the elegant Count La Pérouse and he wrote in the turgid prose of officialdom— although a safe return to England spoke well for his seamanship. The expedition had a more explicitly military purpose than its predecessors. Vancouver ridiculed Spanish administration of the colony and called it "New Albion" as though it were already part of England. Great Britian was a successful imperial rival of Spain and hoped to extend its purchase on Canada southward to Oregon and, perhaps, California. The presidios were "totally incapable of making any resistance against a foreign invasion" and the colony as a whole was a failure: "why such an extent of territory should have been thus subjugated, and after all the expence and labour that has been bestowed upon its colonization turned to no account whatever, is a mystery in the science of state policy not easily to be explained. The Spaniards . . . have only cleared the way for the ambitious enterprizes of those maritime powers, who, in the avidity of commercial pursuit, may seek to be benefitted by the advantages which the fertile soil of New Albion seems calculated to afford."[94]

En route to these strategic, even prophetic, conclusions, Vancouver provided an exiguous description of the coastal settlements. In Monterey he stepped off the rustic presidio's dimensions and took a horseback ride to Carmel Mission, which he considered a "benevolent institution." By contrast to La Pérouse, Vancouver had little or no interest in Indians. Although the Indians did not "seem in any respect to have benefitted by the instruction they had received," the colonists were no better as measured by their accomplishments: "The Spaniards in the missions and Presidios, being the two principal distinctions of Spanish inhabitants, lead a confined, and in most respects a very indolent, life; the religious part of the society within a cloister, and the military in barracks. The last mentioned order do nothing, in the strictist sense of the expression; for they neither till, sow, nor reap, but wholly depend upon the labour of the inhabitants of the missions and pueblos for their subsistence and the common necessaries of life." Vancouver was a severe observer and, despite his formal courtesy, something of a xenophobe. His diary omits description of a dinner and dance prepared by the presidio women for their visitors and featuring a performance of the Spanish fandango. Another ship's officer described the dance "with such wanton attitudes, such leering looks, sparkling eyes & trembling limbs, as would decompose the gravity of a stoic." Following this spectacle, Vancouver requested an encore to the performance featuring a hula by two Sandwich Island women, a display that the Spanish ladies took as an insult to their culture and hospitality. Before departing Vancouver offered a fireworks show from his ship that he believed "afforded a very high degree of satisfaction [as] an entertainment to which most of them were before intire strangers."[95]

George Vancouver's *A Voyage of Discovery to the North Pacific Ocean and Round the World, 1791-1795,* was published in May 1798 with extensive publicity and just days before his death from a lingering illness. Not only was Vancouver a famous naval figure at a time of growing public interest in expeditionary narratives, but news of the voyage was spiced by London gossip. Vancouver had dismissed one of his officers, Thomas Pitt (later the second baron of Camelford) in the Sandwich Islands for insubordination and eccentricity. Back in London, Vancouver and his brother had an altercation in Conduit Street with the deranged and resentful Camelford, who attacked the brothers and was beaten back with their canes. The incident was caricatured in a famous newspaper cartoon, "The Caneing in Conduit Street," and fanned public rumors of mutiny during the expedition, which were vigorously denied. All these events resulted in an eager reception of the *Voyage* and more press coverage. The *Naval Chronicle* called it a classic, although another reader considered it tedious in contrast to La Pérouse. The *Annual Register* gave it a long review, which, nevertheless, minimized the importance of Vancouver's discoveries, notably his refutation of claims about a Northwest Passage. At all events, the book and the voyage were widely chronicled in England. "Vancouver's narrative aroused considerable interest abroad; within three years versions of it had been published in four languages"— French, German, Danish, and Swedish (but not Spanish)—and a second English edition appeared in 1801.[96] The reputations of George Vancouver, his crew, and their voyage grew during the nineteenth century when the major island and city of western Canada were named for the captain.

The portrait of California that emerged in the early years of its colonial settlement bore a selective resemblance to the complex and contradictory events that conditioned their first observers and narratives. The Indian voice was silenced—replaced with naturalistic field studies of Europeans who understood the Indian as a feature of the landscape tantamount to a species of animal, interesting to note but inconceivable as a conscious participant. Paradoxically, the story of Spanish civil authority was minimized for different reasons. Soldiers and colonial officials wrote official reports and private memoirs that easily rivaled the quality of travelers' accounts. But these documents were delivered to the Spanish government, which either suppressed them for strategic reasons or neglected them as trivial accounts of a remote and troublesome frontier.

The church history of Palóu stepped into the breach, establishing its place as an important contemporary document because, indeed, it was an extraordinary work and because it had institutional support from the Franciscan Order and the Spanish Crown. Palóu's *Life* circulated throughout the realm and probably stimulated critical discussion in the enlightened salons of Mexico City and Europe. These were the vital centers of public opinion in the late eighteenth century and precisely the audiences for popular travel narratives in the genre of La Pérouse and Vancouver.

Church and expeditionary histories differ widely, as we have seen, yet they also share the European imperial eye.[97] They are contested histories insofar as the Spanish clergy related events from the standpoint of supernatural intervention and missionary paternalism while European explorers saw the world in terms of geopolitics, Enlightenment philosophy, and nascent economic liberalism. Yet they are complementary Eurocentric histories that dovetail in mutually understood debates about nationalism, imperialism, politics, humanism, and religion.

By 1800 California appears to the cosmopolitan world as both a rustic Spanish colony and a strategic node in the European imperial network. It is a land of pliant aborigines and self-sacrificing priests given to harsh discipline of their charges and one another. The natives are known for their alleged deficits (less aggressive than the Yuma or Apache and less commercial than the Northwest tribes) rather than for the fruits of their labor or cultural resistance. Civil authorities appear through travel accounts as upright but incapable of military defense and economic development. Judging from primary sources, the *events* that constitute Spanish California history portray a tenuous colony, a three-way power struggle, deep-seated contradictions, and persistent conflict. Real actors fought over culture, survival, the environment, labor, gender, politics, and religion. The *narratives* that emerge from this process, by contrast, silence key actors, truncate the natural and social world within a narrow Eurocentric discourse, and portray California as a land of benign missionaries, ineffectual soldiers, and looming imperialists—stories dictated by the institutional purposes of the respective authors and publicists.

THREE

Revolutionary California

I am seeking to rescue the poor stockinger, the Luddite
cropper, the "obsolete" hand-loom weaver, the "utopian"
artisan . . . from the enormous condescension of posterity.
Their crafts and traditions may have been dying. Their
hostility to the new industrialism may have been backward-
looking. Their communitarian ideals may have been fan-
tasies. Their insurrectionary conspiracies may have been
foolhardy. But they lived through these times of acute social
disturbance, and we did not. Their aspirations were valid in
terms of their own experience.

E. P. Thompson, *The Making of the English
Working Class*

Monterey's provincial elite was out in small force for the performance
of *maromeros* (rope dancers) at the presidio on the eventful evening in
June 1836. California's nascent bourgeoisie was well represented by
landowners, merchants, and their friends and relatives in public office.
According to custom, the recently appointed governor, Mariano Chico,
would preside over the gala, despite his unpopularity as an imposed administrator from the opprobrious Mexican state—he was not one of
them, not a Californio. As the guests arrived, calamity ensued. The governor's companion, Doña Cruz, whom he introduced to disbelieving citizens as his niece, had brought along a friend, one Ildefonsa Gonzales
Herrera. Doña Ildefonsa, the wife of a presidio official, recently had been
placed under house arrest by Monterey's alcalde (mayor-judge) for her
role in the capital's most outrageous scandal of the day. She had been
carrying on an adulterous liaison with José María Castañares, clerk of
the Custom House who was now doing his penance as a prisoner in the
town jail. The affair had shaken local society, involving as it did two families in public office with dense linkages to others in the capital. Governor Chico's choice to indulge his mistress's friend and flout local authority
concerning the house arrest deeply offended Alcalde Ramon Estrada. The

alcalde promptly released Casteñares from jail, marched him to the presidio, and seated him in the front row for the performance, where he saluted the governor and his former lover. Chico understood the defiant act, went into a rage, demanded the mayor's seal of office, and, with a military escort, put Estrada under house arrest. The governor's impulsive actions in the close-knit town, where he was doubly disadvantaged as a stranger and a Mexican, escalated local resistance. The town's second in command, Regidor Teodoro Gonzalez, came forward to encourage citizens to oppose the governor's encroachment on the rights of municipal authorities. The presidio's military detachment sided with the mayor. Great public excitement was expressed in support of the Californios. Governor Chico belatedly came to understand the recalcitrant public mood and resigned his post, citing popular opposition as the reason for his return to Mexico, with Doña Cruz. Behind the small incident lurked California's revolutionary mood.[1]

The Mexican independence movement launched by Father Miguel Hidalgo in 1810 began an eleven-year struggle that ultimately ended Spanish colonial rule in Mexico and California. By 1821 national liberation movements had swept the South American continent. Yet hemispheric geopolitical realignment and the emerging nations of Latin America had little effect on California and Mexico's northern frontier, at least initially. The principal consequence of political turmoil in Mexico during the first two decades of the nineteenth century was neglect in the colonial territories. The beleaguered Spanish state suffered Napoleonic invasion at home, breakaway republics in Gran Colombia and Rio de la Plata, and far more demands on the military and treasury than could be met by the wounded state. Alta California suffered as essential supply ships failed to appear, military payrolls ceased, and any semblance of central political direction gave way to local ingenuity. Taken unaware by the Mexican independence movement, California maintained its loyalty to Spain during the crisis and found itself alone in the aftermath.

Neglect at the hands of Spain and the fledgling Mexican Republic during the first quarter of the nineteenth century had differential effects on local society. Military and civil government suffered most as the number of officials and soldiers declined, salaries and public investment dwindled, and effective central government collapsed. The missions also experienced a loss of support from the Church's Pious Fund but, as economically productive institutions, were better equipped to confront the crisis. In the absence of imported provisions and given the meager output of pueblo settlements and royal ranches, the missions practically supported California. Indians suffered accelerating mortality rates and growing depredations. On the one hand, the economically depressed settlements had desperate need of Indian workers, no money to pay them, and thus greater recourse to labor coercion. On the other hand, Indians were under siege, their numbers declining and their villages disappearing, conditions disposing them to more ambitious livestock raiding for food and commercial exchange. Livestock theft was a faithful barometer of the Indian condition. Measured levels during the Spanish period now rose sharply as the struggle for survival turned grim. California belonged to Mexico for a mere twenty-five years (1821–46), yet in that period the native population was cut in half (to roughly 100,000).

If the absence of material support and political direction characterized the early decades of nineteenth-century California, a new and influential presence, merchant sailors, began to fill the void. Following the expeditionary voyages of La Pérouse, Malaspina, and Vancouver, commercial shipping became increasingly common at the turn of the nineteenth century. The first U.S. ship, the frigate *Otter* sailing out of Boston, was provisioned at Mission San Carlos in 1796. The *Otter* was one of a growing number of vessels involved in trading sea otter pelts harvested along the northwest Pacific Coast with China. "With the arrival in 1796 of the first Boston vessel, the contest between the otter men and the upholders of the Spanish mercantile system began."[2] Although it flourished for only a decade, the sea otter trade had the important effect of incorporating missions and Indians into the world economic system. Missionaries exchanged pelts harvested by Indians for trade goods and cash, albeit as "smugglers" under restrictive Spanish customs regulations still technically in effect. After 1810 the California trade expanded rapidly in both the diversity of nations represented (Britain, Russia, the United States, France, South America) and the products exchanged.

The fur trade was soon overshadowed by Mexican California's defining industry, hide and tallow export coordinated from Lima, Peru, Santiago, Chile, and Tepic, Mexico. The "Lima merchants," including many English and North American firms, shipped California hides to shoemakers in New England and tallow for soap and candles to Europe and South America in exchange for cash, manufactures, and domestic goods. The implications of the hide and tallow trade were enormous. It was at once a solution to California's economic isolation, a brief lease on life for the missions, a breakthrough for economic liberalism, the basis for a new class of Californio ranchers and merchants (many of them international immigrants), the impetus for a far-reaching property regime based on secularization of church properties and public land grants, and the inspiration for a political culture predicated on local autonomy.

With the consolidation of Mexican independence after 1824, political developments in the new republic began to be felt on the northern frontier. The introduction of liberal reform practices varied by time and place. Policies in support of Mexican federalism during the early years (1821–35) precipitated conflicts on the frontier. Revolt in Texas contrasted with democratization in New Mexico and a hybrid form of independence in California.[3] In general, however, the Mexican period introduced sweeping changes, particularly in California where a variety of international forces intersected. Representative political institutions were adopted and began to flourish. The principle, if not always the fact, of racial equality among Spanish, creole, mestizo, and Indian was recognized in the Constitution of 1824. Economic liberalism and free trade became official, if ambivalently implemented, policy. Colonization plans were renewed, drawing on Mexican peasants, convicts, and soldiers with politically explosive effects. Private land grants were distributed generously, creating in a few decades a powerful landed class. And church properties were gradually secularized in a political transformation with far-reaching implications for Indians, landownership, production, and power. It was a revolutionary time.

Alta California was incorporated into the new Mexican federal system as a territory. Initially, local government was unaffected and continued to practice limited democracy based on the Spanish Cortes and the Constitution of 1812, which established the *ayuntamiento,* or municipal government. In 1822 Alta California was granted representation in the Mexican Congress. A territorial legislature, or *diputación,* was established that consisted of five to seven persons who met irregularly, handled only minor matters, and did little harm. Monterey continued to be governed as a military establishment, although town government was initiated in 1826 and loyalties, even among soldiers, were divided between the town council and the presidio. In 1824 a political junta met in Monterey and adopted a "plan of government" that lacked legal status in Mexico yet represented California's first constitution and a determination to take charge of local affairs. If the governor was a Californio, as in the case of Luis Arguello from 1823 to 1825, then local politics might be harmonious. When governors came from Mexico with an agenda that ignored local preferences, as was typical until the mid-1830s, then there was trouble—and trouble was increasingly the rule.

Mexican California took shape from 1821 to 1846 as a distinctive society; a land of contrasts, pastoral yet tied to the global economy, revolutionary but acquiescent in the face of encroaching foreign powers, liberal and reformist but underpinned by a quasi-feudal property regime, Roman Catholic but dedicated to secularization of church property, democratic but elitist. The new society represented a thorough institutional transformation of Spanish California. The missionary church lost its political power in the early going, persevered in its economic role as long as it was needed, and ended the period in propertyless defeat. The military saw the decline of its institutional prominence and authority over civil society. The Indian population no longer formed a social space in its own right, having been reduced by high mortality and mestizoization. Indians were still numerous, but, rather than form their own society, they lived on the fringes of Mexican towns and ranches. In place of these institutional pillars of Spanish California a new civil society began to emerge in the 1820s—a population of hijos del país, sons and daughters of the country, natives in short. They called themselves Californios, the native-born sons and daughters of colonial sojourners who chose to remain in the frontier settlements. Frequently they were the offspring of lower-class mestizo soldiers who had been awarded small plots of land at the end of their military service. In the early 1800s the families of Ignacio Vallejo, José Francisco Alvarado, and José Macario Castro, sergeants in the Monterey company of the King's Army, each produced a son (or grandson) who became a governor of California. Other children of mestizo soldiers and Indian wives intermarried with influential Californios and foreign merchants to form a well-defined arriviste elite. As the territorial capital and major port, Monterey was an important locus of Californio society but not the only one. San Diego, Los Angeles, Santa Barbara, and San José were growing towns and, in the case of the first two, sometimes rivals for Monterey's political leadership. But Monterey was the center as well as a representative showcase of the new politics and economy that defined the Mexican period. It was in Monterey that Mexico officially gained California, and later lost it.

LOCAL SOCIETY: MONTEREY AS CAPITAL AND CALIFORNIA MICROCOSM

Monterey developed slowly as a town beyond presidio walls. Retired soldiers in domestic unions with native women were the first to settle on town lots (*solares*) granted at the end of their service. On those increasingly rare occasions when salaries were paid at the presidio, petty trade in food and entertainment appeared in the town. One of the first local enterprises was the bar and gambling house of Tio Armenta, a retired soldier. The French trader Auguste Duhaut-Cilly described the humble settlement as seen from the bay in 1827.

> Whoever should arrive at Monterey expecting to see a considerable town would suppose he had made a mistake about the anchorage. The first buildings seen on rounding Point Pinos are those of the presidio which present a quadrangle of two hundred yards, and which, being a single story, resemble long warehouses covered with tiles. On the right of the presidio, on a little verdant plain are some forty scattered houses of a quite pretty appearance, also covered with tiles and whitewashed. This, with a few straw huts, is what constitutes the capital of Alta California.[4]

Fifteen citizens of Monterey petitioned territorial governor José María de Echeandía (1825–31) in May 1826 to appoint a judge with civil jurisdiction over 114 local residents not associated with the military. The settlement included another 80 soldiers and presidio officials (surgeon, accountant, customs officer) and 11 foreigners whose commercial activities came under military jurisdiction. Beyond the town's common lands were twelve private land grant ranches that employed approximately 350 persons, including extended-family owners, ranch hands, servants, and their families. Ranches were established at a slow rate initially, increasing from just six to twelve or fourteen in the first thirty years of the nineteenth century, owing to the threat of marauding Indians and limited commercial opportunities. As the town organized in 1826, Mission San Carlos was losing its Indian population, down to less than 300, or one-third of its historic high, even as the padres prospered in the cattle and trading business. Overall, Monterey and vicinity embraced a population of about 850 souls when the town began operating as a Mexican pueblo. These figures do not include an estimated 2,000 Indians who had either resisted the mission labor draft or abandoned it for the remnants of village life or wage employment in the new commercial sector.[5]

The population grew dramatically during the next fourteen years. Stimulated by the hide and tallow trade, immigration, and the incorporation of former neophytes, the number of Monterey town citizens reached 700 in 1840, not including another 75 foreigners resident in the area. Fifty private ranches had been granted, with 550 persons living on properties that included a number of family farms. In addition to these 1,325 whites and mestizos, a growing number of Indians were now in town and on the ranches. In the Monterey vicinity, continuing high death rates had reduced the Indian population by half since the turn of the century, to 1,740. Perhaps 1,000 of these lived in communities, bringing the total reconstituted area population to approximately 2,300.[6]

Monterey was physically unprepossessing in the mid-1830s, its spatial form reflecting its social organization. The town was oriented toward the bay and port. Many of the early verbal descriptions and drawings are done from the vantage of ships in the harbor. In 1827 the English captain Frederick William Beechey observed about the presidio, "[W]hether viewed at a distance or near, the establishment impresses a spectator with any other sentiment than that of its being a place of authority. . . . [B]ut for a tottering flag-staff, upon which was occasionally displayed the tricolored flag of Mexico, three rusty field pieces, and a half accoutred sentinel parading the gateway in charge of a few poor wretches heavily shackled, a visitor would be ignorant of the importance of the place." Beechey notes perceptively that the neglect of official quarters reflected popular dissatisfaction with government.[7]

Beechey and Duhaut-Cilly agree on the tumbledown appearance of the presidio but neglect the larger social and physical landscape. A more revealing sketch by a crew member of the U.S. ship of Commodore Thomas A. C. Jones, albeit from 1842, shows the town's functional pattern. Principal streets run to the harbor and the Custom House. The harbor faces north, with protected anchorage to the west (or left side of the drawing) overlooked by the landmark Vizcaíno hill on which now resides El Castillo, the fort. Homes and business headquarters of the town's leading merchants cluster around the Custom House and shoreline. Other residences and the church spread out to the east, which was considered more desirable in the town known for its fog and chill breezes. Located back from the bay to the east and south were the homes and small farms of town residents. Food, as opposed to livestock, production was largely an urban enterprise.

The best-known description of Monterey, and indeed of the entire California coast, comes from Richard Henry Dana's journal, *Two Years Before the Mast*, which relates the author's travels on a Boston merchant ship in 1835–36. The youthful adventurer saw California from a more ingenuous and descriptive vantage than his salty predecessors.

> Monterey, as far as my observation goes, is decidedly the pleasantest and most civilized-looking place in California. In the center of it is an open square, surrounded by four lines of one-story buildings, with half a dozen canons in the center; some mounted and some not. This is the presidio, or fort. Every town has a presidio in its centre, or rather every presidio has a town built around it. . . . The houses here, as everywhere in California, are one story, built of

10. *Harbor and City of Monterey, California, 1842*, lithograph by Charles (Karl) Gildemeister. Commissioned by Thomas Larkin and drawn from an original of uncertain authorship. The scene shows Calle Principal (Main Street) running to the harbor, Larkin's prominent two-story house at the left, the Mexican Presidio above it, and commercial houses, many of them connected with the hide and tallow trade that dominated the region's active economy. (Courtesy of the Bancroft Library)

adobes, that is, clay made into large bricks, about a foot and a half square, and three or four inches thick, and hardened in the sun. . . . The floors are generally of earth, the windows grafted and without glass; and the doors, which are seldom shut, open directly into the common room, there being no entries. Some of the wealthy inhabitants have glass to their windows and board floors; and in Monterey nearly all the houses are whitewashed on the outside. The better houses, too, have red tiles upon the roof. The common ones have two or three rooms, which open into each other, and are furnished with a bed or two, a few chairs and tables, a looking glass, a crucifix, and small daubs of paintings enclosed in glass, representing some miracle of martyrdom. They have no chimneys or fireplaces in the houses, the climate being such as to make a fire unnecessary; and all their cooking is done in a kitchen, separated from the house. The Indians . . . do all the hard work, two or three being attached to the better house; and the poorest person able to keep one at least.[8]

In 1836 an exhaustive census was conducted of the Monterey *munici-palidad* (municipality), which at the time embraced both the town and the surrounding ranches for a considerable distance.[9] The survey (*Padrón General*) was based on eighty-eight town residences and the two military barracks, a total of 700 people, and twenty-eight ranches, with 587 people—1,287 people in all. The great sociological value of this census lies in its listing of town and ranch households and all of their occupants (parents, children, servants, and nonfamily residents) by name, sex, age, occupation, and place of birth.

Urban households are distinctively extended-family units. They are large, averaging 7.4 persons, and typically include married spouses and a goodly number of children as well as additional persons identified as *criados* (servants) and *aggregados* (others "aggregated" with the family, including relatives, friends, apprentices, and perhaps renters). There are a few single-person and married-couple households as well as a few unusual bachelors or widows who shared their homes with others. But the rule is a large extended family consisting of couples, large sibling sets, relatives, friends or servants, and sometimes both. Most of the household servants were probably Indians, although given Spanish names often obscure their origins. Of the eighty-eight households, two-thirds fit this extended-family pattern; thirty-two having servants and forty (including some or overlap) having others in the home.

Monterey households in 1836 demonstrated a diversity of occupations. Soldiers constitute the largest single category of urban *oficios* (jobs) with 67 individuals, of whom 52 were single men living in barracks, or *cuarteles,* separated by rank, and 15 family men or retirees living in houses. The military presence was palpable in the small town. Farmers were second in occupational prominence, including town residents who cultivated small garden plots and tended a few chickens and pigs. Artisans were numerous, representing a variety of essential trades: saddle maker, carpenter, tailor, shoemaker, bricklayer, blacksmith, cigar maker, silversmith, tailor, baker, painter, and carriage maker. Merchants, in fourth place, constituted an important occupational segment of Monterey's commercial economy and included various commission and shipping agents associated with international trade as well as storekeepers who bartered consumer goods for hides. Professionals in this setting were white-collar workers and clerks connected with either government or commerce; lawyers, notaries, a surgeon and a blood letter, a tax collector, a customs agent, several clerks, and a manufacturer. Cooks were identified by occupation in the census while most servants (criados) were considered simply as household members. It is probably the case that a category of "domestic worker" would include a much larger number, although, of course, considerable significance attaches to the definition of servants as household, even family, members (criado derives from the Spanish verb criar, to raise or bring up, as families do with their children). Laborers were uncommon among town workers, probably because most of the physical labor was done by farmers and servants. Other reports suggest that Indians were employed loading ships or carting goods, and one suspects that they were neglected by the census taker. The census does identify seventy-six persons as servants, concentrated in one-third of the households (two servants are typical of these households, many have only one, and a few have five or six). The servant category is a very mixed group: adult men who may also have an occupation (e.g., baker); women and children who keep house, wash, and tend to child care (e.g., an Ecuadorian nanny); and some identified with names that suggest they are Indians. Finally, a large number of married women are listed by name, age, and place of birth but without occupation.

Forty-five percent of Monterey's municipal population lived on twenty-eight ranches outside of town. Although these were large properties (many in the 2,000- to 4,000-acre range, some 6,000 to 8,000 acres, and a few in excess of 15,000), the census refers to their proprietors as "farmers" (labradores) rather than the more imposing titles ranchero or hacendado used in Mexico at the time. These ranches were home to extended families and even small communities. The average number of inhabitants was twenty-one but varied widely. Typically, the ranches were not the great estates that existed in parts of Mexico or in fictional accounts of the colonial period. On the contrary, most California ranches

TABLE I
OCCUPATIONS OF MONTEREY
HOUSEHOLDERS, 1836

Military	67
Farmer	35
Artisan	27
Merchant	20
Professional	17
Cook	11
Laborer	7
Total	184

SOURCE: *Padron General,* Municipalidad de Monterey,
1836 (Bancroft Library, University of California, Berkeley).

were family enterprises, moderately sized properties worked by one or
two (often related) families and their (sometimes adult) children. Many
of these also had a few servants who were almost surely Indians. This
pattern characterized roughly two-thirds of the ranches and stood in clear
contrast to large operations based on 20,000 to 30,000 acres with a labor force of thirty to eighty family members and workers. The big ranches
had a number of resident families in addition to foremen (*mayordomos*),
workers, aggregados, servants, and even a teacher in one case. Here, too,
we encounter solid evidence of Indian ranch hands in the use of the term
"neophyte," referring to Indians who were either hired from the mission
or former mission residents. Approximately thirty persons are identified
as neophytes and another forty-six as servants, some of whom are also
Indians, suggesting at this transitional time several classes of Indian
worker. Two observations are supported by these data: Indians composed
an important part of the labor force, even if their identity was sometimes
obscured in census terminology (criados, aggregados), but they were by
no means a majority of the working class. The poorer Mexican and mestizo families provided a large share of the labor force and some Indians
doubtless lived outside of the settled communities in which convention-
ally defined work was performed and surveys taken.

Monterey society in 1836 was intimate, stratified, entrepreneurial, and
contentious. Among the small but diverse citizenry, a Californio elite began to take shape with the developing economy. Local prominence depended on some combination of the assets conveyed by property, public office, California longevity, family connections, arguably "Spanish"
descent, and position in the commercial economy. Juan Bautista Alvarado
was the son of Spanish soldier, a Monterey native, a political activist,

the owner of the 8,940-acre El Sur Rancho, and, in his late twenties, about to become governor. Nicholas Gutierrez, the forty-two-year-old reigning military commander and political head, was a bachelor whose household of six servants included an older widower, a family of three, and a young widow all engaged in farming. José Mariano Estrada, former soldier and public official, a widow at forty-three, owned the 7,726-acre Buenavista ranch in Salinas Valley, which employed thirty hands including at least five Indians. His son, José Ramon, was alcalde of Monterey at twenty-five, owned the 5,668-acre El Toro ranch, and lived in town with his wife, María, and three servants. José María Herrera, an educated man from Mexico and subcommissioner of government at thirty-three, suffered the infidelities of his wife, Ildefonsa Gonzales, and the enmity of Governor Alvarado, which led to his exile. Some of the elite were recent arrivals and foreigners. The Spanish Basque José Amesti came to Monterey in 1824, married well, became a successful merchant in the hide and tallow trade, and received a land grant of 15,440 acres in Santa Cruz. Captain John Rogers Cooper, British turned American, sailed the *Rover* into Monterey Bay in 1823 and remained to become a prominent merchant, shipping-business partner of former Governor Arguello, ranch owner, and a rechristened Catholic and Mexican citizen who adopted the *nom de California* Juan Bautista Rogers Cooper.[10]

Local society was mapped not by individuals and occupations so much as by family and kinship networks. A pattern of dense linkages is illustrated by the family of Ignacio Vallejo. A sergeant at the Monterey Presidio who arrived initially at San Diego with the Rivera party in 1774, Ignacio married María Antonia Lugo, the Santa Barbara–born daughter of a soldier who was with one of the first expeditions in 1769. The Vallejo-Lugo marriage of forty years was fruitful, producing thirteen children and scores of third-generation families. Firstborn María Isidora married Mariano Soberanes, a soldier and later Monterey alcalde, who was granted the 8,900-acre Ojitos ranch. María Isidora died young, but her sister, Josefa María, survived three husbands, including two from the prominent Alvarado and Estrada families. She was the mother of the famous Californio governor and revolutionary, Juan Bautista Alvarado. Eighth in the sibling order, Mariano Guadalupe Vallejo later became military governor, general, one of the three leading figures in California's revolutionary movement (with his nephew and contemporary J. B. Alvarado and José Castro), and owner of the 66,622-acre Petaluma ranch north of San Francisco. His older brother, Josef de Jesus, inherited the family's 8,868-acre Bolsa de San Cayetano ranch just north of the Salinas River and held several government positions. Three other sisters were married to prominent immigrant merchants: María Prudencia to the Spaniard José Amesti, María Paula to the American Jacob Leese (against the wishes of her brother, General Vallejo), and Geronima to the British-American-Mexican Juan Bautista Rogers Cooper. The pattern of family connectedness and elite qualification exhibited in some detail by the Vallejo-Lugo clan was not unusual. The marriage of Josef Macario Castro and María Potenciana Ramirez, who came to California with Governor Pedro Fages in 1783, produced twelve children, a number of branch families, and a grandson governor, José Castro.[11] Through Monterey's network of kinship and connected families flowed the wellsprings of political influence, commercial opportunity, and social honor.

Elite networks were bound together by distinctive gender relations in the form of well-considered marriages. Virtually all of the immigrant British and American merchants married into important, landed Californio families. They joined the Catholic Church, adopted Hispanicized names, learned the language, pledged their loyalty to Mexico with the rebellious ambivalence of their Californio in-laws, and through these means became naturalized citizens qualified to own property. Families arranged these alliances and daughters found themselves married in their midteens, usually to men in their thirties. Californio women were raised to enhance family status by their marriages. Ironically, families only one generation removed from the lowly rank of mestizo soldiers now defined themselves as "Spanish," socially superior to Mexicans, and properly matched with ambitious Yankee businessmen. Yet the women who effected these alliances were more than pawns in a status game. They cared for large numbers of children and dependents, participated in the family enterprise, and frequently ended up as household heads. Widowed and unmarried women headed 10 percent of Monterey households in 1836, including two ranches and a number of town farms with sizable retinues of relatives, workers, and servants.

The fortunes of Monterey's small elite depended on a diverse laboring class. At the bottom rung of the occupational ladder were Indians, who constituted an important segment of ranch labor managing cattle or kitchens and town workers in domestic service or manual labor. As servants and persons without political status, Indians usually labored outside the wage economy in relations of barter and exploitation. Yet the growing cattle herds required attention, resulting in the steady departure of Indians from mission supervision and elimination of laws restricting their horseback riding. The demand for labor helped to bring

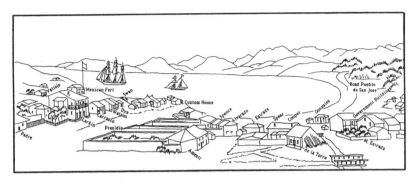

11. *Town Buildings and Residences, 1842.* This copy of a sketch identifies major town structures and residences showing the Custom House, fort, government buildings, and the mix of Californio and European-American homes and businesses. (Illustration by Beverly Lozano)

about wage work for Indians. In addition to Indians, a larger segment of the working class consisted of mestizo cooks, artisans, and casual laborers around the active port. A great deal of labor was required to support the growing local population and agrarian export economy. Indian and mestizo vaqueros not only herded the cattle but also conducted the labor-intensive *matanza* in which animals were slaughtered and skinned, hides prepared for shipment, and fat boiled down to tallow in great pots. Teamsters and muleteers hauled export products to the harbor where crews loaded the ships. Manual labor was also in demand for road building, timber cutting, and construction. As the immigrant population grew and sailors abandoned their ships for employment on land, Anglos (i.e., European Americans) began to join the local working class.

Dana's *Two Years Before the Mast* claims that all of this work was done by Indians. Although there is an element of truth to his observations made around the ports, surviving business records tell a more nuanced tale.[12] Juan B. R. Cooper's store served the gamut of local residents, from poor Indians to the elite Castro, Sobranes, and Osio families, in the late 1820s and 1830s. The detailed accounts kept by Cooper and his half brother, Thomas O. Larkin, indicate that the store was actually a full-service economic brokerage firm, acting as bank, credit bureau, labor exchange, and export entrepot. Ledger entries show "Indian cook," "Esteban the Indian," "old washer woman," "Carlos el Indio," "John the cook," "ditch digger," and "Atamacio the Indian" all receiving store credit for labor performed, sometimes for a named employer (e.g., "for Mr. [Nathan] Spear," a local merchant). The wage was sometimes paid "in cash" but more often entered as a credit against purchases such as "1 1/2 pint grog [liquor]," "knife," "20 yards gingham," "flask grog." The store mediated labor arrangements, paying the worker in cash or kind and charging it to the employer's account—as a bank, in effect. In an economy that was only partially monetized, mercantile companies did much of their business by barter and credit. Hides could be delivered to the store for exchange in kind, credit, third-party transactions, and even cash.

There were also money wages paid to a variety of individuals and services. An Indian woman referred to in the ledger as "Ramonda the blood letter" was paid, not for her medical skills, but as a laundress at the rate of $3 per month, sometimes in cash (the terms "peso" and "dollar" were used interchangeably for the same unit of Mexican money, which was equivalent in value to the U.S. dollar). She received "credit for washing to TOL [probably Thomas O. Larkin] 2 1/2 mos. 7–4 [pesos]." Seferina also worked as a washerwoman. "Vicente the Indian" appears frequently, credited ("to portuguese") for $10 in payment for ten days of work, or "Vicente from Spear, 2," and an accrued $62 paid in cash, although the precise labor performed is not mentioned. Vicente often took partial payment in grog, cigars, and merchandise for his wife. European-American workers included John Matthews and Juan Hogard, who were paid variously for "hauling timber 26," "hauling pitch and gum 15," "10 days hauling loads 10," or generally $1 per day for heavy lifting. Alpheus Stetson and Charles Farmer cut timber at the rate of $18 per month. By 1840 Thomas Larkin's commercial activities eclipsed those of Captain Cooper, including a mercantile store, an export-import business, and a Santa Cruz–based lumbering operation. Larkin contracted with two carpenters, William Trevethan (English and Cornish, judging by his surname) and William Brander (a Scot), to cut and hew one hundred thousand feet of redwood for $1,000 over a period of five months. Indians were employed in the operation, perhaps as servants or nonwaged workers judging from references to "my Indians."[13] In summary, an ethnically diverse working class took shape in these years, toiled under varying degrees of free labor, and earned modest wages in the subsistence sector and emerging cash economy.

The tenor of local life appears in the actions of the ayuntamiento, begun inauspiciously in the early 1820s and granted Mexican pueblo status with town common lands in 1835.[14] Public order concerned the city council, which enacted a series of measures banning gambling and cockfighting (one wonders how successfully), limiting and taxing liquor

sales, prohibiting display of weapons in town, imposing fines for entering stores or taverns on horseback, and ordering a late-night curfew that
made citizens responsible for themselves and for their Indian household
servants. In addition to blue laws, local government displayed a sense of
social responsibility. Pawning was banned because it preyed on the poor.
It was illegal for persons to sell hides who did not produce them, a measure designed to discourage theft. Bread laws stipulated proper weight
and content for public sale. Road-building projects employed Indians for
wages in cash. A school for girls was established, only shortly after the
education of boys had been provided. Books and a schoolteacher were
supplied at public expense. As early as 1824 Juan B. Alvarado proposed
the establishment of a historical society in order that the experience of
their pioneer parents not be forgotten.

Spanish tradition practiced in California granted four square leagues
(ten square miles contoured to local geography) of common land to established towns. The land could not be alienated from the public domain,
but municipal government assigned plots for certain uses such as agriculture (*ejidos*), water supply, or public buildings. Commons rights to
the use of pueblo lands were observed in activities critical to the subsistence of humble citizens such as livestock grazing and woodcutting.
Townspeople regularly cut firewood and hewed lumber in designated
woodlots on the forested hills around Monterey for a small tariff paid
to the public treasury. Lumber sold commercially was taxed at the rate
of 10 percent. After 1835 the town council introduced more systematic
methods for allocating lands that, in effect, became private properties.
A new map was commissioned to fix the town boundaries and a book
of deeds was established. Citizens petitioned the council for town lots,
which were routinely approved free of charge. The local Lands Commission was established to regulate these increasingly important transactions. The city council also took a role in land grants by recommending applicants to the governor, who had legal authority to assign ranches
outside of town.

The definition and treatment of crime speaks clearly to questions of
governance, the economy, and social inequality. The city council prom-
ulgated a number of "police ordinances" that were enforced as common
customs by local citizens and justices of the peace in the absence of any
police force. Drunkenness, curfew violations, stealing, and vagrancy were
petty crimes punished by fines and sentences to labor on public works
projects. Indians, of course, experienced the full fury of law enforcement,
but they were not the only ones put to work at street repair and bridge

building. Public works gangs were integrated. A permeable prison housed up to forty malefactors, including a number of Mexicans and the odd European who had jumped ship as a result, or cause, of drunken abandon. The language in municipal records turns menacing, however, when describing livestock theft by Indians. In February 1835 the town council appealed to the governor for "the arms and munitions of warfare necessary for citizens" to put an end to the depredations. Three Indians were shot for stealing in May. But draconian measures against Indian cattle raiding backfired when a group of white mercenaries under the command of Isaac Graham resorted to unspecified "scandalous and reprehensible conduct" that the council now wanted stopped by the military.[15] Cattle rustling threatened the economic foundation of local life and, when perpetrated by Indians, social order. From the Indians' standpoint, it provided a rare opportunity to participate in the new affluence. The police power of the state, meager as it was, mobilized around the problem, although it also recognized civil and humanitarian limits to its racially differential law enforcement.

After work, politics, and law, Montereyans turned to leisure—or the other way around according to visiting Yankee puritans. The presidio and the Custom House hosted parties, dances (fandangos), performances, and formal balls honoring Mexican officials. Taverns and gaming parlors provided diversion for the working class. Ship arrivals excited the town and occasioned market days at which people from the region came to trade local products for housewares, farm implements, and perhaps a luxury piece of cloth. Descriptions of local life invariably comment on the equestrian skills of the Californio *caballero* (horseman and, colloquially, gentleman), Indian vaquero, and some of the bolder women. Legend has it that Californios seldom left the saddle except to sleep, an observation supported by laws against entering places of business on horseback. Riding and roping skills developed in ranch work were also displayed in festive rodeos and contests. The favorite sporting event pitted a range-savvy bull against the common black bear. Horsemen roped the animals, dragged them to a rustic arena, and set them on one another in a contest of bear claws and bull horns. The bull usually prevailed against the docile black bear, but upsets were sufficiently frequent to make it entertaining—at least to a Californio. Visitors remark on the gracious hospitality of California households, whether in the countryside or in town, often enough that we may take it as a fact, explained, perhaps, by frequent travel in a land of few public accommodations at the time. Foreign visitors and travel writers typically noted these customs but read them inaccurately as evidence of indolence or a carefree lifestyle. Californios had style, to be sure, but they also had plenty of cares.

OPENING TO THE WORLD

The merchant schooner was to California what the covered wagon was to the interior American West. Expeditionary flagships of France, England, and Russia in the late eighteenth century were soon replaced by a growing fleet of commercial vessels. In 1818 Monterey was invaded, looted, and burned by the Argentine captain Hypolite Bouchard, who sympathized with South American independence and hoped to disrupt Spanish shipping. Sea otter pelts were the prize sought by early Spanish mercantile companies engaged in triangular trade with China via the Sandwich (Hawaiian) Islands, exchanging the valued Pacific Coast fur for Chinese quicksilver, essential to mining in Mexico. Pelts were traded between ships' captains and the missions, usually with official mediation by presidio officials. With a contract on offer, including promises of rare imports such as religious artifacts and manufacturing equipment, the padres then turned to Indians for the collection of otter skins. As the trade flourished in the 1790s, English and U.S. ships began cruising the coast in search of direct hide deals with missions and Indians. This avenue of exchange also prospered judging from local observations about better prices from British and Americans traders and Spanish concern over "contraband" trade. Mission San Carlos played a prominent role in the otter trade and joined the smuggling with a Boston ship in 1796.

Although the trade continued into the 1820s, when the sea otter population declined, it never became a major industry for California. On the one hand, otters from these southern waters produced a less valuable grade of pelt than did their British Columbia cousins; on the other, even moderate success in this venture gave the missionaries cause to worry over loss of their labor force to the attractions of successful freelancing. Yet if the otter trade fell short of economic transformation, it provided valuable precedents for the immediate future. The fur trade initiated California's participation in the global economy and began undermining Spain's mercantile monopoly. It introduced English, U.S., and South American merchant sailors to the coast, preparing the way for trade expansion in the Mexican period. Missions and Indian communities found new opportunities in commercial relations with the outside world, including experience with shipping contracts that would prove useful in subsequent transactions.[16]

California's second great economic transformation, which followed and eventually replaced the mission estates, came in the 1820s with the hide and tallow trade. Several changes explain the onset of this new commercial society. Mexican independence was key. Launched in the name of political and economic liberalism, it promoted free trade from the status of discouraged smuggling to development policy. The new regime promoted massive land reform, granting private owners vast chunks of public domain and eventually secularizing church property. Although the notion of "Spanish land grants" infuses California history, in fact very few ranchos were granted by Spanish governors (perhaps thirty statewide, mainly to retiring soldiers). In the Mexican period, by contrast, more than eight hundred grants were awarded to a growing number of immigrants from Mexico and assorted foreign countries.[17] The new trade depended on markets in South America for tallow (for soap, candles, lubricants) and in Liverpool and Boston for hides consumed in the expanding industrialization of shoes, wearing apparel, and sundry leather goods. An essential link in the commodity chain were Lima merchant houses such as John Begg and Company. Lima traders, representing England, Spain, Boston, and the nascent republics of South America, incorporated California into global commerce following the demise of Spanish mercantilism in the Americas.

John Begg and Company originated from Liverpool and employed such ambitious young clerks and future Californians as William Perry Hartnell from England, Hugh McCulloch of Scotland, and Faxon Dean Atherton, a native of Massachusetts. In June 1822 Hartnell and McCulloch sailed into Monterey Bay with plans to start their own California trading firm as agents of John Begg and Company. In the team known to Spanish speakers as "Macala y Arnel," McCulloch was the accountant and astute businessman while Hartnell combined a taste for adventure, liquor, and romance with linguistic (German, Spanish, and rudimentary Ohlone) and scholarly interests. Hartnell drew on several years of South American experience in his negotiations with Father Mariano Payeras, who now headed the prosperous mission system, and Governor Pablo Vicente de Sola. Promising that "a new world opens for us," Hartnell secured official approval to contract for hide and tallow consignments from the separate missions. Success depended on volume and timing. The ships dispatched from Lima were costly to maintain on trips lasting many months. A profitable voyage depended on filling the holds at each mission-port without delay and returning fully loaded—which often meant supplementing cargoes with other products of mission labor such as wheat, hemp, beef

12. *Trying the Tallow, Monterey,* by William Rich Hutton, ca. 1848. A rare depiction of the actual labor involved in the hide and tallow production that flourished during the Mexican period. (Reproduced by permission of the Huntington Library, San Marino, California, HM 43214, #61)

in brine, horse hair, brandy, and soap. Hartnell traveled the California mission circuit arranging long-term contracts that would keep the firm in business beyond the initial mishaps and eventually assure steady production, set prices, and routine collection at a series of depots from San Francisco to San Diego. It was a tough business. The large number of actors and events requiring coordination often went awry; ships languished in port without a cargo, hides rotted without a ship, yields were too small, and when things went well competing merchant sailors tried to lure away suppliers with better prices. After six years in the business, McCulloch, Hartnell and Company closed their operation, complaining that their deal with John Begg left all the hazards and little of the profit with the working partners. The explanation was only partly true, as suggested by other merchants who took up the trade successfully. It was true that the remarkable Hartnell had no talent for commerce and was now drinking seriously, the combination leading to his business failure. Yet the young Englishman had pioneered the trade that made fortunes for others, earning in the process the respect of Franciscans, officials, and competitors alike.[18]

Commerce introduced thoroughgoing changes in California society. Missions became industrial and commercial enterprises. Town governments sought a role as commission agents. European-American merchants invaded the territory. And the countryside hosted a series of export-oriented ranch workshops. David Spence, another in the growing line of Monterey Scots, came to process salted beef for export in the service of John Begg and Company. Cooper, Larkin, and Spear were shipping hides from Monterey in 1828 when the Boston firm Bryant, Sturgis and Company arrived and soon assumed the leadership role vacated by McCulloch and Hartnell. Dana's *Two Years Before the Mast* describes the voyage of the Bryant and Sturgis ship *Pilgrim*. William Gale managed the company from San Diego, employing Cooper as their Monterey agent. New competition and demand complicated the trade over time, with 1835 dividing qualitatively different, early and late periods. From 1822 to 1835 both competition and volume were limited, McCulloch and Hartnell dominated most of the contracts that were with missions, and profits were elusive. The mid-1830s were a watershed as the hide and tallow trade became simultaneously more competitive, extensive, and profitable.

After 1828 Bryant and Sturgis commanded roughly half the trade volume, but a variety of other agents curbed any monopoly. George Allen and Edward Watson were small-time traders in Monterey who married into Californio families and held a number of municipal positions. Trade destinations became more differentiated: Boston receiving hides, horns (for buttons), and agricultural products (e.g., olives); South America, mainly tallow and small amounts of soap, wheat, and hides; and Hawaii, a wide variety of products for consumption and triangular trade. In California, private ranches replaced the secularized missions as suppliers after 1835.[19] Finally, the money value of this trade was big, although the absence of complete records prevents any precise estimate of how big. One study calculates annual revenues for hides and tallow at $1.5 million,[20] but another finds that figure highly exaggerated.[21] Nevertheless, after the early years of uncertainty and experimentation, profits were obviously significant, sufficient to attract large numbers of eager producers, brokers, and customers. Between 1822 and 1840 Bryant and Sturgis alone sent fifteen or sixteen ships to California carrying perhaps half a million hides (acquired at $1–$2 each) along with other products (tallow was valued at $3–$4 per *arroba*, or 25-pound leather container). Different ships were reported to carry cargoes valued from $30,000 to $80,000.

Merchants and Mexican officials were continuously at odds over customs regulations and duties. Mexico encouraged free trade but also wanted to regulate the traffic and collect the required import duties at the official customhouse, headquartered at Monterey and with a branch in San Diego. Customs duties were the principal source of public revenue, and officials who were paid a percentage of what they collected were motivated to clear all shipments through a few closely supervised ports. Ship captains, conversely, preferred coasting the various mission depots or town harbors as supply dictated and moving along as expeditiously as possible to reduce expenses—an objective furthered by avoidance of customs. The whole business made for a subtle diplomatic game. Incoming vessels brought manufactures and consumer goods sold at ships' stores as outgoing cargoes were gathered at each port. Smuggling was common and sometimes justified by excessive duties. Formally high rates might also have served as a standard against which negotiations of de facto rates were conducted. Legend holds that captains learned to offload much of their cargo before clearing customs, then reload and visit a series of ports to sell and collect merchandise. Simpler solutions involved bribes and falsified bills of lading. In the end, merchants and officials worked out a modus operandi whereby the number of customs-clearing ports was increased and significant duties were paid. According to Hubert Howe Bancroft, "In 1839–40 a great improvement is observable, something of order and system being introduced by [officials José] Abrego and [Antonio María] Osio in the financial management and keeping of accounts. . . . [R]evenues increased to $158,000 for the two years."[22] Although trade policy was sometimes a contentious issue between Californios and the Mexican government, many local merchants and landowners also held key positions in government and promoted a stable commercial policy. Californio Luis Arguello left the governorship in 1825 to become a trader, bought Cooper's ship *Rover*, and hired the captain to continue sailing the China circuit. Merchants Hartnell, Cooper, Larkin, and Spence all served on Monterey's town council along with propertied officials such as Alvarado, Estrada, Osio, and Soberanes.

The flourishing international trade materially transformed the California countryside. The number of private land grants in the Monterey district increased from twelve to ninety-five during the 1830s, when most of the great ranches were established.[23] Virtually every prominent family, public official, and naturalized foreigner is listed among the decade's grantees (e.g., Soberanes, Hartnell, de la Torre, Vallejo, Estrada, Soto, Malarin, Figueroa, Spence, Munras, Boronda, Cantua, Lugo, Castro, Alvarado). The rural population increased, with ranches housing multiple families, former neophytes, and the new mestizo laboring class epitomized by vaqueros and female domestics. Although nostalgic accounts would later portray the ranches as pastoral redoubts, in fact they were serious enterprises that produced and elaborated a variety of products for local consumption and export. John F. Dana, a relative of the Boston sailor-author and son of retired Captain William G. Dana and Josefa Carillo, described the family ranch near San Luis Obispo:

> Each rancho was a kingdom of its own. At ours, my father did a lot of man-ufacturing and supplied other ranchos with flour, soap, candles, brandy, lard, sugar, chocolate, cornmeal and other staples. He also had stores of furni-ture, clothing, and implements made in our blacksmith shop. . . . We also had great looms to weave cloth and serapes. . . . The blacksmith shop was generally worked by Indians who made bridle bits, spurs and points for the wooden ploughs. . . . The big boiler in the soap factory held five thousand gallons. We would put all the fatty refuse into this huge boiler such as ren-dered lard and tallow, and boil it down. . . . When the soap was made it was very much like Castile soap and was very good and solid. My father ex-changed it for hides and other produce among his friends. . . . It was really surprising how the Indians did take to a daily program of work. . . . [T]hey built their homes around the outskirts of the rancho and learned to plow, weave, and work in the blacksmith shop and saddle shop. My father paid them $8.00 a month and board besides rationing to the families items like flour, beans and meat.[24]

Monterey, at the intersection of global market and productive country-side, fostered a cosmopolitan society. Its population of one thousand persons was international. Spaniards and South Americans merged with varied sorts of British and North American immigrants. The leaders were Californios with mixed loyalties to their ancestral Mexico and their own increasingly independent land. Thomas O. Larkin became the principal merchant and consular representative of the U.S. government. William Hartnell, the multilingual Englishman, served as a diplomat for several governors, hosted the international community at his elegant home, and established a college for Monterey's youth—twenty-one of whom were born to him and Doña Teresa da la Guerra.[25] Some of the English-speaking families sent their children to boarding school in Honolulu and subscribed to its newspaper, the *Honolulu Polynesian,* for information about world events.[26] Coastal settlements like Monterey, previously con-nected to the world mainly by sea, now witnessed their first overland mi-grants. The Kentucky fur trapper Isaac Graham established a tavern and distillery in the Salinas Valley that seemed to attract ship deserters and motley rogues. From self-styled Spaniards to Indians in surviving tradi-

13. *Monterey, California, Rancho Scene,* by Alfred Sully, ca. 1849. Sully came to California with the U.S. Army and was stationed in Monterey as quartermaster when he married into a Mexican family whose ranch is pictured here. The rancheros seem to enjoy their leisure while Indians chop wood and butcher a cow. (Courtesy of the Oakland Museum of California Kahn Collection)

tional villages and assorted foreigners, California in the 1830s and 1840s was ebullient, multicultural, mobile, progressive, and politically volatile.

THE UNCOMPLETED REVOLUTION

The revolution in California consisted of a series of uprisings from 1828 to 1844 that aspired to political autonomy from Mexico, achieved a good measure of home rule, yet fell short of independent statehood on the contemporaneous Texas model. Californios sought control over their own affairs, notably in the areas of finance and trade and the redistribution of church lands under secularization. Although some among the expatriate community called for a republic, none of the Californio leadership believed full independence provided either a practical solution to their problems or a feasible objective given the divisions among regions, groups, and loyalties within the territory. Nevertheless, "revolution" is an appropriate description for these events. It was the term employed by contemporary supporters and opponents alike. The political movement began with an assertion of independence—"California is free"—a demand for replacement of Mexican authority, and self-determination by a people who saw themselves increasingly as a distinct society—no longer a colony and never really a part of the Mexican nation. The political transformation of California in the 1830s and 1840s, moreover, transcended the coup d'état or local rebellion by fostering a revolutionary conception of citizenship that permeated all ranks of society, reaching down to the humblest mestizo and Indian. And revolution is how it all ended in a series of events, unplanned by Californios, that witnessed the semiautonomous Mexican territory fall to incorporation by the United States in 1846.

The revolutionary tide was pushed by a variety of accumulating grievances and pulled by new opportunities for intrepid action. After 1825, as before, the leading California complaint about political rule was neglect of the frontier. Mexican independence failed to bring new state investment to California. Military and territorial officials were paid irregularly, if at all, and forced to generate their subsistence through levies on the profitable missions and merchant trade. The situation generated resentments, degraded public institutions, and encouraged corruption. Democratic promises in the Mexican Constitution concerning universal citizenship and territorial governance were unfulfilled in California. Out of necessity, the missions continued to produce most of the wealth under the old system of Indian servitude. The diputación, or territorial legislature (consisting of six or seven prominent figures), seldom met and legitimate channels for expressing public opinion were blocked. Civil and military authority was still combined in the governor, who was imposed from Mexico City according to the interests of contending factions and with little regard for local preference. Californios frequently judged the actions of their governors as harsh, insensitive, and, above all, offensive to regional pride. In an odd turn of self-perception, these Californio descendants of frontier Spanish mestizos began to construe their lineage as independent of and superior to that of the Mexican. They were Californios, while Mexicans were *de la otra banda,* of the other party. In the late 1820s small but increasing numbers of former convicts came to settle as troops in new military detachments or as colonists. Californios called them "cholos," a term for persons of mixed race that was transformed on the frontier to an insult akin to "vagabond" or "bum." California was being invaded by Mexican riffraff! These newly invented ethnic distinctions expressed local resentments derived from a compound of political and economic grievances.

Yet Californio "protonationalism"[27] was ambiguous and opportunistic. On the one hand, interests in the territory fostered an independent mood with respect to home rule, customs, and trade. On the other hand, Alta California, like Texas and New Mexico, was integrated in a vast patronage network extending outward from Mexico City. Californio regional identity carried the territory up to, but not over, the brink of independence.[28]

As grievances took shape, the wages of success in the political game were escalating. The hide and tallow trade generated revenues for producers, traders, and customs officials, which were becoming a vital resource for whomever had control of territorial fortunes. And at the economic base of the trade was the greatest prize of all—the vast lands and great cattle herds belonging to the missions but scheduled for secular redistribution by laws going back to the Spanish Cortes of 1813 and reaffirmed in Mexican policy up to enabling legislation in 1833. If the California revolution sometimes appeared as a series of comic military engagements and trivial spats like the Governor Chico affair, at bottom it was a high stakes struggle for land and power.

The rebellion began in a small way over official neglect and local resentment. José Maria de Echeandía, an engineer and Mexican republican, replaced Californio Luis Arguello as governor in 1825. Although Echeandía's policy on secularization was supported locally, the new governor antagonized the Monterey group with his preference for residing in southern California and his inefficient financial management. In October 1828 soldiers at Monterey walked off their presidio and mission posts in a job action demanding back pay. Having won no satisfaction, in the following year the troops seized the presidio, jailed local officials, took possession of Monterey, and issued a proclamation calling for removal of Echeandía and appointment by the legislature of a proper financial manager. Known as the Solis Revolt after their chosen leader, this agitation involved a good deal of intrigue among customs officials and did not represent the Californio political elite, some of whom were involved in the recapture of Monterey two months later. Nevertheless, the soldiers' rising convulsed the territory with troop mobilizations, armed skirmishes, a significant countermovement, and dissension sufficient to earn the title "California's first revolution."[29]

Echeandía's mainstream approach to secularization combined economic realities with liberal republican principles in a policy of gradual reform. The territory depended on mission production for subsistence and trade revenues, yet the missions would soon be required to conform to historical intentions and law (both Spanish and Mexican) by ceding land and property to Indian pueblos. Secularization raised a host of practical problems. Popular sentiment favored retaining the friars as parish priests, but the Franciscans resisted separation from their missions and the oath of allegiance to Mexico required to avoid expulsion. The friars argued that Indians were not ready for self-governing peasant villages, citing drunkenness, indolence, and thriftlessness as evidence for the continuing need for pastoral supervision. Indeed, with some justification they claimed that secularization proponents were interested in grabbing land, herds, and slave labor. The servile condition of former neophytes in ranch and town households was cited in support of mission paternalism. If the question of whether to secularize the missions was foregone, the matter of how was wide open. Tradition, honored in the breach, held that the land belonged to the Indian, but would others such as colonists or poor Mexicans share the largesse? Who would supervise the redistribution, on what schedule, with which priorities? In July 1830 the territorial legislature approved Echeandía's cautious program, which allowed that mission Indians could apply for a "license" conveying emancipation and a parcel of land within their means to cultivate (in effect a garden plot) provided they were Christians, married adults, with fifteen years of mission service, and the means to earn their own livelihood. Although Echeandía seems to have promoted emancipation, and attracted strong political support among southern California Indians, few Indians were awarded emancipation and only a few Indian pueblos were established in the San Diego area.

Revolutionary ferment accelerated when Echeandía was replaced by Manuel Victoria, a military man whom Californians believed to be associated with the ascendant conservative faction in Mexico City and the church's agenda locally. Victoria brought a law-and-order regime justified by the Solis Revolt but experienced locally as brutal and capricious. When Victoria suspended the territorial legislature in September 1831, Monterey's town government assumed its place as a popular forum by complaining of arbitrary rule to the governor and Mexico City. While Monterey petitioned, San Diego mustered the revolution of 1831, which reconvened the legislature and exiled Victoria after a clash of troops near Los Angeles. An incipient split between northern and southern California political interests is apparent from now on, beginning with a dispute over who would succeed Victoria—Pio Pico, the influential political figure in

San Diego, Echeandía, who claimed an army of Indian partisans, or Augustin Zamorano, who raised support from the Company of Monterey Foreigners, including Hartnell and fifty others. The impasse was solved when José Figueroa arrived from Mexico to end the rivalry, impose order, and get on with a reform program resembling Echeandía's policy of gradual secularization in cooperation with the legislature.

Figueroa's brief reign (January 1833–August 1835) witnessed a convergence of complex forces that have received deserved extended treatment elsewhere.[30] From the standpoint of the revolutionary movement, the essential events of the period concern the politics of land reform. Although described as an immoral man in reference to his domestic arrangements, in Monterey Figueroa was surprisingly popular for a Mexican governor. His mestizo origins marked him as a man of the people, his intervention brought order among local factions, he respected the territorial legislature, and he was a good administrator. Bancroft says, "His partisans were then and later the controlling element of the population. He was liberal in the matter of land grants and in his policy toward foreigners. He antagonized no class, but flattered all. . . . [H]e is probably entitled to his position in history as the best Mexican governor ever sent to rule California."[31] Yet it is also true that Figueroa bitterly opposed efforts by the Mexican government to colonize California and he played into the hands of local elites who coveted mission lands. If Figueroa had lived longer, a revolution might have been unnecessary.

In Mexico, the Gómez Farías administration took up an elaborate legislative program for the secularization and colonization of California. One bill passed by the congress rapidly in 1833 called for immediate secularization. The missions would become parish churches, although the legislation said nothing about how the task was to be accomplished. Another bill, which ultimately failed, stipulated that mission lands would be divided according to a schedule of priorities in the following order: Indian families living in California, active military in California, resident Mexican smallholders (i.e., owning less than 52 acres of irrigated land, 826 acres of rainfall land, or 1,860 acres of arid land), new Mexican immigrant families, entrepreneurs, and released convicts. Figueroa and members of the territorial legislature received news of the first bill and assumed that the second one specifying priorities was still under discussion. Those preferences, of course, were viewed with alarm by Figueroa and powerful Californios, who typically owned far more land than the guidelines specified for new recipients. In their view, the whole scheme threatened to turn over California's most valuable resource to incompetent Indians and poor Mexicans. To head off that prospect, the legislature pressured Figueroa to take a hand in the procedural details for accomplishing secularization. In this way, a de facto policy began to emerge from the legislature whereby the territorial government would take charge of mission finances, a commissioner assigned to each mission would supervise the transition, former neophyte families could be granted an inalienable plot of up to thirty-three acres, Indian pueblos with common lands would be established, and the remaining lands would be managed by an official of the state responsible for maintaining stipends for the priests, schools, and good government out of proceeds. In fact, very little of this program ever materialized. Some indication of where things were headed was provided when the legislature granted Figueroa a 26,000-acre ranch near Los Angeles for the trivial sum of five hundred pesos (governors were paid a yearly salary of $4,000).[32]

Figueroa spent much of his governorship battling the Mexican government over a plan to colonize California north of San Francisco with a group of settlers from Mexico City led by José María Híjar, a prominent associate of Gómez Farías, and José María Padrés, a republican reformer and old hand in Monterey politics. The story of the ill-fated Híjar-Padrés colony is rich with intrigue, factionalism, and lessons on Mexico's continuing failure to settle and control its northern frontier. In California, the colony was in bad repute from the start. On his arrival Híjar was to assume the governorship, replacing the popular Figueroa. Although the appointment was effectively canceled by a change of Mexican administrations, local sentiment supported Figueroa's claims that the settlers were ill prepared for their agrarian mission and covertly intent on other political purposes. The prospective colony figured in the unfolding revolution as another source of conflict between Californios and Mexican rule. The precise connection lay in the rumor, disingenuously fostered by Figueroa, that colonization was aimed at former mission lands and that Híjar and Padrés aspired to political power. Figueroa argued these charges in his polemical 1835 manuscript, *Manifesto to the Mexican Republic,* the first book published in California (or second after a related pamphlet) and a fair statement of Californio views on Mexican policy. In the end, the colonization scheme failed and its leaders were deported in the revolutionary uprising. During a critical period, it added fuel to the fires of political discontent.

The revolution of 1836 emerged from a series of intersecting events in California and Mexico. Figueroa died in office at the end of September 1835, depriving Californios of a friend and political ally. Juan B. Alvarado, now the key insurgent leader, proposed to the legislature that a portrait be commissioned and hung in their chamber to honor Figueroa, and a joint resolution with Monterey's town council authorized that "a durable monument with a suitable inscription be raised in one of the most public and unobstructed sites in Monterey."[33] Although both proposals were buried with their namesake, this was the first attempt to commemorate a figure in California history and it testified to the palpable spirit of regional independence that now prevailed. Figueroa's administration had been good for Californios. Local interests were prevailing in secularization and territorial finances were on a sound footing. In a gesture freighted with symbolic power, Figueroa had split the military and civil command into two offices and designated the ranking officer, Nicolás Gutiérrez, and a member of the legislature, José Castro, as twin successors. But trouble loomed on the horizon. Mexico was undergoing a conservative counterrevolution under Antonio López de Santa Anna that repudiated the federalist principles of 1824 in a new centralist constitution of 1836. This was the context in which the otherwise merely tiresome Mariano Chico was considered loathsome in the governorship. Chico lasted only a few months, until the tempestuous events at the presidio when an aroused citizenry sent him packing. But his chosen successor, Gutiérrez, a Mexican of Spanish birth, was scarcely an improvement. Fears of reimposed Mexican centralism were supported when Gutiérrez recombined the positions of military and political head of government and refused to hear appeals from the legislature. The Monterey elite was especially aroused about a proposal to move the capital to Los Angeles. California's struggle for self-government, begun with the demise of Spanish colonialism and consolidated under Figueroa, now appeared in danger of reversal by an increasingly alien state.

The rebellion played out in a series of prosaic actions. In fall 1836 Alvarado was working as an inspector at the Custom House when he had an altercation with the governor over a minor question of revenue collection. Other tensions must have surrounded the event, for Gutiérrez overreacted by ordering Alvarado arrested. Alvarado left town for nearby San Juan Bautista, met his fellow members of the legislature who had also fled (six in all, including Montereyans Castro and Spence), and together they called for the governor's removal. The palace revolt was part of an established protest repertoire, having been staged in Monterey and Los Angeles previously, and was simply carried further in this instance. A battalion of insurgent ranchers and civilians was raised in the area between San José and San Francisco. Alvarado then took the unusual and serious step of enlisting Isaac Graham and his rough-hewn company of trappers and deserters whose reputation as riflemen (*rifleros americanos*) commanded fear throughout the territory. Alvarado then traveled north to Sonoma for an endorsement of the revolution from his uncle and the most respected Californio, Mariano Guadalupe Vallejo, hoping to return to Monterey with a heavy arsenal of military and political authority. But Vallejo, content in his own domain, equivocated at the thought of a disruptive war. Nevertheless, Alvarado returned south, claiming Vallejo's blessing. One hundred supporters led by Castro marched on the Monterey Presidio where Gutierrez was ensconced with fifty loyal troops and officials. The showdown was harmless. With the presidio surrounded and one well-placed cannon shot from El Castillo, Gutiérrez and his supporters surrendered and agreed to exile.

The rising of 1836 was simultaneously California's most far-reaching revolutionary act and largely a local campaign of the Monterey group—modest in conception and incomplete in execution. The Monterey elite consisted of socially mobile families of former soldiers and colonial officials and immigrant merchants of Anglo-American and Hispanic origin, both groups now substantial landowners. At twenty-seven when the revolt began, Alvarado was the revolution's talented and undisputed leader. In his immediate circle were boyhood friends José Castro and (uncle) Mariano Guadalupe Vallejo—the triumvirate in popular parlance. Many more were central to the group, including Antonio Osio, the former customs official, Monterey alcalde Antonio Buelna, Vallejo's brother José de Jesus, former priest and customs official Angel Ramirez, and merchants Spence and Munras. Many of the elite, particularly the immigrants, were connected by marriage and kinship bonds. They lived in close association, played together, and had a history. They were united, moreover, by a *patria chica* (regional or local loyalty) that entailed both a sense of personal identity and pride of place. In his memoirs Alvarado recalls getting into youthful fights over insults directed at Californios.[34] Alvarado and Castro were believed to be authors of *pasquinades*, or satirical broadsides ridiculing Mexican governors and posted on Monterey's street corners.

Revolutionary aspirations were always a bit uncertain. The classical pronouncement came from four members of the legislature (Alvarado, Castro, Buelna, and José Antonio Noriega from San José) immediately after victory at the presidio on November 6: "Federation or Death is the destiny of California. . . . California is free, and will sever her relations with Mexico until she ceases to be oppressed by the present dominant faction called the central government. . . . [W]e are firm in our purpose that we are free and federalists." The following day the more detailed *Plan of California Independence,* consisting of six points, was adopted by the legislature (i.e., by four of the six). The first point repeated the proviso, "Alta California is declared independent of Mexico *until* the federal system of 1824 shall be reestablished," and the second continued in a more assertive vein: "The said California is erected into a sovereign state, establishing a congress which shall pass all the particular laws of the country."[35] The remaining articles said California would be Roman Catholic, have a constitution, communicate through the municipalities, and be headed by Vallejo. So California was a sovereign state like Texas—but only until Mexico returned to a federal system. Nothing specific was said about what would happen in the interim or in the event that Mexico did not come to its senses. At the level of routine governmental affairs things went along pretty much as they would under a governor like Figueroa who favored California interests. Home rule flourished, and no one made an issue of precisely what California independence entailed.

If we assume some connection between purpose and action, then the revolution's aspirations are more fully revealed in the record of Alvarado's government during the next six years. Top priority went to consolidating land, power, and financial control in the hands of Californios—and northerners, perhaps, as critics in Los Angeles and San Diego soon began to argue. Trade prospered as Alvarado introduced reforms to rationalize commercial transactions and increase customs. The land boom peaked in these years, with Alvarado awarding an unprecedented 170 grants.[36] Many of the new ranchos were cut out of former mission lands. *Plunder* is the word critics employ to describe Alvarado's secularization program. The government administered these estates through appointed commissioners and mayordomos on the ground. Mission cattle were expropriated for payment of loans and service to the state. Indians who remained on mission lands and surrounding villages, the purported beneficiaries of land reform, rarely received title to their small plots. Instead they were rented out as field labor to private ranches for the mayordomo's profit. The missions went to ruin as productive entities and in many cases were gradually abandoned as parishes. Alvarado endeavored to restrain the worst features of despoliation, employing Hartnell to conduct an inspection tour of the missions in 1839 and implement reforms in response to complaints by clerics, Indians, and local citizens. Hartnell's report documented contract labor abuses and deterioration of the properties. It moved Alvarado to issue a new set of regulations in 1840

14. *Carmel Mission,* 1854 lithograph by Cyrille Pierre Théodore Laplace. From an 1839 original by François Edmond Paris. Drawing shows the mission with the Carmel Valley and Santa Lucia range in the background at a time when Mexican secularization would have left the grounds abandoned to a few remaining Indians and encroaching ranches. (Courtesy of the Bancroft Library)

aimed at taking the profit out of the mayordomo's position. From all accounts, nothing changed except for the continuing depopulation of the former mission settlements. Perhaps five thousand Indians still lived on at these sites, down from fifteen thousand in 1834. Mission San Carlos had stopped recruiting neophytes much earlier and by 1840 retained only thirty Indians tending garden plots.[37]

The apogee of Alvarado's revolutionary movement in the late 1830s soon passed into domestic strife. Rival factions in Los Angeles now echoed complaints of neglect and corruption previously voiced by Montereyans about Mexican rule. Alvarado found Graham's riflemen conspiring with enemies and had them briefly exiled to Mexico. Ironically, the legislature met less frequently, the popular movement for self-government dissipated, and the governor's closest supporters, including Castro and Vallejo, found themselves at odds with the political drift. For his part, Alvarado seemed to lose interest, an assessment readily explained by his growing addiction to alcohol (a problem he shared with a number of political figures, including Gutiérrez and Castro). As the Californios succumbed to regional strife, the population of foreigners was growing in numbers and power. By 1840 overland migration had become a significant factor affecting the population and the tenor of political discourse. Alvarado granted a huge tract in the Sacramento Valley to Swiss John A. Sutter's New Helvetia colony. Annexation was already a topic of conversation in the United States and among prescient Californios like Vallejo, who came to the reluctant conclusion that Mexico was powerless to resist the expansionary force from the east. But Vallejo remained loyal to Mexico and petitioned authorities to replace Alvarado with a strong governor and military force who might hold the territory. In 1842 Mexico sent Manuel Micheltorena with another cholo army, the question of California's independence having evaporated along with support for Alvarado and the movement. Two years later the last Mexican ruler would be deposed by a popular uprising. California's revolutionary temper was not quite exhausted, but the movement had lost the influence over events that it attained in the midthirties and then dissipated in provincial wrangling.

The incomplete revolution in California grew out of a conjuncture of colonial grievance and commercial opportunity. The Mexican territory suffered from neglect followed by heavy-handed attempts to appropriate its fledgling prosperity. As California became modestly self-sufficient, its population developed a sense of their patria—a regional identity as sons and daughters of a country whose provenance they imagined as more grand than benighted Mexico with its corrupt officials and cholo soldiers. The inaccuracy of these perceptions only emphasized their ideological importance. Californios were themselves the offspring of enterprising cholos, and Mexico's military and convict settlers were on the whole well behaved. Through the good fortune of Figueroa's regime, California achieved a measure of home rule before the attempted reimposition of state centralism. The revolt that followed was impelled by a strong dose of protonationalism and a clear-eyed assessment of the rewards to political control of land, commercial revenue, and public office.

It was a bourgeois revolution. But it was also a sectional rebellion, centered in Monterey and bound up in the lineaments of family, kinship, and place. California lacked any bases of territorial unity beyond self-interest or common grievances against Mexico. Although the insurgents of 1836 reached out to other northern settlements, the rebellions of this period were strictly local affairs. With the exception of the desultory legislature and declining missions, there were no territory-wide institutions with which to build a broader movement. Life was organized in towns and ranches that traded unilaterally with the insinuating global economy.

For want of institutional mechanisms or unifying interest, those who attained political power used it to consolidate their own regional bases. In the end, revolutionary California never had a vision, strategy, or plan for its future. Californios resigned themselves to wait for something to happen, and it did.

REVOLUTION WITHIN THE REVOLUTION

Although California's revolution lacked a dramatic overthrow of the old regime, its cumulative effects were nevertheless revolutionary when measured by the spread of a new conception of political freedom and citizenship. This development is easily overlooked in a history dominated by elite struggles over property, power, and commercial privilege. Insofar as a revolution in political culture occurred at the grassroots, its development was further obscured by contemporary histories that neglected or denigrated the lower orders. Many of the primary-source documents on early California were recorded by Franciscans with a vested interest in maintaining the missions as protectors of the allegedly incompetent Indian or by public officials who belonged to the commercial elite that depended on an available labor force. It is hardly surprising that contemporary descriptions of secularization portray Indians as indifferent to land reform and emancipation. Yet the same sources contain inconsistencies that belie the official line. Indians and lower "castas" (mixed-bloods) act in unexpected ways, and their expected actions yield to alternative interpretations. After sixty years of missionary socialization, some Indians doubtless did not want individual freedom while others, like the rebellious Chumash who seized Mission La Purísima in 1824, forcefully demanded it. Between these poles, the lower orders demonstrated a range of political action. The question is whether the bourgeois revolution had its counterpart in the rank and file: was there a popular revolution for citizenship rights within California's bourgeois revolution?

Evidence on the subject appears in connection with secularization and petitions for licenses of emancipation, which the law required of Indian families requesting a grant of former mission land and property (e.g., livestock). Introduced in 1826, the law evolved from restricted to potentially general eligibility.[38] Indian communities at the missions were advised of their rights under the new law during visits by Mexican officials dedicated to reform. Governor Echeandía carried the message of emancipation to southern California missions and is said to have attracted a large following. Bancroft describes mission visits to promote secularization by both Figueroa and Alvarado, although he also seems determined to trivialize their results: "[Figueroa] visited the southern missions in person, exhorting assembled neophytes and explaining to them the advantages of proffered freedom. Of one hundred and sixty families at San Diego and San Luis, qualified according to the standard established [then involving adult Christians with long service], only ten could be induced to accept emancipation before Figueroa started on his return to the north." Bancroft's source for the item, Padre President Narciso Duran, was a vigorous critic of emancipation. The statement itself is oddly confined to a brief period between the Indians' first news of the opportunity and Figueroa's departure, implying that the consequential decision should have been reached precipitously. No allowance is made for the possibility that additional families chose emancipation after time for proper reflection.

Alvarado spoke to a crowd of neophytes at Mission San Miguel "where from a cart in the mission courtyard he vividly pictured the advantages of freedom to the Indians; then requested those who wished to remain under the padre to stand on the left and those preferring freedom on the right. Nearly all went to the left at first, where they were soon joined by the small minority who had not the courage of their convictions." Here again, Bancroft attaches no significance to the fact that an unspecified "small minority" under pressure to make an immediate choice in front of priests and officials nevertheless did choose emancipation initially and may have reversed themselves more than once as time and circumstance permitted. Elsewhere, Bancroft reports as unremarkable that "no secularization was yet attempted at Sta Clara, though many neophytes were given licenses of emancipation." The verb *given* is patronizing by contrast to alternatives like *petitioned* or *sought*, which would be more consistent with the legal procedure for attaining emancipation. Bancroft's consistent editorial bias on the subject of political agency is not surprising given his frank conviction of Indian inferiority: "[S]uch was the inherent stupidity of the native Californian character that no great revolts or outrages have to be chronicled. Thousands toiled on patiently year after year, and the evidence is but slight that any great number realized that their lot was a hard one."[39] But the evidence can be made to seem slight by cursory and blunt readings. Bancroft's pessimism does not seem to be supported, although his evidence alone cannot be turned to the opposite conclusion. So far only two facts are clear: a new conception of citizenship rights was conveyed, even advocated, to the Indian population, and people were listening judging from the choices of some and indecision of others.

Closer scrutiny indicates that significant, if not overwhelming, numbers pursued legal emancipation with its entailed property rights. Several secondary sources provide comparative evidence. Elisabeth Haas studied Mission San Juan Capistrano, perhaps the best example of a self-determined Indian pueblo, where "the alcaldes for the Juaneños requested that the 891 neophytes at the mission be given land surrounding the mission proper. This land, they argued, had irrigated lots on which they were supporting themselves without the aid of the mission. This claim to the land articulates their sense of rightful possession derived from their labor."[40] C. Alan Hutchinson cites a petition to Governor Echeandía from Mission San Buenaventura in which a group of Indian artisans requested emancipation. When the governor consulted with Father Duran, the padre president allowed that these petitioners might have the skills to support themselves, but their loss would hurt the mission and could lead to wholesale defection, which was something clearly to be avoided. This case suggests a different context altogether from Bancroft's dismissive examples, one in which Indian agency and church institutional power are pitted in a self-conscious struggle over the control of labor and property. Finally, George Phillips cites several petitions from neophytes in the San Diego area requesting that they be allowed to continue farming their mission plots where they had "plantings of wheat, barley, corn, beans, peas and other plants for their sustenance, and two vineyards, with their gardens."[41]

If nascent citizenship may be gauged by Indians' assertions of a right to land and the fruit of their labor, then several changes demonstrate the development of this political consciousness. First, Indian land use practices changed as self-provisioning grounds and productive exploitation of common land grew. Although the data are lamentably indirect, references in provincial records and mission inventories point to self-provisioning. Missions had gardens, and neophyte labor supplied food for its own consumption. Indians whose departure from mission control was resisted or decried had obviously proven their capacity to support themselves and others in agricultural and artisanal production.[42] Complementary evidence based on the institution of common land demonstrates the existence of new town statutes defining a widening range of common rights to water, woods, wood(cutting) lots, grass, pasture, and ejido (cultivation) plots. Moreover, people exercised these rights in a developing moral economy, as shown by town council proceedings dealing with access, fees, public regulation, and legal prerogatives (e.g., concerning the difference between woodcutting privileges in commons woodlots and prohibition on private land grants).[43] Common land, of course, was available for use by all citizens, not only Indians, but the point is precisely that Indians began to think and to act as citizens.[44]

A second source of evidence on the development of political rights are the local "Mexican Archives" of legal papers for the Monterey district from 1835 to 1846 dealing with all aspects of civil and criminal procedure adjudicated by local alcaldes, courts of first instance, justices of the peace, and grassroots "perfects" who investigated legal complaints.[45] Sometimes referred to as the "Monterey Archives," the collection was indexed and bound in 1859 by Alex Taylor for preservation by Monterey County under the title Mexican Archives (which also distinguishes it from D. R. Ashley's Monterey Archives of Town Council [Ayuntamiento] proceedings in the Bancroft Library). David Langum, who examined these records with special reference to the treatment of Anglo-Americans under Mexican law, describes the archive as "by far more nearly complete than those for other California localities" and so, for present purposes, a richer source than has previously been brought to bear on the question of revolutionary political consciousness.[46]

The index to the Mexican Archives employs a cross-referenced system based on individual names and topics such as municipal affairs, political affairs, and land. One of these subjects, "Indians," itemizes documents pertaining to all manner of contacts between Indians and the legal system. There are fifty-five Indian cases during the decade that encompass everything from homicide, rape, and drunkenness to petitions for emancipation, land, and complaints about labor conditions and unpaid wages. Criminal matters run the gamut of actions and punishments. Conviction for homicide could result in a sentence ranging from ten years in prison to death. Petty crimes of theft and disorderly conduct are common and routinely result in fines or penal servitude on public works for short periods. The Negro Francisco, for example, was sentenced to four months of public works for robbing Thomas Larkin's house.

Yet many legal transactions describe Indians self-consciously exercising their citizenship rights. The Indian Ignacio claimed a piece of land in Carmel Valley where he had a house and was raising crops in 1837. María and José Cassia petitioned for their freedom, while Iliseo asked for custody of a child. When the fifty-five cases are classified by general subject matter, three categories emerge (as well as an unclassifiable miscellaneous group): misdemeanors (drunkenness, family disputes and violence, petty theft, etc.), felonies (murder, rape, robbery), and citizenship claims (petitions for emancipation, protests, flight, etc). Although felonies are common (20 cases), the other two categories are roughly equal (12–14 cases each) and especially significant. When Indians came to the rudimentary California court system, in about 25 percent of the cases they did so on their own initiative to appeal for redress of their rights. They knew two critical things: that there was a code of law that dispensed justice and that they now qualified for its attentions despite their past disenfranchisement. The speed and depth of the change should not be exaggerated on this evidence. Few former neophytes became civil libertarians overnight (although it seems a few did), and the large majority may never have fully grasped the change. But there is good evidence that a new consciousness of political citizenship had taken root and was spreading to an extent not properly acknowledged by contemporaries and subsequent analysts.

If that assessment is bold, consider the Indian and mestizo voices in the following cases. Thirty neophytes at Mission Santa Clara issued an undated "notice to the public" (probably in the late 1830s) complaining of the treatment from the mayordomo and threatening action if their protestations were not addressed. They came forward as witnesses for the people of the pueblo whom they served, demanding "that the mayordomo Vic*te* [Vicente] leave because he is going around alienating [literally, "unmarrying"] us from our wives. We give our administrator 8 days to remove him and put another in his place. If this is not done as we state, one of two things will happen: Either this man will experience some misforture or 30 of us men will walk off until we can meet with [two authorities] making them aware of the public notices that there are on the ranch, all of them pertaining to Vicente and our wives." The notice appears designed for public posting and is signed with thirty crosses.[47]

In another case, Indians in private employment moved well beyond petitions for justice on the secularized mission estates. Jeronimo, Altarsiano, Proto, and Albana in the pueblo of San José de Guadalupe complained in 1843 that Don José de Jesus Vallejo (the general's influential brother and a landed rancher on the Pajaro River north of Monterey) was not respecting their status "as Indians" and wage workers. The document's narrative voice alternates between the justice of the peace, who is recording the charges, and the petitioners themselves, but all of the representations come from Indians.

> They are employees in his [Vallejo's] service and until now he has not satisfied [treated] them as Indians (indigenas) according to the law [authority] but as servants (criados) to whom he offers payment for personal services so scant that they cannot live satisfactorily. In virtue of this they left the employ of this gentleman imploring the justice due them as Indians and for their misery they find themselves exposed to mistreatment as men and in truth they believe that

all subservient people are enslaved as Indians to suffer until death: for fear
we have abandoned our families and sustenance awaiting the disposition of
superiors and government. In the meantime, we subject ourselves to the orders of the court.[48]

The judicial voice returns in the final lines of the document, approving
the petitioners' claim and recommending retribution.

The striking features of this case show Indians *using* the newly elaborated legal system for redress and self-consciously demanding rightful
treatment, not as servants but *as Indians*—as members of a group that,
they understand, enjoys the rights of citizens and does not have to suffer the patronage of subjects in the old regime. They are pessimistic about
the chances of subordinated people generally, or perhaps this is a rhetorical device, but they are also content to place themselves at the disposition of the new authority. Until very recently, their options had been exhausted by the choices of flight, sabotage, malingering, or resistance. As
they begin to pursue new avenues with petitions, local justices, courts,
and citizenship statutes, they simultaneously demonstrate a revolutionary sea change in political rights.

Indians, it should be stressed, were not the only beneficiaries or measure of the new political consciousness. Mestizos, women, and the low
born also experienced the desire for citizenship. María Guadalupe
Castillo was a Monterey native of Hispanic mestiza ancestry who married the English carpenter Ed Watson at the age of fifteen or sixteen. Baptized José Eduardo María, Watson became a trader and elected member
of the town council. The couple had two children and a debt-ridden life
together before their divorce in 1842—the same year María Guadalupe
ran afoul of a powerful enemy. Although the full details are lacking, it
appears that after an amicable divorce María Guadalupe and the children went to live in the household of Gabriel de la Torre, a member of
the Monterey crowd, former soldier, revolutionary, land grantee, rancher,
and town official. Within months she had moved to the household of
Rafael Gonzales, a former alcalde of Monterey and customs official who
was briefly arrested in 1837 and seems to have been on the wrong side
of a quarrel over revenues. On November 9, 1842, in the waning days
of his governorship, Juan Alvarado demanded officially that Monterey
Justice of the Peace José Fernandes execute an order of banishment from
the town against María Guadalupe Castillo.

> The recent outrage that my household has suffered, caused by the prostituted
> Guadalupe Castillo, who lives in the household of Don Rafael Gonsales, with

whose tribunal you are already acquainted, and as I wish to avoid any new insult on this matter, I expect that within twenty four hours after receiving this order, you will order the aforementioned Guadalupe to be banished twenty five leagues from this town to the cardinal [compass] point that she chooses . . . that you will continue the formalities to cover the complicity of the aforementioned Don Rafael Gonsales in whose household has twice appeared, at odd hours of the night, one of the orphan girls who reside in my house receiving education.[49]

The force of Alvarado's outrage is not explained by the circumstances cited; an orphan girl under his and his wife's protection is making nocturnal visits to the home of a possible political opponent or to a woman whose reputation had been damaged by divorce. Yet clearly the beleaguered governor feels some personal insult, an offense against his honor, and "outrage that [his] household has suffered" (has the girl rejected the family's charity?).

We may never know the specifics beyond this suggestive amalgam of personal affect, family status, and political will—and the important fact that Alvarado was now a troubled shadow of his 1836 revolutionary self. Yet the more important lesson of the case lies in the reaction of less powerful citizens. In the first instance, Justice Fernandes looked into matters and replied to Alvarado the following day: "[T]here has not been a formal charge or denunciation resulting in sufficient proof of a crime of Guadalupe Castillo regarding the kidnapping and flight of the young woman Josefa from Your Excellency's household. . . . I don't believe it just to sentence Castillo to banishment from this city when she hasn't been accused nor your evidence to be reasonable." An angry Alvardo fired back the next day: "When I opened, just now, your official note, I believed that its content would be an act of subordination and obedience to superior orders, but it is with feeling that I have seen the contrary. . . . My honor and that of my household and all that is conducive to respect for the dignity of the post that I occupy obliges me to warn you again to execute that mandated in my first note, the contrary being the narrowest irresponsibility." Despite his misgivings, Fernandes acquiesced to the governor's power and ordered Guadalupe into exile on November 12.[50]

Guadalupe Castillo had the last word, answering Fernandes, "I obey the order in spite of great illnesses I have as caused [or perhaps as a "casta" or mestiza] by the enclosed petition protesting against you as a judge who has attacked my individual liberty, giving judgment to a despotic, servile, tyrannical, violent and unconstitutional order [and] will carry my protest to a competent judge for his [Fernandes's] having been sentenced me without hearing me and without formation of cause and due to whose violence and infraction of laws, in due time I will press claims for the harm and damages that result."[51] We know that Guadalupe was illiterate and must assume that the statement's prolixity derives from a legal adviser. Yet her sense of injustice moves the cumbersome lines and her choice of the legal protest vehicle demonstrates that she, like her humble fellows, had achieved a new understanding of the justice to which she was rightfully entitled. Equally important, California's legal system had evolved in the space of a few years since the 1824 constitution. A staff of advocates in the field had been created, perfects and justices of the peace who, despite their own humble origins revealed in the language of their petitions, actively represented the weak against the strong. Such were the nourishing fruits of revolution.

REMAKING AND UNMAKING HISTORY

The great irony of Mexican California's contemporary recorded history was that few of its revolutionary accomplishments were chronicled or credited. On the contrary, the revolution was silenced, along with the perspective of the Mexican state on these events and the voice of the mestizo and Indian concerning the experience of change. The rich, if self-aggrandizing, church history of the Spanish period faltered in the nineteenth century in tandem with the missions themselves. The whole configuration of contested histories produced during the Spanish period shifted in the direction of fewer competing narratives and greater dominance of the expatriate vision that looked on events from the outside in and from one culture to another without empathy. In the nineteenth century, moreover, the expatriate vision was no longer that of an urbane Count La Pérouse or a worldly Vancouver but one centered on Anglo-American commercial interests and territorial designs. Nevertheless, there were still two narratives, however unequally matched, one the view of Californio partisans and the other of Yankee critics.

The early nineteenth century witnessed the emergence of an identity and a culture, underpinned by the new regime of bourgeois property and commerce, that contemporaries called "Californio." It constituted for the young revolutionaries a sense of "patria," a cultural distance from and superiority to Mexican society and its motley immigrants. Although one might expect to find the origins of Californioismo in the anticlerical accounts of civil society in the Spanish period, in fact the connection is

weak. Far from building on a tradition of historical interpretation initiated by Miguel Costansó or Pedro Fages, the Californio narrative began
with problems of the moment, the whole range of conflicts with Mexico, and then rummaged among the relics of an imagined Spanish past
in search of principles fit for useful application in the present. This
method of historical reconstruction is illustrated in the only specific documentary source on Californio partisanship, José Figueroa's *Manifesto
to the Mexican Republic* of 1835—the first proper book published in
California and a defense of local interests that reflected the views of
revolutionaries.

Figueroa's *Manifesto* comprised a series of letters the governor wrote
to the territorial legislature, Mexico City, and José María de Híjar, Mexico's embattled director of colonization in California. The letters are often passionate, self-serving, and one-sided, if not erroneous. These features are of less concern here than the actual content of Californioismo
that they articulate. As Figueroa attempts to sort through a welter of
conflicting communiqués from Mexico and seeming subversive threats
to California self-government, he continually looks back to legal foundations established in "the Spanish Constitution, which is in effect in this
Territory, and the law of June 23, 1813," involving the legislature. Since
becoming governor, Figueroa says, "I have been regarding with pleasure
the constitutional progress being made by these peaceful inhabitants without any obstacle or disturbance. . . . I have held in veneration the laws
containing the social guarantees. But one of those misfortunes by which
the genius of evil extends its malign influence seeks to take away from
us the enviable tranquillity which only Californians are permitted to enjoy." [52] The evil influence, of course, is Mexican intervention in the presence of the Híjar-Padrés colony and the threat it represents to mission
land and Indian labor, specifically the radical schemes of Mexican political theorists who have no acquaintance with California and would
ruin decades of progress by redistributing profitable lands among un-
skilled poor colonists and turning Indians loose to the ravages of unem-
ployment, drunkenness, and exploitation by unscrupulous masters. Californians, by contrast, were enjoying constitutional progress, economic
prosperity, and social tranquillity under home rule.

Figueroa's stated purpose in the *Manifesto* is to set forth a Californio
"narrative of events" consistent with progress based on Spanish social
principles and, with regard to Mexican intervention, to provide a "refutation of the antisocial doctrines which they have used to corrupt virgin
California." In this document we encounter the first explicit invocation

of a California history—the first claim to a tradition that resides in California's past and carries moral force as a guide to present action. For his vision as well as his skillful political leadership, Figueroa was praised by the legislature as "the father of our California."[53] If that were true, he was also the father of a California whose days were as numbered as its detractors were numerous. The *Manifesto* lacked a program for the imminent revolution, just as the revolution lacked a plan for social reorganization, and both faded from memory for want of any connection to an institutional framework. The Californio narrative, like Figueroa's monument, was approved but never built.

The expatriate narrative was developed in a variety of words and deeds. Expeditionary accounts continued to pour forth in the early nineteenth century. Authors such as Beechey and Duhart-Cilly provided original portraits of Monterey, as we have seen, while others such as William Shaler (the first extended account of California, published in the United States in 1808) borrowed extensively from La Pérouse and Vancouver. During the 1830s, Anglo-American accounts began to appear that would soon enjoy great commercial success, occlude indigenous histories, and become the dominant story of Mexican California. In 1839 Alexander Forbes published the first work that would qualify by today's standards (overlooking its garrulous nineteenth-century subtitle) as a history text, *California: A History of Upper and Lower California from Their First Discovery to the Present Time, Comprising an Account of the Climate, Soil, Natural Productions, Agriculture, Commerce, &c. A Full View of the Missionary Establishments and Condition of the Free and Domesticated Indians. With an Appendix Relating to Stein Navigation in the Pacific.* Although Forbes never set foot in Alta California, he acquired a thorough knowledge of his subject as a partner in one of the largest trading houses on the west coast, Barron, Forbes and Company of Tepic, Mexico. The assured Scotsman wields a businesslike pen and clearly read extensively in the Spanish, French, and English sources. The more historical sections are composed of long quotations from Palóu, Beechey, and others.

Yet, in the introductory words of Herbert Priestley, Forbes's "history with a purpose" is less a scholarly examination of California society than it is an evaluation of the region's economic prospects and a cultural critique of their management by Spain and Mexico. The mission system is credited with having educated the comparatively backward California Indian and attaining great productivity under humanistic Franciscan stewardship. Nevertheless, like La Pérouse, Forbes regards mission servitude as slavery contrary to the rights of humankind: "[O]ne of the finest countries on earth has been doomed to be the abode of men reclaimed from one state of misery and barbarism only to be plunged into another sort of barbarism and an aggravated state of misery; whereas under other management, it might now have been the abode of millions of the human race, enjoying all the advantages and comforts of civilization. . . . [W]e entirely condemn their system and its results." The fundamental flaw in the mission system is its reliance on religious superstition ("a sort of dumb show"), and he wonders if better results would not obtain by alternatives such as British colonialism that proceed "by other means than religion." Forbes is equally critical of Mexican government and the territorial legislature, which he considers "a set of ill-informed and rapacious men, united into a democratic council, and daily manufacturing absurd laws and regulations which, after a very short time, are laid aside for some fresh whim, as a child throws away its plaything at the sight of a new one. . . . Any foreign power if disposed to take possession of California could easily do so."[54]

Forbes's *California* is a major turning point. It builds on previous traditions and then leaps to a new cultural interpretation, if not a new historiographic genre. In Forbes, Palóu's Franciscan history is absorbed, exploited, and then placed in the background as the product of a retrograde religious institution. An emphasis on the rights of man is drawn from Le Pérouse, along with Vancouver's preoccupation about military defenses. Forbes carries these influences to a new level, however, in his ridicule of Mexican government and his prophetic judgment that California is a rich prize awaiting the nation capable of taking charge. Indeed, Alexander Forbes was in regular contact with James Alexander Forbes (no relation), British vice-council for California from 1843 to 1851, about various schemes for British acquisition of the Mexican territory. At bottom *California* was an imperial narrative, the portrait of a land containing great resources but a benighted history of Hispanic misrule inviting conquest for the benefit of nature, humanity, and commerce. California will never progress under the weight of Spanish culture and Mexican rule, relics of the past in any case. *California* enjoyed great commercial success after its 1839 publication in London, appearing in a number of subsequent editions and in the United States. Among its attractions was a set of splendid illustrations by William Smyth sketched during his earlier voyage with Captain Beechey. Smyth became a popular illustrator for various works on California, and his drawings presented the world with a pastoral image of the frontier circa 1830 that invited comparison with the English countryside. Bancroft notes, "Forbes book was not only the first ever published in English relating exclusively to California, and more than any other the means of making known to English readers the country's advantages, but it has always maintained its reputation of being one of the best extant on the subject."[55]

The classic Yankee narrative of early California, of course, was Richard Henry Dana's 1840 *Two Years Before the Mast*. Still read with profit one hundred sixty years later, Dana's book was the first bestseller in the United States set primarily in California. *Two Years Before the Mast* is at once a nonfiction sea story rivaling *Moby Dick* in contemporary popularity and a travel account that took the East Coast audience ashore in the rustic ports of Monterey, Santa Barbara, San Pedro, and San Diego. Dana was raised in the shadow of Harvard University by an elite Boston family. At the age of nineteen and in poor health, he left the university for a taste of adventure at sea to restore his spirits. As a merchant seaman on the *Pilgrim*, Dana experienced fierce storms, picaresque shipmates, floggings, a worker's introduction to the hide and tallow trade, and the exotic charms of California's ports.

Although much of the book's appeal is as a sea adventure, it is also a remarkable ethnography of commerce and society in early California— a description of local life superior to anything written by a contemporary Mexican, Californio, or expatriate resident. Dana witnessed California from the docks and harbor, not really understanding the social and political forces at work in the territory. But from his vantage he saw clearly and recorded eloquently events that escaped others. Dana attended to the physical surroundings and townscapes, as we saw in previous passages about Monterey, but was equally keen on social structure: "Among the Mexicans there is no working class (the Indians being practically serfs and doing all the hard work); and every rich man looks like a grandee, and every poor scamp like a broken-down gentleman." In a sharp insight on Monterey's parvenu society, he notes that the exclusive, intermarrying upper class "can be distinguished, not only by their complexion, dress, and manners, but also by their speech; for calling themselves Castillians [Spaniards], they are very ambitious of speaking the pure Castillian, while all Spanish is spoken in a somewhat corrupted dialect by the lower classes."[56] For all his acuity, however, Dana did not hesitate to judge Californios by the austere standard of New England Puritanism.

> The Californians are an idle, thriftless people, and can make nothing for themselves. The country abounds in grapes, yet they buy, at a great price, bad wine

made in Boston and brought round by us, and retail it among themselves at a real (12 1/2 cents) by the small wine glass. Their hides, too, which they value at two dollars in money, they barter for something which costs seventy-five cents in Boston; and buy shoes (as like as not made of their own hides, which have been carried twice around Cape Horn) at three and four dollars a pair.

And echoing a refrain from Vancouver and Forbes, "In the hands of an enterprising people, what a country this might be!"[57]

A bestseller on publication, *Two Years Before the Mast* has remained continuously in print since 1840 with hundreds of thousands of copies read around the world. Fifty-four U.S. publishers have issued seventy-seven editions, twenty-three editions have been published in England, and translations have appeared in a dozen languages.[58] In addition to enduring as a classic of American letters, Dana's work received enthusiastic contemporary reviews and the attentions of reformers shocked by the severe punishments suffered by merchant seamen. The historian Kevin Starr goes so far as to speculate that "as the author of the first best-selling book about California, Dana did much to bring on [U.S.] annexation."[59]

Yet, if *Two Years Before the Mast* was easily the most influential account of Mexican California, it also contributed to a broader movement of public history by complementing and extending the critical Anglo-American narrative present in Vancouver, Forbes, and others to come. Dana epitomized a socially constructed history that was developed by various authors and historical actors, a movement in nineteenth-century thought that surveyed a very narrow range of California experience and judged it harshly by alien standards. The Yankee critique readily eclipsed the fragile Californio narrative of Figueroa and his supporters but not because it provided a more complete or accurate survey of events. On the contrary, despite its partisan stance and strategic purposes, the Californio narrative was far more attentive to the decisive social conditions, political issues, and revolutionary currents of the day. But it was the story of history's losers, a people who were being invaded and absorbed by the ascendant Yankees.

From the Spanish to the Mexican period, a substantial shift has occurred in the story of California, a change constituted by new events, to be sure, but also a reconfiguration of the past. History as understood at the close of the Spanish period, the contested narratives of the church, civil authorities, and expeditionaries, has been truncated and reordered. The Franciscan tradition fades, except in unsympathetic caricatures, and with it the use of primary sources. The state narrative almost fades, and except for the defensive voices of local officials we begin to lose an appreciation for political action, constraint, and struggle. The diplomatic and scientific investigations of La Pérouse are replaced by commercial, aggrandizing, and, above all, judgmental portraits. The reconstruction of history is underpinned by political changes beginning with the collapse of Spain in the Americas, Mexican independence and state turmoil, neglect of California, and the emergence of a self-governing but divided territory. Beyond these broad forces, however, the social construction of a new California history is a two-part process. On the one hand, the old history wanes because its institutional bases have washed away: the church with its scholars, archives, and vested interests in recording (perhaps exaggerating) its deeds is in effect gone, along with the materially supported military. Figueroa's plaintive and mercurial manifesto is the revealing exception. On the other hand, a new institutional presence and a new set of interests developed in Mexican California around the fateful incorporation of the region into the global economy. The commercial opening generated a cascade of changes in land, social class, politics, and, ultimately, in the cultural reinterpretation of the California story at the hands of Forbes and Dana and the social forces they represented. In the absence of an institutionally grounded competitive narrative, the Anglo-American critique overshadowed other views and earlier traditions, producing expatriate histories that largely excluded Californio society, its revolutionary experience, and its voice.

EPILOGUE

The defining fact of Californio society in the Mexican period is that it ended not in a moment of revolutionary victory, or defeat, but through a process of desultory resistance and the steady dissipation of political initiative after 1836. The Californios had one more revolt in them; they rose in 1844 to expel the last Mexican governor, Manuel Micheltorena, sent at the request of Alvarado's former allies to salvage a worsening situation of internal strife. But it was too late for Micheltorena, who confronted new resentment of his cholo forces, shifting local loyalties, and a growing U.S. presence (U.S. Navy commodore Thomas Ap Catesby Jones seized Monterey in October 1842 in the mistaken belief that the Mexican-American War had already begun, thus anticipating by nearly four years the decisive invasion of Commodore John Drake Sloat in July 1846). The fateful events affecting California were no longer taking place in Monterey or Los Angeles but in Washington, D.C., and along the Mexican border where President James Polk's imperial chess game drew the careening Mexican regime into a territorial war it was bound to lose badly.[60] But events of the 1840s did less to change the character of Mexican California than to create a watershed for changes in the latter half of the nineteenth century. When Commodore Sloat raised the Stars and Stripes over the old Mexican Custom House, the event projected the American future instead of culminating the Mexican past. California was not so much conquered in 1846 as it was steadily absorbed in a new political and cultural amalgam after the incomplete revolution of 1836 collapsed into strife and indirection. This fact, too, is typically obscured in conventional narratives of war and western expansion.

FOUR

American Property

What is a paisano? He is a mixture of Spanish, Indian,
Mexican, and assorted Caucasian bloods. His ancestors have
lived in California for a hundred or two years. He speaks
English with a paisano accent and Spanish with a paisano
accent. When questioned concerning his race, he indignantly
claims pure Spanish blood. . . . In Monterey, that old city on
the coast of California, these things are well known, and they
are repeated and sometimes elaborated. It is well that this
cycle be put down on paper so that in a future time scholars,
hearing the legends, may not say as they say of Arthur and of
Roland and of Robin Hood—"There was no Danny nor any
group of Danny's friends, nor any house. Danny is a nature
god and his friends primitive symbols of the wind, the sky,
the sun." This history is designed now and ever to keep the
sneers from the lips of sour scholars.

John Steinbeck, *Tortilla Flat*

SUSPENDED ANIMATION

In the latter half of the nineteenth century, California experienced the
creation of a new property regime controlled by a few speculators and
railroad tycoons whose vast landholdings dwarfed those of the dwin-
dling and sometimes dispossessed Mexican rancheros. Monterey County
was no exception to this pattern as several land empires took shape on
the peninsula and in the Salinas Valley. The most notorious of these was
assembled by the Scot David Jacks who arrived in 1850 with $4,000 and
within a decade owned thirty thousand acres of former city lands and a
growing number of ranches that eventually brought his estate to ninety
thousand acres. Where there were huge concentrations of land there
inevitably large numbers of landless. And their ranks grew in the 1860s
and 1870s as more U.S. citizens sought public lands and a new start in
the west. In Monterey, however, public lands were scarce given the dense

pattern of Mexican land grants that were now being defended before the
U.S. Land Commission just as they were coveted by new speculators.
Among his many acquisitions, Jacks purchased from the Hispanic grantee
one of these tracts, the nine-thousand-acre Rancho Chualar. Like many
Salinas Valley ranches, Chualar was imprecisely bounded, poorly surveyed, underoccupied, and generally an open invitation to the growing
numbers of squatters who believed themselves entitled to settlement on
"government land," as they perceived the open western range. Jacks attempted to fight back the invasion by suing the squatters for adverse possession and damages in the amount of $1,300 each. As the case dragged
through the courts, the settlers mobilized and delivered a feisty coun-
terdemand and obscure threat to the penurious Scot:

MONTEREY COUNTY OCT 4, 1872

Mr David Jack—Sir

near four years have we waited for a decission in the Choualar case in
order to arrive at a decission in your case. Now that this case has been
decided in favor of the Squatters on that land which you pretend to claim
as a part of the Choualar Grant and you have there by been the cause of
great deal of unnecessary annoyance and expense to those settlers—some
of them you have actually sued for tresspass and damages putting that
damage at $1300.00 cts at the time that said suit was brought with an
addition $100 per month for every month that they occupied that land
there after.

now you low lifed son of Birth you have sued them for that amount
of damage—to you—for occupying United States government land that
happened to join your grant land.

now you Son of a bitch if you dont make good that amount of damage
to each and every one of those settlers which you sued as well as a reasonable amount for compensation to each of the other settlers—if you dont do
this inside of ten days you son of a bitch—we shall suspend your animation
between daylight and hell.

By order of the Executive Committee of the Squatters' League of Monterey
County.[1]

The Squatters' League was only one among a variety of popular movements fostered by rapacious practices of late-nineteenth-century economic
development. As poor settlers challenged land magnates, townspeople
trespassed on privatized woodlands, marginalized social bandits preyed
on nascent commerce, vigilantes retaliated, and a growing immigrant
working class fought among themselves as often as against their bosses.
American California was reorganized along new and sharper lines of

class, race, gender, and power. Toward the end of the century a reconfigured historical narrative emerged that silenced contemporary social strife in a story that celebrated California's progressive ascent from
Spanish pastoralism to Yankee efficiency. Indeed, local histories constructed a mythic Spanish arcadia in tandem with promotion of the new
property regime—a pastoral epic that delighted investors but never
squared with the dissenting voices of popular recusants.

The story begins with conquest and its aftermath, particularly in the
transformation of landownership under American rule. The transition
introduced a new culture of land use as well as a more concentrated distribution of wealth and property. The expanding labor force, conversely,
became more polarized in the form of a large ethnic working class (Hispanic, Chinese, Italian, Portuguese). The pattern of cultural change and
social inequality generated a variety of conflicts, from social banditry
and vigilantism to squatter movements and nativistic labor disputes. In
addition to protest movements, a transformative struggle developed during the 1880s for the control of the city of Monterey. In an alliance with
railroad interests, local business and civic groups mounted a successful
struggle against land monopolists to incorporate the city, strengthen municipal government, and develop Monterey as an elite resort and property market. The transformation was enabled by a resurgence of local
history celebrating such Monterey attractions as the old Spanish capital
and mission. The development boom, however, was not shared by Monterey's poor and ethnic communities. Town modernization for the benefit
of real estate and resort interests demanded urban renewal aimed at rustic waterfront housing and Chinatown business. The working class suffered gentrification, although it appears that they also avenged their grievances. That, at least, is one plausible explanation for an enduring local
mystery that I propose to solve.

CONQUEST AND ITS AMBIVALENT AFTERMATH

Acting under orders from President James Polk and Secretary of War
George Bancroft, Commodore John Drake Sloat entered Monterey Bay
with a fleet of ships in early July 1846. At the Custom House on July 7,
Sloat claimed California for the United States by right of conquest in re-
sponse to alleged aggressions that precipitated the Mexican-American
War. In fact, the war was a pretext and Mexico's "invasion" of south
Texas a debatable interpretation of border skirmishing. For years the
United States had made clear its expansive interests in California and the

15. *Raising the Stars and Stripes above the Monterey Custom House, 1846.*
This 1961 painting by Hardy imitates the style of military artists who accompanied Commodore Sloat's landing at Monterey on July 7, 1846. Sloat's marines claimed California for the United States by raising the flag over the Mexican Custom House while a peaceful and well-dressed crowd looked on. Hardy captures the reported mood, although critics say the women's dress is more typical of a later time. Many Californios had resigned themselves to U.S. conquest, and Monterey's large foreign community welcomed the change. (Courtesy of Monterey State Historical Park)

Oregon territory—its "manifest destiny to overspread the continent allotted by Providence for the free development of our yearly multiplying millions," in the prophetic phrase penned by John O'Sullivan in 1845.

Sloat's conquest was hesitant and mild. His orders, dictated in 1845 and renewed over months before conflict on the border, called for immediate seizure of California if the United States was forced to move against Mexico. With his Pacific squadron anchored at Mazatlán, Sloat received reports of growing tensions and a U.S. blockade of Mexico's Atlantic ports but saw nothing in these maneuvers that would constitute an act of war or sufficient provocation for invasion. Sloat had clearly missed Washington's intentions, broad hints, and between-the-lines message about taking California. His indecision prompted Secretary Bancroft to send new orders relieving Sloat of command, but before they reached the west coast the commodore set sail, acting finally on reports of Mexican troop movements. The strategy unfolding in Washington (including Captain John Charles Frémont's military-diplomatic expedition to California begun in 1845) testifies to a well-considered plan for annexation calculated to provoke as little resistance as possible.

The character of conquest is further demonstrated in Sloat's proclamation "to the inhabitants of California" delivered at Monterey. Because Mexico had commenced hostilities against the United States by invading its territory north of the Rio Grande and attacking its troops, Sloat explained, the two nations were at war. Accordingly,

> I shall hoist the standard of the United States at Monterey immediately, and shall carry it throughout California. I declare to the inhabitants of California that, although I come in arms with a powerful force, I do not come among them as an enemy to California; on the contrary, I come as their best friend, as California will be a portion of the United States, and its peaceful inhabitants will enjoy the same rights and privileges as the citizens of any other portion of the territory. . . . They will also enjoy a permanent government, under which life, property, and the constitutional right and lawful security to worship the creator in the way most congenial to each one's sense of duty, will be secured, which unfortunately the central government of Mexico cannot afford them, destroyed as her resources are by internal factions and corrupt officers, who created constant revolutions to promote their own interests and oppress the people. Under the flag of the United States California will be free from all such troubles and expenses; consequently the country will rapidly advance and improve, both in agriculture and commerce, as, of course, the revenue laws will be the same in California as in all other parts of the United States, affording them all manufactures and produce of the United States free of any duty, and all foreign goods at one quarter of the duty they now pay. A great increase in the value of real estate and the products of California may also be anticipated. With great interest and kind feelings I know the government and people of the United States possess toward the citizens of California, the country cannot but improve more rapidly than any other continent of America. . . . With full confidence in the honor and integrity of the inhabitants of the country, I invite the judges, alcaldes, and other civil officers to retain their offices, and to execute their functions as heretofore, that the public tranquillity may not be disturbed. . . . All persons holding titles to real estate, or in quite possession of lands under a color of right, shall have those titles and rights guaranteed to them.[2]

The spirit of Sloat's proclamation, much of which was incorporated into the 1848 Treaty of Guadalupe Hidalgo ending the war, is clearly one of reconciliation, even presumptuous congratulations to those who may now consider themselves citizens of such an advanced country. But the language is tactical at the same time, reflecting diplomatic intelligence as much as the vulnerable position of Sloat's small force. The authors know that Californios have suffered under Mexico's central government, customs duties that burden commerce, and shifting land grant policies. Under U.S. sovereignty, the statement promises, Californios will enjoy continued home rule free of Mexican interference and the prosperous influence of a permanent government that assures constitutional rights. At bottom, Sloat's appeal was for a peaceful transition to U.S. rule, and in that he was largely successful. The conquest became more aggressive when Commodore Robert Field Stockton succeeded Sloat and without compelling cause deployed a force of Marines against the home guard under José Castro. Stockton and Frémont replaced Sloat's passivity with bullying adventurism. Some Californios resisted the conquest militarily, first on the plains east of Monterey and then more vigorously in southern California. But the fighting was generally symbolic, light, and short-lived. When conflict ceased in January 1847, some partisans returned to Mexico, but they were the exception to the Californio majority who received U.S. rule, as they had foreign residents for two decades, with a mixture of resignation, relief, resentment, grace, worry, and wonder.

Ironically, in the early years of U.S. rule very little changed in the traditional areas of Mexican California that were unaffected by the gold rush. A series of military governors followed Sloat, but they came with no resources or political mandate from the Congress in Washington mired in a struggle over slavery and states rights. Effective government was scarce, existing mainly in towns like Monterey, San Francisco, and Los Angeles where the Mexican system of alcalde and town council carried on improvisationally with an admixture of Yankee and Californio officials interpreting legal tradition as they adopted new municipal statutes. A civil government for the state under Frémont (and including redoubtables such as Alvarado, Spence, M. G. Vallejo, and Larkin) was proposed in early 1847 but never met. This scene was confused further by the discovery of gold in the Sierra foothills in January 1848. Californios and argonauts from around the world rushed to San Francisco, Sacramento, and the goldfields, leaving coastal towns like Monterey partially abandoned and commercially moribund. Growing disorder and appeals for effective government finally brought action in April 1848 with the arrival of the last military governor, General Bennet Riley, who urged adoption of a civil government and suggested the electoral mechanism by which delegates to the Constitutional Convention were chosen from regions around the state.

California's Constitutional Convention was eventually held in Monterey during September and October 1849 but not before a spirited debate in San Francisco centered on the authority of a military governor to, in effect, suspend Mexican law guaranteed by treaty and order into existence a civilian government. The impasse, of course, was the responsibility of Congress, which failed to act for another year until presented with the fait accompli of a democratically constructed constitution. Meanwhile, a mass meeting and discussion in San Francisco provided the popular legitimacy necessary for Governor Riley to move forward with the election of convention delegates. The convention finally gathered at Colton Hall, the government headquarters and public school in Monterey, for deliberations. Forty-eight men constituted the delegation, many of them Yankees and relatively new arrivals but others experienced politicians from frontier states, six European Americans of long residence in California, including Larkin who was also official translator, and seven Californios such as M. G. Vallejo who were large landowners. The convention was bilingual, multicultural, and, surprisingly, antislavery to a delegate. Any speculation about whether California might become a slave state and so upset the delicate balance in Washington was dispelled in the early going when the antislavery article was accepted unanimously, in part because several delegates with southern sympathies had accurately read the public mood expressed in mass meetings and local initiatives. (One material explanation for the strong antislavery mood was that miners feared the introduction of slave labor in the goldfields.) The constitution recognized separate property rights of wives and required that all state documents be published in Spanish and English. After a delegate-sponsored dance in the meeting hall, the constitution was signed on October 13. Through its own initiative, California was on its way to statehood in 1850 without having gone through a territorial phase.

In the transition from Mexican to U.S. sovereignty, Californios and the growing Yankee immigrant population confronted one fundamental question: who owned the land? What was the status of property granted under Mexican law, particularly the large number of eleventh-hour (1840s) titles awarded in an effort to shore up Mexican political control? What would happen to church lands, including some secularized in transactions illegal under prevailing Mexican law? What about the waning Indian population on marginal rancherías alongside sprawling haciendas of thirty thousand to fifty thousand acres? How to convert the rude sketches and gross descriptions of properties in Mexican *deseños* into the rectangular ordinance survey system required in the United States? How to render justice among competing interests in a situation replete with fraudulent deeds, legal grants of extensive tracts, rapid turnover of property and population, growing numbers of squatters claiming rights, and a good many valid deeds held by Californios and Anglos but clouded by the transition itself? How, in short, to create a new property regime in law and custom?

That was the work of the next thirty or forty years, and it began with the California Land Act of 1851. After debating the merits of blanket recognition of all Mexican land grants, which some considered a guarantee of the Treaty of Guadalupe Hidalgo, versus approval based on proof of title to avoid fraud, the U.S. Congress took the latter course. The U.S. Land Commission, a board of three judges, was established to evaluate all claims for confirmation of ownership, which, if successful, was followed by a new survey and U.S. land patent. Appeal to the California District and U.S. Supreme Courts was provided for claims denied by the Land Commission.[3]

Was justice done? The question has been debated for one hundred fifty years without complete resolution. Early and influential classics of California history denounced the Land Commission for its alleged presumption of fraud by requiring proof of title, for long delays in the confirmation process, and for the resulting loss of land by Californios saddled with attorneys' fees, taxes, and squatter invasions during years of uncertainty. Josiah Royce bemoans "the poor native whom the general government thus so shamefully harassed" and Hubert Howe Bancroft rumbles that a "great wrong was done. . . . [Californians] were virtually robbed by the government that was bound to protect them. *As a rule,* they lost nearly all their possessions in the struggle before the successive tribunals"—views also shared by certain modern authors.[4] Subsequent analysts who have actually studied the hundreds of court cases disagree. Paul Gates, a leading authority, concludes that "there was no such thing as a 'needless persecution of grant holders' . . . [and] Bancroft's 'spoliation of the grant-holders' is sheer nonsense. . . . [T]he Land Act of 1851 was a statesmanlike measure to apply the time-tried system of adjudicating land claims and to make the courts responsible for the entire process"—a conclusion recently endorsed by Donald J. Pisani.[5] To some extent, these divergent judgments stem from different ways of assigning causal responsibility and moral blame to the multivocal facts of economic transition in the early American period. The facts provided in recent analyses are not themselves in dispute.

One datum addresses many questions: the Land Commission upheld more than 75 percent of the 813 claims it processed, and, while most of those were carried further to the district court (e.g., by rival claimants or the government itself), the overall number of successful claims was actually increased in the appeals process. Beyond that blunt result, detailed points begin to show the legal and moral complexity of the problem. Royce's concern for the "poor native" was belied by two facts. First, the native claimants included three Vallejo brothers in Monterey and Sonoma who claimed 218,000 acres, the Pico family in Los Angeles (532,000 acres), the De La Guerra (326,000 acres) and Carrillo (320,000 acres) families from Santa Barbara, and many more who were far from poor. Second, a number of foreigners were recipients of Mexican land grants and others purchased properties from native grantees in the years between conquest and claims processing. Gates estimates that 42 percent of land claims were presented by non-Mexicans, a conservative figure given that some claims were pursued in the name of the original grantee even though they had been sold to Yankees in the interim and others were held jointly with U.S. citizens.[6] Fraud was common during this scramble for wealth, sometimes in blatantly falsified deeds, but more often in claims to enlarged boundaries by otherwise legal grantees fearful of having their vaguely defined ranchos reduced. From these data we may assume that relatively few Californios were dispossessed by the Land Commission and courts per se.

What of the argument that losses were the result of the expensive and protracted confirmation process? The average duration for a successful claim to move from filing to patent was seventeen years, and the burdensome delay was made worse by taxes, attorneys' fees, costly surveys, and improvements that went on irrespective of the legal strength of the title. Some claimants were ruined financially and others forced to sell off portions of their land or trade it for legal services. Equally important, squatters were moving on to unused parcels, requiring ejectment proceedings that were costly and sometimes difficult to enforce in a political climate sympathetic to settlers. Conversely, however, most of these circumstances contained reciprocal advantages. Claimants retained possession and full use rights during the confirmation process with potential benefits from production, rental, and sales of surplus land. And the delays themselves were created by claimant choices—to prepare a stronger case, stall scrutiny of dubious titles, speculate on property sales and price rises, settle family and inheritance disputes, or any number of additional reasons lying outside the responsibility of the commission and the courts. Meanwhile, of course, the economy was moving forward, placing new demands for capital and modernization on all producers who hoped to survive the competition. Gates summarizes the complex question as follows:

> That numerous Spanish speaking Californios lost their great ranchos or at least part of them in the first generation after American control was established is probably true. Progress meant more intensive use of land. Extension

of the land tax assured division. . . . Litigation was another factor contributing to the breakup of large holdings, not only that involved in the adjudication of the Mexican claims but also court action from intra-family disputes, conflicts with the squatters whose attorneys found numerous flaws in titles long after they were confirmed and patented, and the anxiety of claimants to stretch their ill-defined boundaries to the utmost, thereby involving them in legal conflicts with other owners.[7]

Given the mixed nationality of claimants, it also follows that a good many Yankee immigrants also suffered in the bruising transition to competitive capitalism and a new property regime. Squatters lost out, too, despite federal and state legislation following the 1851 act designed to extend public domain settlement, open to preemption those lands denied confirmation, and vest new legal rights in settlers. "The squatters were victims as well as victimizers and it is not easy to sort out winners and losers when two or more versions of law collide."[8]

It is not only difficult to sort out winners and losers in the broad transition from Mexican to American rule, it is also to a large extent illusory given the great variety of regional and local experience. The transformation was not experienced generally but concretely as brutal or enriching, insult or reward, windfall or hard work by particular people in local places. The full meaning of these events must be sought in the details of situated action and participant experience. Cogent interpretation is built up from, not imposed on, the case. In the microcosmic case of Monterey, all of the decisive forces played themselves out on the local tableau and left a revealing record for those who would read it.

LOCAL SOCIETY: CALIFORNIA IN TRANSITION

Shortly after the military occupation of Monterey, Commodore Stockton appointed his ship's chaplain, Reverend Walter Colton, as the town's first American alcalde. The genial Colton was a fortunate choice. He liked Californians and respected the office: "[I]t never entered my visions that I should succeed to the dignity of a Spanish alcalde." Colton moved into the elegant home of U.S. Counsel Larkin, fortunately as there was "not a public table or hotel in all California," and began to mix with people, "high and low, rich and poor, [who] are thrown together on the private liberality of the citizens."[9]

The town appeared much as it had to Richard Henry Dana eleven years earlier. "Nearly all the houses in Monterey are of one story, with a corridor. The walls are built of adobes, or sun-baked brick, with tile roofs.

The centre is occupied by a large hall, to which the dining-room and sleeping apartments seem mere appurtenances. Every thing is in subordination to the hall, and this is designed and used for dancing." Like Dana, Colton viewed California's rustic commerce through the blinkered eyes of a New England bourgeois. Indolent Californians valued dancing and horses above all else. Yet, somewhat inconsistently, Colton also reported that "they drive their ox-carts, loaded with lumber or provisions, two hundred miles to market." Through the immigrant lens we see a pre-capitalist, partially monetized society still governed in many respects by the moral economy of frontier communalism. Monterey is surrounded by pueblo common lands where citizens, including Colton, hunt game and cut wood. Indians spear three-foot-long salmon in the Carmel River and lug them three miles to market in Monterey. Yet cash is in short supply and wage labor the exception to various forms of artisan trade, independent proprietorship, and subsistence work.

> The usual rate of interest for money loaned here on good security, is twenty-four per cent. This is sufficient evidence of its scarcity , and yet it is almost valueless when you come to the question of labor. A foreigner may be induced to work for money, but not a Californian, so long as he has a pound of beef or a pint of beans left. Nor is it much better with the Indian. . . . Hunger is unknown here; the man who has not a foot of land seems about as independent as he who has his ten-league farm, and has vastly less trouble and vexation. [Yet the state was underdeveloped and so fortunately filling up with Yankee immigrants,] a sturdy band whose enterprise will cover these fertile hills with golden harvest.[10]

Economic transformation was both cause and consequence of social dislocation introduced by American conquest. Increasingly, two cultures and two legal systems ran afoul of one another with damaging results. Colton's diary records the experience of transition as it was felt across the social hierarchy. A group of Californians took up arms, "not to make war on the American flag, but to protect themselves from the depredations of those who, under color of that flag, were plundering their cattle, horses, and grain." As alcalde, Colton was called on to settle disputes. For example: "The presiding priest of this jurisdiction applied to me a few days since to protect the property of San Antonio Mission. A Spaniard, it seems, who owns a neighboring rancho, had, under color of some authority of the late administration, extended his claims over the grounds and buildings." In a similar case, "a ranchero, living some forty miles distant, not liking his own land, had lifted his boundary line, and projected it some six miles over that of his neighbor."[11]

Property disputes were not the sole concern of large landowners. Colton adjudicated a dispute between two "unmanageable" Indian women who earned their living washing clothes and quarreled over which one had the right to a certain section of the pool where they worked. In another case, "an Indian woman of good appearance" appealed to Colton for custody of her own child. She had been working for a Mexican family when her husband died and the father of the family "claimed, according to custom here, a sort of guardianship over [the child], as well as a right to a portion of its services." The woman was about to remarry and wanted her child back. The alcalde agreed with her claim but also hedged by suggesting that she first give the marriage a trial, and if the new man was a good provider, then he would restore custody. In his capacity as custodian of the town jail, Colton discovered that "the custom has been to fine Spanish and whip Indians." He wrote, "The discrimination is unjust, and the punishments ill suited to the ends proposed. I have substituted labor; and have now eight Indians, three Californians, and one Englishman at work making adobes." Although the ratio of native to immigrant arrests suggest differential law enforcement, a group of English gamblers was fined heavily and the proceeds used to build the school. Under the three-year rule of Colton's law, justice was administered in a style both democratic and personal. The reverend navigated wisely in uncharted legal waters, but settlers pressed for clearer statutes and government services that were customary in the United States.[12]

Early in 1850 Monterey's traditional ayuntamiento was reconstituted as a common council of seven to ten members, most of them local Anglo-American merchants. The alcalde was rechristened mayor and regidores became aldermen as the common council took up a welter of problems concerning public order, municipal services, and government finance. New ordinances evoke a portrait of town life: swine running free in the streets caused their owner a $6 fine ($12 for a second offense), slaughtering animals within one mile in any direction of Colton Hall was prohibited (a $5 fine per animal), firearms could not be discharged in town, horses could not be raced on city streets, open wells had to be enclosed with a three-foot wall, houses had to be lit by lanterns on dark nights, and the sale of liquor to Indians was forbidden—evidently with little success given the number of Indians in jail who were charged with drunkenness. Taxes were imposed on stores, liquor sales in hostels and taverns, gambling establishments, auctioneers and peddlers, and traveling circuses. Local merchants regarded street hawkers as a particular menace and submitted a petition with fifty signatures to the council citing the "necessity and justice of protecting the trading community of Monterey." With new responsibilities the costs of local government grew. The common council maintained three standing committees: roads, bridges, and police; laws and ordinances; and ways and means. The rustic Mexican town needed to bridge culverts, channel drainage, improve roads, rebuild the porous jail, provide a hospital, and pay a variety of contractors, from physicians tending the poor to surveyors laying down precise property lines. Meanwhile, the salaried city workforce grew to include the mayor, tax collector, recorder, marshal, harbormaster, and night watchman.[13]

Local growth and municipal finance were closely bound up with the land question, particularly with public land. Initially, the common council appointed a special town lots committee to examine Mexican records, to survey public lands, and generally to determine who was in rightful possession of what parcels and who was eligible to apply for standard-sized (six hundred square yards) vacant lots. Each citizen was allowed one town-lot grant. The committee entertained petitions from residents and judged them with dispatch: "granted," "this claim is correct," "having had already land granted, he is not entitled to more," "grant his petition if vacant," "petition cannot be granted the land having an owner."[14] Approximately sixty of these claims were processed. A report of town receipts dated March 18, 1850, indicates that $1,602 had been realized from the sale of "town" and "garden" lots.[15]

But controversy surrounded the allocation of land traditionally belonging to the "pueblo"—the Spanish word signifying both town and people. Monterey mayor Philip A. Roach wrote the council in April, noting that the practice of the previous ayuntamiento had been "to grant the vacant Town land to actual settlers at a price required by law, upon the condition that the land ceded should be built upon within two years or else they would revert to the Town." Subsequent to that practice, California governor Burnett had written Roach observing that state law required all public land sales (excluding common lands) be held at auction and go to the highest bidder. The mayor's letter to the council continued with a clear indication of his position and spirit of local independence: "The question is, shall the lands be sold at auction to speculators or shall they be granted to our citizens as homesteads." Two weeks later he added, "I still adhere to my opinion that the vacant lands referred to should be sold at 31 1/2 ¢ per yard to actual settlers, in preference to disposing of them at auction for speculative prices of town lands can never confer the benefits upon the town that can be realized from the improving spirit of actual settlers."[16]

A related question was how the city would manage traditional common lands. Merchant and longtime resident David Spence joined the debate in his official capacity as town perfect in charge of public welfare.

> I have this day seen a notice informing the public that the "wood lands" surveyed by Mr. Snyder will be sold in lots of 300 yards at 31 1/2 ¢ on or about the 1st day of February. I again inform you that according to the law of the 20th of March 1837 the Perfects only have power under certain restrictions to distribute common lands for temporary occupation and as Perfect of this district I claim the above mentioned portion of the woods as a part of the pueblo lands under my control, and therefore by these presents do publicly and solemnly protest against any steps that the Ayuntamiento takes to sell or dispose of these or any other lands in the vicinity of Monterey except those that are considered within the limits of the town.[17]

Nevertheless, the traditional commons defended by long-term residents steadily lost force under the twin influences of real estate speculation and growing municipal debt. Sometimes the two forces combined in a single agent. Key to these developments was a local attorney, Delos R. Ashley, who simultaneously held public office, organized the Democratic Party of Monterey County, defended the city's pueblo land grant before the Land Commission, and speculated in town property. Ashley had plenty of allies, including his young protégé David Jacks, who was elected city treasurer in 1853. Public debt became a growing problem as local officials endeavored to meet a variety of needs (roads, bridges, indigent medical care, law enforcement) for a population that resisted taxes. Spending outpaced revenues and officials looked for a financial fix. In December 1851 voters (in a bilingual ballot) approved a measure authorizing the council to mortgage city property for a loan of $2,500 to pay the debt. Although council records do not show who loaned the city money and in what amounts, throughout 1852 the aldermen received communications from Jacks and attorney Andrew Randall about a proposal "to negotiate in regard to the wood lots of the city." Other notices show that Jacks actively loaned money to the city, the county, and private individuals on property collateral. At a sheriff's sale in November 1852, Jacks purchased a tract corresponding closely in description to the city lands, although at this point there were several claims in the area.[18] By July 1853 Ashley had risen to president of the council and proposed that some twenty "unsold wood lots of the city of Monterey be sold at public auction."[19] During the same year, Randall won a debt foreclosure judgment against the city on behalf of his San Francisco client Daniel Murphy.[20] Randall and Murphy thus became co-owners or part owners of the city lands for several years, although Randall went bankrupt and their taxes fell delinquent. Jacks and Ashley purchased the property belonging to Randall and Murphy at a city tax sale in May 1853. In July 1855 the *Monterey Sentinel* advertised a sheriff's sale of Rancho Punto de Pinos, two square leagues (8,888 acres) of prime coastal property once held by Andrew Randall. Jacks eventually acquired this parcel of former city land.[21]

All of these men were involved at an early date in schemes to acquire the extensive and strategic lands of the original pueblo grant. The plan encouraged the city to mortgage and sell its valuable property to political insiders. No other long-term solutions to the debt crisis were proposed (e.g., additional taxes, user fees, spending cuts), suggesting that foreclosure and private sale of city land was the desired end. An entry in the 1854 Monterey County Assessment Roll suggesting that this process was officially recognized lists "Andrew Randall, Daniel Murphy, David Jacks, D. R. Ashley, and the City of Monterey" as owners of the city lands—an entry, moreover, in which the last line has been crossed out and a note added saying, "ordered by the court that the words 'and the City of Monterey' be stricken out." This patent land grab would become clearer and more brazen in the next few years.

SOCIAL CLASS DIVISION

The 1854 county tax assessment roll provides a snapshot of Monterey society in transition. Monterey in 1854 is still Hispanic, judging from the makeup of the population and ownership of land. Measured by assessed property valuation, the wealthiest individuals possess fortunes in land and commerce acquired during the Mexican period. Francisco Pacheco, who came to the country as a Mexican soldier and lived near San Juan Bautista in what would become San Benito County, headed the list of landed gentry. Pacheco and his daughter (who married sixth-richest Mariano Malarín) owned nearly 60,000 well-stocked acres and several town lots, including a house in Monterey. Other elite Californios derived their wealth from land and cattle, including Teodore Gonzales (17,776 acres), Mauricio Gonzales (22,220 acres), and Mariano Malarín (32,298 acres). The Italian immigrant and silversmith Alberto Tresconi owned a ranch, five town lots, and the leading Washington Hotel, the sum of which placed him sixteenth on the list of worthies. Yankee immigrants who had married into Californio families were among the top twenty in wealth and their holdings were diversified. David Spence, Juan B. R. Cooper, and Jacob Leese were prosperous merchants with business properties, inventory, town lots, and extensive ranches. In monetary terms, Pacheco's holdings were estimated at more than $150,000, three to four times the assessed worth of other land barons and merchants (the Gonzaleses, Malarín, Spence, Cooper, etc.), who averaged $30,000 to $40,000.

A cut below these established family fortunes was a solid and diverse middle class. Leading figures of the Mexican period lived on in comfort: former Governor José Castro on a 3,000-acre ranch and former treasurer Antonio Osio in downtown Monterey (the streets forming his corner had already been given the bicultural names Franklin and Alvarado). William Hartnell had a 4,447-acre ranch and town house (on Hartnell Street), and José Abrego lived on one of his nine town lots (on Abrego Street). These families were comfortable, if not rich, with assessed property valued between $20,000 and $30,000. Equal in assets were the ambitious recent arrivals: storekeeper Joseph Boston, who also owned a town lot and a woodlot, retired army surgeon James Stokes, who had twelve lots and an 8,000-acre ranch, storekeeper Milton Little and butcher Francis Doud, both of whom were plowing their proceeds into real estate. In 1854 Jacks and Ashley ranked below these burghers with modest four-figure fortunes, if more ambitious plans.

At the bottom of the assessor's list, but still among property tax payers, were a large number of Californios, Mexicans, and Yankee immigrants. Carmen Barretta and José Madariago each owned a $50 town lot and dwelling—the latter next door to a like accommodation of his brother Juan. Mayor Philip Roach owned four town lots (on Washington, Abrego, and Scott Streets) with a total value of $250. John Morris, who worked for Spence, lived in a house valued at $500 on Monroe Street, while Jack Swan ran a rooming house on Pacific and Scott worth $1,200. And there were humble folk in the countryside. Clara Martinez and Eulojio Martinez held adjoining forty-acre farms on the Salinas River valued at a few hundred dollars. Uniah and Jonathan Burns were among a number of squatters whose only assets were a wagon, oxen, and improvements on a "claim on Salinas plains."[22]

Women are obscured in local records that subsume them within households headed by men and, in the early years, assign them no independent occupational role. Yet available evidence and some inference reveal distinctive patterns. Women were a minority in frontier society and even by 1880, when the U.S. Census first published a breakdown by sex for the county population of 11,302, they constituted an unbalanced 41 percent. The ratio would have been more skewed in 1850 when the county had a mere 1,872 residents and Monterey's population numbered 1,008.[23] Very few women were active in the formal, wage-labor economy in 1850, although they obviously performed essential work in the household and informal economy. Working white women discernible in official records kept boardinghouses and served families as governesses, while Indians and mestizas worked as household servants and laundresses. In time, a few professional women appeared. Mrs. S. Nichols M.D. Homeopathic Physician of Monterey featured "special attention to diseases of women, children, and midwifery." Dr. C. Loewen of Salinas specialized in "female and chronic diseases," and Mrs. Jane Allen offered "her services to the Ladies of Monterey and vicinity" as a midwife.[24] Occasionally women divorced and took out newspaper advertisements declaring their legal and financial independence.

NOTICE

Know all men by these presents that I, CHLOE L. STRODE, a married woman, wife of Leander Strode, a resident of San Juan township, county of Monterey, State of California, do hereby declare, that it is my intention to carry on in my own name, and on my own account, the business of farming and raising stock and poultry, at my residence.[25]

The notice is dated October 11, 1855, and declared bona fide by Justice of the Peace J. P. Lane.

Single women headed approximately 10 percent of Monterey families. The 1850 manuscript census suggests three distinct types of female household. First are the widowed and divorced women of middle age with children in the home. Second are a very few single women living alone, such as Sarah King, age twenty, from England and Manetta Rankell, an eighteen-year-old Californian. Third, and surprisingly numerous, are households composed largely of women close in age and a few youngsters of both sexes including offspring and siblings. The pattern is striking, if not common, and suggests that vulnerable single women created communal households for support of one another and their dependent children.

In some instances, women inherited fortunes from their husbands, but propertied wealth did not ensure tranquillity. José María Sanchez was one of the county's rich men, owning two 6,666-acre ranches, when he drowned accidentally in 1852. At the age of twenty-eight with three children, Incarnación (Concha) Sanchez inherited an estate valued at $29,000 in Monterey County properties and perhaps twice that in holdings elsewhere. Sheriff William Roach administered the estate in collaboration with his bondsman, Louis Belcher. Incarnación remarried twice in rapid succession, first to Gordon Williams who died in a steamboat explosion and then to Monterey lawyer Dr. Sanford. Sanford teamed up with Belcher in legal proceedings that charged Roach with having improperly taken possession of the widow's money and property. A bloody feud began, each side employing enforcers, with the resulting death of Sanford and Belcher in separate barroom shoot-outs, the assassination of Roach, and collateral carnage involving nine others. Widowed for the third time, Incarnación married again to George Crane (known locally as George IV), who seems to have taken most of the fortune, gotten himself elected to Congress, and died in New York. Incarnación, the only survivor of this lethal greed, salvaged some of her inheritance and settled down to a quiet fifth marriage on the ranch near San Juan Bautista.[26] The Belcher-Roach feud is legendary in local annals and doubtless an extreme case of property transfer from Mexican to American control. Yet it illuminates something essential about the struggle for land and the predatory pressures on Californio owners, particularly if they were women.

Patterns of wealth and employment shifted significantly after midcentury as American society consolidated its control of California. Land was changing hands, agriculture converting to wool production and field crops, new industries developing (timber, coal, and fishing), and town commerce slowly attaining respectability. The portrait of California landed wealth presented in the public record of 1854 had been thoroughly redrawn a dozen years later. Of the former economic notables, the assessment roll of 1866 shows only J. B. R. Cooper (3d), Mariano Malarín (7th), David Spence (13th), and Teodore Gonzales (20th) still ranked in the top twenty. Monterey's old Californio families (J. Vallejo, M. Gonzales, Leese, Abrego, Bernal, Tresconi, Estrada, Soberanes) have been supplanted by Yankee land barons such as U.S. senator Thomas Flint; W. W. Hollister, who was starting his own town near San Juan Bautista; Hollister's Irish neighbor, Patrick Breen; Faxton D. Atherton, who owned vast properties near Missions San Antonio and San Mateo; J. D. Carr, the rising power in the Salinas Valley; and Monterey's own David Jacks, who had risen from store clerk to twelfth in assessed worth in sixteen years. Jacks would top the list in 1880.

The changing occupational structure demonstrates another facet of transition. Table 2 groups a variety of census-enumerated occupations under a delimited set of categories for two widely separated years, 1850 and 1880. In both years, generally, professionals are few, including physicians, lawyers, engineers, judges, and one self-identified "capitalist" (Jacks). Merchants are more common, including sales agents, traders, and merchandise store owners. Town services involve jobs such as clerks, innkeepers, barbers, waiters, and railroad agents. Artisans number a good many carpenters and all the characteristic skilled trades of the time such as blacksmith, mason, tailor, printer, gunsmith, shoemaker, saddler, bookmaker, and even a photographer. "Labor" refers to the less skilled work of teamsters, fishers, cooks, shepherds, and miners. Servants are household labor and dependents of inns and rooming houses. The familiar category "farmer" refers to people within the town limits who run dairies and truck farms, rather than the larger operations of the countryside. Two anomalies appear in the table that affect comparison over time. The large contingent of U.S. Army troops bivouacked in Monterey after the Mexican-American War had left town by 1880, altering the local economy. In the latter year, the census taker began recording the work of women "at home" or "keeping house." For the sake of cross-category comparison, housekeepers are separated from the base number (488) for the 1880 percentage figures.

A comparison of the occupational structure over this thirty-year period demonstrates a marked tendency toward social polarization. In 1850 there are a wide variety of jobs, a number of well-represented categories, and little concentration. Two relatively large categories are in fact diverse: that is, "soldiers and sailors" (25 percent) includes a variety of services and ranks, some living in the barracks, or Quartel, and others in town, and the group of artisans (24 percent) embraces a score of different trades. By 1880, however, the labor force exhibits greater inequality. Labor and servant categories comprise half of the employed (only a combined 11 percent in 1850) and the upper-rank professional and merchant groups contain fewer persons (a combined 7 percent, down from 20 percent in 1850). Only the services grow to balance slightly this result. Generally, the trend in wealth and social class structure during the late nineteenth century is toward less occupational diversity and growing inequality—a change orchestrated by movements in the land and capital markets.

Yet this is a thirty-year period during which changes in local society were experienced gradually. Monterey's population remained virtually stationary in the early American years. Newspapers came and went, beginning in 1847 with the *Californian* edited by Walter Colton and constitutional convention president Robert Semple. Each new editor praised

TABLE 2

OCCUPATIONAL STRUCTURE, CITY OF MONTEREY,
1850–1880

Occupation	1850 N	1850 %	1880 N	1880 %
Professional	15	7	21	4
Merchant	28	13	17	3
Services	17	8	74	15
Artisan, skilled	54	24	113	23
Labor	20	9	194	40
Servant	6	2	49	10
Farmer	25	11	20	4
Soldier/sailor	61	25	—	—
Subtotal	226	99	488	99
Housekeeper	—	—	245	—
Total	226	99	733	99

SOURCE: Seventh U.S. Census of Population, Monterey County, California 1850 (manuscript); Tenth U.S. Census of Population, 1880 (manuscript). (Percentage columns total 99 because of rounding.)

some local virtue (climate, harbor, scenery, railroad) as the key to progress in the town repeatedly labeled "sleepy hollow." The early years were difficult. The gold rush drew attention away from coastal settlements. Civil war and national depression slowed the California economy. Yet subtler undercurrents were at work in local society. A clever, if unknown, Scot who spent fall 1879 in Monterey noted, "[T]he town . . . was essentially and wholly Mexican; and yet almost all the land in the neighborhood was held by Americans, and it was from the same class, numerically so small, that the principal officials were selected. . . . Spanish was the language of the streets. Physically the Americans have triumphed; but it is not entirely seen how far they have themselves been morally conquered."[27]

Robert Louis Stevenson stayed for three months courting his future wife, Fanny Osbourne (who lived with her sister in Monterey while deciding to divorce her current husband), nursing his chronic asthma, and contributing the odd piece (signed "Barbarian") to Crevole Bronson's paper, the *Monterey Californian.* Whether it was his European perspective or writer's insight, Stevenson saw features of social relations lost on the new American settlers. The native population was a thorough mix of Spanish and Indian: "I do not suppose there was one pure blood of either race in all the country." Referring to these Indian-mestizo-Californios collectively, Stevenson went on to observe, "[T]he Mexicans although in the State are out of it. They still preserve a sort of international independence, and keep their affairs snug to themselves."[28] A few Mexican Californians who were prominent before 1846 retained their wealth and social standing into the 1870s and 1880s as new generations diluted their assets. In Monterey, particularly, many prestigious Californio families lived on in comfort, if not luxury.

At the same time, however, an ethnic working class was growing in the wake of social polarization. Race, ethnicity, and national origin continued to influence social rank, but increasingly in combination with class, which was becoming the more potent discriminator of privilege. A growing Anglo-American population and sharper socioeconomic divisions left most Mexican Californios at the bottom, if not outside, of the social order. A new status and social problem appear in local discourse: the poor Mexican, "natives," "paisanos." Whatever term the brusque Americans employed, they referred to that vast reservoir of people whom they considered vagabonds, derelicts, drunks, and bandits still living in California's benighted past.

RACIAL CONFLICT

Good evidence of nineteenth-century intergroup relations comes from the annals of law enforcement. Matters of conduct and culture found their way into the courts or the sheriff's bailiwick and thereby became part of the historical record. Actions considered self-defense in one group were prosecuted as crimes in the other. Stevenson had this in mind when he observed that Mexicans were in, yet out, of the state. Monterey County Coroner C. A. Canfield had discovered the same thing in his efforts to solve the murder of an Indian named Laurencio: "Heretofore it has been almost impossible to procure evidence of any crime committed by Californians, as even the eye witness of it would furnish no information to guide the officers in their efforts to ferret out and punish the perpetrator." In the particular case, the body of an Indian named José Laurencio had been found with stab wounds buried on the beach about a half mile from town. Laurencio had been drinking behind Gerardin's store with a few friends and fellow farmworkers, including José Morales, Juan Alverez, Jacinto, and Feliciano. Jacinto recalled to the coroner, "[W]e all got drunk, together, and I got drunk and they cut my hand. I don't know who cut me. José Morales did not say anything about José Laurencio." Somehow, the coroner concluded from these sketchy accounts and the prior friendship of Morales and the deceased "that the killing was done by José Morales."[29] The presumption of guilt may have been inferred from recent stints in the town jail for larceny by both Laurencio and Morales. The record shows that on May 27, 1868, José Morales was "sent to God on a rope."[30]

The jail register is a revealing document. Of more than six hundred inmates handled over a twenty-two-year period, 10 percent are identified as Indian. That figure is probably an underestimate given that some known Indians (e.g., José Morales) were not identified as such. More important, a large and disproportionate number are mestizos. The register included several columns describing physical features of arrestees, including complexion. At first the jailer seems uncertain about the category and enters a variety of incommensurate terms: "Californian," "Indian," "dark," "Sonoran." Seven persons are described as "negro," "black," or, in one case, "black as my hat." As time goes on, the record settles into a perfunctory distinction of "light" and "dark." Nevertheless, where there are meaningful distinctions and surnames, it is clear that accused criminals are predominantly paisanos, although Americans appear also. Most of their crimes are petty: drunkenness, larceny, assault, "threats," stealing, fighting, "insanitation" (i.e., pissing in the street). Yet there are striking numbers of homicides and cases of horse stealing. Depending on the victim, local sentiment considers these equally grievous crimes. Punishment was racially mediated. For petty crimes, Indians frequently "received 25 lashes" while whites were given a fine or period of days in jail. In a few cases, all involving Indians or mestizos, prisoners were "found hung in jail yard" or "strangled in his cell," whether the victims of vigilantes, fellow prisoners, or both we do not know. No wonder a goodly number "broke jail."

Injustice was common and frequently meted out along ethnic lines. Indians were arrested without clear evidence of their guilt when whites were murdered. In one 1856 case several Indians were hung by vigilantes when charged circumstantially with two separate killings. In 1865 a sheriff's posse descended on "two outlawed villains accreted in a house about a mile from town" one of whom was Juan Iguera, "said to be the fellow who shot Dep. Sheriff Brooks of Santa Clara county, some months ago, at New Almaden Mines, and for whom it is said there is a reward of $800." When his companion (Francisco Alviso, "a desperate fellow who killed a man some years ago") was wounded, Iguera fled with the help of a mare pastured nearby. That afternoon the fugitive was captured by a group of citizens and hung on the spot, whether for the shooting or horse stealing is unclear. That he was guilty of something was never in doubt: "He was an abandoned wretch, only twenty years of age, but old in crime. His father we learn was hung by the people of this town some twelve years ago, for murder."[31] The following year, José Maria Arceo was found guilty of murder and ordered hung. When his jury on second thought expressed doubts about his guilt, the sentence was reduced to thirty years in state prison.[32] Ironically, José Maria's brother, Laureano, was killed a week later by William Switzer, a farmer who assumed Laureano was stealing horses when he was only leading his own mount from Switzer's corral where he had stopped and asked a ranch hand for permission to rest. "Switzer is blamed for the precipitation exhibited in the shooting" but not charged with a crime, even though Laureano "is reputed to have been an honest and industrious man."[33] Toribio, "a half crazy Indian" was arrested, convicted of battery, and sentenced to ninety days in jail for throwing a stone at a boy in the streets. "We learn that it is the practice of boys in this city to amuse themselves by stoning these poor devils of Indians that roam about the streets, thereby provoking them to retaliation in kind."[34]

In this intolerant climate, it is not surprising that the mestizo minority would feel themselves oppressed and moved to threaten revenge. Although we know nothing of the circumstance or parties (other than their Hispanic and Anglo-American identities respectively), the following anonymous letter was received by a Monterey man and printed in the newspaper as a worrisome event:

> "hagame el favor de dejar vivir la gente pacíficamente si no usted encontrara su sepultura debajo de un encino muy pronto. Sus varios amigos." [Which the newspaper translated] "do me the favor to let the people live peaceably, if not you will find your grave under an oak tree very soon. Your numerous friends."[35]

The author's Spanish is literate, suggesting a good education, which only a few enjoyed, and the recipient was clearly in a position to affect the daily lives of the people—perhaps as a property owner claiming title or rents. The anonymous threatening letter is another indication of ethnic strife and paisano resistance to acts of perceived injustice.

Paisanos subject to the combined influence of socioeconomic inequality, racial prejudice, and institutional injustice understandably resorted to varied measures of self-defense and resistance—retributive crime among them. In California, as in transitional peasant societies around the world, the soil nurtured social bandits—figures perceived as criminals by the dominant society but as folk heroes by the oppressed.[36] Legend commonly reported that bandits avenged atrocities against the

people (rapes, land seizures, labor drafts) and were protected from authorities by their neighbors. Monterey had its criminal gangs, "young
scoundrels in this city, associated together for the purpose of stealing,
and annoying the peaceable portion of the community." These were not
just any scoundrels but ones organized under the name "La Compañía
del Orillo—so called, undoubtedly, because like crickets, its members hide
in their dens and holes all day and come out to infest the city at night."[37]
Another gang led by Francisco "Mexico" Cordero robbed the home of
local merchant Santiago Rossi, making off with a sizable haul of twenty-
dollar gold pieces and heirlooms. When news of the crime spread, former gang member Dionicio "Choriso" Garcia rode into town to protest
his innocence. "By this strategic set, he escaped being driven through the
streets as a felon, and also gained the sympathy of the community."
Meanwhile, the culprit Cordero was arrested with three others not involved in the crime whom the honorable robber cleared by confessing
his own guilt.[38]

California's most celebrated social bandit (of more certain provenance
than the romanticized Joaquín Murieta) was Tiburcio Vasquez, a native
of Monterey and revered figure in the Hispanic community. His exploits
as highwayman and rustler took place mainly in the areas of San José,
Hollister, and Los Angeles, although his reputation spread across the
country in newspapers and penny dreadfuls. Sought by law officers
throughout the state, in his Monterey County home he walked with im-
punity. On a visit to Salinas in 1874, "he was very enthusiastically received there, the citizens turning out *en mass* to celebrate the arrival. . . .
Tiburcio arrived here Thursday, and all the talk around is Vasquez."[39]
A contemporary reported that "when young Vasquez started out on his
career of crime, it was the assistance that he received from the [Hispanic]
ranchers over the state that kept him out of the clutches of the law so
long."[40] Like other noble robbers, Vasquez went to the gallows in 1875
without remorse, malice, or revelation of the names of his comrades still
at liberty. Admitting to acts of revenge, Vasquez claimed, "I had numerous fights in defense of what I believed to be my rights and those of
my countrymen."[41]

The record of law enforcement provides a unique window on group
conflict and cultural difference. We must not infer from these fragmentary data that all paisanos resisted their subordination through crime,
or that all Hispanic criminals were engaged in cultural defense. But the
evidence demonstrates that many paisanos lived in a linguistic, moral,
and cultural world apart from the American majority. That culture sanc-

tioned resistance, criminal and otherwise, and protected its own. Like much of California in the late nineteenth century, Monterey was a divided society.

LAND: BARONS, SQUATTERS, AND RECUSANTS

Land was key to the transition from Hispanic to American society. Control of the urban property market and sprawling ranches both reflected and enabled a shift in social power. A fine-grained analysis of these changes on the land shows how new meanings of place emerged in tandem with a new understanding of local society.

Any examination of the land question in Monterey County during the latter half of the nineteenth century must revolve around the figure and business dealings of David Jacks. On the one hand, Jacks built huge holdings in farmland, urban properties, and a dozen enterprises, demonstrating along the way how fortunes were made in American California. On the other hand, Jacks kept records of his legal, business, political, and philanthropic endeavors so massive in detail that many remain uncataloged in the Stanford University and Huntington Libraries. Jacks was a dour man—serious to a fault, hard to like, a caricature of the tight-fisted Scot, devoted to church and family, and easily the most despised figure on the central coast. His life was threatened repeatedly, if never seriously, and his severe control of the local property market was a rallying cry for political movements in the 1870s and 1880s.

David Jacks emigrated from Grieff, in Perthshire, Scotland (where the family name was simply Jack), in 1842 at the age of nineteen. After plying several trades on the East Coast, he worked as an accountant for the U.S. Army and was shipped to San Francisco, where he became a naturalized citizen in 1849. At the beginning of the following year, he came to Monterey, where he remained for the next sixty years with the exception of one return visit to Scotland. He was already wealthy and nearing forty in 1861 when he married María Christina de la Soledad Romie. Fifteen years his junior, María came from a German family that had been in Mexico and California since the 1830s. Jacks seems to have acquired some knowledge of Spanish and local custom judging from his incoming correspondence and business dealings with the Romie, Malarín, and other prominent Californio families. In an effort to rehabilitate his memory, modern biographers emphasize that Jacks gave prodigious sums to the Methodist church, worked for the cause of temperance, helped destitute friends, and through his dairy business gave the world Monterey

Jack cheese.[42] Jacks's voluminous correspondence reveals a complex man: shrewd, austere, clannish, self-assured, petulant, charitable, obsessive, puzzled by others' resentment, and master of a thousand details, from the county list of tax delinquent properties to the names and dispositions of every horse on his farm.

The decisive event leading to a new property regime was the acquisition of thirty thousand acres of Monterey's ancestral pueblo lands by David Jacks and Delos Ashley. These two public servants were conspiring to acquire city lands as early as 1852 by arranging mortgage loans to the debt-ridden common council. They exploited insider connections for privileged access to sheriff's sales and private purchases. Other speculators were playing the same game, but they lacked the Ashley-Jacks combination of financial acumen and political influence. While Jacks generated capital through leases and several business ventures (timber, sand, dairy), Ashley worked the public sphere as alderman and city attorney. At Ashley's urging, in 1853 the town council resolved to seek confirmation of the pueblo lands title before the U.S. Board of Land Commissioners. Title was confirmed in 1856, although legal maneuvering continued until 1858 when an appeal entered by the United States was dismissed.[43] Meanwhile, Ashley had run successfully for the state senate, where he was in a position to offer legislation affecting Monterey's municipal organization and finance. Ashley proposed two amendments to the original city incorporation act. One changed the council form of government to a weaker board of trustees. The second provided that "the trustees may also pay for the expenses of prosecuting the title of the city before the United States land commission and before the United States courts, and for that purpose may sell and transfer any property, right, or franchise, upon such terms and for such price as may by them be deemed reasonable."[44] That is, Ashley's law said the city could sell its land to pay Ashley's legal fees. Only one step remained. On February 9, 1859, the entire (29,698-acre) parcel of pueblo land was offered at public auction on the steps of city hall. Ashley and Jacks were the successful and only bidders with an offer of $1,002.50, or three cents an acre. The "reasonable" amount mentioned in the legislation was calculated to satisfy attorney's fees of $991.50, $11 for the cost of the sale, and nothing more for the impoverished city coffers.

Privatization of traditional common land and forests offended the moral economy governing land use practices of old residents and the Californio majority. As early as 1855, Jacob Leese and Andrew Randall had published warnings in the newspaper against trespass and woodcutting on their coastal ranches.[45] That townspeople customarily used the wood-lands is clear from efforts to enjoin them in the early 1860s. Jacks and Ashley posted an undated announcement: "All persons are notified not to trespass on lands of the undersigned in the township of Monterey, and all persons are prohibited cutting trees thereon and removing wood or timber therefrom—and any person doing the contrary will be proceded against at law." A flurry of notices in 1863 charging "you have trespassed and are still trespassing. . . . and have committed waste by cutting trees, and are still doing so" were addressed personally to Pedro Gonzales, John Myers, Eugenio Martinez, and Grácia Martinez. The latter two were also warned that "any buildings or improvements you may place on the lands will be forfeited," suggesting that they were squatters.[46] Owners and claimants of these coastal woodlands took out newspaper ads warning against trespass and timber cutting, suggesting that the conflict was pervasive.[47] Jacks and Ashley repeatedly brought damage suits against a class of named individuals (Felipe Garcia, Francisco Martinez, Fulgencio Valenzuela, Graciano Martinez, James Jackson, James Younglove, Peter Janex, Silas Tracy, Stephen Song, and Thomas Meaker, all sued in October 1869) for various amounts, from $500 to $2,000, for "cutting oak, madrone, laurel, baywood, and other valuable trees and converting same to their own use."[48]

Acquisition of the city lands entitled Jacks and Ashley to all those town tracts lacking proof of ownership. The number of properties involved was significant given the informal deeds and casual record keeping employed during the Mexican period. Matters were never rectified, owing to the alienation of paisanos from the legal system. Jacks challenged the title to a good many town lots, taking them up piecemeal as his development or sale plans evolved. He sued Abel and Placida Espinosa for a lot "in back of the Catholic church" that the couple claimed had passed to Placida through her family line, Dutra. Basilio Gonzales and Carmelo Reid owned a plot between Larkin and Madison Streets that Basilio claimed his father had purchased from Rafael Cano and willed to him via his mother. Jacks denied the claim and fenced the property when it became valuable as a gravel quarry. The record is not always clear on how these cases were settled, although it appears that Jacks usually won in court. The Martinez family had adjoining lots in the Catholic church neighborhood, passed down from an older sibling, which Jacks successfully reclaimed as pueblo land when Grácia Martinez tried to sell her lot to W. A. Kearney.[49] The state sued Jacks on behalf of a Portuguese fisherman when Jacks demolished the poor man's house and charged him with adverse possession but lost the case.[50] Local opposition to the penurious landlord overflowed legal channels. When Jacks put up fences they were routinely torn down and angry citizens confronted him in the streets with threats and denunciations. An account provided by the "Spanish lady" Mrs. Trip describes a general pattern.

> About eight years ago I bought a piece of land, about 6 1/2 acres, from Martinez for $250, during which time I have been what, under the law, might be termed peaceful possession of the premises, but according to Mr. Jacks' way of doing things I have had anything but peace since I bought the place. He has harassed me at every turn; surrounded me with fences, attempted to intimidate me, and by every means imaginable has tried to get my little piece of property away from me. All this time I have had to carry water for house use a long distance just because he would not give the water company permission to put their pipes through his lots to reach me. He claims my place under the so-called Aguajito grant, and once erected a tent on my ground, but I fired the tent over the fence and warned him to keep away. Time and again he has been to me with this and that proposition, but each time he has had a mysterious paper for me to sign. It is undoubtedly his old game to have me recognize his title in some respect and then he would have me. This last attempt in this direction was made a few days ago when he called at my house and said that if I would sign a certain agreement with him he would allow the water pipes to be laid through the grounds to my place. I told him I would sign nothing, and he said I would have to go without water then. He has even gone so far as to say I am crazy and one time reported me as being so to the sheriff of this county, but I am not half as crazy as he thinks. At another time I told him not to be such a hog about land, to leave me and my four children in peace.[51]

The piece appeared during the height of a newspaper campaign against Jacks, and Mrs. Trip may have had encouragement from editor Bradford who catered to popular resentment at the time. Yet accounts of this sort are common and consistent with private correspondence in which Jacks is constantly devising schemes to secure and enhance his landholdings. Mrs. Trip's rebellious mood, moreover, had been spreading. A twenty-year tide of discontent broke over Monterey in the late 1880s challenging Jacks and the control he had wielded over local government since he and Ashley first joined forces.

SQUATTERS' RIGHTS

Meanwhile, the countryside experienced parallel struggles over landownership and settlement. As in other parts of the state, American settlers arrived in growing numbers looking for public and cheap land. In the act of occupying lands claimed by holders or purchasers of Mexican grants, they became "squatters," a status not altogether disdained in the new political climate. Many of the new state's elected leaders repudiated Mexican claims to large ranches and proposed legislation, such as the short-lived settlers' bill of 1856, that encouraged squatters. In July 1855 a squatters' meeting took place in San Juan Bautista that attracted delegates from the Salinas Valley who hoped to justify and propagate their cause. Representatives claimed that squatters alone gave value to the land by using it productively, paying taxes, and eventually purchasing the invaded properties. Drawing on ten years of experience with California settlers, Mr. H. Cocks informed the crowd that "in nine cases out of ten, where they had squatted on private property, they had done it with full knowledge that it was covered with a Spanish or Mexican grant . . . and in nearly all cases, the land owners were willing to sell land at a fair valuation."[52] The methods seemed to work for Mr. Cocks, who accumulated a 1,100-acre tract. Whether landowners were willing to sell, or felt the political climate gave them no other choice, is an open question. But the observation faithfully reflects squatter insouciance that helped to spread the conflict. Many of the big ranches were invaded and their owners (including Atherton, Cooper, Castro) retaliated with lawsuits for adverse possession, damages, and partition.[53] Jacks successfully sued Carlos Baldez, Gregoria Vasquez, Graciano Martinez, and twenty-two other Anglos and Hispanics for adverse possession of Rancho Aguajito.[54] Squatter-owner encounters led to forceful eviction and bloodshed. Squatters, in turn, sabotaged properties by filling up watering holes or running off livestock before being expelled themselves.[55] Jacks warned the public against purchasing cattle taken from his land by Marcelino Joseph, and he had Manuel Padilla and José Maria Torres arrested for herding their sheep on his ranches.[56] The squatter question was pervasive and tempestuous.

The most vivid, and certainly the best-documented case of squatter conflict was played out on the nine-thousand-acre Rancho Chualar in the Salinas Valley. Jacks acquired the ranch in a deal with Mariano Malarín who had inherited his father's 1839 grant comprising two square leagues, now divided into the Chualar and Guadalupe ranches. Typical of the Jacks method for leveraging property acquisitions, he first lent $3,000 to Malarín, who was planning to build a commercial grain mill, with the ranch as collateral. Jacks was also after Guadalupe and had a lien on the second ranch. The grain mill flopped and Malarín settled with Jacks by signing over Chualar in exchange for the note and clear title to Guadalupe.

Once in possession of Chualar, Jacks resorted to the common strategy of attempting to extend the boundaries of the original grant. This
involved having the property resurveyed and obtaining a new patent for
the larger parcel. In private correspondence, Jacks states his case and seeks
political support from influential friends. The original grant to Juan
Malarín, he argues, was larger than that described by the U.S. Surveyor
General and approved by the district court in the confirmation process.
More than three thousand acres had been cut out when Mexican square
leagues were converted to U.S. acres (in fact, the difference between the
two measurement systems in this case would have been only about 100
acres). Jacks's resurvey indicated that Chualar should measure 12,906
rather than 8,890 acres.[57] The difference was critical, not only because
squatters were gathering, but also in light of maneuvers by the Salinas
Valley land baron Jesse Carr to locate state school land warrants on the
ranch. Jacks suspected Carr of sabotaging his claim and perhaps brib-
ing officials at the Surveyor General's office in San Francisco. Jacks wrote
to his old partner Delos Ashley, now the U.S. congressional representative for Nevada, asking for help, and Ashley, in turn, wrote California
senator Cornelius Cole with a long explanation and plea: "If you can
possibly induce the Commissioner to give Mr. Jacks the full amount of
the Chualar about 19,000 [sic] acres I shall feel very much obliged." Ashley notes that Carr was "an out and out Copperhead [Republican sympathetic to the Confederacy]" during the war while "Jacks was a Republican when it was considered a disgrace to be called one."[58] Similar
phrases in Ashley's letter and others that Jacks sent to federal officials in
San Francisco suggest that Jacks was orchestrating the whole campaign.
Indeed, Jacks wrote Ashley asking, "[I]f there is any possible way of getting my Chualar Ranch enlarged survey patented, I hope you will aid
[Washington lawyer] Mr. Chester in getting it done. If it cannot be done
in any other way you might get a bill through congress allowing me to
purchase at government price." The congressman may have felt put upon
at that point and answered briefly by telegram, "I think not."[59] Ultimately,
the expanded claim was denied in one of Jacks's uncommon legal defeats.

That the claim was disputed by squatters on the ground is suggested
in a letter from Jacks to Jesus Alonzo "at Mr Spences Ranch": "You are
hereby notified that the frame house in the Chualar Canon formerly occupied by the Portuguese is mine and on my ranch. . . . You are further
notified that in case you go into or on the Chualar Canon with sheep
that I will charge you 500$ per year in gold coin payable in advance."
Alonzo replied politely in Spanish, saying he had bought the house, had

not intended to take anyone's land, and invited Jacks to visit the site so
that they might "reach an understanding."[60]

Squatters were alert to contested spaces and doubtful claims. In late
1868, as Jacks was pressing his claim in Washington, he wrote San Francisco attorney and real estate agent James Stuart: "I have just received
word that there are a number of squatters on that part of the Chualar."[61]
This was very likely the origin of the ephemeral Squatters' League of
Monterey County proclaimed in the 1872 threatening letter to Jacks. Evidence suggests that there was organization behind the squatter invasion.
In a subsequent letter, Stuart informed Jacks, "I saw one of the squatters who recently jumped your land in the US archives examining your
papers and I gave him a good lecture. He seemed to be a Captain among
them who had come up to see where they were." Stuart hints further at
some kind of sponsorship behind the movement, saying they were "being made fools of by others."[62]

The insurgency of 1872 failed, but squatter problems at Chualar persisted. All of the large landowners including Jacks were faced with the
problem of making the land pay, or at least cover taxes, until they might
realize profitable sales through subdivision. This was the ruin of many
Mexican grantees who failed to evolve from ranchers in the hide and tallow trade to commercial farmers. The other side of the problem was the
cash-poor settler and aspiring small farmer. The solution practiced increasingly in the 1870s was tenancy. Smallholders leased land on a yearly
cash contract to raise grains and sheep. When cash and new tenants were
short, owners accepted in-kind payment of wool and grain. Tenant farmers lived close to the subsistence margin and frequently failed, but ever-
hopeful recruits took their places. In the late 1870s Jacks had upwards
of twenty tenants on Chualar in addition to a number of shepherds tending his own sheep.[63] Most tenants were docile and blamed themselves
for their sorry fortunes. But some accused the system of injustice. John
Whitworth, the tenant overseer at Chualar, notified Jacks in March 1878,
"[T]hat Spanish man alneso [sic] that lives up the Chualar Canon that
there was trouble with last year as staked out 160 acers of your land an
moved is house on it."[64] This was probably Jesus Alonzo who had stood
up to Jacks twelve years earlier and perhaps now intended to file a preemption claim (as other paisanos had done in Carmel Valley).

Early in 1880 the most colorful of all settlers appeared at Chualar.
On February 10, writing in a fine hand, the poet of Monterey County's
squatter movement informed A. Sanborn, the local hardware store
owner,

I am going to settle upon Government Land claimed by David Jacks the robber of the Widow the Orphan and Government land. I have the proofs that will dispossess him of his fraudulent claims, also Jose Pilolo (alias Teodero Gonzalez) who was sent from Mexico in Irons a Convicted felon who claims a Grant from a Governor he was in Irons under.

Will you please forward the following Pile of Lumber at as reasonable figure as you can afford. I will pay $210.00 down and the balance at your usual extension of time. Viz [there follows a list with dimensions of boards, rafters, flooring, etc.]

I am Sir Very respectfully Your Obt. Servt. Jno. A. Douglas[65]

Jonathan Douglas settled at Chualar, although it does not appear that Sanborn forwarded the lumber for him to build a house. During the summer, Jacks employee R. E. Bowen reported that he had found Douglas's horse grazing in his field of stubble, which "made words" between them. "He claims that the land belongs to the people but I told him if it does he does not own it." Douglas had not signed a lease, saying, "Jacks wouldn't dare collect money from a poor man."[66] Some months later, judging from the account he provided Jacks, overseer Whitworth seems to have been ordered to evict Douglas: "I saw Duglass with sum furneter in is waggon so I watched him and he went wright to earricks and thare got the Black woman and started far the unruh place [a tenant farm]. . . . Just as I got thare duglas went in the house. I saw that one of the leoks was brokin. I sent sanclare to telegrafh to you and to send me Mr. Boan so that we could get him out of the house."[67] It appears that Douglas and his "Black woman" companion were living on the former Unruh tenancy and, although evicted by Jacks's employees Whitworth and Bowen, returned the next day with new locks for the doors.

Douglas's perseverance is demonstrated in a supremely confident letter to Jacks written from Chualar eight months later.

David Jacks Esqr.

Dear Sir

Enclosed please find An Abstract of title of the Gonzalez Rancho. I have not published an Abstract of the Chualar & Zanjones yet but only denounced it in a general way. The land outside of your Two League Survey and Your Three League Survey, also your protracted survey over Government Land all of which you know to be a gross fraud. I would not take posesion of until you got the crop from it. Notwithstanding this concession on my part. One of your sycophants that is detested by nearly all on the ranch, took my horse off the stubble, has he done so by your authority, If so it is a very small matter on your part, recall it. I am not so much against

you as I am against Gonzalez who stole Land that you claimed, and holds
Land that I own and am bound to get.[68]

The enclosed "Abstract" is a well-drafted map of the ranch area along
the Salinas River divided into sections and labeled according to Douglas's interpretation of their legal status. At the upper left is a wide swath
of "Government Land" which includes the "Douglas Claim." On two
sides of that are "Decree of Chualar Ranch manufactured by D. Ashley
in 1852. Patent of this two leagues recalled by the Government as a fraud"
and "Zanjones Rancho, manufactured by Lawyer Ashley in 1852 not
patented." To the west are two sections described as "Protracted survey
[i.e., of Jacks] over rejected land" and "Part of Chualar Ranch jumped
by Settlers who had the courage to hold their natural rights." The letter
and map make a powerful statement about popular justice. Douglas does
not repudiate all of Jacks's property claims (or even Jacks himself as the
principal malefactor) but identifies specific questionable claims (of which
there were many) and celebrates the settlers' "natural rights" to take possession of a fair share of the land. Judging from his language and actions,
Douglas was an unusual man. We do not know what happened to him
after 1881. Yet he left a record that demonstrates that squatters understood the politicized system of land distribution and acted with some
effect to establish a place for themselves in the new society.

What can we conclude from the Squatters' League, the Douglas case,
and other instances of protest action? It is important, first, to recognize
that organized resistance to practices of land concentration did take place,
probably on a scale greater than what we know from the documented
record that relies heavily on Jacks's papers. Second, like town residents
who understood the moral economy of the commons, squatters acted on
ideas about justice drawn from the American frontier. Their resistance
was principled, pragmatic, and aimed at inclusion rather than repudiation of the property regime as a whole. Finally, the squatter movement
was relatively weak, episodic, legally overmatched, and palliative—a far
cry from the agrarian revolt tenants would soon mount in populist sections of the South and Midwest. In Monterey County, settlers were
steadily incorporated into the inequitable land tenure system through a
combination of tenancy, successful squatting, small-parcel purchase, and
public land (preemption and homestead) claims.

Accommodation of growing numbers of settlers was made possible
by the efforts to promote economic development by local elites. On the
one hand, they looked for ways to put people on the land profitably in

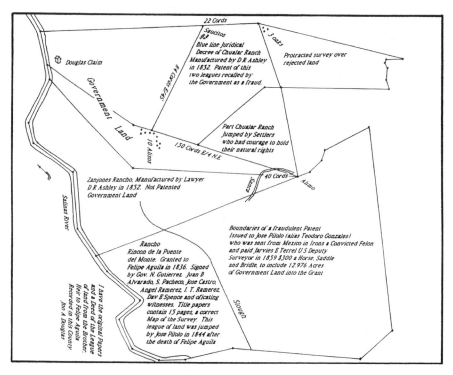

Within the map, the following labels appear:

22 Cords

Saucios
&s

Blue line Juridical
Decree of Chualar Ranch
Manufactured by D R Ashley
in 1852. Patent of this
two leagues recalled by
the Government as a fraud.

3 oaks

Protracted survey over
rejected land

Douglas Claim

Government Land

10 Alisos

150 Cords E/4 N.E.

Part Chualar Ranch
Jumped by Settlers
who had courage to hold
their natural rights

40 Cords

Aliso

Salinas River

Zanjones Rancho, Manufactured by Lawyer
D R Ashley in 1852. Not Patented
Government Land

Rancho
Rincon de la Puente
del Monte. Granted to
Felipe Aguila in 1836. Signed
by Gov. N. Gutierrez. Juan B
Alvarado, S. Pacheco, Jose Castro.
Angel Ramerez, I. T. Ramerez,
Dav E Spence and oficating
witnesses. Title papers
contain 15 pages, a correct
Map of the Survey. This
league of land was jumped
by Jose Pilolo in 1844 after
the death of Felipe Aguila

Boundaries of a fraudulent Patent
Issued to Jose Pilolo (alias Teodoro Gonzales)
who was sent from Mexico in Irons a Convicted Felon
and paid Jarvies E Terrel U S Deputy
Surveyor in 1859 $300 a Horse, Saddle
and Bridle, to include 12.976 Acres
of Government Land into the Grant

I have the original Papers
and a Deed of the League
of land from the Brother,
Heir to Felipe Aguila
Recorded in this County
Jno A Douglas

Slough

16.   Squatter's Map, 1881. Jonathan Douglas, a squatter on David Jacks's
Chualar Ranch, drew the original of this map and sent it to Jacks, claiming his
title was fraudulent and the property subject to homesteading. Douglas had
clearly researched the various patents in support of "settlers who had courage
to hold their natural rights." (Illustration by Beverly Lozano)

arrangements such as annual leases for tenants and wage employment
for shepherds. Jacks was among those progressive farmers who adopted
new forms of production, technical assistance, and wholesale merchandising. On the other hand, local capital attacked the county's major in-
frastructural problem, the lack of rail access to urban markets.

Unserved by the state's Southern Pacific railroad octopus, a countywide group organized the Monterey and Salinas Valley Railroad Company (M&SVRR). In September 1874 the narrow-gauge M&SVRR began service between Salinas and Monterey, an hour-and-fifteen-minute
trip with two stops. The railhead at Monterey fronted the wharf and the
coastal steamship service and connected with the Southern Pacific at Salinas. The company's capital stock of $300,000 was subscribed by seventy-
two investors led by the county's great land engrossers—Jesse Carr
(45,000 acres), David Jacks (30,000 acres at the time), C. S. Abbot (10,000
acres), A. and M. Gonzales (13,000 acres), Robert McKee and the

Munras family (19,000 acres), Mariano Malarín (5,000 acres), and B. V. Sargent (13,000 acres). The syndicate included seven of the county's top eighteen income earners as well as many smaller investors who hoped all boats would rise with the tide of increasing land values.[69] The railroad was an expensive project, plagued by Salinas River floods and washed-out bridges. Although it reported earnings of $9,000 in 1876, the road's passenger traffic, volume of freight, and rate savings to shippers never came up to booster expectations. Investors lost money during the brief life span of the M&SVRR before it was taken over by Southern Pacific.

The transition to a new property regime effected by land concentration and settler accommodation did not eliminate squatter conflicts. Jacks was still engaged in a protracted legal battle with a dozen settlers at Cañada de la Segunda in Carmel Valley as late as 1898. The settlers had been in possession of their farms for up to ten years, operated commercially successful activities like Kaspar Henneken's apiary, and scoffed at Jacks's claim that their properties were within the city lands grant. Anyone could see that they were located south of the ridgeline specified in the original pueblo deed. But Jacks's San Francisco attorney argued that the 1866 "Act to Quiet Land Titles in California. . . . allows David Jacks the privilege of purchasing for a nominal sum certain lands that were once included in the Mexican grant of the Pueblo of Monterey and excluded from the grant by a government survey in 1887" given that Jacks had paid taxes on the land since 1864, used it for grazing, and made improvements. The case was decided by the U.S. Land Commission in San Francisco in favor of the settlers but reversed in Washington on Jacks's appeal.[70] Local sensibilities were outraged. Further appeal to the secretary of the interior brought no satisfaction. Bad blood between the men grew as Jacks tried to win a waste-removal contract with the local army post held by Henneken. Meanwhile, Jacks had ordered all the Cañada de la Segunda settlers to leave the land, allowing that they might take their crops and improvements with them. Henneken, the last of the settlers, still refused to leave. Without support for any collective protest, Henneken struck out at Jacks, first in a threatening letter dated October 2, 1902.[71]

David Jacks Esq

Monterey, Cal

Sir

I want to communicate to you that I will have no more of your persecution, but peace; no more law but my Rights and Justice; no more starving my Family by Reason of your oppression.

This town cannot hold both of us under present conditions, but settle as is just between man and man.

Remember this and act quickly and all will be well but no other way.

KW Henneken

On the following day, Henneken accosted Jacks on Alvarado Street in Monterey, pulled a revolver, and demanded, "You sign this deed or I will kill you, or I will take money from you." Ignoring the deed, which presumably would have returned Henneken's farm, Jacks called for help from bystanders, who separated the antagonists. Jacks survived and the desperate attempt at revindication failed. Henneken was later tried in Justice Court, although no one wanted to pursue the unfortunate incident.[72]

Henneken disappears from the historical record along with Douglas and other advocates of squatters' rights. By the turn of the century, a new property regime is consolidated with a few owners with extensive holdings at the top, a preponderance of struggling tenants, smallholders, and rural wage workers at the bottom, and not much between. Social inequality on the land was reinforced by legal and political practice— but not without demands for justice from the squatters' league, legal challenges, and determined recusancy. The new regime was erected on contested ground where squatters and Californios persevered alongside successful engrossers.

LABOR: MAKING AND MALIGNING AN ETHNIC WORKING CLASS

The transition to American society also entailed wholesale changes in the labor force as the comparison of 1850 and 1880 census figures demonstrates (see table 2). The working class expanded significantly and, in combination with servants, made up fully half of Monterey's employed population. At the same time, the working class became more diverse, populated by immigrants of varied ethnic and national origin. Initially, these laborers filled a critical shortage and were hailed for their industry. As the half century wore on, however, class antagonisms fanned by political opportunism grew, ethnic labor generally and the Chinese in particular were disparaged, discriminatory acts further segregated groups, and a pernicious class society took root. Yet discrimination was met with determination in the new groups. Communities formed, nurtured their own, improved their lot, and found ways to defend themselves. Unknowingly, they began the development of Monterey's future industrial wealth. Although the day of the ethnic working class lay a half century ahead, its foundations were established here.

Mestizo vaqueros and household servants who made up the original working class expanded their field of endeavor in the American period. Women in domestic service, along with others in casual work such as laundry and cooking, increased their numbers. As the agricultural economy shifted from cattle ranching, former vaqueros joined European immigrants on the farms as shepherds, sheep shearers, and general hands. David Jacks used the labor contracting firm of C. R. Hansen in San Francisco to recruit specialized farmworkers such as Basque shepherds. Hansen had trouble filling the request but sent "the nearest to Basques we could find in the city this time—they are regular French shepherds & we hope they will prove to be #1 men. . . . [And in a later postscript:] We have had Irish shepherds who wanted to go but we would not send them."[73] Good shepherds were in short supply, and shepherds as a group were known for their independence and preference to "quit their wages" as often as the mood or an overbearing foreman dictated. Even more in demand were the rural labor specialists who castrated and sheared sheep. One fall a foreman reported that shearers were getting very independent and "everyone is complaining—some will wait till spring to shear," although he was trying to get Santana Alviso, whose men were scattered, or "another company." He ended up with Ramon Romero, who brought a crew of eight other Hispanics and insisted on payment at the going rate of five cents a sheep. Skilled workers were scarce, and they prospered during the fall harvest, although employment was seasonal.

The fishing industry developed slowly in Monterey. Native Americans used the oceans and rivers for subsistence and even dabbled in commercial catches of sea otter and salmon. An authentic industry began with the Portuguese whalers who maintained a community of fifteen fishers during the 1850s.[74] When the Portuguese set up a whaling station at Point Lobos, the Chinese were already fishing the bay for squid, which they dried and prepared for export on the beach. Fishing was a family enterprise among the Chinese. Women worked alongside men on the boats and dressed fish on shore.[75] Although there are early accounts of the bay teeming with palatable fish such as sardines and salmon, commercial fishing for domestic consumption seems to begin in earnest only with the arrival of the Genoese Italians in the early 1870s. According to one contemporary account, "A company of Italian fishermen from up the coast [probably Santa Cruz] have made their headquarters in this bay, and intend going into the fish business on a large scale. They have made arrangements with Wells, Fargo & Co. to ship 2,000 pounds each day to San Francisco."[76] Later, Japanese fishers would join the industry, specializing in the canning and export of abalone. Workers in various aspects of the industry soon numbered in the hundreds.

The massive introduction of Chinese workers into California grew out of demand for manual labor in railroad construction and mining. Monterey County followed this pattern, adding to its Chinese fishing community. Eighty Chinese miners were employed in the San Antonio district in 1866 and on construction crews of the narrow-gauge railroad in 1874. Railroad labor demand escalated when the Southern Pacific purchased the M&SVRR in 1879, converting to broad gauge and adding a Monterey-Castroville line with the help of "14 white and 150 Chinamen,"[77] As criticism of the use of Chinese labor began to mount in the 1870s, local editor W. L. La Rose made an inspection tour of the Carmelo Coal Mine and reported, "Mr. Strader says that he has 23 Chinamen employed altogether, and about 60 white men. His defense for employing any of the Mongolians is that the Company could not afford to erect buildings and employ cooks for white workers for the short period of time which will be consumed in the construction of the road." Presumably the Chinese could live in tents and cook for themselves, thereby cutting labor costs. In a previous editorial, La Rose had already arrived at the axiom, "[I]t is impossible, therefore, for Caucasians to contend with the moon-eyed lepers in the walks of cheap labor."[78]

Demeaning references to Chinese labor were actually something new at this time. Until the late 1860s, Chinese work habits and achievements were lauded repeatedly. For example: "It is doubtful if on the whole we have a more industrious people in our state than the Chinamen. . . . [T]he Chinese throughout the mines are a sober, honest, industrious class, who seldom interfere with others in any way, and who are content to work where the Anglo-Saxon will not labor."[79] And even as the nativist movement got under way, a number of local citizens individually, and the Republican Party organizationally, defended Chinese labor, albeit as faithful workers. "Thus far, the Chinaman has been not a curse, but a blessing to California. He has contributed largely to our prosperity, our comfort, and our wealth."[80] But times were changing as class conflict and political demagoguery escalated in the 1870s.

California's nativist movement began in San Francisco under a unique set of conditions, including an overcrowded labor market, a relatively high proportion of Chinese workers, Democratic Party co-optation of "anticoolie clubs," and a challenge to the city's Democratic machine by the Workingmen's Party of California—both vying for potential support mobilized by the "Chinese threat."[81] The Workingmen's Party of California (WPC), which bore little relation to the national one, was first in the field with heated rhetoric about the "Mongolian" influx that drew on an inexhaustible supply of cheap labor and threatened soon to replace all American workers. With the nation suffering economic depression in the late 1870s, political party battles intensified in California cities as the Workingmen took to the campaign trail and local Democrats responded with incantations such as "The Chinese Must Go."

Early in 1878 a "grand anti-Chinese meeting" was held in Salinas sponsored by "The Caucasion Society" [sic], which soon became a local chapter of the Workingmen's Party.[82] One year later, "quite a large and respectable looking crowd of people assembled in the [Monterey city] hall, not withstanding the rain and frigid character of the night, and a very enthusiastic meeting was the result." Calling itself the Monterey Labor Union, two hundred members elected blacksmith Walter Dodge president and butcher Thomas Doud secretary.[83] As in Salinas, the Monterey Labor Union transformed itself into a WPC affiliate and ran a slate of local candidates, headed by barman and constable Rosario Duarte, in the next election. County politics were raucous and factionalized. Democrats usually won elections with the help of Salinas landowners and a large segment of the working population who were arrayed against Monterey Republicans, among them Jacks and a number of local newspaper editors. Energized by the fiery anti-Chinese rhetoric of the Irish labor leader Denis Kearney, the WPC challenged both political parties from its San Francisco headquarters. But it posed a particular threat to "the Democracy" by appealing to its working-class constituency. The same dynamic was at work in Monterey when Kearney visited for a memorable speech that demonstrated a keen knowledge of local conditions. Although no transcript survives, *Monterey Californian* editor La Rose caught the bombastic flavor.

> Denis Kearney made his appearance and opened the seance by reading Chapter V of James, it being the evening of the Sabbath. He then branched off on the subject of the land sharks and robbers of Monterey, giving their history since the first landing of the missionaries, and wound up christening David Jacks as the last missionary who had arrived, and dubbed him "Captain Jacks, the chief of the Monterey highwaymen." Denis characterized Jacks as one of the most notorious land pirates and robbers known to-day in the whole world. That Vasquez was hung because he killed a man or two, but was a gentleman compared with Jacks. He denounced the citizens of Monterey for suffering Jacks' rule as abject slaves. . . . He also charged Jacks with defeating the in-

corporation of the town; with charging poor washwomen 50 cents per month for washing their clothes at Huerta Vieja[,]. . . . robbing the town of its city lands[,] . . . burning up old trees and limbs, hiring Chinese to do it, to prevent the poor people from obtaining firewood. . . . Kearney then took up land monopolists in this county, told what they paid in the way of taxes and what they ought to pay. . . . Kearney closed an hour and a quarter's speech, and he told many killing truths on some of the old citizens, proving them by a vote of the audience.[84]

The charismatic Kearney did not sway everyone. Agreeing with many of his points, La Rose nevertheless judged him "a communist of the worst kind." A Chinese friend known to the editor as Tim Wong (Wong Wah Foo), an outspoken leader and rights advocate among local Asians, indicated that the community was not worried: "the Chinese [do] not give a darn for Kearney."[85]

Jacks had employed Chinese for many years to clear roads, cut timber, and do laundry and field work. On his Pescadero Ranch fronting Carmel Bay, he leased property to a company of Chinese organized in a fishing village. But the nativist movement was making things difficult for everyone. A Chinese laundry man whom Jacks knew as Ah Chew left his employ. Jacks wrote to Robert McElroy, a San Francisco friend and business associate, asking if Ah Chew might be found among relatives in Oakland and enticed back. Ah Chew, as it turned out, had taken advantage of a special railroad fare and gone to New York. McElroy reported to Jacks: "[I] took the laundry matter to an Intelligence Office and was informed that it would be impossible to obtain Chinamen from here who would go down and take the risk, as they are now very different since this agitation has intimidated them. I am informed that the only way that you can get laundry men from here will be to hire them at so much a month and take them down to work in the laundry. You could hire them for about $25 or $30 per month and they board themselves."[86]

In Monterey, persecution of Chinese begun during the brief popularity of the WPC persisted well into the future. Chinese fishers were assailed by their Italian rivals and local authorities for allegedly using illegal nets that destroyed small fish. Whaling vessels attempted to run down Chinese fishing craft. These altercations typically resulted in mass arrests of Chinese disputants, but no others.[87] The Chinese were singled out in charges of smuggling, and, as the city began to require licenses of tradespeople, Chinese vegetable peddlers and laundry men were selectively harassed. Residents of New Monterey next to the Point Alones Chinatown (there was another one downtown) successfully petitioned the city to ban aromatic squid drying on the shoreline, a traditional practice essential to the Chinese fishing business.[88]

The anti-Chinese agitation introduced a new mood of racial intolerance to local society. If Hispanics, mestizos, and kindred paisanos were denigrated, they were also a majority with whom Anglos were forced to deal owing to their pervasive language, culture, and representation among the landed upper class. Now the nativist movement divided the working class, setting white and Chinese tradespeople or Italian and Chinese fishers against one another. Efforts to segregate and vilify the Chinese begun at this juncture would soon spread to a general campaign against the working poor.

Ironically, the popular mobilization that denied poor people also began to challenge monopolistic control. The two outcomes need not have been linked, but in fact they became so under the particular conditions of local development. Monterey's Anglo-American middle class was growing, organizing itself in business and civic associations, chafing under the developmental restraints of weak government and land monopoly. The old Spanish capital was on the verge of reinventing itself in a political struggle for city independence.

THE CITY RISING

When Robert Louis Stevenson described Monterey in 1879 as "a place of two or three streets," he explained its tumbledown appearance as the result of historical decline, "a Mexican capital continually wrested by one faction from another, an American capital when the first House of Representatives held its deliberations, and then falling lower and lower from the capital of the State to the capital of a county, and from that again, by the loss of its charter and town lands, to a mere bankrupt village."[89] He refers to the decision to establish California's first capital in San José, transfer of the county seat to Salinas by vote in 1872, and changes in the city charter engineered by Ashley and associates that reduced its assets, fiscal authority, and governing powers to a minimum. So Monterey languished. From 1850 to 1890 the county population increased tenfold to 18,637 while the city less than doubled to 1,662. An optimistic account in 1874 observed that the number of business establishments was double the previous year, yet most of these covered, and duplicated, a narrow range of consumer services: 9 groceries, 5 saloons,

2 clothing stores, 2 hotels, 2 real estate offices, 2 barber shops, 2 fruit stores, 2 butchers, 2 lumber yards, 2 drugstores, 1 physician, 1 law office, 1 blacksmith, 1 millinery establishment, 1 tin and stove shop, 1 saddlery, 1 printing office, 1 China wash house.[90]

Yet the midseventies saw definite stirrings of development. The M&SVRR inspired conviction that progress was imminent. For at least a decade, promoters had sung the virtues of Monterey as a "watering place—a place of summer recreation and resort. . . . [W]e have fine bathing, fine fishing, yachting, splendid beach drives, romantic old town, picturesque scenery and places of curiosity." Later the appeal was extended to "tourists, invalids, and pleasure seekers." Only a luxury resort hotel was lacking, but there were rumors that "monied men were already prospecting Monterey for a site."[91] In a major initiative promising trainloads of visitors, David Jacks gave five acres at Pacific Grove to the Methodist Episcopal Church for a summer retreat and Chautauqua conference center. Before long a town grew up around the camp and Jacks began selling suburban lots. A new *Hand Book of Monterey and Vicinity* celebrated these achievements and commended the church retreat at Pacific Grove: "The eastern boundary is about one-half mile west of Chinatown. . . . [T]he encampment commands a splendid view of the Bay of Monterey, and the magnificent scenery surrounding it, with pretty bays for bathing places and beautiful groves for rambles. . . . with opportunities for every kind of outdoor occupation and enjoyment; and all within three miles of Monterey, and its railroad and steamboat connections. . . . [A] location so healthy that doctors scarcely make a living, it bids fair to become an unrivaled summer resort."[92]

With development at hand, the city still lacked paved streets, lighting, rudimentary services, and, critically, the municipal authority to provide them through taxation. State legislation promoted by Ashley in 1853 and 1857 had amended the original act of city incorporation (April 1851), reducing the common council to a three-person board of trustees, prohibiting municipal indebtedness, and limiting the means of raising revenue to public land sales and leases. The question of reincorporation was raised in 1875, as it had been on several previous occasions without success. Town trustees and a citizens committee rallied public backing and succeeded in drafting an incorporation bill that provided a series of (property, road, dog) taxes for "street grades, laying out and opening new streets, requiring sidewalks, sewerage, etc.[,] . . . City Clerk, Attorney, Surveyor, and such policemen as they deem necessary." Jacks and a small circle of associates systematically opposed any attempt to alter weak

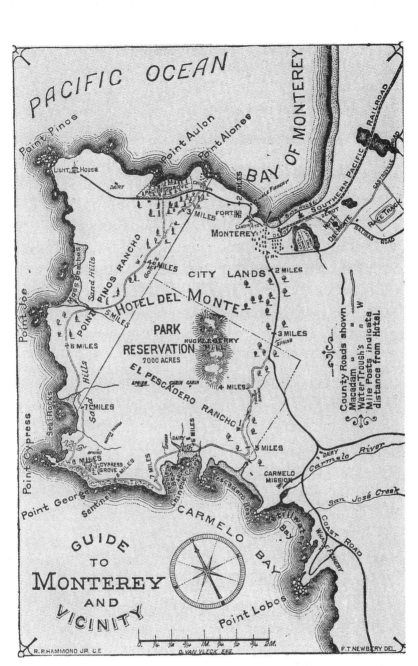

17. Monterey Peninsula Map, ca. 1890. This map by D. Van Vleck from the promotional *Souvenir Guide to Monterey and Vicinity* (1886) reflects local politics of the late nineteenth century by representing the peninsula as centered on the Hotel Del Monte. The city of Monterey is pictured as an appendage to the hotel and railroad. The area's central attraction is the Hotel Del Monte's 7,000-acre "Park Reservation" encircled by the Seventeen-Mile Drive and available real estate. (Courtesy of the Monterey Public Library, Local History Collection)

municipal powers, particularly any prospect of opprobrious property taxes. The proposed bill went forward from the town council and passed the state assembly but failed in the senate, where, one suspects, political influence came into play.[93]

But the local empowerment movement was moving simultaneously on a parallel course. For a number of years, city trustees had considered ways of recovering the pueblo lands including purchase and litigation charging that the original sale to Jacks and Ashley was illegal. Several years previously, Jacks and a few other important town property owners (e.g., Gonzales, Serrano, De la Torre, Geradin, Cuellar, Leese, Abrego) had resisted similar efforts locally and petitioned Sacramento, saying, "[W]e do not want any more taxation for city purposes."[94] Now the trustees tried a new approach, contracting with attorney Robert Forbes to divide equally the profits of a suit against Jacks to recover city land (Ashley had long since sold all his interests in Monterey to his partner). Popular pressure was mounting with the promise of development. Forbes addressed a mass meeting at city hall, saying that Jacks's title was worthless and noting that one hundred citizens had already signed a petition to the Senate Judiciary Committee where a new bill on the land question was stuck after clearing the assembly. Jacks debated Forbes at a subsequent meeting held in the Union Saloon, arguing that his ownership of the city lands was perfectly legal. When the city's recovery lawsuit made no headway, dragging through the courts for another twenty years, a determined political movement turned again to the incorporation question.[95]

This time the results of local mobilization would be different. Monterey had arrived at a pivotal moment with the introduction of big California capital on the local stage. Within a calendar year of summer 1879, three events created the watershed change, all associated with the Southern Pacific Railroad (SP) of Collis Huntington, Leland Stanford, Charles Crocker, and Mark Hopkins (who died in the same year). First, the SP bought the railbed of the ruined M&SVRR and upgraded the line with a broad-gauge connection between Monterey and the SP station at Castroville, and on to San Francisco. Analysts at the time reasoned that the SP had noted the success of Santa Cruz tourism and hoped to steal a march on the South Pacific Coast Railroad, which was building a San Francisco–Santa Cruz line.[96] Second, acting through its landholding subsidiary, the Pacific Improvement Company (P.I. Co.), the railroad bought from David Jacks more than 7,000 acres of his prime (Pescadero and Point Pinos) coastal property and 148 acres in Monterey for $35,800.[97] Third, the P.I. Co. purchased the 144-acre Toombs tract in Monterey

18. Hotel Del Monte, ca. 1880. Collis Huntington and his Southern Pacific Railroad built the luxurious hotel to make the line from San Francisco profitable by converting the old Spanish capital into a tourist attraction and elite real estate development. From the *Souvenir Guide to Monterey and Vicinity,* 1886. (Courtesy of the Monterey Public Library, Local History Collection)

for $5,300 and announced plans for the much-anticipated luxury resort hotel.[98]

Unbounded enthusiasm greeted the railroad and its striking Gothic-design Hotel Del Monte—"one of the most elegant seaside establishments in the world," as illustrated spreads on the newspaper's front page announced. In addition to the architecturally extravagant hotel, the resort advertised that "seven thousand acres of lands have also been reserved especially as an adjunct . . . skirting the ocean shore and passing through extensive forests." Adjacent to the Del Monte Forest lay such attractions as the Pacific Grove retreat and Carmel Mission. The Del Monte promised to reveal the "true character [of Monterey] as a favorite summer resort." And the credit for this peerless achievement belonged to the Southern Pacific Railroad, "the managers of the road having taken much interest in the old town . . . [T]he completion of this road, on New Years Day, sealed the destiny of 'the sleepy hollow of California.' It was the beginning of the new era—the epoch of prosperity."[99]

The P.I. Co. also went into the real estate business, developing suburban lots next to the hotel as the Forest Grove tract and explaining in great detail how their legal title traced from the city lands through Jacks's rightful ownership to the present seller. As one observer noted, the great significance of these developments was that Monterey had finally "got Jacks' boot off its neck."[100] Increasingly, city leaders and entrepreneurs hailed the progress engendered by the P.I. Co. and, as a reflection of the hotel's role in local transformation, began to equate Monterey with the

Del Monte. Hotel advertising sometimes used the postal address "Del Monte, California."

Over the next few years the forces of incorporation regrouped, emboldened by the protective cover of the P.I. Co. The hotel laid in its own infrastructure, including rail, ship, and road connections. A twenty-five-mile scenic carriage drive along the shoreline and through the forest was the centerpiece of hotel attractions. The critical water supply was constructed by transporting river water from the Laureles Ranch (which the P.I. Co. bought) deep in Carmel Valley for use by both the hotel and the city. Yet each impressive achievement recalled public deficiencies and reaffirmed the need for an effective city government.

The incorporation fight began in earnest at the outset of 1889 with a new team of political leaders and vigorous press in H. L. Bradford's crusading *Monterey Cypress*. A large public meeting produced a draft bill for submission to the state legislature that would, in effect, reincorporate the city by repealing earlier amendments to the original incorporation act. The plan was complicated, involving steps to first officially disincorporate, then incorporate anew under the desired stronger form of government, approve these changes in the legislature, and finally institute them by local election. With popular support, a delegation went to Sacramento to argue their case before the Municipal Corporation Committee. There they encountered David Jacks and several associates presenting the opposition's side. As supporters called attention to the city's need for modernization, Jacks cannily took up the egalitarian cause, noting that the plan "does not propose to include [within] the new boundaries, the magnificent grounds and spacious buildings of Del Monte. That property will not be taxed for the improvement of our streets, but the poor fisherman will have to pay"—as would Jacks.

But this tax concession to the city's new benefactor did not trouble supporters and, in any case, Jacks's argument was transparently hypocritical. Another town meeting at Bagby's Opera House, convened by a marching band, ratified an amended version of the bill and sent it forward to the legislature. New Monterey including the Point Alones Chinatown up to the boundary with Pacific Grove and the Del Monte Forest would be within city boundaries, the Hotel Del Monte grounds excluded (but not its bathhouse on the city beach). The meeting resolved, "[A]ppreciating the many favors done our city by the P.I. Co., and the great advantages derived from the location of the beautiful Del Monte in our midst we believe it the part of justice to our friend the Company and advantageous to ourselves that the world famous Del Monte and her grounds proper should be excluded from the city limits . . . but the bathhouse grounds should be included." With forthcoming legislative approval of the revised bill, the deal seemed final.

Monterey supporters were understandably shocked when newly elected Governor Robert N. Waterman vetoed the bill. Although the governor gave no explanation, a Sacramento observer told the *Cypress*, "[I]t is evident that your esteemed fellow townsman, David Jacks, has been pulling every wire in his power to defeat the will of your people." Supporters hastened to Sacramento and pressed the novice governor, who conceded he had been misled (presumably by Jacks) on the extent of property-owner opposition. Now he was given to understand that supporters included the great majority of property owners and business-persons while "Mr. Jacks' delegation consisted of himself, a Monterey minister of the gospel, his squirrel poisoner and his sheep dipper." In a face-saving maneuver, the veto was left standing and the governor agreed to sign a new bill to the same effect.[101]

Monterey was jubilant in the victory of "a grand revolution of progress." In a baroque turn of phrase, the "silurians" (geologically aged or old-fashioned) were defeated. A carnival mood erupted in the city, suggesting the depth of resentment it held for nearly forty years of Jacks's oppressive influence on civic life.

> Bon fires lighted up the atmosphere at various portions of the town. Public and private houses were illuminated and the streets were thronged with people of all sexes and ages, sheltered under umbrellas, all anxious to witness the grand demonstrations. The firing of anvils in front of Bagby's Opera House attracted the throng in that direction and lighted transparencies bearing many comical and original mottos were greeted with cheers as they made their appearance amid the crowd. Among them the most attractive was "The Silurian, last week" represented by a happy looking Jacks, while on the other side "The Silurian this week" appeared with heels up, showing that the animal was dead.[102]

The required vote in June favored incorporation by a margin of 341 to 24. The *Cypress* noted augustly, "Since the landing of Padre Serra, at the little beach north of the Custom House, just one hundred and nineteen years ago to a day, nothing of so much importance to Monterey had occurred."[103]

In some respects, however, local business and progressive interests traded one patron for another. In the interests of joining with a powerful ally in the incorporation fight, the city conceded a great deal by exempting its richest enterprise from property taxes levied on humble shops and households. The railroad had been embraced as a friend and "shield" against Jacks without reflection on the long-term implications of the alliance.[104] One effect of progress was a series of new suburban developments that would require the standard infrastructure of streets, drainage, sewage, and lighting. New Monterey was laid out in small lots extending from the old fort to Pacific Grove, and the equally modest Oak Grove was projected east of downtown between Lake El Estero (the original presidio site) and the Del Monte. The P.I. Co had its own upscale suburban tract. Beyond the hotel lay East Monterey and the Doud tract. Following the Pacific Grove model, a Catholic seaside resort and suburban development initially named Paradise Park was announced to a gathering of the Catholic Ladies Aid Society meeting at the Del Monte in September 1890. The special attraction of Paradise Park was its proximity to the historic Carmel Mission, currently undergoing renovation. Paradise Park failed to materialize, but other developers were at work planning Carmel City for the same area.[105] The suburban boom would alter Monterey's historical character and put new service demands on the treasury.

Another consequence of the alliance with "our friend the [P.I.] company" was a tendency on the part of local influentials to equate the hotel and the city, to assume a commonality of interests and even to reconfigure the town's identity as the location of the "world famous Hotel Del Monte." Although this enhanced the advertised appeal of the hotel, with a quaint "old town" as one of the sights on the shoreline drive to Chinatown and the mission, it posed a problem for local institutions. When "our future" was discussed, leaders in business and government invariably identified local priorities with the P.I. Co., visitors, tourist attractions, appearances, and such urban services as directly served these interests. The newspaper, for example, ran an engraving of the Del Monte front-page center for several years in the early 1890s and regularly reported on such hotel news as the number of debutante engagements in the "season," tennis and polo matches, and visitations by such elite families as the Crockers or Vanderbilts. The town assumed an obsequious posture toward the P.I. Co. and its municipal agenda.

Several courses of action followed from the assimilation of hotel and city interests. In an ironic turn of events, the emboldened city government recast David Jacks as an impediment to progress and began tearing down fences that Jacks built around lots he claimed to own. The city's objective was to see more town lots turned over to smallholders who would develop them. For the next three years, Jacks was vilified in the press and vigorously pursued by the tax collector.

19. Chinese Fishing Village, Monterey, 1875. The Chinese were among the
first to develop Monterey's commercial fishing industry, specializing in squid
for the export market. The makeshift village and the smell of drying squid
near the heart of town led to a series of attempts to remove the Chinese from
this site. (Courtesy of the Monterey Public Library, Local History Collection)

Greater consequences derived from a campaign to rid the town of the
disreputable poor, their unsightly shanties, drying fish and laundry,
tramps, and other eyesores that might offend visitors. Among the taxes
levied by the new city government were licensing fees for ambulant peddlers and laundries, most of whom were Chinese conducting business on
city streets. Punitive fees, selective enforcement, and arrests were clearly
intended to drive these practices out of sight.[106] Petitions from New Monterey neighbors against drying squid in the Point Alones Chinatown resulted in a city ban at that location.[107] An epidemic of tramps was de-
tected "over running" the city, leading railroad conductors to throw them
off in-bound trains and constables to arrest them.

In the most draconian attack on blight and poverty, city government
and property owners attempted to remove low-rent housing on the waterfront near the train depot. Progress, the *Cypress* ruminated, was
defined by orderly urban space: "[I]t means the obliteration of the shape-
less adobes. It means good government, symmetrical architecture, graded
streets, beautiful avenues, attractive lawns." When the city disclosed plans
to clear the shanties that Portuguese and Italian fishing families had rented

near the wharf for the last twenty years, a protest was mounted and dissenting petitions gathered. On the official side, "advocates of removal of the shanties claim . . . that it is high time that they [the fishers] were made to feel that if they expect to live here and peacefully enjoy the rights and privileges of citizens, they must not persist in being a stumbling block in the way of progress." The resistance movement seems to have had an effect in delaying adverse action. The P.I. Co. was involved in these negotiations and settled on a piecemeal approach to urban renewal. The company's discretion was probably informed by the housing needs of its own sizable staff (including kitchen, laundry, and garden workers) many of whom lived in Monterey's central Chinatown. Yet rumors of pending slum clearance continued. Within a few years, a shack on land leased from Jacks near the railroad tracks was torn down after the unfortunate occupant, a fisherman, was run over by a locomotive. Soon the community learned "there is a plan on foot to remove the fisherman's houses from the railroad lands near the wharf." The question of where to house the urban poor persisted into the twentieth century when the policy of removal bore tragic results.[108]

The "grand revolution of progress" proclaimed with Monterey's victorious reincorporation may not have delivered benefits to all segments of the population, but it certainly signified a thoroughgoing transformation in economic organization and political power. Local business and government had taken control of their fate and then cast it with the interests of railroad capital and its subsidiary land and development company. In the process, Montereyans arrived at a new understanding of themselves and their history. The town that engaged the likes of Richard Henry Dana and Robert Louis Stevenson now trumpeted a story of cosmopolitan connections and a prepossessing past. History was becoming Monterey's most valuable asset.

MAKING LOCAL HISTORY

In the late nineteenth century, Monterey's public history was thoroughly reconstructed as a local story expressed in a variety of civic and creative forms. The prerequisite for having a story is having an audience, something Monterey qua Monterey lacked until the 1880s. Its former notoriety derived from the mission or political system of which Monterey happened to be the headquarters. Now, as the "old city" attracted investors, visitors, and interests from abroad, a uniquely local story was called forth. One source of the new history was the local press, which ran regular features on Monterey's romantic Spanish past, its mission, or Sloat's triumphant arrival—events that conferred historical importance and supported promotional efforts. Local history was also produced in the commemorative activities of civic associations: churches, lodges, patriotic groups, and business associations. A new form of commercial publishing offered elegantly bound volumes combining local history and biography. Known as "mug books," these county histories were prepared by urban firms by patching together standard versions of California history with county-specific material, local data (from climate to agricultural production), and short biographies of leading citizens. The books were sold by subscription, sometimes with previous agreement that the subscriber would be profiled in the biographical section. Finally, we have the beginnings of a local artistic movement of painters and writers who portrayed the area in their creative works. As the accumulation of these varied representations of the region's character combined with promotional efforts of the civic associations, a public history took shape—a portrait of Monterey inscribed in handbooks, literature, painting, architecture, and the changing spatial form of community and environs.

General histories of California also flourished in the late nineteenth century, providing the background and often the narrative tone for local works. Central to this genre was Franklin Tuthill's *The History of California* published by H. H. Bancroft & Company of San Francisco in 1866, the first survey since Forbes's work appeared in England twenty-seven years earlier and the beginning of a homegrown history industry that Tuthill's publisher would bring to fruition. Tuthill was a New York physician who took up a career in journalism with the San Francisco *Bulletin* and pursued his "literary interests" at night. The volume contains six hundred fifty authoritative pages reaching from the early Pacific voyages and "discovery" to the U.S. Land Commission and state politics. Tuthill acknowledges a debt to Forbes and Miguel Venegas, the Jesuit historian of Baja California, although most of his sources are documentary, including ships' records, Spanish and Mexican archives, official reports, congressional papers, and "oral evidence of natives and early immigrants." Palóu's *Life* is cited along with high praise for Father Serra's "wonderful faculty for attaching to himself the affections of the natives . . . to charm them into a new mode of life." Native Americans, however, were beneath contempt, too "cowardly" to resist domination (which he, like Forbes, claims would have inspired respect). "Of all wretchedly debased and utterly brutal beings, the Indians of California were the farthest fallen below the average Indian type." His account of Mexican rule and California rebellion is informed but skewed in a manner that gives foreigners credit for effective action. Californios had a "characteristic dread of all changes, except in the one item of governors [perhaps because they] were dashing and careless, fond of fandangoes, always ready for a dance." Frémont is made the hero of the American conquest, although California was ready to "drop from the impotent hand of the sick man, Mexico, into the palm of the United American States." In the end, Tuthill develops further the position of Dana and Forbes, arguing that Californios were inherently incapable of developing the country and that superior Americans were rightful masters.[109]

Bancroft's seven-volume *History of California* that appeared between 1884 and 1890, from which I have quoted liberally, was a very different historiographic endeavor—a detailed compendium of its subject that resembles a primary source more than a synthetic history. Bancroft began his career as a bookseller, eventually making his fortune as the largest distributor of books and stationery on the West Coast. A high school dropout, he became an institution in western history by acquiring an enormous collection of official documents and private papers, many at auctions in Europe, relating to California and the west, and then hiring a research and editorial staff that cataloged the collection and, in the end, actually wrote many of the volumes attributed to the publisher. When reading Bancroft we are more likely to be reading Henry Oak, William Nemos, or Frances Fuller Victor—the only woman on the staff. The failure to credit these and other essential staff writers was an ethical lapse by the driving entrepreneur. Yet, whatever the mix of authorial and editorial responsibility, reading these prolix volumes evokes awe, respect, satisfaction, occasional tedium, and no small amount of humor. Opinions are freely aired, sacred cows lampooned (both Serra and Frémont are subjects of heavy satire), and decent men and women unsentimentally acknowledged (another volume, *California Pastoral*, contained the pioneering chapter "Woman and Her Sphere").[110]

Yet in other ways Bancroft reinforced the American-centered construction of California's past typical in the work of his predecessors. Comparative study of civilizations, Bancroft claimed, demonstrated the scientific truth of social evolution with all the certainty of Darwin's evolution of the species. California history spanned the evolutionary continuum as it moved from aboriginal to Spanish, Mexican, and American society.

Half-way between savagism and civilization, California's pastoral days swept by, midst the dreamy reveries of a race half-way between the proud Castilian and the lowly root-digger. . . . This California country suited the Mexican settler, with his inherent indolence, relieved only by slow, spasmodic energy. . . . Spoiled partly by bountiful nature [the man] yielded his best efforts to profitless pursuits, heedless of the morrow [while] the women do all the work and rear the family [although] the character of the Californian was what in the main would be called good—mild, well-meaning enough, though not very pronounced, kind-hearted and liberal.[111]

These stereotypes, to be sure, appear in one ancillary book, while Bancroft's actual history provides detailed analyses of political movements and the thriving export economy—developments hardly consistent with indolence. Part of the contradiction lay in Bancroft's merchandising schemes intended to hook readers on continuing subscriptions with breezy sequels to the history. Whatever the explanation, in serious and popular treatments Bancroft helped to institutionalize an evolutionary narrative that simultaneously patronized and romanticized California's Hispanic past. As Bancroft's work, and that of Theodore Hittell (his only serious competitor whom he also published), established the interpretive standard, local historians drew on them for legitimacy.

This thematic trickle-down is illustrated in the work of Monterey historians and writers. Excited by the promise of railroad development, the *Monterey Herald* publishers Emmet Curtis and W. H. Walton issued *The Hand Book of Monterey and Vicinity*, billed as "a complete guide book for tourists, campers, and visitors." The compact paperback book provided a fund of information, from a business directory to meteorological data, and descriptions of interesting local places such as Carmel Valley and Mission, Pacific Grove Retreat, Chinese Colony, Cypress Point, and surrounding towns. Curtis provided a poem titled "Monterey" on the inscription page that likened the city to Sleeping Beauty, "her passions wrapped in slumber" until the "fairy Prince of Progress" frees her to realize her destiny as "a queen among the cities that adorn our golden coast." The historical sketch that follows draws heavily on Tuthill and shares his bias, crediting Alvarado's revolution to American riflemen and lauding Sloat's conquest as a glorious act of liberation. From the American annexation in 1846 until the railroad in 1874, Monterey experienced its lowest ebb: "Business of every description was almost stagnant. . . . She rested in peaceful somnolence—a veritable land of lotus eaters. . . . The sleepy hollow of California." But the railroad promised "great improvements" based on "all the natural advantages for becom-

ing one of the leading watering places and summer resorts"—advantages
such as the old town, Carmel Mission, the shoreline and lighthouse at
Point Pinos.

This basic narrative, moving in stages from aboriginal darkness and
Franciscan charity to Hispanic indolence, necessary conquest, and American progress, is repeated in a spate of newspaper features that provide
the prehistory of Monterey's transformation into a world-famous seaside resort. The new Monterey story has no place for Native Americans,
Spanish officials, Californio rebels, American squatters, or a diverse working class. Monterey's romantic past is commodified for the visitor and
increasingly accepted by townspeople.

The new history was celebrated in a variety of representational forms
beyond the print media. Commemorative events began in the 1870s with
the Firemen's Ball in recognition of the Serra landing 105 years earlier.[112]
Robert Louis Stevenson wrote a short piece for the local paper describing the annual celebration of San Carlos Day at Carmel Mission, then
in ruins. Stevenson's lament about the state of collapse into which the
old mission headquarters had fallen may have spurred a preservationist
effort. In the following year, a celebration of the mission's foundation
noted that parish priest Father Casanova had begun a fund-raising drive
to save the church.[113] The priest's efforts met with success, attracting support not only for mission reconstruction but also for a monument to Father Junípero Serra donated by Mrs. Leland Stanford. The statue of Serra
was erected at the site of his landing and first mass on the hillside overlooking Monterey Bay. Dedication of the monument in June 1891 drew
a crowd of five thousand, many coming by train from San Francisco, a
military band, several California heritage groups, church representatives,
and a local judge who informed the audience, "verily shall this place be
a spot for the pilgrimage for all nations."[114]

In the 1890s there was much to commemorate in the secular arena as
well. A group of Mexican-American War veterans headed by Edwin Sherman of Oakland proposed a monument to Commodore Sloat on the occasion of the fiftieth anniversary of the conquest of California. Sloat's
monument would share the same bay outlook with Serra but dominate
the humble padre's likeness with a massive pyramid erected at the top
of the hill. Just as the organizers were making headway on a bill to provide congressional funding, scandal threatened the project when organizers discovered Bancroft's less than complimentary discussion of Sloat's
indecision and near-dismissal prior to the invasion. The veterans fought
back, denouncing Bancroft and his chief of staff, Henry Oak, and mar-

shaling other evidence from military records and supporters that testified to Sloat's heroism. A four-day California Jubilee in July 1896, spanning the Fourth and the landing date of the seventh, was planned by Monterey's Native Daughters of the Golden West and local businessmen at which the cornerstone of the Sloat monument would be laid. Public opinion sided with the patriotic mobilization over Bancroft's libel. A cast of military men graced the ceremonies, although women representing various heritage groups gave most of the speeches. "The people of Monterey themselves prepared for the occasion as they never did before. The town was beautifully, if not expensively, decorated. . . . Alvarado Street was crowded with an expectant throng."[115] Despite the Jubilee's success, the Sloat monument ran into funding problems and delays lasting until the San Francisco earthquake of 1906 when a bronze-cast eagle that would have topped the pyramid was destroyed. Shortly thereafter the final design was completed with a more modest, if ferocious-looking, concrete eagle topping the monument. Both Serra's statue and Sloat's pyramid now looked over the bay, projecting an eclectic and revered historical presence over Monterey and Pacific Grove.

Monterey's public history was embodied in generous contributions from the arts—literary, graphic, and architectural representations of the region that shared with the print media a blend of fact and imagination. A group of artists congregated at the Bohemian Club restaurant of Jules Simoneau, Stevenson's friend and host during his months in Monterey. Among the painters attracted to Simoneau's table were fellow Frenchmen Jules Tavernier, who established a local studio, and Leon Trousset, who had relatives at nearby Moss Landing. Many European artists painted the western United States as they had come to expect it—large landscapes, romanticized pastoral settings, oceans and mountains. Trousset's uncommon and striking treatment of a historical subject portrays Father Serra's landing with the padre president celebrating Pentecostal mass in an idyllic setting. The secular world is arranged before him, on their knees and in ranks according to their importance: governor and lieutenants in the center, soldiers in the front lines, a few civilians and Christian Indians on the edges, and two curious heathens looking on from the forest. The church and subservient state lend order to a remarkably tidy social landscape. The Spanish conquest is a natural event, the spiritual union of pastoral setting and social order. It is a world without church-state conflict, coerced labor, disease, Indian resistance, and commercial exploitation.

Local history was also expressed in architectural works that popu-

20. *Father Serra Celebrates Mass at Monterey,* by Leon Trousset, ca. 1870.
Trousset was one of a small colony of artists who came to Monterey in the late
nineteenth century and congregated around Jules Simoneau's restaurant. European artists contributed significantly to a romanticized portrait of the colonial
period. (Courtesy of the California Historical Society, X68-56-1-2, FN-31586)

larized Monterey's contribution to California design. Ironically, the
Monterey Colonial–style house, featuring two-story balcony overhangs
and generally thought to derive from Spanish manorial tradition, was
actually the invention of Thomas Larkin in the 1830s. The architectural
style was popular among American immigrants, who frequently gave
Spanish names to their houses and called them "adobes" (authentic Mexican adobes were of a much earthier appearance). As the architectural
historian Harold Kirker explains, "Far from representing the pastoral
life of the rancho, the Monterey Colonial house represents the first important victory in the inevitable struggle between the mutually antago-
nistic Spanish-Mexican and American cultures."[116] In the late nineteenth
century a Mission Revival movement captured California architecture.
Public buildings such as the Custom House and Colton Hall were restored and new structures built emulating the imposing Monterey Colonial. The "old Spanish capital" was artfully reproduced in more picturesque style with the town's new commercial development.

The most sustained literary treatment of Monterey subject matter in the late nineteenth century was the work of the novelist Gertrude Atherton. Born Gertrude Hunt in 1857, the San Francisco native was married in her late teens to George Atherton. George was the son of Faxon Dean Atherton, a Yankee trader in the hide and tallow business who rose from clerk in Chile to land baron in California. At one time, Gertrude's father-in-law was the wealthiest landowner on the Monterey County tax rolls, although the family lived in San Mateo. Despite affluent support, Gertrude's marriage was dismal. George was phlegmatic, unsure of what to do with his life, while Gertrude was independent and energetic. She took up writing in the interests of self-expression, her financial security assured, while George returned to South America and died of an illness. On her own as a writer, Gertrude soon found her literary purpose, to be a "correct historian." She approached the novel as "a memoir of contemporary life in the form of fiction."[117] As a native Californian experienced in elite-family business and political affairs, she incorporated local history into her novels not simply as backdrop but as the "contemporary life" she intended to examine. In preparation for a novel, she would take up residence in a place (Monterey or Santa Barbara, for example), study its history, and develop a circle of informants among older residents, particularly women.

> We went first to Monterey, then a far more picturesque town than now, for fashion had not discovered it and many of the old adobe houses, built in the early days of the century before the American conquest, were standing. . . . Pursuing a plan I had formed, I roamed about until I saw a house that looked moderately comfortable, a two-story adobe with a balcony, walked in, and asked the large dark bearded relic to take us as boarders. The old lady had married an American, but she belonged to one of the best-known of the Spanish (or Mexican) families, and as I soon persuaded her to talk, she gave me much information of the manners and customs and personalities of the days when California was a Department of Mexico.[118]

Atherton's first novel drew on her experience of a squatter rebellion on her father-in-law's forty-five-thousand acre ranch in southern Monterey County near Mission San Antonio. In *Los Cerritos: A Romance of Modern Times,* a mixed group of Hispanic and American squatters have settled on an unoccupied land grant that has recently been purchased by a San Francisco millionaire (just as the elder Atherton acquired his Rancho Milpitas). The squatters refuse eviction, claim the land belongs to the government, organize under the leadership of the cunning vaquero Castro, and present owner Tremaine with a threatening proclamation in "an almost unintelligible jargon of Spanish and English." The San Fran-

cisco millionaire is unimpressed and calmly faces down sixty armed squatters attempting to invade the hacienda. "The squatters, poor wretches,
were intimidated by the determination and contempt of Tremaine and
his men, and stood back like whipped curs." Tremaine has meanwhile
fallen in love with Carmelita, a local teenager and "child of nature" determined to save a redwood forest in the area. Tremaine decides not only
to help her save the redwoods but also to divide his land among the settlers in fifty-acre farms "to such applicants as investigation proves are
worthy." But not before offering some avuncular thoughts on the affair
to the acquiescing local priest: "There will never be a concerted movement. . . . [W]e rich men hold our wealth because the poor man fosters
the conditions which enable us to do so. Why does he foster them? Because he intends to be a rich man himself, some day, and if he destroyed
the conditions he would destroy his own hopes." In search of meaning
beyond the settlers' petty concerns, Carmelita persuades her lover to
abandon society for the redwoods. Later Atherton would acknowledge,
"[The novel] did not amount to much, but I wrote it with a certain fer-
vor as it dealt with the wrongs of helpless squatters at the mercy of the
rich."[119]

Atherton's historically informed treatment of Mexican California in
The Doomswoman reflects similar ethnocentric and patrimonial themes.
She knew the writings of Hittel and Bancroft and incorporated their dis-
paraging views of Mexican character and society. Her heroine, Chonita
Iturbi y Moncada, is the self-described doomswoman—beautiful, white-
skinned, iron-willed, but trapped in a web of elite-family intrigue and
languid associates. Although their families are divided by some ancient
feud, she is attracted to Don Diego Estenega because "he is tall and
straight and very strong, not so indolent as most of our men. They call
him the American because he moves so quickly and gets so cross when
people do not think fast enough." The story unfolds in Monterey of the
1840s where dances at the Custom House and dinner parties at the home
of Governor Alvarado provide distraction from the impending demise
of the Californio way of life. But Estenega sees it coming, welcomes it,
and shares his views with the understanding governor.

> [I]n American occupation lies the hope of California. What have we done with
> it in our seventy years of occupation? Built a few missions, which are rotting,
> terrorized or cajoled a few thousand worthless Indians into civilized imbecil-
> ity, and raised a respectable number of horses and cattle. . . . The women of
> California are admirable in every way—chaste, strong of character, indus-
> trious, devoted wives and mothers, born with sufficient capacity for small

pleasures. But what of our men? Idle, thriftless, unambitious, too lazy to walk across the street, but with a horse for every step, sleeping all day in a hammock, gambling and drinking all night. Our women will marry Americans [and then] a race will be born worthy of California.[120]

Atherton's work was intimately bound up with her time and social position. She was close to the events she described and understood them as many other influential actors did at the time. During her long and successful career, Atherton's novels were read as reliable portraits of early California society. She helped to make history in her art, and her art bore strong similarities to the important histories of the period. We read Atherton with profit today, not for any special insight into squatter movements or Californio society, but for what she helped to create—the late-nineteenth-century understanding of California history and the ideological basis for remaking that history in the moment. As Kevin Starr notes, "One returns to her novels not for accomplished art, but for the record. California would have to await the fiction of John Steinbeck to receive a comparably integrated coverage."[121]

Standing back from the varied contributions to Monterey's public history, a distinctive new interpretation emerges in the late nineteenth century: a narrative of American progress. In general, the Franciscan missionaries are admired as the founders of California at Monterey. Indians disappear from historical chronology except perhaps as backdrop. A few critics believed the missionaries were slave masters, but most commentators considered them merely naive. Their missionary communities were utopian, dedicated to civilizing incorrigible natives in the face of opposition from their own government. Following secularization, Mexican California was chaotic and directionless. The men, we hear over and over, are "indolent" and the women long-suffering. In a gendered reading of the dilemma, male Californios are incapable of arousing the full passion and possibility of the region's female nature. But Americans are up to the manly task. They inspire progress and realize all of the state's dormant potential. Indeed, progress is evident in the 1880s, manifest in railroads, property development, business activity, national recognition, and, perhaps above all, status. Monterey is the site of a world-famous watering hole and an impressive history inscribed on the landscape of town, mission, and shoreline monuments.

The new history is more developed than previously, expressed in a greater variety of forms and products, more univocal, less challenged by oppositional narratives, and more locally rooted, albeit with derivations from general sources. The narrative of American progress is closely tied to collective action. The new story is developed in the context of public action intended to control the disorderly conduct of Mexican Californios, the threat of Chinese immigration, and the urban blight presented by the fishing industry and the poor. Actions aimed at eliminating these social problems are the logical complement of self-congratulatory celebrations of the American conquest, the hotel and railroad, or the progressive development of town and suburb. In this two-way dialogue, the new narrative informs and explains action. Yet we still confront the question of how this new history was constructed and how it relates to the earlier narratives that were equally compelling in their time.

The answer begins with broad historical changes, especially the conquest and annexation of California by the United States. The geopolitical shift calls for historical reorientation in conventional histories that take the nation-state as the unit of analysis and plot national trajectories. California is resituated in the unfolding American narrative, no longer a product of Mexican rule except insofar as Mexico "lost" (or never rightly possessed) territory in the wake of manifest destiny. Earlier narratives centered on church or colonial historical development have no place in this trajectory. The point now is not what the missionaries and Mexican civil authorities actually did but how their failings led inexorably to subordination under the naturally expanding American republic. Winners in the imperial game found ample reason to explain and justify their actions—metaphysical notions such as manifest destiny in tandem with social and economic ideas about liberating the subject population, developing the natural resources, and enlightening the culture.

But these are general changes and the answer we want is palpable, local. In fact, a number of concrete interests shaped the new history. Americans brought to California a vastly more commercial society, one that commodified property and use rights in a fashion that conflicted with the moral economy of Spanish tradition. The acquisition, concentration, legalization, and exploitation of property orchestrated a great deal of local history during this period. Conflict centered on the appropriation of common lands for exclusionary use. As the dust of squatter struggle and the incorporation fight settled, a new image of Monterey was built on a reconfiguration of land use and ownership. Key to the change was the Southern Pacific Railroad, its Pacific Improvement land company, and its highly publicized Hotel Del Monte. The P.I. Co. supported and opened the door of town and suburban development. A great deal of the new history was generated at this intersection of interests. County "mug books" sold by subscription, like Bancroft's weighty tomes, were commercially marketed histories. Potted versions of local history were produced "for tourists, campers, and visitors," providing an account of the Del Monte's surroundings and an explanation of the sites that would interest visitors from the outside world. Local developers of the new suburbs brought groups to the Del Monte for a civic welcome and tour. The hotel, of course, offered the shoreline (carriage) drive via the Del Monte Forest to Carmel Mission (later the Seventeen Mile Drive) for the purposes of both entertainment and real estate promotion. All of these activities were grist for the local newspaper mill that published and republished items of historical interest.

The mission and its history were refurbished owing to the intersection of P.I. Co. interests and the local clergy's ambition to regain some of the importance once attached to Carmel and Monterey as the Catholic Plymouth Rock. "An effort is being made to preserve the old Mission San Carlos at Carmelo. . . . The priest at Monterey, Father Casanova, Major Hammond, of the Southern Pacific Railway, with others, have been appointed upon a committee to seek assistance in this matter."[122]

Convergent interests in the narrative of American progress multiplied as the town found a new purpose in development. Like the church, civic and patriotic groups realized their own psychic income from building a community. Women found an accessible avenue for citizen participation in groups such as the Catholic Ladies Aid Society, Native Daughters of the American West, lodge auxiliaries, and commemorative events committees. Even David Jacks, once he had paid his overdue city property taxes, was brought on board as president of the new Progressive Association, devoted to projects of civic improvement. In 1901 President William McKinley visited Monterey, lodged at the Hotel Del Monte, and declared, "This is indeed historic ground. This quaint old town of toil and traffic, of traditions and history, is most interesting to your countrymen generally, and it is especially interesting to me."[123]

That was what they had been striving to realize, their aspiration and reward. They were a place, esteemed in the eyes of the country, historic ground.

THE MYSTERY OF THE DEL MONTE FIRE
AND OTHER UNTOLD STORIES

Late in the evening of April 1, 1887, the luxurious Hotel Del Monte broke out in flames. At the sound of the fire alarm around 11:00 P.M., two hundred seventy-five guests were evacuated, some joining the hotel staff

21.   President McKinley's Visit to Monterey, 1901. The president's visit was an unprecedented honor for the small town. McKinley's recognition of Monterey as "historic ground" confirmed the ambitions of local business and civic elites. (Courtesy of the Monterey Public Library, Local History Collection)

and the Monterey Fire Department in an all-night battle against the consuming flames. By morning, exhausted, sodden, and sooty volunteers surveyed a scene of complete waste. Only chimneys and beams rose from the smoldering foundation of the queen of American watering places.

As investigators assembled the evidence, it became apparent that the fire was the work of one or more arsonists. The blaze originated on the basement floor directly below the lobby and somewhere in the vicinity of the "circulating room" (providing access to water and gas pipes), an ice closet, and the (staff) "China dining room"—none of them the likely source of an accidental fire. More incriminating, firefighting efforts were hampered because someone had closed a valve in the water system located in the gardens, not once but three times, causing a loss of pressure to the fire hoses. In addition to these physical suggestions of arson, there were pointed suspicions. As it happened, April 1 was the date of a change in hotel management involving the dismissal of E. T. M. Simmons, longtime clerk promoted to hotel manager during the past year, and his replacement by original manager George Schoenwald on the orders of the P.I. Co. Schoenwald accused Simmons of arson, alleging to police that his motive was revenge for dismissal. Schoenwald supported his suspicions with claims that Simmons needed money to support a style of high living (which further assumed the fire was cover for robbery of the hotel safe), was seen moving about hotel corridors before the fire alarm, and had a bottle of turpentine in his quarters that could have been used to start the fire. Obvious ill will between the two managers prompted these suspicions.

On the strength of Schoenwald's denunciation and P.I. Co. pressure for decisive action, Simmons was arrested, charged with arson, and tried in June at the County Court House in Salinas. Two weeks of testimony from one hundred fifty witnesses demonstrated to nearly everyone's satisfaction that there was no case against Simmons. Hotel employees accounted for his whereabouts up to the sound of the fire alarm, when he was seen salvaging the contents of the safe (which were intact) and assisting the fire brigade. The turpentine had been prescribed by a local physician for his daughter's asthma and the limit of his high living involved purchase of a Pacific Grove lot that he could well afford on his comfortable salary of $200 a month. After the innocent verdict, Simmons countersued the P.I. Co. for $100,000 in damages and won the case but was awarded only court costs of $741.

If Simmons was not the arsonist, who was? Local law enforcement never answered the question. Indeed, the malicious act and bad publicity were soon silenced as the hotel was rebuilt on an even grander scale and promoted anew in extravagant tones. Yet behind the facade of gracious living, trouble continued to plague the Del Monte. The events of April 1887 alone suggest tensions among the staff. Trial testimony indicated that Simmons was well liked, that others including two chambermaids were dismissed at the same time, and that Schoenwald was an abrasive man who, with the assistance of his wife, dealt abruptly with employees. Some, like the stableman, reported previous "unpleasantries." The hotel employed several hundred workers, from bookkeepers and front office staff to housekeepers and chambermaids as well as scores of Chinese gardeners and kitchen workers. The fire was clearly an inside job and probably a collaborative effort judging from coordinated action in the basement and garden water system. If some conspiracy of hotel workers was responsible, then who might they be? Of course, we do not know for sure. Yet one hypothesis incorporates the presumption of several arsonists (with some bond of mutual trust), who were likely to have had a grievance associated with the change of management, who had privileged access to the China dining room and hotel gardens, and who could move about unremarked (shutting valves) during the commotion. The arsonists were probably hotel workers, perhaps Chinese workers.[124]

The hypothesis makes sense in light of historical precedents, labor relations, and intergroup sentiments. Protest arson was a common practice in nineteenth-century California. The Del Monte experienced unexplained fires before and after April 1887. During the previous year, specific conflicts arose in Monterey where the P.I. Co. purchased and leased properties in Chinatown through a community agent. "There is a great deal of jealousy and ill-feeling existing among Chinese just now, which had already led to several incendiary fires. . . . The trouble grew out [of] the collection of rents there by the P.I. Co. through one Choy, who appears to be a sort of head man in the town, but who they think divides up the rent collections with the P.I. Co."[125]

The Chinese working class suffered varied forms of mistreatment in Monterey, ranging from the harassment of peddlers and laundries to evictions. We do not know about labor conflicts involving Chinese at the Del Monte before the fire, but we might suspect their presence given the general local pattern. That inference is supported by a strike of Chinese workers two years later at the El Carmelo, a hotel built in Carmel and managed by the P.I. Co. The incident speaks to labor relations that were arguably similar to those prevailing at the troubled Del Monte. "When the guests at the El Carmelo sat down at breakfast Monday morning they found the course of events interrupted by the refusal of the waiters to serve Dr. Leonard because he had commented upon the character of the immigration pouring into the Golden Gate. The guests were convinced by this miserable manifestation of low spite that the Doctor was fully justified in his strictures. . . . Mr. Seely [the manager] discharged the strikers at once but as the guests were hungry had to placate the strikers by a partial yielding to their contemptible demands."[126]

Someone, and more likely some small group of solidary protesters, fired the Hotel Del Monte in April 1887. My purpose is neither to condemn the agents as lawbreakers nor to romanticize them as avengers. Rather, it is to understand the historical circumstances in which protest arson flourished. Labor and ethnic relations were hostile. The combination of these conditions with precipitous dismissals and the reintroduction of an onerous management may explain the otherwise mysterious fire. In any case, arson by hotel workers, perhaps Chinese workers, is a more plausible hypothesis than any offered at the time. It is a hypothesis, moreover, that opens up the world of working-class and ethnic groups to examination and understanding. For that reason alone it is an avenue of inquiry preferable to the larger conspiracy of silence about these conflicts in the narrative of American progress.

The Del Monte fire is one dramatic example of history that was silenced—evidence of a pattern of group conflict that few had an interest in reporting and many preferred to suppress. Late-nineteenth-century local history, unlike other periods, was characterized by a relatively unanimous dominant voice. A number of groups on the rise shared a material interest and a genuine belief in the progressive nature of the American conquest and property regime. Nevertheless, there were muted voices of dissent. Squatters, bandits, paisanos, Chinese workers, and shantytown residents all spoke in deeds. A few others spoke in Spanish, or tried to, about an alternative historical narrative.

In 1886 the old general Mariano Guadalupe Vallejo was invited to address Monterey's celebration of the fortieth anniversary of the Sloat landing. The invitation was gracious, stating that no one wished to gloat over Mexico's defeat or boast of American triumphs, but to commemorate "three epochs of history" in the symbolic raising and lowering of the Spanish, Mexican, and U.S. flags. Vallejo accepted the literal spirit of the invitation. Taking the podium before a large crowd at the Custom House, close to his birthplace seventy-eight years earlier, the general proposed to read his address as prepared in Spanish. But too few in the audience understood the language, so Vallejo translated as he spoke. With some of the force of his oration already compromised, he then delivered a history of California and Monterey that began with Columbus and Cortés, who opened the continent, carried on with Portolá, who brought Spain to California (Serra never impressed Vallejo and the liberal Californios), credited Hidalgo with the revolutionary independence of Mexico and California, and came forward to the American conquest, which he characterized mainly in the shabby treatment accorded him by Frémont and Larkin at the time.[127] Apart from the personal references, Vallejo's point was to place California in a chronological and cultural stream that ran opposite to the triumphant American narrative. That may have been clear to some of his listeners, but most understood events differently as they celebrated the liberation and progress wrought by Americans in California. As Rosaura Sánchez shows in a perceptive analysis of the *testimonios* given to Bancroft's staff by the old Californios, Mexican California produced a "proto-nationalist" account of those times that survivors perpetuated (and altered in memory) but never published.[128] The accounts of Vallejo and his compatriots languished in Bancroft's library. The Californio narrative had no constituency or institutional sponsorship. No organization supported Vallejo or Alvarado or María Ord or María Amparo Ruiz de Burton. No one encouraged them to write their histories or offered to publish their work in the way the Catholic Church sponsored Palóu. Otherwise, history might have been different. But it was not, then.

CONCLUSION

The American conquest in 1846 led to a thorough transformation of California society and its history as contemporaries understood it. The revolution began on the land where entrepreneurial investors used their skill and political influence to engross large properties at the expense of Californio grantees, common lands, and less adept speculators. The emerging regime of landownership and use was challenged by customary commons users, squatters, and disaffected outlaws. If the new property elites tended to prevail in struggles over land, they were dependent for labor on a growing and ethnically diverse working class. Like squatters, the laboring poor suffered ill treatment but persevered in their ethnic communities and even enjoyed a measure of social mobility. Indeed, the town finally began to prosper as a result of railroad investment and a new middle class in local commerce and services catering to the large working population.

Yet growth was constrained by weak government and the monopolistic control of city land. Under these conditions, a successful political movement was mobilized by business and civic groups to reincorporate the city, raise tax revenue for needed services and infrastructure, enter into an alliance with railroad capital, and clear the downtown of unsightly low-income neighborhoods. Here, too, coercive measures met with resistance from the poor, including, evidently, protest arson.

Monterey's "revolution of progress" was celebrated in a variety of published chronicles, artistic works, and commemorative events that, taken together, constituted a new public history—a story of American progress over the last half century that relegated the Hispanic past to a place of quaint origins now on display to visitors. The occasional dissenting voices of paisano recusants or veteran Californios like Vallejo were easily ignored. The narrative of American progress enjoyed a vigor derived from the collective action in which it emerged and the local achievements it convincingly explained.

FIVE

Industry and Community

An Irishman must think like that, I daresay. We feel in
England that we have treated you rather unfairly. It seems
history is to blame.

James Joyce, *Ulysses*

THE ODOR OF PROSPERITY

In *Tortilla Flat,* John Steinbeck remarks, "[T]here is a changeless quality about Monterey. Nearly every day in the morning the sun shines in
the windows on the west side of the streets; and, in the afternoons, on
the east side of the streets. Every day the red bus clangs back and forth
between Monterey and Pacific Grove. Every day the canneries send a stink
of reducing fish into the air." If not exactly changeless, the potent odor
of fish processing was a nuisance of long standing. At the turn of the
twentieth century, local residents offended by squid drying in the Chinese waterfront village urged the city council to ban the practice. During the early decades of the century, an extensive industry developed in
Monterey devoted to fishing, canning, and reduction (to fish meal and
oil) of sardines. The new plants, particularly the reduction process, were
far more aromatic than their Asian predecessors. As industry expanded
with the stimulus of wartime demand and the addition of reduction facilities to the initial canneries, the stench grew proportionately. By 1917
waterfront property owners in New Monterey (where the plants were
proliferating) and around the harbor (where they began) were demanding that city officials put a stop to air and water pollution.

The controversy came to a head in 1917 when the Western California Fisheries Company requested a city lease to waterfront property for
a new plant next to the original Booth Cannery on the harbor. Opposition was prompt and vigorous, led by the Pacific Improvement Company,

which owned extensive coastal real estate and the famous Hotel Del
Monte. At a prophetic meeting of the city council, a company representative "protested against the project [and] declared that the Hotel Del
Monte was Monterey's greatest asset—in fact greater than any other two
or three institutions in Monterey. He dwelt at length upon what the company spent here and then stated that any further encroachment of the
canneries toward the Hotel Del Monte would drive the hotel away from
this place where it has been established for forty years." A property owner
on Alvarado Street, Monterey's main artery, which terminated at the harbor, objected to the new cannery "on the ground that it would raise a
great deal of evil smell." The newspaper noted, "[T]his smell question
seemed to be the one strong feature [of the protest]." Then something
unprecedented happened. T. A. Work, a rising star in local business, took
the floor, complimented the P.I. Co. for its many contributions to the community, "but at the same time held that all the benefits of the presence
of the Hotel Del Monte could not begin to compare with what the canneries were bringing."[1] The fishing industry was now Monterey's greatest asset. The perceptive Mr. Work announced a new era, a period of
industrial prosperity that would alter substantially the structure of community power and the sympathies of local culture.

The Pacific Improvement Company and its allies in real estate were
unbowed. Property interests continued to wield influence, if no longer
the decisive power they exercised in the late nineteenth century. But they
were strong enough to defeat the harbor lease in 1917, confine industrial expansion to New Monterey as the city council itself favored, and
pass a local ordinance in 1918 (No. 106) making it unlawful to permit
the discharge within city limits of "any unwholesome, offensive, dis-
agreeable, nauseous, or obnoxious smell, odors or gases." The odor ordinance had little effect. Complaints continued, and the polluting practices of industry went unrestrained. A Monterey fisherman, Sal Colletto,
who had worked as a fish cutter in the canneries when he was a young
man, recalls, "[T]he cutting tables had holes where the heads of the fish
were thrown in the bay, to be washed up on the beaches, and the fish
heads underneath the canneries would be a foot risk [pedestrian hazard]
all along cannery row. The heads and grease from the fish would pile up
on the beach from the Custom House all the way to Seaside. The City
of Monterey did not do anything about it because it was during the
war years and that was the main industry that sustained the economy
of the city."[2]

The odor controversy returned periodically throughout the 1920s and

1930s, usually in the fall when reduction plants were at peak production. In October 1926 S. F. B. Morse, nephew of the inventor Samuel F. B. Morse and president of Del Monte Properties, which succeeded the P.I. Co., addressed a broadside at "weak and inefficient" city officials. The occasion was revealing. "Next week there will be 1400 of the most prominent real estate men of the United States on the Monterey Peninsula. They will be greeted with the smell of dead fish."[3] Morse's indictment was promptly disputed by the mayor and the city manager who claimed they were in the midst of ameliorative action, including the appointment of a San Francisco chemist who would study the problem and recommend necessary changes. The continuing clout of real estate interests is suggested by an announcement from the cannery owners pledging to limit their operations while the state realtors' convention was in session and "to eliminate all odors during that time." Morse published an apology for his strong language and underestimation of city concern, but the mayor was not mollified. The mayor was on top of the problem, and he bristled that the "communication from S. F. B. Morse . . . had no bearing on the canners' action."[4]

Although some of the plants installed deodorizing equipment, the stench returned during the 1928 season with such force that the city issued warrants charging violation of Ordinance 106, a misdemeanor punishable by ninety days in the county jail and/or a $300 fine. Max Schaefer, plant superintendent of the Monterey Fish Products Company, was arrested by the keen-nosed "detection squad," composed of police, the city's cannery inspector, and an employee of Del Monte Properties, "which bore down on the reduction plants." The city made it clear that this was only the first step in its campaign to eliminate cannery odors. The get-tough policy involved creation of a "permanent smelling committee . . . composed of representative citizens of the community on call at all times to trace objectionable odors and testify against reduction and canning plants held responsible for them."[5]

Yet even the permanent smelling committee made little headway against the incorrigible stench. Indeed, it appears that everyone save the hotel owners had accepted seasonal pungency as the cost of industrial prosperity. In 1929 a variety of hotels complained that visitors were leaving in droves, causing them financial harm. "The Hotel Del Monte suffers a considerable loss every year due to the terrible odor."[6] A new city ordinance made permits to operate reduction plants contingent on installation of odor abatement equipment, and the county health department was put on inspection duty. But the smell continued.[7] Del Monte

Properties (which now owned the hotel, real estate, and affiliated business enterprises) brought suit against the canners' association in 1934 and achieved a settlement with eleven firms calling for comprehensive changes in odor prevention (hoods, scrubbers, ventilators) and waste disposal (affecting the bay and seashore).[8]

If the new measures had any appreciable effect, it was lost on the City of Pacific Grove, which threatened another lawsuit against the canneries in 1937 with the support of Del Monte Properties. This time, in the midst of the depression, the campaign failed altogether. A coalition of local citizens spoke up for the industry by way of a petition asking the city to abandon odor abatement action: "The petition is reportedly sponsored by leading merchants, business men and cannery employees. W. R. Holman, owner of Holman's department store, was the first to sign the petition. . . . [T]he canning industry should be encouraged instead of discouraged."[9] The petition went on to note that of the total cannery workforce, more than six hundred lived and spent their wages in Pacific Grove. The smell seemed less offensive these days. In local parlance it was "the odor of prosperity."

COMMUNITIES: TEXTURE AND DIVISION

Monterey's twentieth century began where the nineteenth left off. A small but coherent group of boosters in business and government continued to press for economic growth, notably in commerce and real estate. A large group of working people pursued economic opportunity, particularly as it began to appear in the fishing and canning industry. Nascent industry suffused every aspect of the local community. A bona fide working class emerged in the presence of factory workers, fishermen, and support personnel, including transport operatives, maintenance workers, and dockhands who repaired boats and cleaned nets. Industry followed the grooves laid down in earlier racial and ethnic encounters, incorporating Japanese, Italian, and Chinese fishing communities as well as Asian, Hispanic, and white laboring groups. Gender developed as a fundamental division between fishermen, female housekeepers, and segregated male and female workers in the canneries. All of these divisions were mapped onto the spatial structure. Ethnic working-class communities grew up alongside the factories, around the waterfront, and between commercial zones bordered by middle-class suburbs, which, in turn, melded into elite neighborhoods. This was the moment in which new social spaces were laid down and set on the road to becoming the living places of Cannery

Row, Old and New Monterey, and the suburban villages of Pacific Grove and Carmel.

The key to these developments lies in social divisions of the late nineteenth century and their articulation with emergent industry. The 1890s witnessed repeated efforts by downtown commercial interests to clear the waterfront of unsightly low-income housing, ethnic enterprise (e.g., Chinese laundries, gaming parlors, and brothels), unsavory transients, and, generally, perceived blight in all its human and architectural forms. Typically these efforts were unsuccessful, both because people resisted removal and because the neighborhoods performed useful functions by housing low-wage labor and providing needed services. Attempts to ban squid drying at the Point Alones Chinese village on the New Monterey–Pacific Grove boundary in 1890 were unsuccessful judging from renewed efforts in 1904.[10] Chinatown in central Monterey suffered recurrent harassment at the hands of police, city license inspectors, and unruly citizens. Yon Slim Ham, the proprietor of a brothel on Washington Street, was beaten and his house set on fire by a mob of soldiers from the newly recommissioned Presidio. The *Monterey New Era* observed, "[T]he crime is a serious one, but no sympathy is being wasted on the victim, who has a most unsavory record."[11] While familiar practices of social exclusion continued into the twentieth century, they met new obstacles, not the least of which was the determination of ethnic minorities to defend their social and economic position.

CHINATOWN

Although the nativist anti-Chinese movement had subsided by the turn of the century, racism remained pervasive and found a new target in the Japanese community. Reflecting a trend throughout the West Coast, Monterey's Japanese population was growing in 1900. Modernization programs in Japan's Meiji state after 1886 dislocated segments of its rural population, and this "push" factor combined ironically with the "pull" of the U.S. labor market, which was denied an important stream of immigrant workers by the Chinese Exclusion Act of 1882. Monterey experienced a steady influx of Japanese who took up diverse pursuits, notably fishing, abalone canning, tenant farming, and contract labor. Japanese middlemen helped to recruit and place laborers. Onojiro Uchida advertised "Japanese Boys" available for domestic, garden, and ranch work.[12]

Ethnic tension developed within the expanding ranks of labor. In

March 1904 the Southern Pacific Railroad Company "discharged a number of Italians employed in the local section and put Japs in their
places."[13] In retaliation, Italian section hands dynamited a shack housing six Japanese workers, destroying the building but only bruising its
occupants. Japanese salmon fishermen were well organized and contracted with Monterey's early canneries to sell their catch at competitive
low prices. Italian fishermen, who had quarreled for years with Chinese
net fishermen, extended their rivalry to the Japanese. Lawsuits were
brought against the Japanese cannery, but the proprietors successfully defended themselves in court. Japanese-owned fishing boats were burned
in an arson fire at a waterfront warehouse, presumably the work of rival
fishermen.[14] Although the original cannery employed Japanese fishermen,
owner F. E. Booth promised concerned citizens in 1905 that he "will not
hire Japs." The local newspaper commended the policy in language implying that Japanese were not part of the community: "The employment
of Japanese in the cannery would be a distinct loss to Monterey, for the
place carries at least fifty people on the payroll during the entire season."[15]

Point Alones Chinatown on the beach in New Monterey had been an
established fishing village since the mid-nineteenth century, long before
suburban encroachment and the sale of the property by David Jacks to
the Pacific Improvement Company. The P.I. Co. continued Jacks's practice of leasing land to the Chinese as a site for their community and base
of operations for fishing, market sale, squid drying, and export business.[16]
The fishing village became an inconvenience as Pacific Grove grew from
church retreat to puritan town, working-class tracts developed in New
Monterey, and the Presidio reopened in 1902 to the Ninth U.S. Cavalry
home from the Philippine campaign. The odor of drying squid, of
course, was a problem, but more important were the neighbors' prejudice and P.I. Co. plans for a choice real estate development. In November 1905 the P.I. Co. notified the Chinese that their lease would not be
renewed and ordered them to vacate in the next three months. Echoing
popular opinion, the *Monterey New Era* considered this "one of the best
pieces of news we have heard for a long time. It not only means that an
eyesore will be removed from one of the most beautiful and picturesque
spots on the bayshore, but that a highly desirable residence tract will be
opened."[17] The company proposed a new site for the village, first at Seaside on Monterey Bay, then at Pescadero Beach on Carmel Bay. The Chinese, however, resisted eviction. When the deadline arrived three months
later, they had not budged.[18] Indeed, the village population swelled with
refugees from the San Francisco earthquake and fire in March 1906.

Calamity struck Monterey on the night of May 16 when fire consumed Point Alones Chinatown. Within hours all but sixteen of more than one hundred buildings were destroyed. Given Chinese opposition to eviction efforts, rumors of arson flourished in the aftermath. Supposition held that the company or its agents turned to incendiary means as a last resort to clear the property. The theory was nourished by looting of the charred remains at the hands of "the thugs and rough element" of Monterey and Pacific Grove—"a disgrace to decency," in the words of the Salinas press.[19] Yet there was no direct evidence of arson and, on the contrary, a history of accidental fires in the village.[20] In any case, looting, reports of bystanders cheering the fire, town pressure on the P.I. Co. to enforce eviction, and the failure of law enforcement to punish looters, all demonstrated antipathy toward the Chinese and the proximity of their communities.

Racial bigotry and economic competition were unhappy facts of local life. But they were not the only facts or, in the end, the deciding ones. Compassion for the victims and feelings of disgrace about the looting were demonstrated in popular responses to the tragedy. A relief fund was started that collected a paltry $29, but a charity baseball game organized by Pacific Grove mayor Will Jacks produced a hefty $180. The Pacific House Hotel in Monterey offered shelter to the homeless, and "ladies and gentlemen occupying fine residences offered and took Chinese women and children home with them for the night and cared for them." Mayor Jacks, son of the great land baron, took a family of six into his Pacific Grove cottage.[21]

While iniquity and grace combined in public responses to the crisis, the Chinese persevered. They erected tents on the ruins and began to rebuild. When the P.I. Co. reiterated the eviction order and fenced the property, residents breached the fences, erected makeshift shacks from scrap lumber, and hauled in new building material. From Oakland the company's general manager, A. D. Shepard, wired, "[D]o anything necessary to prevent rebuilding."[22] Local police were ordered to clear the site, although at least one refused the order and helped tear down fences. The Chinese went to court to retain possession of their lease while the company responded with a countersuit as well as an offer of the 1.5-acre Pescadero Beach site for a monthly rental of fifty cents. In the end, the Pescadero yearly lease was signed on July 3, 1906 (and renewed twice), by general manager Shepard and San Choy, who spoke for the community.[23] Activities of the fishing village were continued on a small plot leased at McAbee Beach, one quarter mile east of Point Alones. New

Monterey residents protested once more, but the P.I. Co. and the new landlord were equally satisfied with the profitable solution.

The Chinatown fire and relocation struggle convey an essential truth about ethnic relations in Monterey. The community was divided over what to do, some sympathizing with the underdog and others practicing mean-spirited segregation. For their part, the Chinese resisted energetically, in large part because their economy was based on the site convenient to local markets and transportation. In the end, they would carry on as part of a diverse community embracing Japanese, Italians, Hispanics, paisanos, and Portuguese. The P.I. Co. won the battle but under compromised terms. The episode was a public relations booby trap for the company, which could not afford the appearance of a bullying landlord to prospective real estate clients. Hence the fifty-cent rental and the subsequent decision to donate the Point Alones property for a university research facility rather than development. In sum, property interests, ethnic minorities, and the involved public all participated in a negotiated accommodation that created a particular kind of multicultural community. The result was not always amiable. Group conflict would recur, and so would generosity. The essential result was that people learned to live together in distinctive ways and locally textured communities.

TOWN AND SUBURB

Monterey welcomed the twentieth century with the élan of progressivism on the national scene, and California's energetic version of the movement focused on political and economic reform. Local groups dedicated to "building up of a greater Monterey" included the business Promotion Committee, the Board of Trade, the Merchants Association, and the newly formed Monterey Chamber of Commerce and its affiliated Monterey Civic Club, managed by women in the interests of charity, conviviality, and bourgeois solidarity.[24] The Civic Club Ball at the Hotel Del Monte in 1907 was "the swellest affair ever held on the Monterey Peninsula. . . . [O]ver 125 couples were present, and these represented polite society of Pacific Grove, Carmel, the Presidio, Monterey, and the surrounding towns."[25] The one hundred twenty-five couples, white Anglo-Americans with but one exception, included the gamut of business owners, real estate agents, developers, bankers, town officials, and the army's officer corps. If not a dominant class, this was an affluent group representing Main Street—a concerted, self-conscious faction, the locus of opposition to smelly canneries and seamy ethnics. Yet this was also a group that included progressive business leaders like T. A. Work who understood that local prosperity relied on a healthy working class. The prevailing philosophy was, "Mechanics receiving good wages are the backbone of the community."[26] It was the political center, replete with its own tensions and inconsistencies.

Property development was the great obsession of local business. The chamber of commerce proclaimed: "There is but 25,000 acres of ground on the whole peninsula. We need it all to build a city upon."[27] Suburban development begun in earnest during the late nineteenth century continued on a wider scale. New tracts were opened in Monterey: Vista Del Rey, with 500 lots on 1,100 acres to the east of downtown, and Monterey Heights on the west. The P.I. Co. continued to promote Pacific Grove home sites and businesses (the El Carmelo cum Pacific Grove Hotel and Chautauqua convention grounds), meanwhile opening the new Hillcrest tract above town. Del Monte Park was developed in the same area by Coast Cities Improvement Company, providing affordable view lots. The maverick developer Frank Devendorf teamed with the financial backing of Frank Powers (more precisely the fortune of his wife, Jane Gallatine Powers) to purchase Santiago Duckworth's foundering investment in Carmel (Paradise Park having been abandoned). The Carmel Development Company projected an arts community lodged in rustic cottages blending with the natural setting.[28] But the jewel in the real estate crown was Pebble Beach, the P.I. Co.'s elite villa housing development and golf course in the six-thousand-acre Del Monte Forest occupying the peninsula between Pacific Grove and Carmel. Pebble Beach was reached by the Seventeen Mile Drive and toll road from the Hotel Del Monte. Opened in 1908, the Pebble Beach Lodge and Club House was described by hopeful management as "society's Mecca." Enthusiasts anticipated, "[I]f the plans of the Pacific Improvement Company do not go amiss the Seventeen Mile drive reservation will be dotted with magnificent homes in the next few years."[29]

As it turned out, the residential community developed slowly and management commitment to the region wavered. The Pacific Improvement Company, which played such a large part in Monterey's development over thirty years, was created originally for the purpose of liquidating property held by the Southern Pacific Railroad. As time went on, its directors vacillated in purpose while their interest in California properties waned. In 1919 the legendary P.I. Co. sold its Monterey holdings to the Del Monte Properties Company, a group of investors anchored by the San Francisco banker Herbert Fleishacker and managed locally by the young

Yale graduate S. F. B. Morse. The new company acquired property valued at $4 million covering eighteen thousand acres on the peninsula and including such diverse enterprises as Rancho Del Monte in Carmel Valley (formerly Rancho Los Laureles of 11,800 acres), its water pipeline to Monterey, Monterey County Water Works, Del Monte Forest (5,272 acres), Hotel Del Monte grounds and polo field (337 acres), Del Monte Forest (Pebble Beach) Lodge and golf course (233 acres), and Pacific Grove city properties (360 acres).

If Del Monte Properties did not equal the land monopoly once owned by David Jacks, it included many of the same valuable tracts and emerged immediately as the most powerful real estate conglomerate in the region. Like its predecessor, Del Monte Properties intended to develop an exclusive residential and recreational redoubt. Having borrowed heavily for the purchase, the new managers noted in their General Plan that "land sales will be pushed as rapidly as seems best." A company planning memo drawn up in May 1919 stresses "high class" advertising and "local sales under a high class specialized salesman" and the need to "get people to [Hotel] Del Monte and Lodge [and to] [l]et them know property is for sale."[30] The private golf club projected selling five hundred proprietary and three hundred associate memberships at $1,000 each. Renewed development efforts required clearing more land and laying out lots. A dozen Japanese crews were employed in the forest to trim, fell, clear, and cut trees into firewood. Gated access roads were built for sales tours and use of the Seventeen Mile Drive was controlled by toll booths.

The Pacific Improvement Company introduced restrictive covenants in property deeds as early as the 1890s, affecting subdivision developments on all of its extensive holdings but concentrating on Del Monte Forest. Other developers adopted the exclusionary practice in Pacific Grove and portions of Monterey and Carmel. A typical deed from Del Rey Oaks stipulated, "No Mongolian, Hindus, Malays, Negroes, or Pilipinos [sic] shall use or occupy any building on any lot, except that this covenant shall not prevent occupancy by domestic servants." Another took the more direct approach, specifying only those who were allowed in: "No use or occupancy shall be made, or permitted by other than a person of the White or Caucasian race." The Del Monte Properties Company spelled out the most rigorous and inventive restrictions for its Pebble Beach development: "Said premises shall not . . . at any time be occupied or used by Asiatics, Negroes, or any person born in the Turkish Empire, nor any lineal descendant of such person." Bryan Taylor, who manages a local title company and discovered these vestigial clauses in current deeds, believes that the category "Turkish Empire" was aimed at Jews. Palestine was part of the Ottoman Empire until its dismemberment after World War I. One suspects that marauding Turks were less an imminent threat to the character of Pebble Beach than prosperous Jews.[31] Restrictive covenants were employed routinely to engineer the social landscape, until 1948 when they were outlawed in California (but surreptitiously used long after).

As the 1920s progressed, Pebble Beach and Del Monte Forest flourished as an elite enclave devoted to golf, polo, the good life, and, what made it all go, property sales. Six thousand acres of privatized forest, coastal plain, and oceanfront separating the coastal connection between Monterey–Pacific Grove and Carmel created a permanent spatial reorganization of the area. Del Monte residents enjoyed free access to local communities. Carmel Mission and "historic old Monterey" were selling points in company publicity. But the reverse was not true. The public paid for the privilege of visiting Pebble Beach by toll road. Del Monte Properties was an influential participant in community politics. If it did not prevail in the odor controversy, it affected the terms of compromise and generally insinuated its interests on local associations. Yet the communities had no say over access to and land use in the Del Monte enclave. As corporate citizen, the company participated in town politics, mission restoration, festivals, and the history and arts association. S. F. B. Morse became a power among mayors and cannery owners. In short, Del Monte Properties loomed as a spatial, political, and institutional presence in local life, representing upper-class propertied interests typically arrayed against the ethnic working class and industry.

BAD LANDS

Interwoven with the laboring communities of Monterey and the affluent suburbs of Pacific Grove and Carmel were diverse neighborhoods of the underclass. Steinbeck insists that "Tortilla Flat" represents a real place occupied by real people.

> Monterey sits on the slope of a hill, with a blue bay below it and a forest of tall dark pine trees at its back. The lower parts of the town are inhabited by Americans, Italians, catchers and canners of fish. But on the hill where the forest and town intermingle, where the streets are innocent of asphalt and the corners free of street lights, the old inhabitants of Monterey are embattled as the Ancient Britons are embattled in Wales. These are the paisanos.[32]

The author is probably taking liberties here. His contemporaries and one authority on Monterey County place-names agree that Tortilla Flat is a composite of several neighborhoods on the fringes of town.[33] But that conclusion only reinforces the point that Monterey's social and spatial structure embraced significant numbers of real disreputable poor—hustlers, hoboes, squatters, gamblers, paisanos, and prostitutes.

Shacks and abandoned adobes near the waterfront were occupied by a floating population of sailors, casual workers, transients, and practitioners of illicit trades. In 1908 three vagabonds were arrested on suspicion of robbing a Japanese bunkhouse near the train depot. It was reported at the time: "For a while the three camped near the Del Monte bath house, but of late have been living in the pines beyond Pacific Grove."[34] Charles Fisher, a self-proclaimed Gypsy and socialist, squatted on P.I. Co. beach property in Pacific Grove claiming that ground within one hundred feet of high tide was government property open to settlement. Rather than contest this inventive claim, the company moved Mr. Fisher's makeshift shelter to another location.[35] The woods were a preferred location for squatter home sites, providing short-run freedom from rent, regulation, and eviction.

The Presidio separating Old and New Monterey attracted illicit commercial activities to its surroundings. Evading federal and city jurisdiction, unlicensed social clubs sold liquor and sex to soldiers. The clubs were plagued by drunken brawling and violent assaults among soldiers, which led to crackdowns by the police. In summer 1907 the local press reported, "Nigger Sue is Arrested [explaining] . . . Nigger Susie, or Mrs. Susie Taylor as she prefers to call herself, [was charged] with selling liquor and conducting a disorderly place." When the court dismissed the case, the newspaper announced more respectfully, "Dark Skinned Susan Free."[36] Ms. Taylor's transformation from pejorative to polite terms of reference illustrates a general historiographic problem. Minorities appear in the record mainly when they are involved in illegal or sensational escapades, seldom when they simply pursue useful lives. Nevertheless, data outcroppings from the criminal record suggest a diverse underclass flourishing in the seams of Monterey's conventional society.

Washington Street near the harbor was Monterey's most colorful neighborhood—an area referred to knowingly as "the Bad Lands." Chinese, Japanese, and shantytowns coexisted in the Bad Lands. Parlors for opium, gambling, and billiards mingled with "resorts" offering sexual companionship. Although the Bad Lands also included proper residences and commercial services, the area was considered unsavory by guardians of public morals. The *Monterey Daily Cypress* urged the police to close a Japanese-owned billiard parlor in the neighborhood because "the dive is visited by negroes and Mexicans and is no place for young boys to frequent."[37] We know of "a pickaninny den in the Bad Lands" only because a drunken city policeman ran amok in the establishment before some visiting soldiers disarmed him and threw him in the bay. A fellow officer arrived on the scene and, for want of anything else to do, arrested the Negro piano player—perhaps the only innocent in sight.[38] White women also owned resorts in the neighborhood and sometimes got mixed up in the excitement: "Gertie Allen, who conducts The Willows at 419 Washington street fired four shots at Billy McGreevey who was residing at the house."[39] This time everyone including the Negro piano player was spared arrest. Two years later, The Willows, now under the proprietorship of Trixie Gilmore, was dynamited by a lovelorn client. Miraculously no one was hurt, although "the shock was of such strength as to shake the resorts along Washington street, and the report was heard over most of Monterey."[40]

From the Bad Lands to Pebble Beach, from Pacific Grove to Tortilla Flat, Monterey was a mosaic of economically specialized, ethnically diverse, and socially interrelated communities. The neighborhoods had their distinctive colors, but Monterey society derived its character from their interdependence. A growing working class earned the wages that fueled local commerce and real estate. Japanese labor cleared Del Monte Forest for luxury view lots and built the Seventeen Mile scenic road. Presidio supply contracts stimulated civilian enterprise and soldiers patronized the "resorts" maintained by blacks, Asians, and white working women. Despite its exclusiveness, Del Monte Properties capitalized on local history and the paisano presence. A company brochure designed to lure visitors into the real estate office gushes, "[T]he old town of Monterey is a constant delight and it should be seen by all tourists. . . . On the streets may still be seen the Spanish vaquero on his horse, or the lazy Mexican, with his black pipe, and his red handkerchief knotted around his swarthy neck, dreamily tipped back in his chair before some adobe house; or a dark eyed beauty, a descendant of Spain."[41] National institutions mingled with local actors. Standard Oil built a storage tank facility in New Monterey, despite strenuous neighborhood protest that echoed the odor controversy. The area became a hangout for tramps and muggers until a spectacular fire destroyed the facility in 1924.[42] In 1911 the U.S. Treasury Department, proprietor of the old Custom House, decided to rehabilitate the waterfront by clearing the rented shacks of local fishermen.[43]

It was all of a piece, each community shaped by its relation to the rest and forming in the aggregate a distinct place. Old Monterey was home to labor, trade, and sin; extending outward to Pacific Grove, Pebble Beach, and Carmel, respectively, lay the ordered precincts of God, capital, and culture.

CANNERY ROW:
INDUSTRY, LABOR, COMMUNITY, ACTION

During the first half of the twentieth century, Monterey became the most important fishing port in the United States and the world's third largest, by tonnage of industrially processed fish.[44] Although several kinds of fish were canned and "reduced" to fish oil and meal, the California sardine was emblematic of Monterey's Cannery Row. More than two dozen canneries and reduction plants lined Cannery Row in the peak years of the industry around 1940, each with its own brand name and colorful sardine label decorating cans, quarter-pound tins, pound ovals, packing boxes, and cannery buildings. The October-to-February sardine season experienced wide monthly and yearly fluctuations in the catch but at its zenith employed 3,000 to 4,000 people directly in fishing, canning, and reduction at a time when Monterey's total population numbered 10,000.[45]

> The chief industry in Monterey since the turn of the century has been large-scale commercial fishing, canning, processing, and distribution of sardines. So dependent is Monterey upon the sardine for its livelihood that the industry's seasonal fluctuations now affect the local economy with the precision of a seismograph recording earthquake tremors. Merchants solemnly claim that they observe "a falling off of trade even during full moon periods and in rough weather when the boats do not go out."[46]

The *WPA Guide* (published in 1940 by the Works Progress Administration) notes that "Monterey has never been a Yankee town," an observation all the more true of the fishing industry. From its beginnings at the hands of Portuguese whalers and Chinese marketers, commercial fishing was a multiethnic undertaking, dominated in the 1920s and 1930s by Sicilian boat owners and crews with minority participation of Japanese, Spanish, and North Americans—virtually all men.[47] Not so in the canneries, where women, children, people of motley national origins, and many an Okie migrant worked at specialized ethnic niches along the production line. Women, including many wives, sisters, and daughters of fishermen, packed sardine cans. Until their skills were automated, Asian and Spanish men and women were fish cutters. White males dominated skilled mechanical tasks such as tending boilers that cooked the canned

fish and, until electrification, powered the line. One of the larger canneries boasted of its "all [female] white packers" and hardy Spanish ware-
housemen.[48] Foremen, superintendents, and cannery owners were men of
Anglo-European extraction, with notable exceptions among the several
Sicilians who rose from fishing to cannery ownership and management.

Diverse in gender, nationality, language, and heritage, cannery workers and fishermen nevertheless formed a working-class community with
its own emergent culture. Wedged together in ethnic slices along Monterey's waterfront, Sicilians, Chinese, Portuguese, Japanese, Spanish, and
Anglo families pursued socially segregated lives in full awareness of one
another. On important occasions they came together in churches, labor
unions, and community festivals. Cannery Row took shape during
World War I when business boomed and enough new plants were built
side by side along the beach in New Monterey to form a row. In local
parlance, the term "Cannery Row" dates from this period but enjoyed
no broader recognition until John Steinbeck's 1945 novel of the same
name. Appearing almost at the close of the sardine era, the opening pages
of *Cannery Row* momentarily looked back on the period of industrial
movement and community sentiment.

> Cannery Row in Monterey in California is a poem, a stink, a grating noise,
> a quality of light, a tone, a habit, a nostalgia, a dream. . . . In the morning
> the sardine fleet has made a catch, the purse-seiners waddle heavily into the
> bay blowing their whistles. The deep-laden boats pull in against the coast
> where the canneries dip their tails into the bay. . . . Then cannery whistles
> scream all over the town men and women scramble into their clothes and come
> running down to the row to go to work. Then shining cars bring upper classes
> down: superintendents, accountants, owners who disappear into offices.
> Then from the town pour Wops and Chinamen and Polaks, men and women
> in trousers and rubber coats and oilcloth aprons. They come running to clean
> and pack and cook and can the fish. The whole street rumbles and groans and
> screams and rattles while the silver rivers of fish pour in out of the boats and
> the boats rise higher and higher in the water until they are empty. The can-
> neries rumble and rattle and squeak until the last fish is cleaned and cut and
> cooked and canned and then the whistles scream again and the dripping,
> smelly, tired Wops and Chinamen and Polaks, men and women, straggle out
> and droop their ways up the hill into town and Cannery Row becomes itself
> again—quiet and magical.[49]

Here, however, any resemblance between Steinbeck's *Cannery Row* and
the working-class community on Monterey Bay ends. For artistic purposes, Steinbeck designed his story to work at several thematic "levels"[50]
expressed in friendship and society among a humble lot of bums, pros-

titutes, Chinese, and an exemplary marine biologist who lived along the eponymic street. Although Steinbeck's characters were based on real people, his quixotic tale makes no mention of the industrial surround; of the Sicilian fishermen, cannery women, labor unions, meeting halls, churches, their working day, entertainments, virtues, or iniquities. That is the novelist's privilege. No one on Steinbeck's Cannery Row has a regular job, save perhaps the Chinese storekeeper whose labors are caricatured as sharp trading. The fictional Cannery Row is a tumbledown redoubt of lovable rascals, far from the world of industrial production and working-class family reproduction. Social history must not confuse these two different stories. But cultural history can explore profitably how and why the two stories have been confounded in popular memory.

INDUSTRY

Monterey's industrial era began at the turn of the century and lasted until 1950 when the sardines precipitously vanished. Commercial fishing on the bay dated from the early nineteenth century. Initially Indians traded salmon and sea otter pelts with arriving Europeans, followed by Portuguese (Azorean) whaling, Genoese and Chinese market fishing, and Japanese abalone canning. From the 1870s onward, local observers remarked on the great abundance of marine life in the bay and the untapped potential for commercial exploitation. In 1896 Frank Booth of the Sacramento River Packers Association attempted a salmon cannery without success, owing in part to the reluctance of Monterey fishermen to sell their catch to local upstarts rather than their traditional San Francisco patrons. During the first years of the new century, successful canning operations were started by Joseph and Edward Gayetty in collaboration with Japanese abalone divers at Point Lobos, H. R. Robbins of San Francisco who combined reduction facilities with sardine canning at the harbor, and Harry Malpas who, in 1902 with the financial backing of Otosaburo Noda, built the first plant at what would later become Cannery Row in New Monterey.[51]

Frank Booth returned in 1902, purchased Robbins's plant at Fisherman's Wharf, and solved his earlier supply problem by contracting with Japanese fishermen. In June 1904 the *Monterey New Era* reported, "The Sacramento River Packers Association opened its packing house Monday morning, about seventy-two of the Japanese fishermen in the port have agreed to sell fish at the terms offered. This decision on the part of the Japs was reached through the action of General William Quniton, president of the Monterey Chamber of Commerce [who] realized that every day the packing house was closed meant the loss of so much money to the town and promptly took steps to bring the fishermen and packers together."[52] By this time the size of the daily salmon catch was making headlines and the new industry was recognized as the engine of progress.

Following Robbins's initial efforts, Booth began experimenting with the bay's overabundant sardine. Booth succeeded owing to his own perseverance and the critical contributions of two immigrant men. Knut Hovden was a Norwegian fisheries expert and engineer who designed a modern assembly line operation and much of the machinery for mass production of tinned sardines. Pietro Ferrante was a Sicilian fisherman whose early success on the Sacramento Delta led to conflicts with bay area Genoese and his interest in relocating in Monterey where Booth needed a loyal fleet. Ferrante and his brother-in-law, Orazio Enea, arrived in 1905, quickly attracted members of their extended families from a group of fishing villages in the immediate vicinity of Palermo, and steadily took control of the Monterey fleet by displacing Genoese and Asian competitors.

Race and politics crucially affected the organization of California's fishing industry, following precedents laid down previously in land and mining claims. Commenting on the efforts of Greeks and Italians to claim exclusive fishing grounds in San Francisco Bay, Arthur F. McEvoy notes, "[T]his meant, first and foremost, excluding Chinese workers from fisheries in which Westerners were interested."[53] Government propagated anti-Asian restrictions beginning with the 1880 Act Related to Fishing in Waters of the State, which prohibited Chinese fishing. Although it was soon struck down by the courts, additional measures followed including Asian-specific licensing fees (a "foreign fisher's tax"), restrictions on equipment and nets, and limits on the abalone catch. "When anti-Chinese fishing laws grew so complex as to foster the growth of protection rackets between Chinese merchants and Fish and Game patrol agents, a frustrated legislature dealt the industry a lethal blow by prohibiting the export of its produce."[54] Conflicts between Italian and Chinese fishermen were common and recurrent throughout the late nineteenth century in Monterey. Chinese were routinely arrested and fined for illegal fishing practices, their drying nets cut, and their boats run over in the water or burned on shore. As the Sicilian fishing population grew, a combination of violence, legal restrictions, and town sentiment drove the Chinese from fishing and reduced the Japanese to a minority, if determined, part of the sardine fleet.

With a growing concentration of Sicilian fishermen, mechanized production facilities, a ready cannery labor force including members of

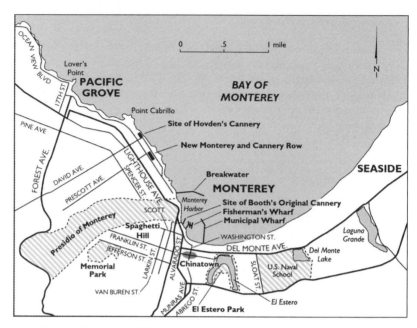

22.   Map of Monterey. This current map of Monterey marks many prominent
sites of the industrial period. (Courtesy of the author)

fishing families and displaced ethnics, and bountiful sardine runs, Booth's
cannery led Monterey into the industrial age. World War I created brisk
demand in the sardine market and a row of eight canneries and reduction plants along the beach in New Monterey about a mile from Booth's
original site at Fisherman's Wharf. Hovden left Booth's employ in 1916
and built a large modern plant at the far end of the street that was soon
christened Cannery Row. The industry expanded in the 1920s as larger
boats and nets were introduced, and an increasing proportion of the catch
was reduced to fish oil, meal, and fertilizer where profits were greater.
Early warnings of depletion from overfishing issued by California's Fish
and Game Division met disbelief and resistance in Monterey. Legislative
limitations on the profligate reduction process, which set a quota or ratio on the volume of canned to reduced product, were persistently attacked in the courts as unconstitutional, in political arenas as a restraint
of free enterprise, and in public as a hardship on workers who needed
jobs during the several economic depressions of the period. Indeed, ecological jeremiads of "the fish and game" seemed to be refuted by peri-
odic upsurges in the catch after several years of decline. In the long run,
however, the state's biologists were right.[55]

Whether the result of overfishing, changes in ocean tides and temperatures, long-term species life cycles, or some combination of all these factors, the annual sardine catch, in excess of 200,000 tons during the boom years of the 1930s, had fallen to 2,000 tons by 1960. The industry collapsed during the 1950s, with exiguous yields, massive plant closings, and property sales to salvage companies and real estate firms. Cannery Row came to an end as an industrial, working-class, ethnic enterprise. In time "Steinbeck's Cannery Row" of property development, service industry, and tourism would eclipse the original.

LABOR

The characteristic feature of Monterey's fish industry is a level of social complexity that defies conventional labor/management, worker/owner dichotomies. In the first instance, the industry consisted of four groups, each with its own organization: cannery owners, cannery workers, fishermen who owned boats, and fishermen who made up the boat crews. Boat owners, who were usually fishermen, were the first to organize in 1914, followed by cannery owners in 1918, crew fishermen in 1925, and cannery workers in 1937. Fragmentary evidence of the Japanese Fishermen's Association, established in 1909, supports the sequential pattern.[56] Hierarchies of skill and occupational prestige governed each of the four sectors, from prosperous cannery owners (including a few absentee corporations) to migratory cannery workers. Individuals and firms crossed sectoral lines. Some boats were owned by several fishermen, by families (brothers, sons, and nephews) who constituted the crew, or even by crew-member collectives. Canneries owned some of the boats and leased them to fishermen, who thus became de facto cannery workers. Similarly, some boat owners compromised their independence by contracting regularly to sell fish to a given cannery. In one case, fishermen owned the San Carlos Cannery, which was founded in 1926 as a cooperative for Sicilian boat owners. Finally, cannery workers were often former fishermen or members of fishing families. Family and kinship ties pervaded the industry; most boat crews comprised fathers, sons, uncles, nephews, and cousins while their families, including wives, mothers, sisters, aunts, nieces, and more cousins, worked in the canneries.

Who were these workers? No simple answer suffices here either. The labor force in fishing had a profile very different from the canneries, and both changed over time. The year 1920 provides a convenient baseline for examining the labor force. The industry had just stabilized after its explosive growth during World War I, although it had not yet taken off with technological advances and generous reduction permits, which did not come along until the 1930s. Nineteen twenty has the additional advantage of being the most recent manuscript census open to public view at this writing.

In the 1920 census 357 persons identified themselves as fishermen, and among them only a very small number said that they were also boat owners. (The census, taken in early January after the peak sardine season, undercounts seasonal migrants to the fishing grounds. The number of boat owners or part-owners may be underestimated because that information was volunteered to census takers who may not have probed the simple response "fisherman.") Half the fishermen were Italian (Sicilian), but in 1920 there were still significant numbers of Japanese and Spanish. Ethnic concentration is even greater if one includes a number of U.S.-born second-generation Italians who fished with their fathers and uncles. That this was largely an immigrant labor force is highlighted by the data on citizenship. Few were citizens by U.S. birth, and fewer yet had become naturalized; fully 83 percent were resident aliens. Some may not have lived in the country long enough to qualify for citizenship, but data on year of immigration indicate that in fact 65 percent had resided in the United States for ten years or more. This is consistent with oral histories of families that indicate most immigrants did not bother to become citizens. Cultural insularity was especially characteristic of fishermen. Forty-two percent did not speak English even after a significant length of residence. In summary, the fishermen were mainly Sicilian, Japanese, and Spanish immigrants who had been in the United States for years yet continued to form close-knit family, language, cultural, and ethnic groups.

Cannery workers were a larger and more diverse lot. Thirty percent were women, a number that increased in canneries as opposed to reduction plants. Although nearly half of all workers described themselves as general "laborers," many others performed specialized tasks on the production line. Canneries had a wage-and-status hierarchy running from casual labor to assembly line work and specialized equipment operation.[57] In 1920, before machines eliminated their jobs, fish cutters were a skilled group of men and women, heavily Asian (Chinese and Japanese) and Spanish. Packers were exclusively women who placed the filleted fish in tins that were then sealed and steam cooked in a boiler, or "retort." Beyond a handful of office workers and laborers, most women were either

TABLE 3
MONTEREY FISHERMEN, 1920

1. Position	Number	Percent
Owner	9	2
Captain	3	1
Fisherman	345	97
Total	357	100

2. National Origin		
Italy	172	49
Japan	79	23
Spain	40	12
United States	37	11
Portugal	9	2
Other (U.K., Yugoslavia)	11	3
Total	348	100

3. Citizenship		
United States	39	11
Naturalized	19	6
Alien	285	83
Total	343	100

4. Immigration Year (Naturalized and Alien)		
1915–19	26	9
1910–14	77	26
1905–9	69	24
1900–1904	83	28
Before 1900	39	13
Total	294	100

5. English Speaking		
Yes	203	58
No	147	42
Total	350	100

SOURCE: Compiled by the author from the 1920 Manuscript Census. Total numbers in each panel vary as a result of incomplete information, illegible entries, or restricted categories.

23.   Bayside Cannery Workers, 1919. Forty-six cannery workers, some
in their best dress, posed outside the plant on Ocean View Avenue for the
customary company picture. The close-up of this relatively small group
allows inferences about the gender and ethnic composition of the labor
force. (Pat Hathaway Collection of California Views)

cutters or packers. White men dominated the high-status (engineer, me-
chanic, cook/fryer) and year-round (maintenance, warehouseman) jobs,
although they were also the largest contingent among the ethnically varied laborers. In sharp contrast to fishermen, the majority of cannery workers are U.S.-born citizens. Although many were aliens, shoreside workers were more enculturated (English speaking) and longer resident than
fishermen. During the sardine season, migratory workers who followed
the summer fruit canning circuit would move into rooming houses and
rental shacks on the waterfront, remaining as long as the canneries provided steady work.

Photographic evidence supports this portrait. A typical group of cannery workers posed outside the Bayside Fish Company in 1919. Dressed
specially for the occasion, the group of eighteen women and twenty-eight
men includes nine Asians, perhaps one African American, and no doubt
a number of Italian and Spanish descent. Most of the women are white,
some quite young. Two appear affectionate—married, perhaps, or anticipating its pleasures. Social surveys revealed that "[t]he average worker
is one of a four member family in which both parents work as they can
and sometimes one of the children if old enough."[58]

The labor force experienced a number of changes over the next several decades. Most important, it increased fourfold to embrace as many as four thousand workers in record seasons like 1941–42. Automation of ethnic specializations such as fish cutting lessened diversity, a trend that paralleled the industry's growing dependence on the reduction of fish oil and meal, which mainly relied on male laborers. The constant number of Japanese fishermen became proportionately a smaller segment of the expanding fleet, falling from 23 to 6 percent in their last season, 1940–41, before wartime internment. Sicilians came to dominate the fleet (86 percent in 1930), but they were increasingly second-generation Monterey men who combined with Japanese and Anglo-Americans from various home ports to produce a majority of U.S.-born fishermen by 1940.[59]

Sardine fishing in Monterey underwent a series of changes in its fifty-year history, but none was more decisive than the shift from the Italian heritage lampara launch and net to the larger and more efficient purse seine boat and net. Sicilians at the turn of the century revolutionized sardine fishing in California with the lampara "outfit" (a launch with a lighter in tow for the catch) and large nets (1,200 feet long by 200 feet deep) that encircled schools of fish. The early lampara boats were small at a length of 20 feet, manually operated by three fishermen, but grew in the 1930s to 45 feet, gasoline engines, a capacity of 40 to 50 tons, and a crew of eleven to fourteen. In 1926 cannery owners introduced purse seiners from southern California in an effort to avoid local labor demands and land more fish in competition with profitable offshore reduction ships (which were eventually outlawed). Seiners of the late 1920s ran 55 to 85 feet in length, carried 80 to 100 tons of fish, used diesel engines that allowed weeklong trips over a much wider area, were safer and more stable in rough seas, used power winches to haul the nets, and carried a crew of seven to nine men.[60] By 1930 purse seiners made up one-third of the fleet and soon took over completely with ever larger boats that averaged 80 to 100 feet and 150 tons capacity by 1940.[61]

Initially, local fishermen opposed the new boats, which represented a much larger capital investment, reduced labor demand, and worried those already alert to the prospects of depletion.[62] But as reduction quotas were eased during the depression, the more efficient seiners rewarded those who borrowed money to purchase or lease larger boats. Some others retained the older boats but replaced lampara nets with larger ring nets that worked in a fashion similar to the purse seine net by closing at the bottom like a drawstring purse. Purse seiner boats clearly had their advantages. Sardine fishing took place on moonless nights when schools of fish revealed themselves by a luminescent glow on the water. Fish hunting

TABLE 4
MONTEREY CANNERY WORKERS, 1920

1. Position	Number	Percent
Owner, manager, foreman	30	4
Clerical	14	2
Engineer/inspector	14	2
Mechanic/craftsman	36	5
Cutter	136	20
Packer	102	15
Fryer	19	3
Labeler	13	2
Warehouse/maintenance	13	2
Laborer	308	45
Total	685	100

2. Gender		
Male	494	70
Female	211	30
Total	705	100

3. National Origin		
United States	351	52
China	94	14
Japan	57	9
Spain	66	10
Italy	28	4
Mexico	13	2
United Kingdom and Canada	27	4
Other (Portugal, Austria/Yugoslavia, Sweden, Germany, Denmark)	33	5
Total	669	100

4. Citizenship		
United States	351	52
Naturalized	24	4
Alien	302	44
Total	677	100

5. Immigration Year (Naturalized and Alien)		
1915–19	29	12
1910–14	41	18
1905–9	49	21
1900–1904	26	11
Before 1900	88	38
Total	233	100

TABLE 4 *(continued)*

6. English Speaking	Number	Percent
Yes	544	81
No	124	19
Total	668	100

SOURCE: Compiled by the author from the 1920 Federal Manuscript Census. Total numbers in each panel vary as a result of incomplete information, illegible entries, or restricted categories.

on dark, cold, and treacherous seas was not only safer and more comfortable aboard the hefty seiners, but fewer hands and larger yields meant greater profits divided among the crew. In addition to many uneventful hours and days spent looking for the glowing schools, the hardest work in fishing involves rapidly setting and hauling the nets. Winches and motorized turn tables that played out the enormous purse seines improved significantly on lampara methods that set the nets by hand from a lighter rowed around the swarming fish. Deep in the water with a good catch, the seiners were less likely to capsize in rough seas on the way home.

Cannery work followed the rhythms of the sardine catch. During full moons, storms, poor runs, and the five spring and summer months, there was little work. But when the boats came in loaded, whether in the middle of the night or at midday, the whistles that distinguished each plant sounded across waterfront neighborhoods summoning workers immediately to the production line. Former workers recall the "clomp-clomp" of women walking down the residential slopes to the New Monterey shoreline in their (self-provided) rubber boots, aprons, and white hair nets. The line ran until every fish was canned or reduced; twelve- to fifteen-hour days were not uncommon when the catch was good. The work was repetitive. Cutters and packers who stood in one place for the entire shift suffered cold and dampness. Yet they also found the irregular tempo and changing fortune an exciting atmosphere. Esther Compoy recalls, "I was awful shy, but in the canneries it was one big family. . . . It was exciting."[63] On the shop floor women developed a work culture that offered identity and collective solutions to daily problems.[64] Women welcomed the independence that came with an income and experienced a spirit of camaraderie, particularly when the union organized.[65] Mavis Lautaret was working in the office at Sea Pride Cannery when she discovered that "the take-home pay of the cutters and canners was quadruple what I earned." She asked for a tryout on the cutting line and a few nights later she was called to the plant at 1:00 A.M. The night's catch was coming in.

The workers all knew me, but I cannot say I received a warm welcome. What was an office worker doing dressed in their mode? Most couldn't (or wouldn't) speak English in those days, and I was getting the message—without understanding what they said—that I was trespassing on their territory. . . . [T]he foreman placed me in back of a rapidly moving conveyor belt, which had many deep slots for the fish. Sardines were pouring out from the hopper onto a platform by the conveyor so fast that they were spilling all over the floor. . . . And cold? It was freezing! I never knew before why the workers wore boots, now I did. The floor was almost knee-high with excess icy ocean water that came in along with the sardines. . . . I started slapping the fish in the right way so they could be canned in a relatively gutless fashion. I slapped sardines for hours, I thought, and my back was breaking and I was freezing. I looked at the clock and only 20 minutes had passed. I slapped, slapped, and slapped pilchards, looked up again and five minutes had slipped by. . . . When the sardines finally stopped coming and the whistles blew again, it was 7:15 A.M. I could barely walk. My fingers were stiff and blue, my back was breaking, my head was splitting, and I was fishy from my hair to the toes of my boots. Dragging myself outside, a funny thing happened. All the workers (who now miraculously spoke English) crowded around me and some pounded me on the back and we all sat down on the curb and drank coffee from a thermos someone had brought. . . . I had hung in and I had become one of the group.[66]

Like most things on Cannery Row, wage rates varied in complexity. Fishermen were paid on the basis of shares in the catch. Boats had a fixed number of shares, often twelve, into which the receipts of the catch were divided after expenses such as gas, oil, and food were deducted. A boat owner-captain would receive, say, four shares (more or less, depending on the period and how much of the operating expense he assumed), the cook and each of the fishing crew one share (a cook who also fished got two). A fisherman who captained a cannery-owned boat and also fished might receive one and one-half shares. Apprentices less than sixteen years old earned half shares. The general principle varied in application. The larger purse seiners, for example, calculated on the basis of nineteen shares, with seven going to the boat. A fisher's seasonal income could vary from nothing up to several thousand dollars, and wages rose over the years. Although earnings from local sardine fishing comprised the largest single income source, some fished in Alaska during the off season while others took shoreside jobs or just maintained their boats and equipment. Data for selected years, nevertheless, indicate that fishermen were the local labor aristocracy. In the 1930s, $1,000 to $2,000 was typical. With wartime prices in effect, the average for 1942 was $3,100. In a bad year like 1947, the range was $100 to $3,000, the mean $800. For-

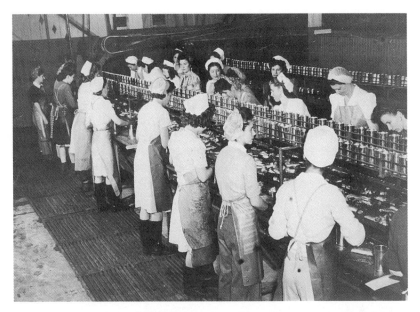

24. Women on the Packing Line, ca. 1940. Women were approximately 30 percent of the cannery labor force, concentrated in assembly line fish cutting and packing. Women came from a variety of racial and ethnic backgrounds in addition to the Italian fishing families. (Courtesy of Colton Hall Museum, City of Monterey Collection)

tunes reversed in 1948 with a range of $1,500 to $4,600 and an average of $3,600. In the best years, crews on the top boats earned $4,000 to $5,000, although that was rare and ephemeral.[67]

Cannery workers were paid in piece-rate and hourly wages. Piece rates were computed for cutters by the bucket of fish and for packers by the dozen tins. Experienced hands made what they considered good money as long as the line was running and the job secure—which often was not for long. Most jobs lacked such an obvious metric and received hourly wages. Wages of men and women differed, but not by much. A survey conducted by the Women's Bureau of the U.S. Department of Labor in 1939 found hourly rates of 63 and 58 cents for men and women respectively.[68] In 1942 wartime restraint held rates to 70 and 65 cents respectively. By 1948 the unions had achieved a substantial increase: $1.21 for women, $1.28 for men, and $1.36 in the reduction plants employing men.[69]

The key to gender differences and seasonal income generally, however, lay in the number of hours worked. The 1939 study showed that

25.   Cannery Row, ca. 1940. George Robinson's classic photograph shows
daily activity on Ocean View Avenue during the industry's most productive
period. The overhead conveyors moved packed and sealed cans (right to left)
from plant to warehouse and delivered empty cans from the opposite direction
for packing. (Pat Hathaway Collection of California Views)

two-thirds of the women worked less than forty hours per week but only
41 percent of the men did so, resulting in a weekly pay difference of
$20.55 for women and $30.85 for men. This was the result, once again,
of the relative concentration of women on the irregular production line
and men in full-time jobs such as maintenance and warehousing. Those
who managed to put in a sixteen- to twenty-week season were doing well,
and within that group men earned $260 but women only $181. Most
were employed for twelve weeks or less, and the average *seasonal income
for all workers,* short and long term, was $189 for men and $71 for
women. Seasonal incomes of less than a couple hundred dollars dramatically demonstrate the humble lot of cannery workers, particularly
those men and women who headed households.

Cannery jobs were physically taxing and differentially rewarded in wages and status. An industry task force in the 1940s reported,

> [T]here is of necessity much dampness and water on the floor, and the chances of slipping are frequent. Sometimes fingers are caught in moving belts and also sometimes there are cuts from fish bones. . . . [T]here is what is known as fish poisoning, and those susceptible to it cannot handle fish. The canneries are somewhat damp and of necessity have to be unheated, but there is a considerable amount of steam from the exhaust and baking ovens, and this sometimes causes respiratory trouble.[70]

In 1943 Monterey's local of the Cannery Workers Union of the Pacific (AFL) appealed to the War Labor Board, as was required under wartime regulations, for a small increase in wages. Union officials submitted, "[T]hese employees have to be subject to call. They don't know when they go to work. They have to wait until the pack comes in. They are not like other workers who have a regular shift." Elsie Cowell, who worked for Hovden's Cannery for seventeen years, testified to the board that the work was wet and messy: "[W]e wear jeans and blouses and rubbers, aprons and boots and sweaters, several of them. . . . [I]t is not very pleasant to pack when you are all wet." Sometimes when the processing line moved unevenly, better-paid and higher-status cutters were moved to packing cans. Shop steward Marian Caveny observed that workers would "lift my scalp" if she failed to report grievances stemming from violations of work rules. She sympathized with the cutters: "[A]fter all, they are wet, as Mrs. Cowell stated, and they are miserable. Naturally have been working hard. Seven or eight hours is pretty good to work piece work, you know, working hard and then come up and pack. They ought to go home. They do come up, I should say, under pressure. . . . [T]hey didn't want to pack."[71] Although the War Labor Board denied the requests for pay hikes, overtime pay, and a closed shop, the union had achieved a loyal following and wages improved as a result of organization.

COMMUNITY

Monterey families involved in the fishing industry were simultaneously participants in a working class, a community, and a culture that integrated these spheres. Their working-class experience was shaped as much by the job as by the local community.

Social class is not simply an occupational phenomenon but also a way of being and acting shaped by institutions ranging from the local neigh-

borhood to the state.[72] And class was not the only dimension of the laboring life. Monterey's working-class communities were also organized
along lines of ethnicity, national origin, culture, associated lifestyles, and
emergent group identities that stemmed from being ethnic minorities in
America.[73]

Well-defined ethnic neighborhoods ringed Cannery Row and the harbor. The social order was reproduced spatially in ways that affected group
life and interaction. The *WPA Guide* observes, "[T]he medley of na-
tionalities, each confined to its own neighborhood, includes Greeks and
Italians, Chinese and Japanese, Spanish and Portuguese and Mexicans.
Even more isolated are Monterey's few Negroes and Filipinos. In the
town's various foreign quarters English is the language least heard. Home
of the Italians is Oak Grove, between El Estero and Del Monte; of the
Chinese in downtown Old Monterey and behind Cannery Row; of the
Spanish, Mexicans, and Portuguese, New Monterey."[74] There were sta-
tus differences between neighborhoods. Beginning with Pietro Ferrante,
Sicilian fishing families concentrated on the promontory across from
Booth's cannery and the boat harbor. In time, a number of captains and
boat owners built view-lot homes on "Spaghetti [some say Garlic] Hill."
On the flat between downtown and the elegant Hotel Del Monte, Oak
Grove housed diverse working-class folk including Italians, Anglos, and
at least one black family. Between Oak Grove and downtown were distinct Chinese and Japanese "towns."

As the canneries located along the beach at New Monterey, an intri-
cate residential and social pattern developed. Sicilian fishermen and cannery workers were of lower status than their "in town" relatives, the boat
owners and captains whose wives and daughters did not work in canneries. Hispanic families were common in New Monterey, and a small
Japanese neighborhood developed near the dividing line with Pacific
Grove. Another Chinatown existed right in the middle of Cannery Row.
Recently arrived from China, Won Yee settled in New Monterey around
1918 and built the well-known Wing Chong ("glorious and successful")
store and a squid export business. "Wing Chong was a general store
geared to serving the cannery workers living and working nearby; Won
Yee stocked not only food but also the equipment the cannery workers
needed—gloves, rubber boots, and fishing tackle."[75] Local legend holds
that Won Yee grew rich and loaned money to Knut Hovden during pe-
riodic crises in the cannery business.

Monterey's ethnic communities were populated with Old Country villagers. The Sicilians, in particular, came from close-knit kinship networks

based in four villages near Palermo. Like the Genoese community at San Francisco's North Beach, local Italians were highly provincial. Dino Cinel observes that these communities were governed not only by generalized notions of nationalism and regionalism but also by a fine-grained *campanilismo*—"the sense of loyalty and attachment to the traditions of one's commune (literally to the local bell tower) rather than to the entire region."[76] Cultural solidarity was all the more intense among fishermen who followed their traditional calling according to old ways, worked and socialized mainly with one another in the native tongue, married women from kindred village families, and brought up their sons in the trade. "Fishermen proved that . . . a group could isolate itself almost totally from the larger society, recreating patterns of economic and social organization almost entirely from the Old World."[77] Supporting evidence for this pattern comes from local women who presided over strong family-centered households yet traveled in wider circles of the town and canneries, leading to their greater proficiency in English. Peter Cutino describes the Sicilian neighborhood in the 1940s.

> Life on Garlic Hill was rather structured. During the day, the men slept to prepare themselves for the night fishing or when awake sewed nets. . . . For many years some of the Old World's ways remained with the residents of Garlic Hill. A good example is the roving vendors who plied their trade through the neighborhoods of Monterey until the late 1950s. In the evenings, if the men were out fishing, the family would sit around the upright, most-up-to-date radio console invented, listening to the "news." Over the short wave band, the boats would broadcast their positions, the fish they were catching, when they expected to unload, and when they would be home. A good catch meant the proverbial "bread on the table." . . . [M]y mother [was] the emotional "fire" in our family. . . . [B]ecause Dad spoke practically no English, she carried the load of disciplining the children.[78]

At its core, Monterey's working-class community was Sicilian, Catholic, and family-centered, owing in large part to the efforts of women. Carol McKibben's study of these women provides testimony to the importance of sewing circles, rosary groups, and the Italian Catholic Federation (ICF), which sponsored the annual Santa Rosalia Festival celebrating the patron saint of their ancestral Sicilian fishing villages. Jenny Russo recalled,

> We wanted something for ourselves. It was the 1930s, 1931 when we started the ICF and 1935 when we started the Santa Rosalia *feste*. The fishing was good and we were all doing good. We wanted to be together, like family. It was all Italian. Only Italian. The Santa Rosalia Festival represented that. The real meaning of the *festa* for all of us, in being Italian, was religious. We didn't allow divorcees to join the ICF. Only married couples. But it didn't matter if

you were Sicilian, Genovese, Napoleon. We wanted to make a social group of Italians in the church. We would gather for a little dessert, coffee, a little dancing, a little singing. It was nice for us.[79]

Russo's ecumenical recollection of Italian participation is at odds with the memory of other women who report, "[W]e were always reminded that we were not Sicilian. My mother was never invited to sew costumes or bake with Sicilian women. I was never in the [Santa Rosalia Festival] parade. I never got to be an angel or a princess. That was for the Sicilian girls."[80]

Italian men associated primarily in work and union activities, although the Knights of Columbus and Sons of Italy attracted some who had moved into mainstream business and community activity. The Sons of Italy was organized in 1928 "along political rather than religious lines . . . [by Antonio Brucia] owner of Brucia's Tavern on Alvarado Street in downtown Monterey to broaden, maximize, and consolidate Sicilian political power."[81] Gradually, Italians achieved professional roles and won positions in local government. In other arenas, associational life mitigated ethnic separation. A Spanish Hall existed in New Monterey, but its patrons joined Italians, Portuguese, and others in a lively round of Catholic church activities. The Roseland ballroom on Prescott and Lighthouse Avenues in New Monterey adjacent to the canneries was a favorite rendezvous for local youths and doubtless the origin of many interethnic romances. The local trade union movement flourished from 1920 to 1950, uniting classes of workers from all ethnic groups.

Monterey enjoyed its public life and entertainments. The fall fishing season began with the blessing of the fleet and the Santa Rosalia Festival. The entire town assembled for the waterfront parade, flotilla of decorated boats, and picnic. Later years saw the development of a season's-end festival, which, in 1940, announced a "gargantuan banquet to feed 4,000 people, music, games, and dancing[,] . . . a celebration [that] promises to surpass any of the historic old world carnivals in color, excitement, and lusty rejoicing."[82] Indeed, no less a lusty rejoicer than John Steinbeck testifies that the extravagant promise was met.

> At the end of the sardine season, canneries and boat owners provide a celebration. There is a huge barbecue on the end of the pier with free beef and beer and salad for all comers. The sardine fleet is decorated with streamers and bunting and serpentine, and the boat with the biggest season catch is queen of a strange nautical parade of boats; and every boat is an open house, receiving friends of owners and of crew. Wine flows beautifully, and the parade of boats that starts with dignity and precision sometimes ends in turmoil. . . .

With five thousand other people we crowded on the pier and ate great chunks of meat and drank beer and heard speeches. It was the biggest barbecue the sardine men had ever given. . . . [T]he speeches rose to a crescendo of patriotism and good feeling beyond anything Monterey had ever heard.[83]

The fishing industry, as well as the working-class community and culture surrounding the industry, defined Monterey society as a whole. Its fishermen were mainly Italian and Japanese, its cannery workers women and ethnics. Industry supported the town and shaped its character. This material fact was recognized in changing cultural symbols. Once the home of the world-famous Hotel Del Monte, by 1940 Monterey was known to residents and visitors alike as the Sardine Capital of the World.

COLLECTIVE ACTION

With four parties to any action affecting the enterprise of fishing and canning, potential conflicts and alliances were already rich before the state became increasingly involved in efforts to regulate the industry. Boat owners struck the canneries regularly over the price of fish and closed-shop demands. Although heterogeneous cannery workers were hardest to organize, the effort that succeeded in 1937 had precedents in a long struggle. Occasionally, crew fishermen struck their fellow-ethnic boat owners and demonstrated solidarity with cannery workers. As the state endeavored to conserve sardines through limits on reduction, fishermen and cannery owners joined forces with civic boosters and agribusiness to bring political pressure on the legislature. Yet even here there were divisions. A few farsighted canners (including the pioneer Booth) and fishermen believed the warnings about depletion issued by Fish and Game scientists and argued with professional pride that their business was to provide food for human consumption, not fertilizer.

In 1915 the new Monterey Fishermen's Association, in cooperation with an established Japanese fishermen's union, refused to fish for salmon until Booth increased the cannery price from three to four cents per pound. Then a 1917 price dispute divided the fishermen as Japanese continued delivering to Booth while Sicilians repudiated their price contract (citing wartime inflation) and won some satisfaction in a court settlement. With nine canneries operating by 1918, owners had reason to form the Monterey Bay Canners Association, although competition and personal rivalries militated against industry solidarity. A postwar cycle of national (and international) labor insurgency boosted local fishermen into the ethnically integrated, industry-specific Sardine Fishermen's Association, which struck the canners unsuccessfully in 1919 and 1920 for $15 a ton and exclusive (closed-shop) contracts.[84]

More dramatic was the 1920 fish cutters strike led by the "more Americanized" Japanese within this ethnically diverse specialization.[85] Workers sought a closed shop, uniform conditions across canneries, and wage guarantees. In a published statement of their aims, the Japanese Fish Cutters of New Monterey cite only restoration of the previous year's piece rate of ten cents a bucket (as opposed to a reduction to eight cents) and uniform rates across canneries.

> The Japanese fish cutters ask for fair treatment only. They do not ask for an increase in pay, but only ask for the same working conditions and the same pay that they received last year, which was 10c a bucket. The [sic] DO ask, however, that all canners pay the same wages. As it is now, one Canner pays one price and one another. Each seems to want to outdo the other and be the favorite one. This makes dissension among the cutters. . . . The Japanese people also would like to state that they were not the only ones responsible for the dissension between Cutters and the Canners. The Chinese, Mexicans, Italians, and Spanish, as well as the Americans, who are cutting fish, are dissatisfied with present conditions.[86]

Canners and the local press reacted in angry racial tones. "Japs Stir Up Strife" headlined the *Monterey Daily Cypress*, "brown men accused of creating dissension among laborers along Cannery Row."[87] The K. Hovden, Bayside Fish, and Monterey Canning companies threatened to import Filipino replacement workers and advertised "permanent positions for men and women" paying as much as $15 to $18 per day and $50 per week for "light work [requiring] only the skills of the ordinary housewife." Cutters acknowledged that the pay was good, yielding the equivalent of something more like $1.00 to $1.25 per hour, but irregular and not uniform—even the size of ten-cent buckets varied across plants, they said. Tacitly conceding their need for skilled workers, the cannery owners gave in after a month and unilaterally announced ten cents a bucket where scaling the fish was required, eight cents without scaling, and uniform wages in the plants of nine signatory members of the Monterey Canners Association (absent Booth). At the same time, however, they threatened to replace all Japanese workers, not only cutters, and continued to hire docile replacements. The fish cutters were not satisfied and resumed their walkout, provoking a special meeting of the community-wide Monterey Japanese Association, which published a statement lamenting the strike, "the deplorable conditions caused by the Fish Cutters," and wholesale dismissals of Japanese workers. "The Japanese Fishermen . . . will remain faithful to the Canners."[88]

This dramatic vertical class division within the Japanese community was neatly complemented by a horizontal alliance across ethnic working-class groups. In sympathy with the strike, Chinese fish cutters staged a "small riot" at the Carmel Canning Company, "throwing rocks at the cannery building, firing revolvers, and [causing] other disturbances" to protest fellow Chinese entering the plant to work.[89] In the end, the canners association stuck by their concessionary wage offer while replacing workers and, before long, eliminating the skilled and feisty cutters altogether. But 1920 marked the beginning of working-class struggle on Cannery Row, a style of conflict that would soon visit the fishing fleet and return again to the canneries in the 1930s.

Class action expressed in strikes and public broadsides routinely shaded into political violence, sabotage, and sullen resistance. Italian fishermen traditionally employed force when necessary to establish and maintain control of fishing grounds. Cinel notes that in San Francisco's Genoese-dominated industry "violence and intimidation . . . helped establish a quasi-monopoly, in a city where anti-Chinese sentiment made these tactics safe and useful ways to achieve economic success." The same methods were used less successfully by Genoese against Sicilians on San Francisco Bay in the 1890s. "Boats were sunk, nets have been cut, and sometimes owners too have been cut," in a pattern of intimidation that led some Sicilians to resettle at the Sacramento Delta town of Pittsburg.[90] Indeed, taking the case a step closer, a family history suggests that Pietro Ferrante left Pittsburg for Monterey owing in part to "envy and jealousy" followed by a fire that destroyed the wharf—arson, one conjectures.[91] Hovden claimed that two destructive fires in his plants were the work of incendiaries,[92] a credible charge given the arson in fruit canneries such as swept nearby Watsonville at the time. Bombs were planted (but failed to explode) on one of the boats and at the home of Angelo Lucido, whose San Carlos Cannery was accused of undercutting the fishermen's contract price during a 1931 strike.[93] Threats of violence and sabotage attended every major conflict of Monterey's industrial period.

The mid-1920s saw all the intricacies of class struggle in operation at once. Important strikes took place in each year from 1923 to 1926 as the canneries recovered from a postwar slump and began expanding again—good fortune that also entailed new labor needs. As an indicator that labor's moment had arrived, the canners agreed in 1925 to the long-standing demand that they employ only union boats.[94] The agreement did not last and was a bit symbolic in any event because unionized Sicilians dominated the fleet. Yet it was a significant symbol.

Success, however, brought new worries. With a growing capacity to can and reduce fish, cannery owners began to consider adoption of the larger and more efficient purse seine boats. A favorable climate for labor rights in 1925, as well as threats posed by the big boats that used mechanized equipment and fewer hands, led to formation of the Monterey Fishermen's Protective Union, an organization of crew members separate from fellow Sicilian boat owners. Ironically, the boat owners retaliated by dismissing their crews and threatening to import fishermen from southern California experienced in the use of purse seine nets. The dispute was settled in time for the 1926 season opening when both organizations of boat owners and fishermen struck for a 25 percent increase in the cannery price for sardines (from $10.00 to $12.50 a ton). Now the canners resisted. To keep his cannery in operation, Hovden brought two purse seiners and their crews from San Pedro, the *Admiral* and *Mariposa,* "larger than any sardine fishing boat ever seen in the bay."[95] Booth brought in strikebreakers, too, but in the form of lampara crews from San Francisco who worked boats Booth had recently repossessed from members of the boat owners' association.[96] Those boats were mysteriously scuttled at anchor while the formidable purse seiners chugged on to victory for the canners in the long strike.

Increasingly, conflicts on Cannery Row among fishermen, boat owners, and canners were shaped, even superseded, by state efforts to regulate the industry. Close observers of Monterey's burgeoning sardine harvest such as the Scofield brothers of the Fish and Game Division began to think that the fishery would be destroyed without state-enforced conservation. In the first decade after World War I, the sardine catch increased from around 30,000 to 100,000 tons just as the industry was on the verge of a new technological revolution based on purse seiner fishing and reduction processing. In McEvoy's compelling analysis, the "fisherman's problem" rested on a resource that was common property: "No one of them owns the resource so as to keep others away from it. As a result, everyone has an incentive to keep fishing so long as there is any money to be made in the effort, whereas no one has an individual incentive to refrain from fishing so as to conserve the stock. Every harvester knows that if he or she leaves a fish in the water someone else will get it and the profit, instead."[97]

A progressive state legislature in the early decades of the century passed the California Fish Conservation Act of 1919, amending it two years later to require that reduction use no more than 25 percent of the total sardine catch (a quota also expressed as fifteen cases of packed tins for each ton of processed fish). The law and its enforcement agents, however, soon found themselves on the weak side of economic logic and political influence. Sardines were never a favorite of American consumers, Europeans preferred the smaller Norwegian species of pilchard, and recent sales increases had depended on wartime conditions (U.S. government purchases for sea rations and exports aided by threats to North Sea fishing). At the same time, however, fish by-products enjoyed growing demand: fish meal for animal feed and fertilizer; fish oil for soap, paint, medicine, salad oil, leather tanning, glycerin, and precision-machine oil. Although manufacturers touted the nutritional wonders of sardines, devised new recipes, advertised creatively with colorful labels, sponsored essay contests in Monterey schools on the value of the California sardine, and actually developed new markets, it was apparent before long that industry profits lay in reduction. Where at one time only the offal was reduced, whole fish were now being used, and later canners would be accused of (and vigorously deny) "putting up a low quality pack" by saving the best fish for reduction. A more plausible rumor held that fish were canned and sold for human consumption below cost in order to increase absolutely the quota amount for reduction.

The reduction dispute was complicated in the 1930s by the advent of offshore, shipboard reduction factories, or "floaters," anchored beyond the three-mile limit and the reach of California law. Canners and civic boosters argued effectively to the legislature for liberalized reduction quotas in order to lift the "handicap" borne by shore-based, tax-paying, job-providing canneries. In 1929 the 25 percent limit on the catch subject to reduction was increased to 32.5 percent (and so the ratio of packed tins *reduced* from 15 to 13.5 cases per ton). More liberalization followed in 1932 and 1933 with appeals for depression jobs in a state legislature "vulnerable to . . . well-organized processors and their allies in agribusiness."[98] Eventually, a popular referendum promoted by conservation groups banning offshore reduction was endorsed by the voters in 1938. By then, however, compromises of the original conservation law favoring the canneries had rendered the floaters uneconomical. As groups constituting the fishing industry joined forces in support of greater reduction, concerted action headed for ecological ruin. In some years during the late 1930s and early 1940s, as many as twenty-six plants processed catches ranging from 230,000 to 250,000 tons, six times the volume of the great 1919–20 season.

A new level of working-class organization was attained in 1937 when cannery workers formed their first real union and struck for recognition. The American Federation of Labor (AFL), which represented cannery workers in San Pedro, sent an organizer to Monterey in fall 1936 who opened an office on Cannery Row, held mass meetings, and launched the Cannery Workers Union Local No. 20305. By January, however, Monterey workers, noted for their independence from the national labor movement and their communal ties to local canneries, rejected AFL control. Retaining formal links to the AFL, the union insisted on autonomy in negotiations with canners and elected their own slate of officers headed by Mrs. Garnet Sture, president, and James Mattingly, business agent.

Meanwhile, fishermen became embroiled in a national struggle over control of the union movement. The Monterey Sardine Fishermen's Protective Union dating from 1925 had no national affiliation, but local men who worked off season on the coast from Oregon to Alaska necessarily held dual membership in the dominant Deep Sea and Purse Seine Fishermen's Union–AFL. When the Deep Sea union began its Monterey organizing efforts in 1936, a potent dilemma was posed for local fishermen. On the one hand, many of them valued off-season employment opportunities contingent on AFL solidarity. On the other hand, they preferred local union autonomy, a condition endorsed by all the canners—except Booth, the individualist who had contracts with the AFL union. When the AFL challenged Monterey canners with a strike call in September 1936, the large majority of local fishermen and canneries announced their opposition and pursued their strikebreaking labors—and Booth's cannery suffered a serious fire of unknown origin. It became clear that the AFL could not break local traditions of autonomy and cannery loyalty. Rival fishing unions made peace in January 1937 based on de facto local autonomy with formal AFL links and called a strike mainly as a show of strength celebrating their newfound unity.

But the Cannery Workers Union sprung a surprise, electing to strike in solidarity with the fishermen. In this, their first job action, cannery workers above all wanted recognition and a closed shop, a minimum wage (50 cents per hour for men and 45 cents for women), overtime (an additional 5 cents per hour), time and a half for Sundays, a shop grievance committee, and preferential hiring of union members. The fishermen's dispute posed no obstacle for prompt settlement with canners, but resumption of fishing and processing was stalled by the awkward honeymoon of the two virgin unions. According to a contemporary account, "It is refusal of the fishermen to work for plants which have not signed up with the cannery workers union that makes the latter strike effective." Under the circumstances, the strike was settled within the week and formalized in a twenty-seven-point document that began, "Wage demands of the cannery workers union are granted. . . . The union is recognized."[99]

Although the closed-shop provision did not win agreement, workers got most of what they wanted and in the process set a new standard of cooperative class action that rose above craft, ethnic, gender, and communal divisions in the labor force. Sarah Sousa, a cutter who joined the union organizers, said, "A small group of us could see that we weren't getting ahead. We wanted to better ourselves. It was a powerful feeling, but I was scared too. We went to a lot of meetings, and the men led, of course. But there were a few women who spoke their piece."[100] Charlie Nonella, who packed cans into cases, recalls, "[I]n 1929–1930 we were makin' 38 cents an hour. In 1936 the unions came in and we were jacked up to $1.08 an hour. When I quit in 1946, we were makin' $1.35."[101]

The union movement also generated conflicts within labor ranks. In 1937 the AFL and the Congress of Industrial Organizations (CIO) waged a bitter national struggle over membership and tactics. Shortly after its establishment in Monterey, the Cannery Workers Union had its charter revoked by the AFL, which charged the local with "communistic and CIO agitation."[102] Although the union reorganized and received a new AFL charter, a group of militants bolted and met with a CIO organizer from San Francisco. At an open meeting in New Monterey's Japanese Hall, 150 to 200 cannery workers determined to form a rival union.[103] As the rivalry continued into 1938, West Coast fishermen also split over AFL versus CIO representation. Traditionally conservative Monterey fishermen bucked the trend toward CIO support among California locals in a statewide election and asserted their "right to defend [themselves] when necessary against the action of radicals and troublemakers who try to dominate the fishermen of Monterey and prevent them from organizing in their own interests." Defending against radicals, Horace "Sparky" Enea, president of the Seine and Line Fishermen's Union (AFL), broke a bottle over the head of Mrs. Augustine Martin, a sympathizer with the United Fishermen's Union (CIO), whom Enea thought was tearing down announcements of his union's meeting. A court crowded with union supporters found Enea guilty of battery despite his protestation that Mrs. Martin's husband was a Red and CIO member.[104]

The CIO enjoyed broader, if not majority, support in the canneries. Following the Cannery Workers Union split, the CIO faction mounted an energetic organizing campaign and called for an election supervised

26.   CIO Strike, 1938. In December 1938 the CIO challenged the AFL's
recent unionization of cannery workers. Families were mobilized for the strike
and children carried placards, some saying that Santa Claus would not be
coming to their house because cannery owners and the AFL refused to hold
an election on union representation. (Courtesy of the Maritime Museum of
Monterey)

by the National Labor Relations Board (NLRB) to select a sole bargaining
agent. The CIO's spirited election drive included a children's demonstration at Christmas, their placards reading "Santa Claus Won't Come
to Our Houses this Christmas. The AFL & Cannery Owners Refuse AN
ELECTION" and "Cannery Owners Won't Hire My Daddy. He Belongs
to the CIO." The CIO urged cannery workers to strike in support of their
union elections. Union violence shifted direction when the New Monterey home of AFL supporter Maria Roman was bombed. None of the
four cannery workers or the family who shared the house was injured,
but Mrs. Roman understood the attack as a warning, having been "threatened recently by rival union members."[105] The NLRB soon agreed to supervised elections, which were held in February 1939 at each of the major canneries (despite CIO demands for one neutral polling place). Given
the conservative leanings of fishermen, cannery operators, and their
friends and families in the labor movement, the outcome was never in
serious doubt. With more than 80 percent of eligible workers, or a total
of 1,855, participating, the AFL received 1,133 (61 percent), the CIO
482 (26 percent), and others 240 (13 percent).[106] In the face of such a

clear result the CIO could still take credit for having provided the opportunity for workers to exercise their choice and for winning the support of a significant minority.

By 1939 the "old Spanish capital" had become an industrial union town. In a nation only slowly recovering from depression, Monterey took pride in its new identity, industrial accomplishments, and escape from idleness.

> There is a population here of hundreds of families supported by the industry of the men who man these vessels. There are thousands of people who make their hard living by packing and reducing tens of thousands of tons of sardines. The old town of Monterey shared with the rest of the country the long and difficult years of the depression. But it was during that period that the town woke up to the fact that it wasn't such a bad idea to be called a "fishing village" after all. Tradesmen and bankers realized to a greater degree than ever before how fundamentally basic to the economic welfare of this region the fishing industry was. . . . This Peninsula is one of the rare places on earth, but it is the reality of labor and productivity that saves this place from being one of those baubles whose beauty [is] at the service of those that neither reap nor sow. . . . The fishing fleet and cannery row remind those that live here and those that come to look and see, that there is something more than scenery, recreation and conversation to the Monterey Peninsula. Monterey's fishermen saved this beautiful area from being damned to be only a "resort."[107]

NEW AND RECONFIGURED LOCAL HISTORIES

The Great Depression and World War II were years of extraordinary cultural florescence. In Monterey as in much of the nation, history was rewritten in light of trials unknown to the expansive and self-assured temper of the late nineteenth century. War and depression fostered a new way of thinking about the national experience, new history as well as styles of art, architecture, literature, design, city planning, preservation, and commemoration—a new public history, broadly understood. The cultural renaissance was realized through equally remarkable institutional innovations at the federal, state, and local levels. Government assumed the responsibility of mobilizing society for economic recovery and national defense through a series of programs ranging from public works to the arts. All of these initiatives converged in Monterey. Local life hummed with the activities of relief agencies, WPA projects, historic preservationists, wartime production, festivals combining patriotism and heritage, policies dispossessing the Japanese and Italian aliens, and sundry efforts to somehow represent contemporary experience in a coherent whole. This was the social milieu that produced Steinbeck's classic stories: a diverse group of talented writers, a school of California impressionist painters, sculptors, architects, mission restoration, and a new city plan anchored in historical memory.

Although the work of cultural production was a broadly collective effort embracing many points of view, the Monterey story unfolded in two major historical narratives: the romance of Spanish California and the working-class story. The first narrative continued and elaborated earlier versions of pastoralism in a new rendition that celebrated the church and Father Serra as never before just as it erased Spanish civil institutions and most of the Mexican period (at least anything praiseworthy about it). The working-class narrative, of course, reflected the new era of industrialization, depression trauma, and wartime recovery. The two narratives were divergent, if not necessarily opposed. They had different empirical foci, distinct sympathies, and separate constituencies. They animated different agendas for civic action. Sometimes they came into conflict, but more often they coexisted on their respective sides of the street. On a few revealing occasions they marched in step, belying hegemonic notions of social memory.

THE ROMANCE OF SPANISH CALIFORNIA

In its twentieth-century formulation, the early California narrative took a new form resembling less its nineteenth-century predecessors than its original construction in the late-eighteenth-century writings of Father Palóu. The new romance drew elements from nineteenth-century narratives of Yankee virtue and American progress but changed their valence. Ranchos, the old capital at Monterey, and the caste society of "Spanish" dons and doñas became sites of intrepid romance and courtly elegance rather than havens of indolence. More central to the new story were the mission settlements, church teachings, the exemplary Father Serra, Indian neophytes, and the pastoral society they combined to form. Like Helen Hunt Jackson's utopian portrait of the pre-Mexican hacienda in *Ramona,* the story excluded church-state conflict, exploitation of Indian labor, and soaring mortality rates. To the extent that the Mexican state, secularization, or Californio revolution received any mention, they were understood as the forces that destroyed a noble experiment. The new story was oddly reverential and idealized. Gone were the gritty facts that peppered the church hagiography of Palóu and imperial warrant of La Pérouse. In their place were piety, sentimentality, and ingenuousness. The purpose now was decidedly celebration, not description. Spanish California was refashioned as a commodity traded among buyers and sellers in the developing heritage market. The results were not all bad. The heritage industry served some useful ends, as we shall see. But a rounded, picaresque, warted history was lost in the endeavor. The new romance obscured other, more lurid stories.

Commemorative activities in the new century continued established traditions. In 1910 the long-awaited Commodore Sloat monument overlooking the bay was dedicated before a large patriotic crowd. A mere hundred yards distant, Father Serra was honored with a second monument in 1908, a Celtic cross marking the spot of the Vizcaíno oak where the first Catholic masses were celebrated. The oak itself had died, but a cross section of its trunk was preserved in the entrance to Monterey's historic San Carlos Church (the original Royal Presidio Chapel). Restoration of the Carmel Mission Church, begun in the 1880s by Father Casanova, continued with growing community support during the long tenure of Father Raymond Maria Mestres as pastor at San Carlos. Reconstruction and commemorative events took place regularly (e.g., a pilgrimage in 1913 celebrating the bicentennial of Serra's birth, the 1919 baptism of Alejandro, Berthold, and Juan Onesimo, the last full-blooded Rumsen and descendants of Indians supposedly baptized by Serra). The mission was reactivated as a functioning parish church in 1933. Mestres, an energetic if abrasive advocate, raised substantial sums and enlisted the talents of the nationally renowned architect Bernard Maybeck and artist-sculptor Jo Mora to draw plans for the restoration. Mestres worked closely with Lady Maria Antonia Field, a descendant of the prominent Munras family and secretary of the Mission Restoration Fund.[108]

In 1924 the great Pilgrimage Week and Pageant of Fray Junípero Serra centered on the unveiling of the padre's sarcophagus, the Serra Cenotaph sculpted by Mora, at the mission and engaged the planning efforts of hundreds of citizens. T. A. Work headed an executive committee charged with drafting the program and raising money for artistic contributions. According to committee plans, "The assistance of local artists [was] sought, in order that the historical, romantic and legendary material in the program should be written by nationally known authors. Artists will be asked to permit reproductions of their paintings in the program."[109] The pageant, written by Father Mestres and Perry Newberry, a Carmel author, featured 750 performers in an outdoor reenactment of the Serra-Portolá expedition, the establishment of the mission, and "the growth of civilization and the death of Serra." The seven-day celebration included repeat performances of the pageant, parades, parties, dances, fireworks, the equestrian Fiesta de Vaqueros, and a water carnival of fishing boats regaled with lanterns and music.[110] Every segment of the community was co-opted. Three hundred fifty employees of Del Monte Properties donned period costumes in response to a notice from company manager C. S. Stanley "asking that the employees enter the spirit of the festival with all the interest and vim they can muster."[111] Local historian Major Rolin Watkins was assistant director of the pilgrimage and ensured the events' authenticity. The parade down Alvarado Street celebrated "Three Generations of Occupation," Spanish, Mexican, and American, but stressed the Spanish romance. As an observer described it,

> [F]or an hour this morning Monterey's past lived again—the glamorous past, when life was high-colored, swift and bold, and hearts throbbed with rich hot blood. . . . Surely men of today they could not have been, those dashing conquistadors, gallant caballeros, those fierce dusky Mexicans, and bronze-skinned glowering Indians. And oh, the senoritas—those red-lipped maidens with the dark desirous eyes, sparkling with the unrepentence of a day when love was unashamed to flaunt resistless banners. . . . It was all so intelligent, [participants] caught the spirit of old Monterey and gave it back to spectators in a wondrous interpretation.[112]

Jo Mora, famed for his Will Rogers Memorial Sculpture in Oklahoma, considered the Serra Cenotaph "the supreme professional effort" of his life. Standing in a chapel entry to the mission church, the reclining bronze figure of Serra lay on top of the sarcophagus with his missionary colleagues Crespí, Palóu, and Lasuén kneeling at head and foot. On the ornamental panels of the sarcophagus Mora carved scenes from California history, processions of settlers and soldiers on horseback recalling the Portolá expedition and Indian and Spanish workers, as well as a remarkable invention of the artist himself that shows Indians attacking the mission—acts that never occurred at Carmel and only very rarely elsewhere (San Diego in 1775, Santa Inés and La Purísima in 1824). Evidently Mora, Uruguayan by birth, had absorbed the western American myth that Indians were aggressors in conflicts with whites. In any case, the myth was literally inscribed on the frieze of Serra's commemorative sculpture.

Like the authors and spectators of the pageant, Mora operated in a context suffused with commercialization of the Serra story and early California generally. Funds for the cenotaph commission were raised from local benefactors and businesses, including Del Monte Properties—which also employed Mora at the Hotel Del Monte for works of sculpture (*La Novia*, a Spanish wedding scene) and commercial art (a visitor's map of

27. Serra Cenotaph. The Uruguayan artist Jo Mora contributed a number of artworks to the Hotel Del Monte and Carmel Mission that celebrated, even invented, Monterey's romantic Spanish past. Father Serra's cenotaph completed in 1924 includes a frieze depicting a fanciful battle between marauding Indians and Spanish soldiers defending the mission settlement. (Photo by the author)

the peninsula). Mora illustrated a popular local history written by Tirey L. Ford titled *Dawn and the Dons: The Romance of Monterey.*

While living at the Hotel Del Monte, Ford was captivated by the "magic lure" of the Monterey Peninsula and after discussions with Samuel F. B. Morse, "himself a profound student of history," decided to write a "painstaking study of this playground of California under his [Morse's] encouragement and with his aid."[113] As these origins might suggest, Ford's book is an idealization of the Spanish period studded with platitudes, oozing avuncular prose, and bereft of documentation.

> Be it said to the credit of the Spaniard that his rule was benign. Through the medium of the missions, harmonious relations between these untutored natives and their self-appointed masters were maintained, Aristotle's ideal aristocracy. . . . The most unique feature [of the society] is the grace and refinement of manner, and the ceremonial courtesies. . . . But they were not indolent. They shied at menial tasks, but were tireless in the larger activities of that period (stock raising, hunting, boating, fishing, and flirting). . . . The Spanish days in California were happy days. Want was unknown.

And so on until "the pastoral peace" is upset by Mexican rule, "greedy foreign powers," and the gold rush. But Monterey was spared ruination by its isolation, artistic bohemians, and visionaries whom Ford describes in tones that recall his patron.

> Happily, those who planned and wrought the more recent changes in this delightful playground sensed the charm of the old Spanish days, and were guided in their work by a desire to preserve and to continue the fascinating delights of California's romantic period. . . . Here is the one place in all California where the Arcadian delights of that elder and carefree time have found a refuge from the onslaughts of commercialism; and where American genius has deftly woven into modern life the romantic pleasures of a Latin race.[114]

Ford failed to notice that Morse and Del Monte Properties were in the commercial business of real estate development. The company's crucial support of civic events such as Pilgrimage Week served its own ends as well as those of others, including the church and citizens genuinely interested in historical preservation. If commercialism contributed to these events, it was not the only element of their success. And conversely, Pilgrimage Week had several purposes, including the enhancement of town prestige (the California Supreme Court was invited), economic promotion, fund-raising for historic preservation (including a new roof for the mission), and sheer entertainment. All that said, it was true nevertheless that commemorative events of the 1920s and 1930s celebrated a new and romanticized version of history and the reason for that choice lay precisely in the activities of the commemorators—the interests of the church in celebrating its own past and winning esteem, the ambition of town boosters to fashion a glamorous identity for themselves, the hope of civic activists to enhance their community through historical preservation, and the diverse calculations that connected these activities with economic prosperity.

The labors of civic promotion and historical preservation reach their apogee in the 1930s. History making received an organizational boost early in 1931 with the establishment of the Monterey History and Art Association (MHAA).

> The movement launched three months ago for more effective means of perpetuating this region's historical and artistic treasures achieved definite and permanent status last night, when the Monterey History and Art Assn. Ltd. . . . began functioning as a going concern. Nearly two score men and women prominent in art circles of Monterey peninsula or enthusiastically committed to a policy of preserving the peninsula's historic landmarks became members at last night's dinner meeting held at Cademartori's restaurant.[115]

In fact, the original membership list contains eighty names, among them artists Armin Hansen and E. (for Euphemia) Charlton Fortune, writers Laura Bride Powers and Amelie Elkington, S. F. B. Morse of Del Monte Properties, and Carmel Martin, the town's leading attorney and a member of the planning commission. Many of the members were socially prominent, women, Anglo-Americans, upper-middle-class civic spirits. The leaders were retired army colonel Roger Fitch and Laura Bride Powers, custodian of the U.S. Custom House (an honorary position at the site now maintained as a state park).

The MHAA was serious, professional, energetic, and elitist, at least in the early years. New members were recommended at meetings and elected to the body, its number increasing to 173 by the end of the second year. About half were from Carmel, Pacific Grove, and Pebble Beach. Most would be described as "society people." Group efforts concentrated on marking and preserving historical sites: the Custom House Museum, the first theater, the old presidio grounds, and the Alvarado and Cooper houses. Powers urged that Main Street be restored to its original name, Calle Principal, which was done, although Colonel Fitch opposed her on additional name changes. Part of the several-hundred-dollar annual budget was earmarked for public lectures by "eminent historians," notably Herbert E. Bolton from the University of California, an acquaintance of Powers.[116]

While the MHAA worked with the county planning commission and state parks department, it expressed a special interest in San Carlos Church and Carmel Mission as living landmarks of local history. The group voted to make the pastors of all area missions members of its board and adopted restoration at Carmel as a major objective—advising the archbishop in San Francisco that the work be conducted "under sympathetic and competent architectural supervision and control."[117] Laura Bride Powers had been advocating for some time the reopening of Carmel Mission as a working parish and visitors' attraction. In a series of letters to Bishop John McGinley in Fresno (headquarters of the diocese at the time), she praised the bishop's decision to begin holding masses again at the mission, noted public interest in "our beloved Junipero's grave," but went on to complain that the numbers at Sunday mass were small and Monsignor Father Mestres was unwelcoming, treating the mission as "his own private business." Indeed, she charged that "the Monsignor is regarded as one of the heaviest speculators in real estate on the peninsula, his holdings are large as shown in the records," with the result that "much ribaldry ensues" whenever he asks for funds. Judging from letters to the bishop, a controversy developed, with several parish women defending the monsignor and the church historian Zephyrin Engelhardt weighing in with the observation that Powers was a person "anxious to shine [who] has injected herself in the affairs of this place[,] . . . a loudmouth [who] will conjure up a scandal."[118] In fact, it seems that both Mestres and Powers were egos in service to a cause.

Community relations improved when Philip Scher, former pastor at San Carlos, was named bishop and Father Michael O'Connell became pastor at the reopened mission church in 1933. Scher initiated two history-making projects. First, he retained the services of friend and cabinet maker Henry John (Harry) Downie to repair some damaged statues in the church attic. One repair job led to another, and Downie spent the remaining fifty years of his life in historical research and restoration of Carmel Mission. He lived at the mission, became a local figure known as "Brother Harry" who conducted mission tours in a friar's robe, studied mission history with the local expert Father James Cullerton, and imparted his artisan skills to the resurrected buildings. Scher's second initiative began with a special effort for the annual Serra Pilgrimage on the sesquicentennial of the padre's death in 1934. The local celebration took a dramatic turn when the bishop announced that the Serra Cause for canonization was being proposed coincidentally in Rome. The plan seems to have been discreetly under way since Scher's consecration as bishop, judging from his correspondence and successful effort to have the California State Assembly pass, one year in advance, a resolution declaring Junípero Serra Day on August 28, 1934.

The Serra Sesquicentennial rivaled the great pageant a decade earlier and set new standards of commemorative display. The five-day celebration featured a pageant and parade through Carmel to the mission, band concerts, a daily High Mass, and performances of the mission play. The Serra Fiesta Committee published an elegant program with text by Harry Downie, testimonial letters from California governor Frank Merriam and Vicar General Michael Sullivan, and a long list of sponsors including J. E. Steinbeck, Bank of Carmel, Carl's Auto Service, Carmel Drug Store, Mission Inn, Mission Cleaners, Pine Inn, Hotel Monterey, and Monterey Chamber of Commerce.[119] The parade was designed as a "historical procession." The *Monterey Peninsula Herald* described it thus: "[D]ifferent periods of civilization in California from primitive Indian days to the gold rush boom of '49 and the stage coach will be faithfully reproduced. . . . [F]ollowing the grand marshall will be the Indians in war paint and feathers beating tom toms to call the warriors for a pow wow to overcome the white invasion." Next in line would be Spanish soldiers and "monks" (which Franciscans were not), followed by "fiesta groups" of ladies of the Spanish court, forty-niners, and "miscellaneous mounted groups."[120]

George Marion's mission play, "The Apostle of California," drew on historical and literary sources, including Garcí Ordoñez de Montalvo's sixteenth-century novel, *Las Sergas de Esplandía,* from which the name California derives. Marion, who had acted and directed in New York and Hollywood before retiring in Carmel, cast himself in the title role as Serra. Helen Ware played Califia, the incongruous Amazon Queen, and a large cast of townspeople performed as wild Indians, Catalan Volunteers, clergy, and native dancers.[121] The play set out a melodramatic account of local history.

> Long ago in the hills of Carmel valley Esselen tribesmen listened as their chief implores their God for rain . . . until an Indian runner excitedly interrupts the ceremony. He tells of men marching toward the valley from over southern hills and fills his hungry tribesmen with fear and apprehension. Into the circle of despair a daughter of the Amazona flings her heroic form, dominating her people with her fearless heritage. Califia calls the Esselen to battle any force that threatens the freedom of their fair land of California. Thus when the monks and soldiers of Spain halt in gratitude upon the grounds where now the mission stands to thank their God . . . they find a band of armed and angry Indians. . . . Between drawn guns and pointed arrows steps the fearless padre, Junipero Serra, whose tones ring with the authority of Christian martyrdom. . . . The great soul wins the wondering Indians by that burning force which knows no defeat—the fire of love. . . . [Together they face hardships, De Anza arrives with reinforcements, and] soon the gay fiesta fills all hearts with courage. . . . Indians sway to the beat of their native music. Senora and senorita of old Mexico swing through the rhythms running in their Spanish blood.[122]

Anthropological flights of fancy aside, the play reprises the essential pastoral myth prevailing in authoritative circles at the time. Like contemporary written history, the parade and pageant privileged the Spanish period, misrepresented the Indian response, caricatured the mercurial Serra, reduced Californio society to one long fiesta, and silenced all the rest—notably Indian contributions to the new society, Mexican rule and reform, trade, revolution, and American conquest. Carmel's "Apostle of Christ" drew on the genre established by Helen Hunt Jackson in *Ramona* and the pageant based on the novel that was presented every summer in southern California. Yet where *Ramona* proceeded from an idealized portrait of Spanish colonialism to the dispossession of indigenous peoples

under Mexico and the United States, the new romance elaborated in the
1930s gives no place to Indians after the fearless padre opens their eyes
to the authority of Christian martyrdom.

By any measure, the Serra Sesquicentennial was a great success:
"Peninsula hotels, auto camps, and rooming houses were well filled with
visitors." The MHAA joined the festivities with an exhibit at the Custom House Museum. Del Monte Properties contributed $1,238 and the
pageant earned $1,730 after expenses, both sums going to the Mission
Restoration Fund.[123] Junípero Serra Day became Serra Year. Locally,
1934 was a watershed marked by initiation ("postulation") of the Serra
Cause for sainthood and the Monterey History and Art Association's
successful institutionalization of local history and preservation.

Published in the same year, Laura Bride Powers's *Old Monterey* became the standard text on local history and the handbook of the MHAA.
The book was an acknowledged product of the activities of "Serra Year"
and the fruit of a "spell" the author fell under when as a child of fourteen she witnessed the opening of Serra's grave in 1882. In her view, "the
great Franciscan's story is best understood as the history of Old Monterey." Powers did her homework, consulted the important sources
(Palóu, Forbes, Engelhardt, Hittell, Bancroft, and Bolton, who provided
a brief foreword to the book), and covered the span of events from the
early voyages to the state constitutional convention in 1849 (neglecting
the next eighty-five years, with the exception of Stevenson's visit). The
histrionic writing is effective for a naive audience. But it constitutes an
unrestrained panegyric to the missionaries and Spanish colonialism, a
lamentation of the demise of their "simple, beautiful civilization," and
a scathing indictment of the Mexican "racketeers" who destroyed the
missions for their own profit. The text drums these themes: dimwitted
Indians were "weaned from their wild life and turned into the ways of
industry[,] . . . taught to sing the simpler songs of the church and to grasp,
however feebly, some of the simple truths of the Christian faith. . . . [A]rt,
music, and the sciences were introduced into the Mission in the Wilderness . . . [until Monterey was] looted at the hands of the paisano politicians under the guise of 'secularization.'" By 1846, as a result of the
"crimes" of "paisano chiefs," at last "the time was ripe for the explain-
able seizure of California by the United States." In an interesting twist
on the gendered reading of American conquest in the late nineteenth century, Powers claims that when the matronly señoras closed their shutters
to parading troops, "no such feeling possessed the young *señoritas,* who
promptly re-opened the shutters and waved to the debonair Yankees as

they marched by. A new promise of romance, to be fulfilled beneath the rose-hung balconies of the old town."[124]

If Powers was given to hyperbole, she nevertheless shared a characteristic historical vision with other, more sophisticated writers of the period. In 1933 Virginia Stivers Bartlett published *Mistress of Monterey,* a novel of the 1780s centered on Eulalia Fages, her stormy marriage to the governor, and the querulous relationship between Pedro Fages and Junípero Serra. Bartlett's story, serialized in the *Monterey Peninsula Herald,* reached a national audience and faithfully employed a long list of academic sources identified in a bibliography. Still a good read nearly seventy years later, Bartlett's novel simultaneously airs church-state arguments over Native American treatment (Serra's corporal punishment and Fages's concubinage) and sentimentalizes the Serra-Fages relationship by supposing tender mutual respect beneath their separate foul tempers.[125] The more celebrated writer Mary Austin was less successful with her story, *Isidro,* written in 1905 in the shadow of *Ramona* and without the historical resources available to Bartlett. Finally, Anne Fisher's 1940 novel, *Cathedral in the Sun,* shares features of Powers and Bartlett. Like the latter, it holds up well owing to her use of historical sources (also listed in a bibliography) and her own research with Isabella Meadows, daughter of a Carmel Mission Indian and a British sailor, who is also the novel's fictionalized heroine. The story is at once an elegy to the enchanted world of Carmel Mission (never a cathedral, the seat of a bishop) and an exposé of Indian dispossession and marginalization on a par with the best reformist arguments of Helen Hunt Jackson in *Ramona.*[126]

From monuments to pageants, parades to restored buildings, entertainments to scholarship, a popular culture of Spanish romance and mission pastoral was elaborated in the first half of Monterey's twentieth century. Not only was the new popular culture thematically unified, it was enthusiastically enacted in a set of organizations and commemorative events. Colonel Fitch of the MHAA expanded an earlier drawing into the *Tourist Map of Monterey* identifying fifty-five historic sites in the downtown area, some being restored by the association, that could be visited on a walking tour. Visitors and residents alike were presented with a pronounced vision of "who we are," "where we came from." It was a selective vision, obscuring the Mexican, Californio, and paisano contributions—not to mention Scots land barons and Sicilian fishermen. But, with few deviations, it was the wisdom of the time. If publicists like Tirey Ford and playwrights like George Marion trivialized the story, they were socially, sympathetically, and thematically in the same league with bona fide historical writers like Powers, Bartlett, and Fisher.

More important, many of those who constructed this popular culture drew their authority from academic sources that firmly supported the spirit of their interpretation. Central to these events was the Berkeley historian Herbert Bolton, an expert who lectured the MHAA, endorsed Powers's book, and later served the Serra Cause on a select committee that testified to the padre's saintly character.[127] And it was Bolton who, in the pages of the *American Historical Review,* described the mission as a "frontier institution" that effectively settled and civilized the Spanish borderlands. His book of that name described Serra as "the outstanding Spanish pioneer of California": "Under the new regime, which curbed every native instinct and changed the whole fashion of their lives the Indians deceased. But, while it is easy to pick flaws in the mission system of dealing with the Indians, it is not so easy to point to any other system which has done better. The problem of civilizing a wild people has baffled others than the padres."[128] Bolton and the rest were, of course, entitled to such views, commonplace at the time. Together they demonstrate that Monterey's public history, far from any parochial distortion, was the locally worked out version of California's official story at the time.

THE WORKING-CLASS STORY

The *WPA Guide* ("Compiled by Workers of the Writers' Program of the Works Progress Administration in Northern California," the title page explains) understood perfectly Monterey's "contradictory character," particularly its "mingling of unlike elements[,] . . . still living on its memories of a never-to-be-forgotten past and yet too hurried by today's less-romantic demands to dwell forever in history[,] . . . ancient capital of Spanish-Mexican California [and] modern 'Sardine Capital of the World.'" In 1941 it appeared to WPA writers that "Monterey [was] torn between irreconcilable impulses" to pursue either historical preservation or industrial expansion. The chamber of commerce was vexed by the realization that "history yields cash returns [but] fish canneries are still worth more than adobe *casas.*"[129] Although the observation is insightful concerning the dual character of local identity, it concludes prematurely that preservationist and industrial "impulses" were irreconcilable. In hindsight we can see that these seemingly inconsistent activities coexisted with little friction beyond the odor controversy. On a few occasions they even commingled, as in the often-remarked attraction of visitors to the

colorful wharf, picturesque fishing boats, and religious festival of blessing the fleet.

The reconcilability of impulses was furthered by development of a
broad working-class narrative embracing not only fishermen and cannery
workers but also paisanos, tradespeople, and relief workers, including
the WPA writers themselves. Monterey had long supported a diverse
community of laboring people, artisans, and, in the language of the time,
"bohemians." Monterey's Building Trades Council was organized in
1906, before the fishing industry, and sponsored lectures and picnics fre-
quented by "workmen who have been the pioneers of the successful union
movement here."[130] From the days of Simoneau, Travernier, and Stevenson, Monterey supported an arts colony that was fortified by the development of Carmel-by-the-Sea (as the more affected suburb began calling
itself). The mission town also supported a John Reed Club where the labor and socialist agenda was discussed. From the early years of the century onward, Carmel attracted artists and intellectuals including some-
time residents such as Mary Austin, Jack London, John Steinbeck,
Robinson Jeffers, and Lincoln Steffens, all of whom celebrated the working class in their writings.

The working-class narrative developed locally was a cultural construction extending far beyond political formulations. Fundamentally it
was the expression of an important segment of the community and of
the institutional mechanisms put at their disposal during the depression.
WPA projects (and their predecessors under the Civil Works Administration [CWA] and the California-supported State Emergency Relief
[SERA] efforts) were an important institutional presence. In Monterey
County they employed as many as 1,600 people at their peak (half the
number in fishing), pumped $900,000 into the region between 1931 and
1938, and employed 900 workers in 1938 with weekly earnings of
$22,585 spent locally. The bulk of this effort was devoted to works of
infrastructure and urban redevelopment. The modern landscapes of Monterey, Pacific Grove, and Carmel were created in this endeavor. Monterey
saw the redesign of El Estero Park and its historic French Consulate, the
Colton Hall grounds, the Central Plaza, and the shoreline promenade.
Municipal recreation facilities were built at Pacific Grove's Lovers' Point
and Carmel received a new road fronting the mission. Works of huge
economic importance beyond the towns included extension of the coast
highway and clearing a ten-thousand-acre parcel for the new Camp Ord
military reservation.[131]

The projects themselves did not overtly celebrate labor or recount a particular historical narrative. But they did make huge contributions to the accessibility, use value, amenities, and symbolic importance of public spaces. They said that ordinary folks were entitled to a waterfront park and ocean view, just like the Pebble Beach crowd. They supported unemployed people to build those facilities. And in both acts they mobilized a constituency around symbols of working-class worthiness.

The WPA did a lot more than build parks and roads. It supported varied types of white-collar work, notably cultural endeavors beginning with the Federal Writer's Project that produced the popular guidebook series. And the WPA *Guide to the Monterey Peninsula* was no mere inventory of places to visit but an engagingly written local history ("Monterey has never been a Yankee town"). As Page Stegner observes in a foreword to the new edition, it was an unsurpassed sociological study and cultural history. The Carmel novelist Fred Bechdolt directed the local writer's group and Carol Steinbeck, the author's wife and editor, supported the couple on WPA wages (ranging from $28 to $44 per week) while *Tortilla Flat* was being written.[132]

In addition to the writer's program, the WPA supported local groups of painters, musicians, performing artists, and historians. The Historical Survey of the Monterey Peninsula employed a staff directed by Frank Thompson that compiled an extensive bibliography of sources relating to all phases of local history, a biographical index to notable people, and a collection of early photographs—all of it contributed to the public library.[133] Miss Dene Denny and Winifred Howe supervised the county unit of the Federal Music Project, which organized the Tipica orchestra for performance of Latin music.[134] A number of nationally recognized artists lived in Carmel and Monterey, some of whom worked for the WPA or Treasury Arts Program. Henrietta Shore was commissioned to paint murals in the post offices of Pacific Grove and Monterey, the latter work portraying the Chinese fishing village and Portuguese whalers.[135] Bruce Ariss was hired to paint a 150-foot "WPA mural" in the Pacific Grove High School Library. His recollection of the period captures nicely the narrative alternatives and the sentiments of the arts community: "I decided that painting another standard mural of early Spanish settlers dancing the fandango would be less important than depicting the vigorous, and probably transitory, life on cannery row."[136]

Artworks that spoke to the working class were not confined to the 1930s or WPA sponsorship. Armin Hansen was a celebrated local artist and teacher who brought his classical training to Monterey's *Men of the Sea*. Charlton Fortune (as she signed her work) studied with Hansen

28. *No Place to Go,* by Maynard Dixon, 1935. Dixon's portrait of a depression era tramp captures the Big Sur headlands and the style of social realism that characterized the period. Through the efforts of a number of artists, many with WPA support, Monterey played an important role in defining the depression for the nation as a whole. (Courtesy of the Brigham Young University Museum of Art. All rights reserved)

and lent her impressionist style to a number of works portraying rustic town scenes. Judith Deim painted rough cannery workers and sybaritic bohemians in the late 1930s. Perhaps the most stunning work of the period was Maynard Dixon's forlorn portrait of a man, bedroll slung over his shoulder, looking out to the ocean from the Big Sur headlands, titled *No Place to Go.* This was art that defined the era for Monterey and for America, cultural history that celebrated its working-class provenance.

One should not infer from sympathetic cultural representations of the depression and laboring poor that harmony prevailed or class conflict was absent from local society. As the Great Depression wore on, Pacific Grove found itself facing an "invasion of undesirables." Aroused citizens determined to "discuss the serious problem of the infiltration of undesirables into Pacific Grove, with resultant effect upon property values, morals, and the welfare of the city" and called for a meeting "at the Forest Hill hotel." Chamber of commerce president and city attorney Reginald Foster explained that the situation was serious, real estate values and summer resort business were threatened, and residents spoke of "visiting certain families with shotguns and setting a deadline for them to be out of town."[137] At the meeting, "for two hours and some minutes everybody beat around the bush" until the Reverend Charles Greenleaf confronted the truth they all knew but feared to speak: "[I]t is not a matter of undesirable tenants, then, but of undesirable landlords. If we can eliminate the 5, 10, and 15 dollar houses, we won't have 5, 10, and 15 dollar people."[138] Low rents meant that Pacific Grove was becoming a dumping ground for relief clients coming from such déclassé parts as Salinas. If the good citizens were satisfied that "slum clearance" would solve the problem, subsequent investigation proved less sanguine. As it turned out, a third of the town's 173 relief clients owned their own homes, and only 15 had lived in town less than five years; many were elderly and depended on rental income in retirement in these days before social security.[139] It might have been added that hardworking writers like Carol and John Steinbeck were among the ten-dollar cottage people.

Pacific Grove was no isolated example of intolerance for the poor. Monterey mounted a campaign to tear down unsightly buildings of occupants owing back taxes. The newspaper featured a "shack of the month" to humiliate owners into renovation or demolition irrespective of their financial means. Although there is no surviving record, certainly some families were evicted. A revealing case was Augustine DeSoto, "73 year old native son of Monterey and descendant of California pioneers," who was evicted and his house demolished by the city for nonpayment of property taxes. The irony was not lost on a town simultaneously celebrating its proud Spanish heritage. In response to critical publicity, local officials moved quickly to rent another house for Augustine and his wife and six children.[140] If the DeSoto family was spared by its heritage, others were not so fortunate.

This was the milieu in which Steinbeck wrote *Tortilla Flat* from a Pacific Grove cottage in 1935. If he did not know Augustine DeSoto (and he may have), he knew others from the same social location—dispossessed paisanos who, like the novel's hero, might have squashed bedbugs on the walls of city jail cells and named each stained corpse after a mayor or council member. Steinbeck dedicated the novel to Susan Gregory, friend, Spanish teacher at Monterey High School, and source of many of the stories woven into the author's modern parable of an outcasts' Camelot.[141] Gregory lived on Johnson Street in the hills above town adjacent to the high school and one of the presumed locations of Tortilla Flat. It was all real, the characters, setting, and sentiments—empirical stuff with traceable social origins. Steinbeck's achievement was to inscribe this people's narrative in the local and national imagination as a portrait of the depression era.

If *Tortilla Flat* reflected the conflict of social classes and historical narratives, other forms of cultural production proceeded from negotiation and collaborative action. The 1930s witnessed broad-based efforts of city planning and landscape design combining historical preservation, commercial activity, and public access. That work built on a tradition begun in the late nineteenth century and carried forward to urban renewal in the 1960s. But the thirties were remarkable for an extensive redevelopment program that laid the foundations of the modern city. The WPA Historical Survey and projects were key components. At the same time, the MHAA was successfully engaged in preservation and its own historical survey in cooperation with Dr. Aubrey Neasham of the Bancroft Library at the University of California. Neasham's research was published in the local newspaper and intended for the "purpose of development of a master plan for preservation of Monterey's historical values."[142] Neasham also appears to have recommended the plan to Dr. John Merriam of Carnegie Institute who visited Monterey, liked its possibilities (second only to St. Augustine in underdeveloped historical attractions), and employed the San Francisco landscape architect Emerson Knight to draft the master plan. The Knight plan, unveiled in summer 1938, proposed a spatially reorganized downtown focused on the beach and harbor with the old Custom House and plaza as centerpiece. The plan was "keyed in with the history path" designed by Colonel Fitch and promoted by the MHAA. Its principal recommendations were (1) restoration of the city beach; (2) reestablishment of the Custom House Plaza; (3) elimination of Fisherman's Wharf and relocation of commercial activities; (4) removal of the adjacent Booth cannery; and (5) construction of a municipal bathhouse at the beach opposite El Estero Park.[143]

Knight's master plan walked into a minefield of local interests and recent controversy. Removal of Fisherman's Wharf had been debated in the city council during the previous year and a waterfront committee had been established to consider alternatives. Business interests called for removal of the dilapidated structure at a savings to the city's maintenance budget. Commercial fishermen and fish markets could be moved to the newer (ca. 1926) Wharf No. 2 and tacky concessions scattered elsewhere. But a cry of protest was raised, not from fishermen and concessionaires, but from the arts community that depended on the picturesque old wharf as a landscape subject and venue for selling their paintings. Armin Hansen put his formidable artistic reputation behind a campaign to save the wharf: "Whatever plan develops must be built around this old wharf, and I say MUST because that old wharf is one of the few real going things which this city of ours possesses." The fishermen themselves were less enamored of the wharf's quaintness and felt that it was designed to serve the concessionaires rather than the workers: "What do we care? This place does us no good. Fui [sic] on it." Colonel Fitch and the MHAA weighed in on the side of the bohemians, arguing it was "premature to even think of destroying it unless something else better is offered."[144]

The preservationists won this round in a redevelopment struggle that involved moments of conflict and cooperation between group interests wedded to contrasting historical narratives. Few recommendations of the Knight plan were adopted in the short run. The Booth cannery was de-molished, but later, when the sardine industry collapsed. The Custom House Plaza awaited a subsequent wave of urban renewal. Fisherman's Wharf persists today. The beach was reclaimed for public use (without a bathhouse) and linked with substantial WPA projects at El Estero Park and the shoreline path. City government and the MHAA restored a number of buildings along the Path of History. City offices and council chambers were adorned with local historical scenes painted by Evelyn McCormick and commissioned by the WPA. Preservationist and industrial activities mingled in the evolving structure of public space.

In 1938 the county fair was opened with a gala pageant organized along the town's main thoroughfare, Alvarado, decorated as the "Street of History." The symbolic importance of this "largest parade in [the] his-tory of the old town" was reflected in a series of decorated murals and costumed figures along the route covering "each era of the old town's colorful past." At one end was "In the Beginning, the Indian," followed by the early explorers, Portolá, Serra, Fages, and the Spanish period gen-erally. Next came a fair representation of the Mexican period, including Figueroa, Alvarado, and Vallejo. Equal, but not greater, emphasis was given to the American conquest—Colton, Larkin, and Hartnell. The late nineteenth century was erased—no David Jacks, Southern Pacific Rail-road, or P.I. Co. But the pageant culminated in the current year with "Ital-ian Fishermen 1938," perhaps the first public commemoration of the town's industry and immigrant labor force. Here, for a time, was a synthesis of romantic Spanish and working-class narratives; the result of diverse and uniquely creative history-making activities during the first half of the twentieth century. They put Monterey on the nation's cultural map, creating material works and imaginative muses that still shape local life.

CONCLUSION

The years spanning two world wars and the Great Depression were uniquely eventful in Monterey history. The town was reconstructed physically and culturally. Its reputation for industry, art, and literature reached around the world. While romanticism flourished in society circles, a new story celebrating ordinary working people gained importance as an identity experienced locally and a reputation perceived abroad. The new working-class narrative, like earlier ones, rested on a particular and transient set of structural conditions (industrialization, immigration, unionization, prosperity, depression), institutional supports (federal contracts, state fishing regulations, WPA projects), and group activities (MHAA preservation, the arts community, unions, civic associations). Celebrated artists such as Austin, Fortune, Hansen, Jeffers, and Steinbeck contributed greatly to the narrative, particularly as it was appreciated from abroad. But many of the less celebrated contributed to the story as it was experienced locally in pageants, commemorative events, plays, schools, and post office murals.

World War II brought the era to its fullest expression and its end. Wartime production accelerated depletion of the fishery. Sardine tonnage mined from the bay soared in the mid-forties, then plummeted with the vanishing fish. Once the town's dominant symbol, the Hotel Del Monte limped through the depression and during the war was converted to a naval training school. The army bought a large ranch bordering Seaside from the Jacks daughters and began building one of the largest military bases on the West Coast. Army and navy installations soon replaced fishing as Monterey's main industry. For years state biologists and the Fish and Game Division had been warning of the damage to the fishery caused by the large purse seiners and quota-busting reduction plants. A nascent environmental movement urged limits. In "The Purse-Seine" Robinson Jeffers compared the inveigling nets to the encroachment of urban populations and government power. The eccentric Carmel poet was a prescient voice for environmental awareness as well as an example of its inconsistencies. In "Carmel Point" he decried "this beautiful place defaced with a crop of suburban houses" (by contrast to his rock house) but urged the town board to extend the new sewer line to his property. Jeffers and the fish biologists anticipated a new narrative that would follow in the wake of industrial collapse.

As conditions changed, the old stories began to lose their command of experience. Steinbeck's compassionate *Cannery Row,* written in 1945, described a declining quarter of the city, peopled not with the men who fished and the women who packed sardine cans but with good-natured bums and prostitutes. The MHAA sought restoration of the old Spanish capital, or at least its aura that would come by relocating state government from Sacramento to Monterey. In 1938 S. F. B. Morse argued to public gatherings that war would be averted (Hitler had better sense and the Italians were bluffing) and that Monterey stood a good chance of attracting the capital.[145] But these were pipe dreams diverting attention from looming disasters—in Europe and the Pacific, of course, but also in Monterey Bay, now facing ecological degradation and wartime internment of Japanese and Italian families. The Japanese were dispossessed, relocated, and imprisoned in places like Manzanar in California's Owens Valley that the historical marker calls a "concentration camp." The little-known Italian internment deprived all aliens (including many of the older generation who had not become citizens) of their fishing boats and radios, required that they move inland twenty miles from the coast (to Salinas for some local families), and even imprisoned a few with suspect past associations.[146]

The wartime experience incubated new forms of ethnic consciousness and affiliation. After the war, those Italians required to move or give up their boats were soon reintegrated into the industry. Although many suffered shame, separation, anguish, and damage to their confiscated boats, the hurt was ameliorated by a welcoming community. The son of a fishing family was elected mayor. The reverse was true for Japanese, who faced an ugly local campaign to prevent their return. A group calling itself Monterey Bay Council on Japanese Relations based in Salinas (with peninsula sympathizers) took out an advertisement in the Monterey paper appealing for support in its campaign "to discourage the return to the Pacific Coast of any person of Japanese ancestry, except those in uniform[,] . . . to insist on deportation [and] strict supervision of Japanese schools, societies, and organizations."

As a flurry of letters to the editor soon demonstrated, many peninsula citizens condemned the expressed sentiments. They promptly mobilized a petition drive urging a cordial welcome for returning Japanese internees and affirming "the democratic way of life for all." Ruth Sparkman of Carmel wrote that it was the duty of every American citizen to oppose the Monterey Bay Council on Japanese Relations. Edward Ricketts, Steinbeck's friend and model for Doc in *Cannery Row,* wrote a satirical piece saying local racism was evidence of "Hitler's essential success as a teacher [for] he lives on in the minds of brave Americans who, despite great personal risk, fire from speeding cars into the homes of fellow Americans." The Carmel photographer Edward Weston asked, "[W]ho are the members of this 'council,' why don't they come out in the open? They hide their real intent by exempting those in uniform. Phooey! I protest with every ounce of decency in me." Progressive citizens went into action, contacting "people who could be reached in limited time," and within weeks published a petition with nearly five hundred signatures, including those of the letter writers mentioned, Robinson and Una Jeffers, Toni Ricketts, writer Fred Bechdolt, MHAA historian Mayo Hayes O'Donnell, department store owner M. C. Holman, future mayor Peter Ferrante, cannery owner Angelo Lucido, and John Steinbeck.[147] Something new was in the wind, an appreciation and defense of diverse ethnic heritages—a good moment in local life.

SIX

The Historical Present

"It's a poor sort of memory that only works backwards," the
Queen remarked.

Lewis Carroll, *Through the Looking-Glass*

TRUE TO HISTORY

On June 22, 1998, the *New York Times* ran a story under the headline
"Cannery Row Struggles to Stay True to Steinbeck." It seems that "developers want to build hotels, malls and parking garages in Cannery Row,
but preservationists fear that the area will lose its flavor." The story and
events surrounding it are doubly ironic. John Steinbeck's novel *Cannery
Row* appeared in 1945 at the close of the industrial period and had very
little to do with fishing, manufacturing, working people, and the historical sense of Cannery Row as it evolved over a half century. *Cannery
Row* is a tender and sometimes profound imaginative work but not true
to life on Ocean View Avenue, as the street was called at the time. Representations true to the historical Cannery Row have little to do with
Steinbeck's portrait, and deserving celebrations of Steinbeck's fiction have
little to do with the history of Cannery Row. Yet Cannery Row has been
reconstructed, true to nothing particularly historical, as a mythical place
that conflates fact with fiction.

The question of what to do with a deindustrialized Cannery Row has
been generating controversy since the old plants closed in the 1950s and
urban renewal schemes began appearing in the 1960s. As a gentrified commercial zone superseded the working-class district of New Monterey, a
number of new structures have been added, sometimes after scrutiny by
preservationists, the City Planning Commission, and the California
Coastal Commission. The recent controversy that caught the attention of

29.   Bust of John Steinbeck. Commercial areas of Cannery
Row are decorated with statues of Steinbeck and marine
biologist Edward Ricketts in memories that identify the
industrial site with *Cannery Row* the novel. Here the author
graces "Steinbeck Plaza" and surrounding shops. The sculpture by Carol V. Brown was dedicated in February 1973.
(Photo by the author)

the *New York Times* involves a proposal to build a shopping and condominium complex on 3.5 vacant acres of beachfront and parking space that
once housed the California Packing Company (Cal-Pac) cannery and the
adjacent reduction plant of the San Xavier Canning Company. The site
has been unoccupied since fires in 1967 and 1973 destroyed most of the
original structures (and aroused suspicion when they occurred in a larger
wave following purchase of abandoned properties by a San Francisco firm).
The new Cannery Row Marketplace would fill the largest remaining open
space on the Row, promising in the process to respect the area's histori-

30.   Abandoned Cannery Site. In places along Cannery Row one can still
see the abandoned foundations of the plants and the platforms where fishing
boats offloaded their catch. Developers propose to rebuild on this site of the
San Xavier Canning Company. (Photo by the author)

cal integrity with appropriate architecture, bay-view corridors between
its cannery-style buildings, a public plaza, and restored San Xavier warehouse as a history center. The developer calls it "a vibrant and architecturally and historically sensitive mixed-use project that has been designed
to provide unmatched views and public spaces along Monterey Bay."[1]

Critics disagree. Four buildings, forty-one condominium units, underground parking for 613 cars, and more than one hundred thousand
square feet of commercial space add up to a project described as "massive" by opponents. The City Planning Commission says it is oversized
and commercially redundant, a threat to the viewscape and established
businesses. Citizens mobilized a "Save Our Waterfront" committee dedicated to stopping the project, which, they argue, is not only too big and
too commercial but a defilement of the area's historical character as well.
Much of the debate centers on what is historic.

The sole remaining structure on the property was built in 1942 as an
addition to the San Xavier Cannery complex. It soon fell into disuse and
was rented to a series of businesses, most recently the Stohan Gallery.
The Marketplace plan calls for remodeling and moving Stohan's to a more
convenient on-site location. Presently, Stohan's is the only surviving

31.   Stohan's Building. The last remaining structure on Cannery Row from
the industrial period, San Xavier's reduction plant later housed Stohan's art
gallery. Local preservationists are divided over proposed development on the
site; one side favors restoring the structure intact, while the other side (represented by the San Xavier Foundation in the sign to the left) supports a commercial marketplace that would remove the building but re-create it on the
site as a history center. (Photo by the author)

original (if latter-day) industrial building on all of Cannery Row. A nearby
warehouse was "deconstructed" by the developer, who plans to re-
assemble it on site in the interests of historical preservation. Several storage tanks remain on the property, although their historical value is dubious. Preservationists argue that all these relics should be maintained
in their original locations. Moving and deconstructing the buildings, they
say, is simply the latest in a long series of assaults on the historical character of Cannery Row.

The issue figured prominently in a recent mayoralty election in which
former law school dean and Save Our Waterfront activist Barbara Evans
challenged former high school coach and longtime mayor Dan Albert.
The city maintained that the abandoned buildings on Cannery Row were
not historic, not shown on their planning maps of the area. Opponents
said that they were historic, as shown on proper maps, and that the city
was violating its own standards of historical preservation by allowing the
warehouse deconstruction. Neil Hotelling, a local executive and president of the Cannery Row Foundation, took it upon himself to meet the

threat by nominating Cannery Row for the National Trust for Historical Preservation's list of the "eleven most endangered historic places" in the United States. The designation is purely symbolic and carries no official directive. Thanks to Steinbeck and to Hotelling's well-prepared application, Cannery Row made the list, producing an altogether new stink over the city. Mayor Albert called a news conference complaining that the National Trust had never consulted the city and that his administration placed a high value on historic preservation, as evidenced by its recreation trail through the area, purchase of the Ed Ricketts ("Doc's") laboratory building featured in *Cannery Row,* construction of a park, and restoration of cannery worker shacks at a historically interpreted site. Who is more historical than whom? the city seemed to suggest rhetorically. Save Our Waterfront countered that parks and recreation trails were not historic, that the problem lies with protecting Cannery Row's heritage.

Not to be outdone, the Marketplace Company established the nonprofit San Xavier Foundation with a well-credentialed local advisory board. It plans to present the true story of Cannery Row rather than commercialized nostalgia. Members of the advisory board claim that local history has been obscured by the obsession with Steinbeck. The History Center will focus on the canneries themselves: the diverse labor force and production processes demonstrated in oral histories, photographs, a remodeled interior of the San Xavier reduction plant, and open-air views of the bay and loading docks. Meanwhile, elimination of insignificant storage tanks with toxic residues will enhance the environment. Skeptics in Save Our Waterfront say the History Center is a stalking horse for the outsized Marketplace, contingent on city approval of the development. Advisory board members say no, the foundation is already in operation and raising money for expansion. The Cannery Row Foundation, a group supported by the area's major property owners, continues to favor the Steinbeck motif, tourism, current businesses, and minimal city regulation—all somewhat at odds with a solution to the controversy. The city hopes for a roundly satisfactory compromise that has yet to emerge. John Steinbeck's son, Tom, supported the project in a letter written to Mayor Albert (and reproduced on the Marketplace Web site) suggesting that this is just the kind of new enterprise that his father favored. But daughter-in-law Nancy Steinbeck says that she and her late husband, John IV, have followed family tradition in opposition to the commercialization of Cannery Row.

What is historic? Who speaks for Steinbeck? Does that matter? What is true to Cannery Row? These are the questions that underpin the contemporary politics of historic preservation and interpretation. Public history is a collection of more and less compelling claims, as we have seen throughout this chronicle. Yet there is something new in today's struggle for the historical present. Not only do rival claims arise from different social constituencies engaged in collective action, but these interests now self-consciously proclaim their historical pedigree. Historical legitimation has become a requirement for effective participation in public decisions that involve the physical environment or social definition of the city. Groups need to demonstrate their historical provenance, even create their own history center, as convincing evidence of their authenticity as claimants and advocates. History is a necessary claim *and* a strategy for groups joined in collective action.

The struggle for the spirit of Cannery Row is only one of a series of public history controversies in contemporary Monterey. New narratives embracing competing ideas have emerged dealing with environment, ethnicity, and local heritage. And those stories have come to play a constitutive role in preservation/development conflicts like Cannery Row. New narratives emerge, like their predecessors, in circumstances of economic transformation, spatial reorganization, and changing patterns of political power. New narratives draw on the old. The romance of early California, for example, perseveres in the vaunted heritage of a thoroughly renovated downtown. Working-class stories are embedded in a new ethnic group consciousness. Once-silenced experiences of Indians and women now suffuse all the narratives. In effect, narratives that reigned in earlier periods have been disassembled, their elements polished and then recombined in contemporary stories. New narratives reconfigure the past—or articulate a new past fitted for exigencies of the present.

The contemporary period is unique in one important respect. Historical reclamation is a self-consciously political process, a witting exercise in cultural democracy. Claims on history become a resource in collective action. Public history is democratized. Groups reinvent themselves by reclaiming their history, advocate for their interests by pointing to the value of that history, and reshape the collective consciousness by advancing a sense of legitimacy for the claims of history. In this process, pasts are created to meet present exigencies.

FORCES OF CHANGE

Changes in the content and salience of Monterey's public history emerge from a set of physical, economic, and political transformations. In the early decades of the twentieth century, Monterey was predominantly an industrial town with important contributions to the economy deriving from its Del Monte resort hotel and Ford Ord military installation. After 1950, these institutions were absent or declining. The region badly needed an alternative economic base, which, most agreed, lay in the new service economy. Tourism was key to the new economic design, although the plan developed along a broader front. Monterey could become a convention town. Its renowned U.S. Army Defense Language Institute might form the nucleus of an educational complex. In time, scientific and marine research seemed an eminently practical undertaking. All of these required a new physical infrastructure and a new conception of the city's future—and its past.

REDESIGNING THE BUILT ENVIRONMENT

In the late 1950s Monterey followed the example of hundreds of American cities by responding to federally supported opportunities for urban renewal. Although Monterey had little of the urban decay that the federal Housing Act of 1949 and its subsequent amendments were designed to eradicate, the city did have two potent motives for joining the new initiative. First, the opportunity for federally assisted downtown reconstruction appeared precisely at the historical moment of industrial collapse and flagging local purpose. Perhaps urban renewal was the proffered way of the future. Second, Monterey knew something about urban renewal. A local tradition of civic improvement dated from the late nineteenth century, when unsightly Chinese businesses and working-class "resorts" were eradicated, to the depression years, when WPA projects intermingled with citizen efforts to preserve the rude waterfront. If the industrial era had protected and proliferated low-income areas downtown, their purpose was now in doubt.

Monterey established a local urban renewal agency in fall 1957 and applied for a federal planning grant that was awarded one year later. The urban renewal agency was composed of five prominent men, civic leaders identified with the business and professional community (a physician, a mortician, two contractors, and a dress shop owner with a graduate degree in political science). As the agency went to work developing its constituency and defining its "study area," a commercial redevelopment orientation quickly emerged. One observer of the first public meeting in January 1958 noted that "the agency appears most interested in correcting blighted conditions in the lower Alvarado street area and in improving the traffic situation about the Custom House [which] promises the greatest benefits at this time in the way of improved property values and solves the immediate problem of the city."[2] Urban renewal was firmly backed by an alliance of city officials, bankers, professionals, a broad spectrum of business with the exception of small retail establishments, and the organized construction industry from labor to contractors and suppliers. Arthur Rathhaus, first chairman of the city's urban renewal agency, estimated that "if the plan goes through it will mean between $25 million and $30 million in remodeling and new construction."[3]

Although the suggested goal of "improved property values" might be construed ominously by the poor, initial descriptions of the project stressed economic revitalization and used code words for any suggestion of blight. One agency director announced, "Monterey is losing $8,694,000 in 'unsatisfied sales' each year. . . . [R]enewal will relieve congestion, remove substandard structures and will make a good downtown out of the lower half of our central business district," an area unprofitably devoted to "bars and barbershops."[4] His predecessor in the agency understood pending changes in broader historical terms: "This is not a Spanish outpost fishing village anymore"; urban renewal is Monterey's "chance to show what cities can really do."[5]

It was not long before potential losers got the message that alert winners had been savoring. Building permits were frozen in the "target area," forty-five downtown acres that included residential, historical, and small business sites. Proprietors reasonably feared condemnation, although the project in its early stages lacked detail, official approval, and funding. In public discussions of plans the local agency would submit for federal approval, a diverse opposition began to coalesce. Marje Eliassen, a former city councilwoman and unsuccessful mayoral candidate, expressed concern about her own art studio on Pacific Street as well as the effects of a multistory parking garage planned for a central location where it would obtrusively dwarf several historical buildings. If Eliassen represented a rival faction in city politics, her concerns were shared by Mrs. W. R. Holman and Mayo Hayes O'Donnell, preservationists and stalwarts in the Monterey History and Art Association. The emerging oppositional alliance was joined by the City Planning Commission, which was worried about the physical plan under development and the urban renewal agency's alleged failure to involve local groups in the planning process.

Small businesses were threatened. Joseph Danyah complained to a meeting of the Monterey Merchants Committee that his Casa Mañana contemporary shop on Calle Principal would be replaced by an 800-car garage (nearly the size of San Francisco's Union Square car park). Santo Pisto's tailor shop, Frank Bruno's Plaza Liquors, Lou Mendez's smoke shop, and twenty other small establishments on lower Alvarado Street would yield to a department store. Two historic buildings currently housing restaurants were involved: Wes Dodge's Old Whaling Station and Hermann's Inn occupying the Osio adobe. In all, an estimated 80 to 130 businesses were likely to be displaced. One breakdown of the casualties listed 11 cafés, 8 bars, 7 card rooms, 5 barbershops, 2 Army-Navy stores, 2 upholstery shops, a shoe shine stand, a tattoo parlor, a used phonograph store, a cab stand, a travel agency, an insurance office, and 13 unclassified, perhaps illicit, others. Nothing fancy; pretty much what would be expected on the workaday waterfront.[6]

The largest group threatened by urban renewal, however, was the neighborhood's working-class residents. One estimate put their number at 124 families and 89 individuals in rooming houses, a total of perhaps 600 persons. The area clearly embraced Monterey's poorest citizens and probably an element of vice. Yet intermingled on its narrow streets were the wood-frame houses of Italian and Portuguese fishing families, Spanish cannery workers, Chinese cooks, Anglo mechanics, former soldiers, and a host of maintenance workers who kept the town and wharf running. In their midst, too, were buildings of historical importance and an ambience that tradition had endeavored to preserve— and even to reinvent.

Conflict erupted in spring and summer 1961 as the local agency was completing the plan it would submit for federal funding and formal recognition as the authority responsible for property acquisition and development contracting. Two hundred citizens attended a public forum at the community college in March that was devoted largely to complaints about the agency's physical plan. Tavern owner Peter Torrente argued that urban renewal was "a move to throw out the small businessman, to bankrupt him." A spokesperson for residents informed planners, "[W]e don't want to move, we are happy where we are." Maria Garcia, forty years working as a cook in the neighborhood since her immigration from Spain, asked, "Where will I go?" The MHAA objected to planned street reroutings, parking lots, and indifference to historical preservation. In April Marje Eliassen called the agency board to a meeting in city council chambers where they were surprised by one hundred residents angry about the mammoth parking garage, condemnation, and the agency's failure to encourage citizen participation.[7]

As the mid-June city council meeting to decide on the urban renewal agency's plan approached, the loosely organized protest movement stepped up its efforts. A "Petition Against the Urban Renewal Plan" garnered 270 signatures from area residents, business owners, representatives from most of the Italian fishing families, and local notables such as Miss Margaret Jacks, daughter of the man who once owned the town. The petition stressed three drawbacks in the plan: the parking garage, a pedestrian shopping mall, and redevelopment on large parcels "freezing out the small businessman who has helped support the City of Monterey for many years." Petition and signatories were published in the local newspaper on facing full pages along with an exacting analysis of the plan and a letter from the City Planning Commission that criticized aspects of the design and planning process while stopping short of rejecting the plan itself. Under pressure of federal schedules, the city council voted by a narrow three-to-two margin to accept the renewal agency plan (later one opponent moved over to make a four-to-one majority).

The split vote and unresolved issues left bitterness on all sides. Target-area residents gathered again at a city council meeting, remonstrated, and applauded the suggestion of a recall election. Dodge and Eliassen sued to stop further work by the urban renewal agency and nullify its plan based on alleged irregularities in public advertisement of its hearings. Neither strategy succeeded. Pro-renewal mayor Sparky Pollard lashed out at his opponents on the planning commission and among community "rabble rousers." In repudiation of his critics, the mayor observed that "bankers and downtown businessmen who realize the tremendous value of the benefit to be derived through the rehabilitation of downtown Monterey have expressed bitter disappointment over the present turn of events."[8]

The next step for urban renewal was federal approval and funding of the local plan. The various contending parties knew that negotiation at this stage would serve their purpose; it would be an occasion for opponents to influence the still-malleable plan and for officials to consolidate community support. Members of the City Planning Commission met with the urban renewal agency in the interest of a "community development plan." The agency hired a new design team, the prominent San Francisco architectural firm of John Warnecke, which had recently been named as the master planner for the University of California campus at Santa Cruz. Warnecke's political instinct matched his considerable aesthetic talent. The new plan was received enthusiastically as a "radical" departure from its controversial predecessor. The fortress parking garage was downsized by half and the pedestrian mall reduced to a single block, and, in its boldest feature, the design proposed a tunnel routing traffic through the waterfront renewal area. The road would pass beneath a new Custom House Plaza, conceived as the centerpiece of a historical preservation complex bordered by Pacific House and the original Custom House, both dating from the 1840s. The design answered the appeals of several opposition groups with the exception of small business and low-income residents. It was a breakthrough. Early in 1962 federal approval was bestowed on the Monterey Urban Renewal Agency in the form of a $6.6 million loan and $4.5 million grant.[9]

If the urban renewal fight in its early stages pitted the substantial business community and one faction of city government against a loosely allied coalition of low-income residents, small business, historical preservationists, and another faction of local government, the broader political landscape included important interests that affected the process. Throughout Monterey's history, Del Monte Properties Company in its various incarnations (from Pacific Improvement Company to Pebble Beach Corporation) has cast a long shadow over local government. As plans for the economic revitalization of Monterey's core area were developing in 1961, Samuel F. B. Morse announced that while Del Monte supported urban renewal, it intended to build its own forty-seven-acre shopping center on Carmel Hill within a mile of downtown. The city's business community regarded the Del Monte move as "disastrous" sabotage. Renewal director Arthur Chang called it a "death warrant," urging the city council to deny zoning approval (without success as the council again split 3–2 in favor of the shopping center). In sympathy with property capital and the Del Monte plan, a conservative group advising the city council as the Conservation and Development Committee began campaigning for termination of urban renewal. Monterey did not need federal assistance, particularly when it preempted the property rights of individuals. Like the popular protest movement, conservative opposition to urban renewal slowed but did not stop the process.

The newly empowered Urban Renewal Agency began condemnation proceedings in the core area late in 1962. Although most residents accepted their fate, some continued the struggle. Local resistance took three forms. First, political activists and preservationists carried on attempts to modify planning and implementation decisions. Second, a half-dozen residents sued the agency seeking what they considered just compensation for their loss. Santo Pisto's case was typical. The tailor had asked $25,000 for his small shop, which he had purchased for $10,000 in 1951 (and improved to the tune of another $3,500), and for business losses entailed in relocating. The agency's appraiser said the shop was worth $11,000. A Salinas jury awarded Pisto $11,500.[10]

Slim hope of redress contributed to a third response, noncooperation. Sebastian Patania, a Sicilian fisherman, and his wife, who had lived at 192 Oliver Street for thirty-nine years when they were served with condemnation papers in 1964, refused to leave their home. Relying on their daughter, Mayme Maciera, for English translation, Patania declared, "I don't want to sell. What about property rights? What about the constitution?" Although he had once been offered $25,000 for the house, and had rented the lower floor for a steady retirement income of $75 per month, urban renewal offered him a mere $11,500. Although the couple had not signed the petition endorsed by many of their neighbors, they refused to move. They could never replace their home and location, within walking distance of daily necessities (neither drove), for the financial compensation offered. Mrs. Patania, acting as her own lawyer, attempted to oppose the condemnation in court on constitutional grounds but was told that her case would have to confine itself to the question of fair market value—$12,000 the court decided by way of silencing her plea. Still the couple refused to sell.[11]

Eviction proceedings were forestalled during the next two years by a combination of the Patanias' intransigence and redevelopment delays. The day of reckoning came early in 1966 when the sheriff arrived with an eviction order and moving van. Barricaded inside, the Patanias still refused to recognize the government's right to seize their property—their $12,000 check from the urban renewal agency had never been collected. At the end of a twelve-hour marathon of packing and persuading, sheriff's deputies finally carried the Patanias out bodily. Several days later, as their daughter, Mayme, created a commotion in city council chambers protesting the eviction, the Patanias reoccupied their home with cots and camping gear. Now the sheriff was angry. On the following day, the Patanias were dragged out again, this time for good as a bulldozer stood by to demolish the house that afternoon. Young Republican supporters of the couple planted a sign on the rubble reading, "Here Lies the Constitution of the United States." A week later, parents and daughter were arrested on charges of contempt, tried, and jailed for thirty-five days. In response, Mayor Minnie Coyle was hung in effigy—unfairly perhaps given her opposition as a councilwoman in the three-to-two vote on the original plan.[12]

The Patania affair ended the popular movement phase of urban renewal in Monterey. As demolition moved forward, the players changed from mobilized citizens confronting their elected representatives to developers negotiating finance and design. Custom House Associates, a limited partnership headed by a firm of Philadelphia developers, was selected as the redevelopment contractor. The firm's proposal followed closely Warnecke's "radical" design featuring the tunnel and plaza that was favored by members of the Urban Renewal Agency, and it involved local architects and investors who had sided with the city in opposition to the Del Monte shopping center. A group of local associates under the name Old Town Development Company offered an alternative plan that would have taken in a larger swath of downtown real estate. Old Town charged insider dealing in the bidding process when the agency selected Custom House Associates and brought suit to halt any further work on the project.

Although the redevelopment area was cleared and the tunnel begun by 1967, the private development side bogged down. Custom House Associates was unable to enlist JC Penney in a department store investment owing to questions about adequate parking and the general uncertainty of the project. Meanwhile, the Del Monte shopping center had no trouble luring Macy's, and its promising future probably discouraged downtown investors. Several lawsuits by Old Town added delay and indecision. In the midst of all that, the Philadelphia financier and developer of Custom House Associates died, creating serious doubts about the partnership's capital assets when his estate went to heirs with no interest in the project. Monterey's Urban Renewal Agency had followed the single-redeveloper strategy without considering its risks. As Custom House Associates staggered and then defaulted, the vision of a new downtown, now ten years on, was fading.

"When a ball team loses as many games as urban renewal has, it's time to get some new players." So spoke city councilman George Clemmens, the original dissenting vote on the proposed urban renewal plan and sole surviving public official in the long war. Mayor Al Madden, the fifth in a line of renewal mayors, agreed: "We're going to catch it right between the eyes anyway, so let's meet it head-on and take over the agency." The city fired its Urban Renewal Agency and took over its functions under the direction of councilman and onetime renewal board member John Bouldry and next-mayor Peter Coniglio. The new team took a series of revitalizing decisions. The single-redeveloper strategy was dropped in favor of more flexible individual-project contracting. In lieu of the fading hope for a department store (Penney had withdrawn) as the project's commercial anchor, the new plan envisioned a convention center and hotel located between the downtown core and historic Custom House Plaza.

Parking could now be dispersed in smaller structures. A new design for the reenvisioned space was commissioned by a team of local architects— and later won an award from *Progressive Architecture* magazine. Meanwhile, the federal government approved a progress grant of $4.8 million to the city, which helped to reduce interest payments on outstanding loans and invigorate rebuilding. Sheraton Hotels entered the competition for the convention site, proposing a design in harmony with local surroundings. Although Sheraton later ceded to Phoenix-based Doubletree Inns, the hotel–convention center finally broke ground in 1977 with a design that delighted the major players.[13]

Downtown urban renewal, the Custom House Redevelopment Project as it was formally known, was the largest and most controversial part of a broader regional modernization plan. Federal urban renewal spread to Cannery Row and was partly responsible for the commercial redevelopment lamented by today's preservationists. During the 1960s, Monterey's languid Highway 1 coast road was replaced by a massive, six-lane freeway. Local opposition to a plan that would have ploughed through downtown neighborhoods succeeded in relocating the artery eastward along the foot of Jacks Peak—and convenient to the Del Monte shopping center. Carmel residents bitterly (and presciently) opposed the freeway and Carmel Hill interchange that would disgorge record numbers of cars at its gates. Both developments followed the pattern of downtown renewal with commercial and expansionary interests dominating the planning process.

Economic motives took over downtown, too, once the convention center became the project's centerpiece. Long before renewal, Monterey had a downtown high-rise hotel, the historic San Carlos, built in 1926 and now owned by a local group that included Mayor Coniglio's family trust. Massive by any standard, the San Carlos commanded Monterey's skyline with a picture of aging elegance that the owners hoped to preserve in remodeling. But it soon became clear that remodeling could not produce a modern convention hotel. The San Carlos was razed, and an even larger structure took its place on a full city block across from the convention center. Sheraton Hotels joined the local partnership in building a ten-story, 344-room blockbuster that local folk began calling "the hospital." Little of the concern for design and historical preservation typically voiced about downtown renewal affected the new Sheraton (later Marriott). True, it replaced an equally obtrusive structure that local society had covered with nostalgia. Nevertheless, the ease with which it sailed through the approval process suggests that city government (which would operate the convention center) had shifted to an aggressive commercial development strategy.

In one important respect, however, urban renewal was an alloyed product, a compound of popular, preservationist, and commercial ambitions. The Patanias, Santo Pisto, Maria Garcia, the poor, generally lost. There is no diminishing that fact. But renewal critics with greater political resources won significant concessions. The Monterey History and Art Association was involved at every juncture, albeit with priorities fixed on historic adobes rather than low-income frame houses, which also played a part in local history. The MHAA represented an influential segment of the community and commanded respect in politics. Its advocacy was doubtless responsible for recognition of a "historical district" in the redevelopment plan with its keystone Custom House Plaza, symbolically capping the underground tunnel diverting traffic from the new heart of the commercial waterfront district. These achievements notwithstanding, one hundred rank-and-file members of the MHAA broke with their board of directors by protesting the "massiveness" of the convention center's design. Further changes were negotiated with preservationists' demands always in the mix.[14]

In the end, an elegant convention center hotel filled the space once crowded with bars and barbershops, working-class frame houses, and marine storage lots. Visitors enjoy it and a new breed of merchants prospers. Pedestrian traffic flows from downtown through the outdoor mall and plaza to the lively Fisherman's Wharf and marina. A plaque commemorating Monterey Harbor chronicles events on the spot from Vizcaíno's landing in 1602, the arrival of Portolá and Serra in 1770 and Sloat in 1846, and the fishing industry circa 1930—more history than the average Californian knows or cares for. Ringing the plaza are the neatly preserved historical Pacific House (built originally as a hotel by Larkin), the Mexican Custom House, and the new Maritime Museum whose fine architectural lines house the capable professional staff of today's Monterey History and Art Association. The building also includes (by popular demand, it is said) a social club where retired fishermen gather every Wednesday for collectively prepared pasta luncheons. Across the plaza, facing the bay, stands a statue of Santa Rosalia, patron saint of Sicilian fishermen. Between Pacific House and Santa Rosalia, about where the Patania house once stood, is the public bocci ball court—province of retired seafarers where Italian is the lingua franca and collective memory the topic of conversation.

Urban renewal created the political mood and spatial design for Mon-

terey's transition to a new service economy. That was the principal objective from the start, and the costly result. But thoroughgoing projects
of economic reorganization, whether sponsored by the WPA or urban
renewal, necessarily entail social and cultural transformations. Urban renewal created a new social space, a new cast of characters, and a wholly
different sense of Monterey's business. At every step of the planning
process, in the very act of preservation, it also re-created a different sense
of local history. Downtown became a new space of historic re-creation—
not the town that Commodore Sloat encountered, not Armin Hansen's
gritty waterfront, no more a working-class town. What it became was
not history, to be sure, but a re-creation suffused with what we believe
is history now—a place where observers are struck by the "amount of
history" that transpired here and the conspicuous attention devoted to it.

PROTECTING THE NATURAL ENVIRONMENT

Downtown Monterey is graced by a one-mile waterfront (from the old
Presidio cum U.S. Army Defense Language Institute to the old Hotel Del
Monte cum Naval Postgraduate School), crowded only on its western
side by Fisherman's Wharf and the marina. On the east, the beach
stretches out toward coastal sand dunes along a gentle viewscape and
city park called Window on the Bay. Although part of the new visitor-
oriented downtown, the oceanfront promenade owes nothing to urban
renewal or the WPA, which built El Estero Park across the street. Window on the Bay is an environmental project by the city that began replacing an unsightly row of used car lots in 1984 thanks to initial funding from the Coastal Conservancy program of the California Coastal
Commission. As the unfolding park acquires additional business properties along the strip, the mayor arrives, sledgehammer in hand and pho-
tographers in tow, and proceeds to demolish disused stucco in a well-
advertised campaign of environmental restoration. Since 1972 protecting
the California coastline has been good politics.
    Concern for the degradation of California's coastline took political
shape in about 1970 in connection with the emergent environmental
movement marked by Earth Day and the National Environmental Protection Act of that year. Signs of environmental trashing along California's coast were on the increase. The population of southern California
coastal counties had doubled in the previous decade. Unregulated and
often unsightly building along the coastline was destroying ocean views
and restricting public access. Water quality and wildlife were palpably

threatened; species vanished and lagoons were polluted with sewage and toxic runoff. Tacky development was most extensive in San Diego, Santa Monica, Malibu, and Ventura but inexorably headed north. The Sea Ranch, a projected development of 5,200 vacation and second homes in Sonoma County, threatened to eliminate public access to ten miles of scenic coastline until an alliance of environmentalists stepped in. Monterey produced a textbook example of the problem when Holiday Inn built a freestanding fortress on the bay.

In response, a broad and politically well-connected California Coastal Alliance began to form owing to the energies of Janet Adams, who led the creation of San Francisco's innovative Bay Conservation and Development Commission (BCDC), and several state representatives who had introduced unsuccessful coastal protection bills in the legislature. In 1971 a statewide "Save Our Coast" campaign united the Coastal Alliance and thirty-four civic organizations behind more energetic legislative efforts. Like previous attempts, the grassroots campaign was stopped at the formidable wall erected by oil companies pressing for additional offshore drilling and onshore land and development companies, both in the embrace of Governor Ronald Reagan's administration. Environmentalists turned of necessity to the popular referendum process.[15]

The 1972 campaign for Proposition 20, the Coastal Initiative, is recalled as a David and Goliath struggle despite the sinewy political connections among environmentalists, the liberal political establishment, bipartisan celebrities, and significant elements in government. The underdog imagery derives largely from a campaign in which corporate opponents (e.g., Southern Pacific Land Company, Standard Oil, Pacific Gas and Electric, Mobil Oil, Gulf Oil, Texaco, General Electric, Southern California Edison, and a number of land companies) concentrated their efforts on mass media, outspending proponents six to one. Misleading ads intoned "Conservation Yes, Confiscation No." Indeed, corporate heavy-handedness became an issue in the media campaign. Initiative supporters effectively claimed popular sympathy by neighborhood leafleting, personal campaigning by senior citizens and Sierra Club youth, and folksy published appeals from Carmel artist Hank Ketchum's "Dennis the Menace": "We went to the beach and it was gone."[16]

Support for Proposition 20 was vigorous in Monterey, where a large Sierra Club chapter mobilized the initiative petition drive. The renowned photographer Ansel Adams, who worked out of a Carmel studio, contributed images to the publicity campaign. Local fears of coastal despoliation were aroused by a mid-1960s fight over proposed construction of an oil refinery at nearby Moss Landing and by the new Holiday Inn, regarded by many as both an eyesore and a harbinger of "Miami Beachization." Monterey was a microcosm of activist support for the Coastal Initiative. The petition drive to place the measure on the ballot garnered more than nine thousand signatures locally. When Proposition 20 won a solid statewide victory in the November 1972 election, matching Richard Nixon's 55 percent majority, Monterey County came in on the high side with 58 percent in favor.

The Coastal Initiative was followed, after new delaying tactics and compromises, by the legislature's California Coastal Act of 1976, which established formal machinery for the Coastal Commission. The commission works in partnership with oceanfront counties and city governments, setting standards for new construction, public access, protection of marine and wildlife, restoration of sensitive habitats, and protection of scenic beauty. The teeth of the Coastal Act lie in its powers to review, deny, and refer back to local developers and governments projects the commission judges in violation of environmental standards. Although the Coastal Commission's fortunes rise and fall with successive state administrations (generally on a supportive Democratic and grudging Republican cycle), for twenty-five years it has been a contending force in environmental politics. Any number of massive building projects and noxious industrial developments have been prevented. The public enjoys expanded use of beaches, thanks also to the exhaustive *Coastal Access Guide,* published by the commission and the University of California Press. Travelers familiar with Miami and Malibu, Spain's Costa del Sol or England's southern shore, are suitably impressed by what they see in northern California by contrast to what might have been. Nevertheless, environmental critics make a case for the argument that much has slipped through the commission, pressures from developers are unrelenting, and new environmental threats unanticipated in the original legislation mount. Michael Fischer, former executive director of the commission who moved over to the Sierra Club, believes the agency lacks the muscle to effect a permanent solution to environmental degradation along the coastline.[17]

The Coastal Commission brought varied and long-term changes to Monterey. Downtown urban renewal paused while the courts decided it enjoyed grandfather exemption from review, but subsequent developments on Cannery Row came under the new standards. The commission rejected large and "development-heavy" hotel and condominium projects, sending others back to planners for architectural revision and downsizing. The Coastal Conservancy began purchasing land in Big Sur, providing permanent protection and a precedent for privately funded conservancy. Offshore oil drilling was prevented on a year-to-year basis.

As the local environmental movement attracted recruits and legitimacy, new initiatives were considered for protection of the entire bay. The movement enjoyed close ties to local representatives, particularly Fred Farr in the state senate and Leon Panetta in Congress. Discussion of a national marine sanctuary program got under way at the federal level in the mid-1970s, and Panetta began paving the way for inclusion of Monterey Bay. Although the program was approved in the early 1980s, with the Santa Barbara Channel Island area and the Gulf of the Farrallones off San Francisco gaining recognition, Monterey Bay failed to qualify owing to opposition from fishermen and oil-drilling interests. By 1988 Panetta's stature in Congress had risen so high (and his career would move on to the Office of Management and Budget and the White House) that he was able to negotiate support for a bill designating a huge area, 5,300 square miles and 200 coastal miles from San Francisco to San Simeon, as the Monterey Bay National Marine Sanctuary—the nation's largest.

Beyond proscription of offshore oil drilling, the sanctuary entails a relatively modest set of protections. Sanctions are imposed on intentionally damaging historic resources, disturbing marine animals, dredging the seabed, polluting the water with fish waste, and overflying bird refuges. More important, perhaps, sanctuary management by the National Oceanic and Atmospheric Administration (NOAA) from offices on Cannery Row has encouraged educational programs and environmental awareness—each with effective links to regional groups and activities. NOAA, for example, works with the voluntary Coastal Watershed Council to restore urban watersheds and prevent runoff contamination of the bay. Colorful literature demonstrates how "Monterey Bay Begins on Your Street" and stenciled messages on street drains warn that house, garden, and auto pollution "Runs to the Bay." Citizens are reminded of the intimate connection between their household and the environment, even encouraged to join the cleanup effort as Urban Watch Monitoring Volunteers: "Urban runoff is one of the leading sources of pollution into the waters of the Monterey Bay Sanctuary." In addition to community outreach, the Monterey Bay National Marine Sanctuary supports a variety of environmental research and monitoring activities ranging from the Mussel Watch Program to agricultural management at Elkhorn

Slough wildlife preserve. Residents are surrounded by reminders that Monterey is green.

After the bay itself, the pearl of Monterey's environmental oyster is the popular aquarium on Cannery Row. The idea that Monterey should acknowledge the source of its good fortune with a marine aquarium was first proposed in 1914 by industry-founder Frank Booth, repeated by his protégé Knute Hovden, and urged again in 1944 by Dr. Lawrence Blinks, who directed the Stanford University Hopkins Marine Station next door to Hovden's cannery. In the late 1970s the idea met the money when a group of graduate students from Hopkins Marine Station got together with University of California, Santa Cruz, marine biology graduate Julie Packard. In addition to a professional interest in the marine environment, the group, including Packard's sister and brother-in-law, had connections. The David and Lucille Packard Foundation, endowed by their parents who owned half of Hewlett-Packard Corporation, liked the project. With an initial endowment of $25 million, the Monterey Bay Aquarium Foundation purchased the defunct Hovden works from Stanford University, which had acquired the property as a buffer for Hopkins. Plans conceived something special, a regional aquarium focused on Monterey Bay and its unique marine ecology characterized by diverse species and deep submarine canyons. "The site was an inspiration to the aquarium," Julie Packard explained. After generally enthusiastic reviews by the Coastal Commission and the cities of Monterey and Pacific Grove (which it overlapped), the building broke ground in 1980. Concerns about historic values were addressed in construction. Portions of the original structure were retained in the design or disassembled and rebuilt in fortified renovations. Former cannery workers were employed to explain how things worked to restorers. The idea was to retain the look and feel of a cannery. A photographic record of the structure and a written account of the canning industry were kept for the National Archives. Next door, the laboratory of Ed Ricketts (*Cannery Row*'s "Doc," but more important here, author of the authoritative marine biology text, *Between Pacific Tides*) was preserved as a historical landmark.[18] Since its opening in 1984, the Monterey Bay Aquarium has attracted millions of visitors, redefined the significance of Cannery Row, and promoted Monterey's growing reputation as a center of environmental protection and education.

Visitors to Cannery Row see only one side of Packard family philanthropy—the architecturally striking aquarium with its exotic creatures, colorful tanks, and touchable invertebrates. Behind the aquarium's public presentation is a serious scientific research complex, the impos-

32. Monterey Bay Aquarium. Centerpiece of Cannery Row, the Monterey Bay Aquarium attracts legions of visitors to its display of regional marine life and carries on a major program of scientific research. (Photo by the author)

ing campus of the Monterey Bay Aquarium Research Institute (MBARI) at Moss Landing. MBARI operates a high-tech research ship, the *Western Flyer* (named for the purse seiner Ricketts and Steinbeck chartered to explore the Sea of Cortez), which gathers data from the two-mile depths of Monterey Canyon. Analyses conducted at the Moss Landing labs eventually reach the public at the aquarium, on the Internet, and in scientific publishing.

The laboratories of NOAA and MBARI are only the beginning of a synergistic network of marine research institutions growing up on Monterey Bay. In addition, there is Hopkins Marine Station (Stanford), Institute of Marine Sciences (University of California, Santa Cruz), Moss Landing Marine Laboratories (California State University), Monterey Marine Resources (California Fish and Game Department), more government agencies, and several private firms—all recently united in the seventeen-member Monterey Bay Ocean Crescent Research Consortium. As the *San Jose Mercury News* reported, "By combining strengths, the scientific community hopes to become a world-class center and achieve the impact of a Woods Hole Oceanographic Institute or a Scripps Institution of Oceanography."[19] With nearly one thousand people currently employed in research and development, Monterey's regional service economy embraces much more than tourism.

Environmentalism has become an equally prevalent feature of local society. The Big Sur Land Trust raises millions for preserving open space in Carmel Valley and along the coast, while the American Cetacean Society conducts whale watching trips. The county Regional Park District offers educational programs and maintains 7,500 acres of public land. There are groups to save the seals, watch the birds, and clean up after the humans. The county publishes a brochure titled "Put Yourself in Paradise, An Eco-Tourist's Guide to Monterey County." The *Marine and Coastal Educational Resources Directory* published by NOAA and the Coastal Commission lists forty-nine environmental groups in Monterey County, the highest number in northern California. All of these are informed by an articulate ecological consciousness and jointly mobilized for political action. Monterey has a uniquely dense conservationist infrastructure, giving rise to its growing reputation as an environmental redoubt.

In June 1998 the federal government sponsored a widely publicized Ocean Conference at Monterey's Naval Postgraduate School. Vice President Al Gore presided over five hundred invited experts and a series of presentations ranging from global warming to national security and commercial uses of the sea. As panelists got down to technical details, Gore took a cruise on MBARI's *Western Flyer* and had a close-up look at the ocean in the ship's remotely operated submersible vehicle (ROV). President Bill Clinton joined the proceedings on the following day, bounded over tidepool rocks at Hopkins Marine Station, and complimented conference participants on their serious purpose. Before departing, the president made a short speech at San Carlos Park on Cannery Row announcing his steadfast commitment to the environment, new federal spending programs, and extension of the ban on offshore drilling—nothing especially newsworthy. The event's significance lay elsewhere, in the arena of historical symbolism.

A far cry from President McKinley's 1901 visit to the luxurious Hotel Del Monte and his description of Monterey as the "historical ground" of frontier expansion, President Clinton's trip emphasized the scientific and economic significance of the conference transpiring on the former hotel site, now devoted to higher education. The symbolism of speeches at the waterfront park, former site of the San Carlos Cannery, superimposed environmentalism on the old industrial landscape. As Gore went kayaking and Clinton flew on to a San Francisco fund-raiser, the grassroots environmental community turned out in force for a daylong Oceans Fair of exhibits, speakers, tours, and recruitment by scores of green causes. Environmentalism had become a defining feature of local society. Oceans Fair crowded the Custom House Plaza—historic ground, urban renewal space, and cultural marketplace.

RECONFIGURING THE CULTURAL ENVIRONMENT

When Monterey's Custom House Plaza is not devoted to special events like Oceans Fair or Whale Fest, it routinely hosts an annual cycle of heritage festivals and commemorative celebrations. Independence Day features reenactments of the early days of California, flag raising in 1846, Sloat's landing marked at his monument on nearby Presidio hill, and fireworks. In September comes the Santa Rosalia Festival, which began as a blessing of the fishing fleet and has grown to the more generically cultural Festa Italia. Christmas recalls Old Monterey with candle-lit openings of historic buildings around the plaza, "actors in the adobes," and performances that associate local history and the holiday season. Springtime brings Greek and Filipino festivals with the plaza given over to ethnic cuisine, music, dancing, shopping, and revelry. These events and more, at the mission, fairgrounds, or Cannery Row, portray a cultural landscape constituted by physical spaces and social groups. Festivals and commemorations result from the labors of people in groups with a purpose. No law requires that Sloat's landing be observed every year or that Italian contributions to local society be recalled in evolving forms. Groups take up these efforts for the enjoyment and satisfaction they derive from associating their interests with history; from expressing a collective identity that unites perceptions of history with pride, self-interest, sentiment, and memory.

Contemporary culture in Monterey is pluralistic and eclectic. A number of interest groups and civic organizations constitute the heritage industry, although they also cluster around a few thematic foci. For longevity and numbers, the California heritage expressed in "Old Monterey" is foremost. Since the early 1930s, the Monterey History and Art Association has cultivated local history in preservation, print, and politics. And its efforts continue today, but now as one in an elaborate network of organizations. Custom House Plaza is maintained as a state historic park that includes a score of preserved structures throughout downtown—the First Theater, Stevenson House, Larkin House, Cooper-Molera home and merchandise store, and many more. The city of Monterey is equally represented, maintaining publicly accessible Colton Hall and Museum, the old jail, Vasquez adobe, and city offices themselves that occupy the original military cuartel (barracks). All of these are signposted

33. Murals of Cannery Row. Today's Cannery Row features various works of art, architecture, and preservation that commemorate the industrial era. Here local sponsors and artists pay tribute to sardine packers. (Photo by the author)

stops on the Path of History, first laid out in 1931 by Colonel Fitch, who founded the MHAA, and now maintained by a consortium of agencies, voluntary associations, and volunteer docents. The Historic Garden League, Old Monterey Preservation Society, Nautical Heritage Society, Old Monterey Business Association, and more collaborate with the MHAA and the government. This profusion of civic organizations and landmarks is one important source of Monterey's deserved reputation as a very historical place.

Yet there is more to this scene than self-evident historical fact. There is a sociology of old California operating, a characteristic pattern of group representation and historical selectivity. Old California as it is displayed in Monterey these days is a joint product of urban renewal, commercial promotion, and civic preservation. It is a shared space of business, government, and aesthetic sensibility—a place of great charm and particular historical sense. It is a pleasant place to be, if not always a realistic one.

The groups that have imagined old Monterey in physical form are predominantly Anglo: middle class, North American, white, good-natured, and self-centered. Old Monterey, in their representation, is not very old.

Father Serra, a European, discovered it, and there followed an uneventful seventy-six years until Commodore Sloat gave it significance. Although downtown markers and the Path of History take note of Mexican family homes (Abrego, Alvarado, Osio, Soberanes, Vasquez), these locations and lives are overshadowed by figures of the American period: U.S. Consulate Larkin's house, Frémont's headquarters, Stevenson's House (a rooming house where the writer spent three months), Colton Hall (where California's constitution was drafted), the first theater started in Jack Swan's saloon, and the homes of American settlers (Doud, Merritt, Stokes). Similarly, local stories of early California begin with the basic origin myth in which Father Serra establishes civilization and then move directly to U.S. occupation. Native Americans seldom appear, except perhaps among the wildlife. The consummate deeds of Fages, Gutierrez, Alvarado, Castro, and Vallejo are unreported, probably unknown. But Stevenson is adopted as a native son. Old Monterey is a contemporary social world maintained by city and state officials, businesspeople, civic-minded volunteers, and senior citizens for public consumption. It is entertainment rather than history. Yet it is also the heritage these groups want and go to some lengths to create.

Monterey's ethnic heritage runs a close second to the physical and social complex of old California when it comes to cultural promotion. The Sicilian community, which now tends to define itself as Italian, is the most numerous, organized, and active nationality group. Established at the turn of the twentieth century by Pietro Ferrante and Orazio Enea, Monterey's Sicilian fishing community grew to include the men's families, women homemakers and cannery workers, and a supporting cast of nonfishing Sicilians and non-Sicilian Italians in various affiliated businesses. In fifty years since the sardines vanished, the Italian community has retained its geographic roots while journeying through the occupational world. Italians are now the mayors and schoolteachers, lawyers and grocers. Former fishing families operate Ferrante's (and Spadaro's and Rappa's) Restaurant, Russo's Insurance Agency, Davi Real Estate, Enea Dairies, Bruno's Business Machines, and Bruno's Market, to name a few. Locally the community is organized in the Italian Heritage Society, the Italian Catholic Federation, Sons of Italy, the Festa Italia Committee, the Monterey Fishermen's Historical Society, the Italian Cultural Center, and various women's and church groups. September's Santa Rosalia/ Festa Italia is the largest single community celebration, but Italians are closely connected (and sometimes divided) in family, school, and church activities.

34. Santa Rosalia Festival, 1995. In Monterey's annual Santa Rosalia Festival, an icon of the patron saint is carried to Fisherman's Wharf for the traditional blessing of the fleet. (Photo by the author)

Visible representation of the Italian heritage is growing thanks to the efforts of these groups. Santa Rosalia's statue overlooking the harbor was erected by the Italian Heritage Society in 1970, "in memory of those courageous Sicilian fishermen whose labors and pioneering spirit at the beginning of the 20th century created and developed a great sardine industry and whose heritage and culture contributed significantly to the growth of this city," as the plaque reads. The Fisherman's Wharf Association and the Monterey Fishermen's Historical Association are raising $50,000 for a statue of a fisherman to be placed near Santa Rosalia on the waterfront. Rosalie Ferrante is working with other volunteers and public agencies on a cultural heritage center, perhaps at the Presidio, where various groups might showcase their role in local history. The Italian contribution is already being assembled in family histories, photos, memorabilia, oral histories, and videos featuring the founding families—the latter being recorded with some urgency "before it's too late." Privately Italians concede that they feel slighted by the disproportionate historical attention paid to filibustering soldiers and philandering writers rather than the hardworking families who built the city's great industry. Those "Steinbeck people" on Cannery Row speak for commercial interests rather than people's history.

In spring 1999 a conference was held in the Ferrante Room of the Monterey Conference Center. Sponsored by the American Italian Historical Association and the Italian Heritage Society of Monterey Peninsula, the conference dealt with "Italian American Fishing in Northern California," bringing together fishermen, families, students, and enthusiasts of the industry from Monterey, Santa Cruz, San Francisco, and Pittsburg (formerly Black Diamond, where canning on the Sacramento River spawned Monterey's industry). Sessions delved into topics such as "The Culture of Italian Fishermen," "Fishermen's Wives," "How Did Italians Shape Fishing in Each Community?" and "What is the Future of Italians in Fishing?" It was an informative, pan-Italian, celebratory event—lectures, panels, photo exhibits, music, food, and plenty of spontaneous participation from an audience of former fishermen and cannery workers, families, men and women whose childhoods were spent in the industry. Yet it was a peculiar event. The industry in these presentations became an exclusively Italian affair. Absent were the Japanese fishermen who made up a majority of the commercial fleet in the early days. Gone were the Anglo cannery owners, Norwegian engineers, Chinese fish cutters, Spanish packers, and Okie warehouse workers. It was not that the Italian conferees were unaware of the multicultural character of their industry but rather that they were now primarily interested in memorializing the Italian contribution to local history, which they believed was mainly about fishing, mainly by Italians. History was being recoded; no longer a working-class experience, not particularly an industrial activity, but something that brought Italians together in a shared memory of ethnic pride and achievement. It seemed to them the natural way to commemorate the past—and it is, provided we draw a distinction between history and memory.

Monterey's cultural landscape has shifted. The working-class town of the 1940s is now experienced as a preserve of California heritage created by its multicultural population. For present purposes, the important point about this representational change is that it results from the socioeconomic realignment of local life. Two fundamental changes distinguish contemporary society. First, Monterey, like the rest of the country, has experienced an equality revolution. Diversity, feminism, and multiculturalism are accorded not simply political recognition but social value. Regional and ethnic heritage is a resource to be cultivated and shared. Educational institutions stress these values, as witnessed in a new state university on the rehabilitated grounds of Fort Ord that has made diversity its mission. Voluntary associations respond to the cultural initiative. New

35.   Santa Rosalia Festival Parade Banner, 1995. The
festival commemorates the fishing industry and its various
constitutents, including the Monterey Fishermen's Protective Union that later affiliated with the AFL. (Photo by the
author)

groups organize and old ones energize among preservationists and in ethnic associations of Italians, Japanese, Filipinos, Greeks, and Scots. Second, the new service economy encourages commemorative events and
heritage festivals that draw crowds to local sites, centers, hotels, restaurants, and stores. Sometimes these events tend toward the purely commercial, as in the case of the Cannery Row Sardine Festival. Frequently,
however, they simultaneously create culture and profit, as in the Santa

Rosalia Festival. The political and economic forces shaping the new cultural landscape scarcely detract from its authenticity.

ACTION AND NARRATIVE

Rancho San Carlos is a vast, virgin, postcard property of twenty thousand acres (thirty-one square miles) lying immediately south of Carmel Valley and running most of its length. In 1990 Daishinpan-USA Company of Osaka, Japan, bought the ranch for $70 million as a hedge against inflation in the hot Japanese economy and for long-term development. Planning proceeded deliberately, provision was made for water and roads, an environmental impact report (EIR) was prepared, permits were obtained, local supporters were cultivated, and a public relations campaign was launched. Carmel Valley residents began to learn about the project in the *Rancho San Carlos Update: A Community Newsletter from the Santa Lucia Preserve.* The attractive newsletter was illustrated, printed on high-quality paper, and mailed bulk rate "To Our Neighbors, Rural Route, Carmel CA."

The news from Rancho San Carlos was birdsong to environmental ears. The land would be devoted to Santa Lucia Preserve whose "fundamental environmental elements" included "(1) 18,000 acres of *Preserved Lands* (90 percent of the ranch), which will be permanently protected and managed for wildlife and scenic values by the new, nonprofit Santa Lucia Conservancy, and (2) no more than 2,000 acres of *Settled Lands* (10 percent of the ranch), consisting of carefully located, minimal-impact clusters, which will be developed for limited residential, neighborhood-commercial, agricultural and recreational purposes and will carry conservation easements on all sides." The preserve would include a nature center, public access to hiking trails, lecture and school programs by the Rancho San Carlos Educational Foundation, a grazing program to preserve native grasses, and "a home for wild animals in their native habitat." The plan, in sum, would answer "the decades-long call of environmentalists and critics of traditional land development by fully incorporating the welfare of wildlife and nature into the enterprise of creating communities for humans."[20]

Although newsletter readers would never know, Rancho San Carlos was also an upscale housing development and resort complex: three hundred fifty home sites spread across the length of the property along with a one-hundred-fifty-room hotel, golf course, and commercial center. Their neighbors were not happy about the news and what seemed to them the

Daishinpan company's less-than-candid description of the project. Carmel Valley was already sensitive to overdevelopment. Its General Plan limited new construction, and water shortages that threatened rationing were common. A proposed new dam on the Carmel River, portending resurgent development, recently had been stalled in an intense referendum campaign. This was no time to be discussing big projects in Carmel Valley— a circumstance doubtless responsible for the anodyne language of corporate publicity. Neighbors began asking where the water would come from, how many automobiles would be added to the congested Carmel Valley Road. The company's EIR said they would pump groundwater from wells completely independent of the Carmel River aquifer, source for the rest of the peninsula, withdrawing water at a rate well below natural replenishment. The Sierra Club didn't believe it and brought suit charging the EIR was inadequate.

When the County Board of Supervisors unanimously approved the housing development and golf course, citizens began organizing a grassroots campaign to challenge their leaders and the power of corporate spending. An initiative campaign set up tables at grocery stores and post offices, gathering signatures for a ballot measure on the project. Volunteers alerted residents to the threats of water rationing, 1,269 additional daily vehicle trips on Carmel Valley Road, loss of open space, and corporate intimidation of people circulating the petition. A map-display showing the ranch property thoroughly dotted with building lots asked, "Where's the Preserve?" The petition garnered ten thousand signatures, more than enough to put Proposition M on the November 1996 ballot. Dave Potter ran for county supervisor on a No-on-M platform that challenged the current board's pro-development stance. Measure M proposed a vote on whether commercial zoning would be allowed at Rancho San Carlos; a "Yes" approved the whole plan, a "No" rejected its commercial features (hotel, stores, and administrative offices) but not the residential development and golf course.

The campaign was predictably vigorous. Proponents, always identified as the preserve or the foundation, mounted a free-spending media effort. The project was represented chiefly as environmental preservation: "Your 'YES' vote on Measure M will approve a community preserve that took six years to create"; "Ninety percent of the ranch will be deeded to and managed by the Santa Lucia Conservancy. It will be off limits to any kind of development forever." Not only that, but if the measure failed, someone (who was not specified) could develop up to 522 homes within the norms of the EIR, a prospect to be avoided by approving the preserve's vision. Yes-on-M advertisements listed six hundred endorsements, including the venerable and retired Senator Fred Farr, five county supervisors, the Carmel Valley Property Owners Association, the Monterey County Hospitality Association, the Monterey County Cattleman's Association, and the Mountain Lion Preservation Foundation (the latter two seemingly at cross purposes). No-on-M was a lightly funded, all-volunteer, high-spirited, righteous crusade. They worked the shopping centers with a populist message: "The average home owner can't get approval for an extra bathroom while supervisors kowtow to corporate capital"; "They're getting huge benefits for land dedicated as a preserve that can't be built on anyway." Behind such sentiments stood the League of Women Voters, the *Monterey Herald*, the Sierra Club, the Carmel Native Plant Society, the Carmel River Steelhead Association, and the Surfrider Foundation.

As the election approached, it was clear that personal campaigning and the underdog image was benefiting the opposition. But the San Carlos team still had a valuable heritage card to play. An article in the Sunday supplement before election day revealed that the ranch included a seemingly insignificant cabin ruin that in fact was the salvageable remains of the historic Goate Ranche. On this site in 1879, farmers and former seamen Jonathan Wright and Anson Smith had found Robert Louis Stevenson wandering lost and ill. In this very cabin the goat keepers nursed the frail Scotsman back to health. Who would have known? Elayne Wareing Fitzpatrick wrote in the Monterey newspaper, "Now a team of volunteers—RLS aficionados and history buffs who call themselves 'The RLS Goate Ranche Group'—is collaborating with the Rancho San Carlos Partnership in Carmel Valley to designate the long-neglected cabin site as an historical landmark. Both groups come under the jurisdiction of the Santa Lucia Conservancy, a nonprofit supporting entity of the Trust for Public Land which has assumed responsibility for preservation, interpretation and education connected with the site." Although owners "assured that the cabin site will be conserved and maintained regardless of the outcome of current development disputes," Fitzpatrick clearly endorsed the project (without mentioning Measure M) and suggested that "cooperation" among groups would ensure permanent protection of the "important landmark."[21]

Voters were not swayed by the promise of a nature preserve or a history center. On the contrary, they were worried about further development in a region stressed to environmental limits. Countywide, Measure M was defeated in a 55 to 45 percent vote, suggesting heavy Monterey-

Carmel opposition in an otherwise pro-development county. Dave Potter won his supervisor's race by the same margin. The clear slow-growth message resonated on the peninsula. Environmentalists savored one in a series of small victories. Yet Rancho San Carlos would go on, after shedding the Sierra Club suit, as a luxury home and golf course development without commercial uses. Developers studied the case in anticipation of future proposals. Measure M opened a new chapter in the perennial struggle over development. Costs and benefits would henceforth be calculated in environmental terms, all sides arguing that their work promises a better planet. Environmental protection, moreover, now embraces historical sites—nature center and history center the bona fides of responsible development. Environment and heritage emerge as the legitimating language of public action.

The controversy around Rancho San Carlos is typical of contemporary politics on the Monterey Peninsula. Development is *the* issue—how fast, by whom, with whose water, where, with what effects on the environment and the character of community. These issues are routinely debated by groups of mobilized citizens and property interests. They cover land and sea. They occupy city councils, county boards, planning commissions, and agencies of state and federal government. They are routinely taken to the electorate for debate and resolution. The courts are usually involved at some stage and the stages span years. In the 1950s, and with gathering force in the late 1960s, a freeway through Hatton Canyon was proposed to link Highway 1 at Carmel Hill and Carmel Valley Road. The state transportation agency pushed unrelentingly to remove the "bottleneck" on old Highway 1, even appropriated the necessary funds, while area residents fought back just as forcefully with broad public support, environmental arguments, and good lawyers. Only after a thirty-year struggle was Hatton Canyon Freeway finally abandoned owing to a combination of skilled opposition and the appearance of a more compelling use for transportation agency funds.

Sometimes positions and results shift. In 1984 the city of Monterey approved a large condominium project on Del Monte Beach but reversed itself two years later based on newfound concern for public access and habitat restoration. The developer went to court and eventually won a $1.45 million award for the loss of unrealized profit. While the city appealed the judgment in federal court, the developer sold the property to the state in 1991 for a $1 million profit and the land became a state park. Eight years later, the United States Supreme Court in a five-to-four decision upheld the original award, meaning that the city still had to compensate the developers $1.45 million (and their lawyers $1.2 million) for a property long since profitably converted to public use.

The case of Measure M notwithstanding, corporate property interests are still potent on the Monterey Peninsula. From the days of David Jacks and the Pacific Improvement Company to Del Monte Properties and the Pebble Beach Company, property owners have played an influential role in local politics. Although the corporation has had ten different owners since Del Monte Properties took over in 1919 (nine of those since 1977), its character has been remarkably consistent (while its market value has risen from $1 million to $800 million). For eighty years, the company has been devoted to commercial property management, real estate development, and maintenance of an exclusive residential community and recreational playground (polo, golf, tennis, dog shows, equestrian events). And it has championed those interests as a public actor in the face of hostile forces ranging from redolent fish processing to odious environmental regulation.[22]

Yet the Pebble Beach Company has also changed with the times, especially in its advertised public posture. It is now environmentally sensitive, ecologically proactive. The handsome *Pebble Beach Company Environmental Annual Report, 1996–1997,* describes the varied conservation programs in operation on the 5,300-acre estate: waste recycling, wastewater reclamation, energy saving, ride sharing, educational outreach, hiking trails, harbor seal protection, a cooperative sanctuary golf course in collaboration with the Audubon Society, and the S. F. B. Morse Botanical Reserve. Over $1 million has been invested in eradicating pitch pine canker, a fungus devastating pine forests around the peninsula. Although automobile access to the company's grounds and Seventeen Mile Drive is controlled by a toll road, miles of hiking and nature trails are open to the pedestrian public (as are golf courses at $300 per round). For its worthy efforts, the company has won two environmental achievement awards.

But it is also big business, an international corporation dependent on profitable returns—particularly during the 1990s when it was owned by Japanese investors suffering an economic crisis at home. Long in germination, a plan was put forward billed as "the final phase of 80 years of real estate development in the world-famous Del Monte Forest." Taking a leaf from Santa Lucia Preserve's public relations book, the project was called simply Del Monte Forest Plan. The plan had several aims: to protect and replant trees, save water, dedicate 690 acres to permanent forest, and, inter alia, build a fifth eighteen-hole golf course and 316 new homes. The latter aspect of the plan, moreover, is described as an actual *reduction by 65 percent* of the housing density allowable in current zoning—a godsend compared to what might have been. Water would come from entitlements already earned from the Carmel Area Water District for financial support and use of reclaimed water on the golf course. All these virtues were paraded in a series of newspaper and television advertisements: "We've protected this forest for 80 years. For the next century we'll do the same." As county supervisors met to consider the plan, the company released the results of its own poll (hired from a San Diego telemarketing firm) indicating that public opinion was leaning in favor of Del Monte Forest Plan by a gratifying two-to-one margin.[23]

Even by that survey, however, one-third of the population disapproved. Outspoken groups included a segment of the estate's 1,600 home owners organized as Concerned Residents of Pebble Beach—concerned about housing density, traffic congestion, and habitat destruction. The Association to Preserve Equestrian Easements protested relocation of the stable and show grounds, part of the ranching heritage that predated Del Monte Properties ownership. The Sierra Club and the Native Plant Society weighed in with worries about clearing trees for a golf course in a forest already falling to fungus. Worse, Lee Otter, chief planner for the Coastal Commission's central district, warned that the company's operative land use plan approved by the commission more than a decade earlier might now be invalid. In the interim, Otter noted, the pitch canker fungus had been discovered in the forest along with several endangered plant species.[24] A new round of Coastal Commission hearings would expose the company to public scrutiny at a more environmentally conscious moment and make it responsible for coping with a whole new set of ecological dangers. And finally, the words "initiative process" had been voiced by the Concerned Residents. Another Proposition M would spell trouble.

Whether as a result of looming restraints on development or continuing doldrums in the Japanese economy, Sumitomo Bank negotiated the sale of Pebble Beach Company in May 1999 to a partnership of U.S. celebrities and sports entrepreneurs. Retaining the same on-site management, the company announced a revised plan. Four hundred forest acres would be designated protected open space and the new golf course would steer clear of precious trees—all pending Coastal Commission approval. This latest maneuver seemed to navigate the tricky ground between new development and heritage-environmental sensitivities. But another condition of the approval process had been brushed aside. County planning commissioners were recommending that fifty-three low-cost homes required for company employees (restaurant workers, groundskeepers, and stable hands, many of them Hispanic) be built on Huckleberry Hill inside Pebble Beach gates. Company plans called for construction of worker housing twenty-five miles away in the Mexican village of Pajaro near Watsonville, "where the county needed it most," according to a company spokesman: "The community of Pajaro wants it. The Del Monte Forest would prefer to have fewer homes." Members of Del Monte Forest Property Owners were equally condescending but more direct. They would "strongly object to putting inclusionary housing in Pebble Beach." After all, the Mexican-American occupants of such homes would be far from "community services," the public transportation and child care that those folks need—and presumably would find in abundance in Pajaro. The days of restrictive covenants at Pebble Beach were not so far away.[25]

Returning to the interpretive argument that connects these cases, the failure of inclusionary housing at Pebble Beach (and elsewhere) reflects a more general neglect of inclusionary heritage in local development. This was the grievance of Italian Americans who saw their history on Monterey's waterfront and Cannery Row being erased by commercialism. It was the motive for action to reclaim their past in heritage stories, commemorative events, and physical markers. It is the same concern that motivates Native Americans to protest their invisibility and recall their central place in Monterey's heritage and environment. A Native American village lies beneath the Custom House and multicultural plaza, although it has yet to be marked.[26] The State Department of Parks and Recreation has excavated an Indian settlement on the Presidio and marked it, somewhat ethnocentrically, with a large cross. Painful exclusion has roused Native Americans to take advantage of new opportunities to commemorate their past by becoming involved in local development politics.

Ironically, given the production made of Robert Louis Stevenson's tenuous connection to Rancho San Carlos during the Proposition M campaign, the property also includes an extensive network of Rumsen settlements. A "lost village" was discovered by Gary Breschini, a local archaeologist who was employed by the Pacific Union Company (predecessor to the Rancho San Carlos Partnership) to survey the ranch. The site corresponds to the village of Echilat, identified in Carmel Mission records as the origin of ninety neophytes baptized between 1773 and 1783.[27] Not only did the discovery confirm Rumsen folklore, it provided a physical location and artifact record of the region's preconquest population—something to commemorate with at least a fraction of the enthusiasm invested in the mission that this village helped to populate and build. Native Americans have begun campaigning for recognition of settlement sites.

In a well-publicized instance, a small band claiming Esselen lineage organized in response to plans for a new dam in the upper Carmel Valley. Twice during the 1990s, residents of the Carmel Valley Water Management District voted against the proposed dam, fearing it would open the gates to uncontrolled development. In association with the Sierra Club, the Carmel River Steelhead Association, the Residents Water Committee, and the State Department of Parks and Recreation, the Esselen group "emerged to challenge the Monterey Peninsula Water Management District's right to build a new dam on the Carmel River."[28]

Appearing before hearings in Monterey of the State Water Control Resources Board in summer 1992, representatives of the Esselen argued that the new Los Padres Reservoir would inundate thousands of acres that included important archaeological sites and sacred burial grounds. Some of this heritage had only recently come to light thanks to an archaeological report by the Breschini-Haversat team and efforts by Esselen descendants over the previous five years "to renew the traditions, language, teaching, and ethnology of the tribe." Tom "Little Bear" Nason, activist and seventh-generation inhabitant of the Santa Lucia Mountains, explained, "We're in the process of tribal revitalization, it's not a full culture, but it's something that is growing. There is a thin thread that has come down to us." Owing to the exiguous Esselen heritage, Nason deems it legitimate to fill in some of the gaps by borrowing rituals from other California Indians such as Pomo and Chumash. In that, Nason has his critics—perhaps a healthy sign of cultural dialogue. Rudolf Rosales, a construction worker from Seaside and an independent Esselen, calls Nason's story "a bunch of crock" and continues, "He's just describing Plains Indians. We never had drums. We used abalone shell and tapped them together." Other spokespersons for various Ohlone groups have subsequently elaborated the culture: Loretta Wyer of Palo Alto believes a case can be made for federal recognition of a composite Esselen Nation, while Rumsen descendant Linda Yamane develops programs for local schools and museums.

The important point about these new contributions to local heritage is that they derive from intertwining efforts on behalf of development and environmental protection. In Carmel Valley, "the group was energized by archaeologists exploring Esselen sites" in connection with the

proposed dam. Anne McGowan, a Carmel environmental attorney involved in the continuing fight over the dam, says, "Local government is
the least appreciative of Native American resources." Yet something new
has been added to the struggle: "[I]f you are an environmentalist you feel
a communality with Native Americans."[29]

A new history of Monterey is under construction, a broad narrative
woven of threads fashioned in commercial development, environmental
politics, and heritage preservation. Sardine capital of the world cedes
imaginative power to environmental sanctuary, industrial town melds
into marine research complex, and working-class culture yields to heritage awareness. Not only do these new controlling images provide lenses
on the present, they rotate around, read backward. The Indians always
were practicing ecologists, the Chinese partisans of affirmative action,
and Anglo-Americans curators of cultural tradition. Old stories are retired or disassembled and new ones are constructed in the practical action of groups that make it their job to build, improve, honor, and live
in a place. Stories change because the purposes for which they are in-
voked change.

In some essential aspects, Monterey history is presently embedded in
an environmental narrative. Natural history is the paradigm integrating
portraits of a region comprising land and sea, populated by fish, mam-
mals in and out of the water, animals that walk and fly over the earth.
It is plant species from kelp to oak, geology, meteorology, and diverse
aspects of the ecosystem, including the mixed blessings of human occupation. A staple in this tradition is Burton Gordon's engaging *Monterey
Bay Area: Natural History and Cultural Imprints*. Continuously in print
since 1974 and something of a handbook for local environmentalists,
Gordon's history focuses on the interplay of humans and nature, "Indian occupancy," and "changes attending American occupancy." An ecological sophisticate, Gordon recognizes that Native Americans were capable of environmental depletion, stripping the coastline of mollusks at
times, although more characteristically they husbanded the land with controlled burns and plant regeneration. The balance tipped toward degradation when Europeans and Americans began commercial exploitation
of particular species (otters, whales, sardines) and alteration of the land
(non-native plant propagation, groundwater extraction, salinating irri-
gation, habitat destruction, chemical pollution). Gordon's book is ex-
pressly aimed at redressing these problems: "to investigate the character
and extent of ecological change produced by humans in the Monterey
Bay area and to suggest applications of such information to land-use plan-

ning."[30] A worthy sequel to Gordon's text is *The Natural History of Big Sur,* a lush naturalist's guide and human history produced with the support of the Big Sur Land Trust, the David and Lucille Packard Foundation, and the Community Foundation for Monterey County, among others.[31]

The environmental narrative infuses a variety of interpretive works on local history. A lively and well-researched history of Carmel revolves around a central theme of environmental protection: "In the wave of environmental awareness that swept across America in the last decades of the 20th century, communities began to look for ways to protect themselves against the advance of commercialization. . . . That kind of effort has been going on in Carmel for more than half a century. Probably nowhere else so early and with such vigor have residents fought for the preservation of their community."[32] Another popular history of the Monterey coast shares this appraisal and organizes its treatment of prominent contributors to regional culture under the heading "Artists, Writers, Environmentalists."[33] In recent reappraisals, Robinson Jeffers is classified an environmental poet and the Big Sur headlands referred to as Jeffers Country.[34] John Steinbeck is reprised as an ecological prophet, his book *The Log of the Sea of Cortez* a prototype for Aldo Leopold, Annie Dillard, Edward Abbey, and John McPhee. It is true, of course, that Jeffers and Steinbeck, like Ansel Adams and Edward Weston, were profoundly affected by the natural environment. But only recently have these artists, once icons of bohemian eccentricity and depression travail, been recast as erstwhile characters in the environmental story.

Equally important, the ethnic heritage paradigm is intertwined with the environmental narrative. General regional histories are uncommon lately, replaced by a profusion of heritage stories celebrating the considerable achievements of Chinese, Japanese, Italians, and Native Americans. *Chinese Gold: The Chinese in the Monterey Bay Region,* Sandy Lydon's outstanding social history of Monterey Bay Chinese since 1850, is a richly textured story of immigrant life, work, community, and self-defense in Santa Cruz, Watsonville, Salinas, and Monterey.[35] A sequel by Lydon, *The Japanese in the Monterey Bay Region: A Brief History,* is equally impressive for its photographic images and illustrations, if not its heft.[36] David Yamada's abundantly illustrated *The Japanese of Monterey Peninsula: Their History and Legacy, 1895–1995,* originated as a commemorative project of the local Japanese American Citizens League.[37] Long chronicled for its industry, the Italian community has lately been recalled in memoirs and oral histories as a close-knit world of extended families, church societies, and ethnic associations.[38] And, of course, the Native American story has recently enjoyed extensive scholarly analysis, public discussion, and popular press.[39] In the best and most abundant work of late, Monterey's social history is understood as the product of congeries of ethnic groups, each carrying its own burden of discrimination, laboring through hard times, achieving social mobility and respectability, and leaving identifiable markers on the cultural landscape. This narrative is advanced with a passion that veils earlier accounts of working-class mobilization.

The heritage narrative is broader than the experience of particular ethnic or "minority" groups. It is an idea, a way of organizing collective memory in terms of living connections to local lore; links between things we can experience in the present and illustrious events in the past. The stories, sites, and refurbished structures of old Monterey root important segments of the population in an estimable past with much the same emotive force of ethnicity. Indeed, the California romance is constructed by and for Anglos—North Americans save Mexicans and Europeans save Italians. It is, moreover, constructed chiefly as the pioneering record of Anglo-Americans. The European Catholic Father Serra got things off to a civilized start, then passed the torch to a procession of Americans (Larkin, Sloat, Colton, Huntington) whose homes, halls, hotels, and monuments still tell their story. This is the account developed in several popular histories[40] and reiterated by volunteer docents in adobes along the Path of History. This is the local heritage preserved, interpreted, and represented by the patrician Monterey History and Art Association in a series of commemorative sites and organizational publications.

The story of Cannery Row also belongs to the heritage narrative, although its parvenu social bases differ from the MHAA. It is recent heritage, largely a product of commercial invention, but important for its wide publicity and power to infuse related accounts of the industrial era. It was created opportunistically in a setting of economic and cultural change. Monterey's sardine fishery faltered in the late 1940s and canneries began closing left and right by the early 1950s. A group called Cannery Row Properties—some, former cannery managers; and others, San Francisco investors—began buying the dormant plants and by 1957 owned fifteen parcels comprising 50 percent of waterfront footage. In that year there were just five functional canneries left, none packing sardines but operating intermittently on tuna, anchovies, mackerel, and other sea products. When Cannery Row Properties began buying up the plants in 1953, its principal business was machine salvage, converting cannery boilers and dryers to other industrial uses or selling them to new fisheries in South America and South Africa. No plan existed to rejuvenate the street as a restaurant row or tourist attraction. On the contrary, the desultory property market took its own course as a series of small local businesses gradually moved in.[41] In 1964 a San Francisco firm calling itself Cannery Row Development Company purchased its predecessor and came forward with a plan for building a tourist mecca, but its efforts became entangled with urban renewal, preservationist aims of the city, and the Coastal Commission. The San Francisco firm slowly ceded its properties to Foursome Development Company, composed of local restaurateurs and realtors.

John Steinbeck's popular novel made the idea of Cannery Row an American commonplace. Long-term residents of the street (always officially Ocean View Avenue until renamed Cannery Row by the city in 1953) reported a steady stream of visitors in search of Mack and the boys, the Bear Flag restaurant and bordello, or Doc's lab. Steinbeck's contribution to local publicity did not end there. In *Sweet Thursday* the author provided a popular sequel in 1954, Richard Rodgers and Oscar Hammerstein used that work as the basis for their lesser-known 1955 musical, *Pipe Dream,* and the two novels were merged in a subsequent stage play and a film each called *Cannery Row.* Curious visitors to the Monterey waterfront encountered small businesses, restaurants and gift shops, as well as the imposing hulks of vacant canneries and covered plant-to-warehouse conveyors bridging the street in a well-defined twenty-city-block area that the city hoped to redevelop as a historical business and office center. These surroundings certainly included Steinbeck's landmarks such that the familiar story was bound to figure in any description of the area and its picaresque past. But those circumstances certainly did not dictate a particular version of history or require that the industrial and working-class experience be excluded and "Steinbeck's Cannery Row" privileged. Steinbeck's work scarcely exhausted the history and character of Monterey's waterfront, nor did it even embrace all those features that might interest visitors—from the imposing industrial architecture to lingering groups of workers and the brilliant bay itself. Potentially, there was a rich history waiting to be developed for tourists, residents, students, Steinbeck buffs, Asian and Italian heritage groups, seafarers, scientists, laborites, and environmentalists. The possibilities were abundant. Nothing determined that one version would predominate.

In fact, however, shortly after the takeover by property developers

36. *Cannery Row in its Heyday, Early 1930's,* by Bruce Ariss. Local artist and
Steinbeck friend Bruce Ariss painted this nostalgic reminiscence of the industrial
period for the Monterey Bay Aquarium in 1971. Ed Ricketts (Doc) is depicted
on the porch of his Pacific Biological Laboratory waving to the passing artist
and his wife, Jean, while Steinbeck naps in the Packard parked in front. The
painting evokes "Steinbeck's Cannery Row" of the imagination more than it
does George Robinson's photograph of workaday life on the street. (Courtesy
of Monterey Bay Aquarium Foundation, © 1984)

"Steinbeck's Cannery Row" began to monopolize popular memory.
Class, ethnicity, gender, the fishermen themselves, cannery women, the
industrial engine of town prosperity—all these were neglected or treated
as props in another play. As Martha Norkunas shows in her study of
Monterey's "public texts," property owners re-created Steinbeck mem-
orabilia in sidewalk murals, a wax museum, and a bust of the author.[42]
A series of guidebooks and local histories written over a period of years
effectively assimilated the complex history of Cannery Row to the simple
story of Steinbeck's savvy nonconformists.[43] In some cases these were
good histories and excellent photographic essays, but they merged two
different realities and increasingly foregrounded the novel to stand for
the larger experience.

This was not Steinbeck's doing. By 1957 he had fallen out with his
Monterey friends and contributed a sarcastic critique of California's
"pseudo-old/new-old" architectural and redevelopment schemes for the
local newspaper addressed to "Cannery Row purchasers."[44] The new
story of Cannery Row was constructed by the commercial interests that
took over the street, their public relations advisers, the newspaper, the
city of Monterey, and a variety of popular writers all of whom discovered cash value and name recognition in this version of events. Norku-

nas describes the transformation: "Steinbeck and his fictional characters, rather than the canneries themselves or the actual cannery workers, have become the referents to Cannery Row. With Steinbeck as focal point of the Row, there is no longer a need to refer to the city's industrial legacy. Rather than anchoring the past in the physical remains of the canneries, it is Steinbeck who is used as the implement of authentication, the anchor to specificity of place, the organizing imagery for tourism on the Row."[45] Publicists for the association of Cannery Row property owners speak knowingly of this imagery as the result of their success at "heritage marketing."

CONCLUSION

Steinbeck already knew about the effect of his popular work on local promotion and legend: "When I wrote *Tortilla Flat,* for instance, the Monterey Chamber of Commerce issued a statement that it was a damned lie and that no such place or people existed. Later, they began running buses to the place where they thought it might be." In 1945, returning from New York, Steinbeck found himself unwelcome in Monterey and old friends unable to deal with his success, jealousy he thought: "[There is] an active hatred of the writers and pseudo-writers around here. . . . This isn't my country any more. It makes me very sad."[46] As time went on, Monterey became even less Steinbeck's country. *Tortilla Flat* was the memory he knew.

> The afternoon came down as imperceptibly as age comes to a happy man. A little gold entered into the sunlight. The bay became bluer and dimpled with shore-wind ripples. Those lonely fishermen who believed that the fish bite at high tide left their rocks, and their places were taken by others, who were convinced that the fish bite at low tide. At three o'clock the wind veered around and blew softly in from the bay, bringing all manner of fine kelp odors. The menders of nets in the vacant lots put down their spindles and rolled cigarettes. . . . On Alvarado Street, Hugo Machado, the tailor, put a sign in his shop door, "Back in Five Minutes," and went home for the day. All Monterey began to make gradual instinctive preparations against the night. Mrs. Gutierrez cut little chiles into the enchilada sauce. . . . The Palace Drug Company wound up its awnings. A little group of men who had spent the afternoon in front of the post office, greeting their friends, moved toward the station to see the Del Monte Express from San Francisco come in. The sea gulls arose glutted from the fish cannery beaches and flew toward the sea rocks. Lines of pelicans pounded doggedly over the water wherever they go to spend the night. On the purse-seine fishing boats the Italian men folded their nets over the big rollers. Little Miss Alma Alvarez, who was ninety years old, took

her daily bouquet of pink geraniums to the Virgin on the outer wall of the
church of San Carlos. In the neighboring and Methodist village of Pacific Grove
the W.C.T.U. met for tea and discussion, listened while a lady described the
vice and prostitution of Monterey with energy and color. She thought a committee should visit these resorts to see exactly how terrible conditions really
were. They had gone over the situation so often, and they needed new facts.[47]

Here is a narrative in which town and environment are one, the rhythms
of daily life familiar, social classes and ethnic groups coextensive, the
known community an enveloping frame of reference. All of that went
the way of urban renewal, the modern service economy, social progress,
awareness. Monterey was no longer Steinbeck's country. It was another
place with another history.

SEVEN

Conclusion

Action, Narrative, History

All history is contemporary history
     Benedetto Croce, *History*
          as the Story of Liberty

SERRA REVISITED

If 1780 had been a bad year for Father Serra, 1987 was worse. It began otherwise, with promising indications that this would be the decisive year in Serra's ascent to sainthood. In response to a 1984 invitation from Monterey's Bishop Thaddeus Shubsda, Pope John Paul II was planning a visit to Carmel Mission in September. The Serra Cause, which was fully documented and delivered to the Vatican's Sacred Congregation for the Causes of Saints in 1949, was finally showing signs of progress. Sainthood in the Roman Catholic Church requires that the "cause" of a nominee pass through three deliberative stages supervised by the Sacred Congregation and joined at points by the promoter of the faith (or Devil's advocate) and the pope: veneration (based on proof of a heroically virtuous life), beatification (requiring proof of having performed a miracle or suffered martyrdom), and canonization (elevation by the pope based on evidence of a miracle since beatification). Father Serra cleared the first hurdle in May 1985. Vatican observers believed that the California priest was moving up the saintly ladder on a schedule keyed to papal diplomacy.

Whatever may be said for the virtuous lives of candidates for sainthood, their fates in a field of more than one thousand "postulated" causes at any given time depends on lobbying, luck, and timing. In 1987 the stars seemed aligned for the Serra Cause. Father Noel Moholy, vice postulator of the Serra Cause and full-time campaign manager for more than thirty years, had successfully raised close to $1 million for his promotional efforts, tapping conservative Republicans (e.g., the *Oakland Tribune*'s Knowland family and PaperMate founder and Technicolor, Inc., chairman Patrick Frawley), California bishops, Los Angeles's Cardinal Peter Manning, and the Franciscan Order (whose Rome-based minister general was Californian John Vaughn). Long a staple of California's elementary school curriculum, Serra recently had been honored with a statue in the state capitol and a U.S. commemorative stamp, all the result of Serra Cause lobbying.[1]

Papal visits are elaborately planned affairs, occasions for defining church policy, mobilizing the rank and file, shoring up organizational networks, recruitment, and regeneration. Like visiting presidents, popes usually come bearing largesse. In a recent visit to Poland, for example, John Paul II announced the beatification of one hundred ten World War II Polish martyrs. Serra's veneration in May 1985 was reasonably interpreted as groundwork for the visit two years ahead. Its timing would allow a proper interval before the announcement of beatification at Carmel Mission in September 1987—or so everyone assumed. When Father Moholy delivered the documentation (*summarium depositionum*) of a Serra-inspired miracle to Cardinal Pietro Palazzini, prefect of the Sacred Congregation, the cardinal asked, "When is the Pope coming to California?" presumably as a guide to the timetable he would have to follow. "Asked in an interview what effect the Pope's travel schedule had on the workings of the Congregation, Cardinal Palazzini said 'a lot.'"[2] The trip itself had broad significance for church politics. The United States is simultaneously the richest contributor to Vatican coffers and one of the most undisciplined of Rome's national churches. In California John Paul II would encourage devotion and reward the faithful, particularly the growing Hispanic immigrant population, which is traditionally Catholic but lately defecting in worrisome numbers to Protestant evangelicalism. Father Serra provided the right symbolic coin to offer the disaffected—a western pioneer, Hispanic hero, and affirmative-action saint.

The planned papal visit energized efforts to burnish Serra's image by Father Moholy, Bishop Shubsda, and Cardinal Manning. The Franciscan Committee in Los Angeles published a comic book version of Serra's story featuring sketches of various imagined scenes of historical and contemporary events.[3] In one panel, the padre advises Captain Portolá, "You must impress on all your men—there are to be no slaves! We must not repeat the sins against the Africans." Later, John Paul II is seen standing over the Serra Cenotaph at Carmel Mission, flanked by actor-politicians

Clint Eastwood and Ronald and Nancy Reagan, saying, "Well done, Father Junípero Serra. Well done for God, well done for the United States of America" (a country that did not exist when the Serra-Portolá expedition came to Alta California).

In 1986 the Monterey Diocese published *The Serra Report,* a set of documents prepared by a public relations firm, released to the press on the 273d anniversary of Serra's birth and designed to quiet persistent criticism of the mission system.[4] The *Report* included a series of claims for Serra's good works (some of them distorted, such as the argument that Serra returned to Mexico in 1783 in order to seek greater protection for Indians rather than support for his own authority over Governor Fages, including his control over Indian labor) and a set of interviews with eight friendly academics specializing in colonial California who responded to leading questions from the interviewer (e.g., "Was Father Serra a brutal man who enslaved the Indians and completely destroyed their culture?" "How accurate are the comments from people today who appear to be hostile to the mission?"). Having determined that the padre was a kind and virtuous servant who beat himself more than he did the neophytes, the *Report* concluded with a challenge to critics that they offer equally credible evidence of Indian mistreatment if, indeed, they had any.[5]

That was a mistake. No one sensitive to the volatile political climate of California in the 1980s would engage in high-profile baiting of civil rights constituencies generally and Native American activists in particular. Serra's veneration in May 1985 had drawn public criticism. A mass celebrating the bicentennial of his birth by twenty-eight bishops at Carmel Mission in August inspired a protest demonstration. A Chumash Indian, Chequeesh Auh-Ho-Oh, came to the altar during Communion, waved an owl's feather, and made her offering: "For my ancestors who are all around you . . . who worked here to build this mission." Later she told reporters, "I think it would be a great insult to canonize Father Serra, a man who was personally responsible for so many people to die, to be locked up like animals, to be used." Cardinal Manning, who served at the mass, said he had "never heard such a thing," and Father Moholy characterized it as the "prattle of historical popularizers" (presumably not those who produced his Serra comic book). But the protest spread. Auh-Ho-Oh, who taught Native American studies at Cabrillo College near Santa Cruz, was supported by college teachers from around the state. The Tekakwitha Conference, an organization of ten thousand Native American Catholics, took a public position against canonization.[6]

The protest found more authoritative voice in 1987 when Rupert and

Jeannette Henry Costa of San Francisco's American Indian Historical Society published *The Missions of California: A Legacy of Genocide,* intended precisely as a response to the challenge for contrary evidence in *The Serra Report.* The Costa volume contained essays and testimony from a number of academics, historical sources, Native American experts, activists, and indigenous groups. Although polemical, it easily rivaled the credibility of its church-sponsored counterpart. Published on the eve of the papal visit, copies were sent to Rome and all U.S. bishops. The introduction clearly demonstrated that the volume originated in the canonization controversy, yet it formulated the problem in broader terms of historical memory.

> A myth has flourished in California for well over a hundred years. It asserts that the history of this state had its beginnings with the Franciscan missions. The myth originated in the works of scholarly propagandists of the Roman Catholic Church. Such clerical historians as Father Palou [and others who] believed they were creating a civilization from a wilderness . . . did not consider, nor would they believe, that the land they had reached was already populated, civilized, subject to authority and law, with a culture of its own. . . . Textbooks proclaim that California history begins with the missions. . . . Serra had become a lodestone for the imperial guard of the academic professionals, and the superstar of California's dominant class history. . . . That these invaders chose mindless exploitation rather than constructive development was the final formulation of that tragedy. [Although they brought benefits such as domesticated animals and agricultural implements, those came] at the price of native mission captivity, enforced labor, extraordinary punishment, imprisonment for offenses not before known, and finally, the genocide of a whole people.[7]

One month before the papal visit, the Vatican reported that the pope would not announce Serra's beatification during the trip owing to bureaucratic delays at the Sacred Congregation. One suspects it was politics, not bureaucracy, that delayed the process. John Paul II managed a late addition to his itinerary and met with the Tekakwitha Conference in Phoenix en route to Carmel in September 1987. The pope acknowledged that the church had committed "mistakes and wrongs" in its treatment of Indians but made no link between those and the heroic missionary work of Father Serra, whom he singled out for praise. Although the pope's gesture scarcely satisfied critics, they were not shy about taking credit for derailing Serra's beatification.[8] That seems a fair inference. The church would want to avoid any unfavorable publicity during the goodwill tour, especially if it involved church relations with Hispanic and Native American groups. It also seems characteristic of Vatican power politics that the beatification was subsequently announced with much fanfare before a crowd of twenty thousand in Rome one year later.[9] A demonstration at Carmel Mission by twenty Costanoan Indians answered the pope, although we have no evidence that it had an effect—other than another twelve years with no canonization, which, however, is not unusual by church time.[10]

This was not the first controversy Serra and the mission system had survived since sainthood was postulated in 1934. Historical criticism of the missions—by Governor Neve in 1780, Count La Pérouse in 1786, and Governor Figueroa in 1834—was revived in the 1940s due chiefly to the research on Indian mortality by Sherburne Cook and its diffusion in the popular history of Carey McWilliams. In McWilliams's unforgettable words, "With the best theological intentions in the world, the Franciscan padres eliminated Indians with the effectiveness of Nazis operating concentration camps."[11] Father Serra's place in history would never be the same afterward. Subsequent historians would have to assess the impact of European contact on California Indian culture and, slowly, their reassessment would penetrate public history. When Native Americans began writing their own histories, the work of La Pérouse, Bancroft, Cook, and others provided essential evidence—documented counter-memories to the missionary narrative.

In addition to public controversy and ideological confrontation over these grand narrative themes, there is a micropolitics of institutional history construction—a struggle over the details on which broad interpretations rest. In some respects, the mundane practices and situational contingencies of action are more revealing than dramatic political events that affect the process. In the voluminous discussion of Father Serra's deeds, for example, one never learns that Serra was not the first California missionary to be postulated for sainthood. That honor went to the Franciscan father Magín Catalá who ministered to the Indians at Mission Santa Clara from 1794 to 1830. Although Catalá's principal virtues appear to have been steadfastness, humility, and stoic acceptance of chronic rheumatism, he got lucky in 1851 when the Society of Jesus took charge of Mission Santa Clara and, in the entrepreneurial fashion of Jesuits, decided to promote their own mission saint in 1882. The process moved in fits and starts until 1908 when the Catalá Cause got another break with the appointment of the prolific Franciscan historian Zephyrin Engelhardt as vice postulator. Engelhardt reactivated the investigation, wrote up its favorable results, and delivered the sealed documents to Rome early in 1909.[12] And that was the last heard of Magín Catalá.

37.   Monterey Catholic Cemetery. The local cemetery
includes burial vaults, which are preferred by Italians. All
of the fishing families are represented on these walls, along
with the great and the humble who made local history.
(Photo by the author)

Evidently his cause died in committee. Perhaps it fell between stools.
Catalá the Franciscan had been nominated by the Jesuits who hoped to
bring celebrity to their mission rather than a rival order. In any case, the
Catalá Cause lacked an active lobby, fund-raising, publicity, and collat-
eral interest-group support. Engelhardt was an energetic scholar but
something of a crank, possessed of none of the organizational and public relations skills that Father Moholy brought to the Serra Cause.

Coincidentally, Charles F. Lummis, the famed Los Angeles publicist and founder of the Landmarks Club ("To save for our children and the world the Old Missions and other Historic Landmarks of California") wrote Engelhardt (at his new assignment to the orphans asylum in Watsonville) in April 1909 inquiring into why Serra had not been canonized, as Lummis believed he richly deserved. In expansive language, Lummis offered to investigate the matter himself and, if miracles were required, as he understood, he would put his own research staff to work on the problem.[13] Although Engelhardt's letter in reply cannot be found in the archives of Santa Barbara or Lummis's own Southwestern Museum, a subsequent letter from Lummis indicates that Engelhardt did reply, saying that Serra was an "improbable" candidate for canonization. Lummis expressed disappointment but noted that he was "obstinate" and would keep after the matter.[14] It would appear that Engelhardt did not mention his own concurrent investment in the Catalá Cause and, perhaps, the reason for his reluctance to encourage competition. Postulation of Serra's cause would wait another twenty-five years for a new set of circumstances. Carmel in 1934 witnessed a fortuitous combination of forces. Serra was well known owing to the variety of interests promoting mission restoration. In 1931 the state legislature had selected the padre (and Thomas Starr King) to represent California at the National Hall of Fame in the U.S. Capitol. A new bishop took up his case with the support of the Monterey community and its powerful property interests.

As investigation into the Serra Cause went forward in the late 1940s, a potentially devastating issue was raised, albeit inadvertently. In 1940 Anne B. Fisher published her popular novel, *Cathedral in the Sun*, a story of Carmel Mission and its Indian builders that bore strong parallels to Helen Hunt Jackson's 1884 classic, *Ramona*. Both Fisher and Jackson identified with the mission Indian, considered the Franciscans a decent and well-intentioned influence, and decried dispossession of the church and Indian landholders under Mexican and American rule. Fisher built her historically researched novel around real characters as remembered by their descendants. Her principal informant was Isabella Meadows, in her eighties at the time of writing, born to English seaman James Meadows and Loreta Onesemo in 1846. The novel focuses on Loreta, her parents, and particularly her father, Juan Onesemo, "the builder" of Carmel Mission. Generally the innocuous story fit neatly into the Spanish romance narrative and won the endorsement of reviewers, including the Catholic press.

In one crucial respect, however, Fisher's novel was heretical. In its concluding chapters dealing with the exhumation of Serra's grave in 1882, bemused Indians reveal to Father Casanova that the padre's remains are not in the grave, that they were carried off secretly by Spaniards, with the help of Indian workers, when the rampaging Mexicans arrived. As Loreta watches Serra's tomb uncovered, no bones appear, nothing but moldy wood and vestments. Fisher was convinced of the story, having heard it from Isabella Meadows, who, in turn, was the contemporary link in a chain of Indian oral tradition. It seems Fisher did not realize that Serra's canonization required that his actual remains be positively identified "to ensure that people had not and would not be erroneously venerating the wrong man."[15]

Indeed, Fisher corresponded freely on the matter with Father Maynard Geiger, archivist and historian at the Santa Barbara Franciscan library and a member of the historical commission for the Serra Cause (with Professor Herbert Bolton and Monsignor James Cullerton). From Pacific Grove, the novelist wrote Geiger at Santa Barbara in February 1948 asking for Franciscan approval of the new edition of *Cathedral in the Sun,* as suggested by parish priest Father O'Connell, in order that it might be sold at Carmel Mission (at 40 percent off), thus capitalizing on the growing tourist trade. Geiger was nettled by the request and denied it, saying, "[Although I found] the major portion of the book well done . . . the dramatic scene of the last two chapters [the exhumation] I consider unfortunate."[16] Geiger, of course, knew the significance of physical evidence confirming Serra's resting place. He chastised Fisher for propagating "legend" and arguing "from tradition" rather than relying on the archaeological and anthropological evidence informing his knowledge—some of which could not be revealed at present. Fisher was not intimidated: "The evidence that Serra's bones are not now at Carmel Mission has been made available [in her transcribed interviews]. It is regrettable that the opposite view still rests on *ex cathedra* opinion, the supporting evidence having been withheld."[17] The Serra Cause went ahead. The historical commission had academic witnesses who outranked novelists and claimed (without revealing) scientific evidence that trumped Native American oral tradition.

History making is a circumstantial and contingent process. Since Francisco Palóu's classic *Life and Apostolic Labors of the Venerable Father Junípero Serra,* published for an interested Mexican reading public in 1787, the story of Serra and the missions has been an integral, if evolving, piece of California history. In its successive renditions, the missionary/Spanish romance/California heritage narrative is the most enduring social construction of California's past. Yet, focusing on the detailed turns of the Serra story alone, it is evident that history unfolds in an unpredictable social process, shaped by action and circumstance but determined neither by authority, "facts," nor special interests alone. Father Serra might not have become the popular embodiment of early California had Father Catalá's cause been better organized and financed. Despite a well-oiled publicity machine, the physical evidence in Serra's saintly grave might have been challenged by more authoritative critics. Conversely, the exigencies of papal travel and diplomacy that energized the Serra Cause might have been directed toward alternative saintly possibilities—Polish or Third World candidates, for example. Even under extraordinarily favorable conditions, the Serra legend and mission narrative were eventually challenged in a highly visible forum.

There is a new early California narrative emerging—ironically, one that recovers the gritty elements of Palóu and La Pérouse while embracing the Native American story as it is being elaborated in archaeology, anthropology, social history, and evolving tradition. Church history, if not the Serra Cause, has been displaced; not dismissed, but moved to a supporting role in a reconfigured narrative of cultural diversity. That development, of course, relates to changes in American society as a whole. But there are important local influences. Native American exclusion from California history has been challenged in Monterey by protest demonstrations, archaeological revelations, and cultural programs. Local public history is being rewritten, re-presented. The Native American experience begins the historical display at the Pacific House Museum maintained by the State Parks and Recreation Department at Custom House Plaza. A recent illustrated history similarly develops the Native American setting into which the Spaniards came, bringing "cataclysmic changes that would permanently destroy age-old ways of life for Indian people."[18] A memorial was recently dedicated at the Sonoma Mission modeled on the Vietnam Veterans Memorial in Washington, D.C., and naming many of the once nameless Indians buried there. The haunting equation of forgotten Indian sacrifices and unappreciated Vietnam casualties of war conjures moral offenses that recent history has tried to redress. The tribute resulted from organizational and fund-raising efforts of the Sonoma Mission Indian Memorial Fund led by author and professor Edward Castillo and local Native Americans with the assistance of the California State Park Foundation, the Diocese of Santa Rosa, and the Sonoma League for Historical Preservation.[19] The idea is bound to spread. It captures the cultural themes, social conditions, and actors who are making today's history.

EXPLAINING COLLECTIVE MEMORY

Earlier in this work, I introduced Michel-Rolph Trouillot's discussion of the ambiguities embodied in the word *history;* the idea that in conventional use history can mean either of two different things. First, there is history in the sense of the facts, events, and what happened in the past. Second, there is history in the sense of accounts, stories, and what is said to have happened. Historical analysis spreads out between two poles represented, respectively, by those who believe that historical events possess an independent reality, implying that historical facts can be known objectively (positivists), and those who argue that history is constructed in stories fashioned from all manner of real and imagined material and projected on the past (constructionists).

Recognizing that there is truth in both these positions, Trouillot suggests a third alternative. The two senses of history and the ambiguity they contain can be embraced, incorporated as a figure-ground relationship in the idea of narrative. He offers an example in the proposition that "the history of the United States is a history of migration." Here the meaning is clear; the history of the United States involves a great many elements, and the best way to know and meaningfully organize them is with a narrative in which migration is the central theme. The narrative is an interpretation, a way of organizing what we accept as facts (provisionally, consensually, and subject to revision). It does not pretend to be an objective representation of those facts.

Viewed in this way, the impasse between positivist and constructionist positions is superseded in a historical method that analyzes the relationship between narrative and social process—the distinctive stories that are fashioned about the past *and* the circumstances that explain the production and use of those stories. As Trouillot remarks, "[T]heories of history rarely examine in detail the concrete production of specific narratives. . . . Narratives are occasionally evoked as illustrations or, at best, deciphered as texts, but the process of their production rarely constitutes the object of study."[20] Such has been the object of this study. What may we conclude from the results?

First, let us recall a few key terms to clarify the focus of this explanation. Public history is our object, meaning something more than bookish, formal, or academic history. Public history is, in the words of Carl Becker,

38.   David Jacks's Headstone. This unprepossessing stone marks the resting
place of Monterey's most influential historical figure. The austere Scot inclined
toward anonymity and local history has been happy to give him that. (Photo
by the author)

"the history that common people carry around in their heads."[21] *Public history* signifies the past of a community (region, country) as it is generally understood by its citizenry; the sum of knowledge about the past as presented in monuments, museums, commemorative sites, popular culture (fiction, film), architecture, and design, as well as in history books ranging from popular chronicles to scholarly texts. Public history is the past known to the informed populace, to persons and groups who want to know who are we? and what is our story? Academic history informs and affects public history but is a less inclusive field. Public history is more likely to affect collective action, politics, and, under certain circumstances, even the more aloof forms of formal history. The importance of public history is attested in a growing interest in the pursuit of historical preservation and family and ethnic origins. The universal importance of knowing who we are is suggested in Alma Guillermoprieto's book, *Samba,* about the lives of Rio de Janeiro's slum dwellers (*favelados*) and their attachment to public history.

> The favela concept of "root" is all about the past buried beneath the visible surface. Favela blacks, with not a single history textbook to claim as their own, or one hero of theirs mentioned by name in white textbooks, with hardly

the literacy to get through whatever rare academic studies are available on black culture, are obsessively concerned with their origins. . . . Sambistas write songs about earlier sambistas so they won't be forgotten; carnival scripts frequently focus on historical events. . . . [F]avelados say proudly, "I am root," meaning, "I belong to my past."[22]

Public history comes packaged in narratives. *Narratives* are stories in a formal sense; stories, with a structure consisting of an origin, a chronology, a plot, a conclusion, and a moral. Narratives select and arrange historical material according to some prefigured interpretation or "emplotment." As Hayden White notes, "[N]arrative is not merely a neutral discursive form . . . but rather entails ontological and epistemic choices with distinct ideological and even specific political implications."[23] Narratives selectively construct stories with a rhetorical purpose in mind, using the devices of narration (timing, direction, emphasis) to take the story in a predetermined direction, all the while giving the appearance that this was the natural outcome, the only objective way to tell the tale. There is nothing especially devious about this practice, provided narrators and consumers understand that it *is* a narrative, an interpretation (a provision only occasionally met in the construction and presentation of public history). The story of the good Father Serra is a narrative just as is the story of the exploited Native American. Narratives vary widely in their allegiance to what many may agree are the facts. And the extent of that allegiance can be evaluated, sometimes dispassionately. It is possible to have more than one narrative at a time in a given historical period or community, even to have coexisting, competing, and oppositional narratives.

We should also distinguish a somewhat more general notion of the *narrative form,* by which I mean culturally standardized stories such as the American social mobility (Horatio Alger) story or the ethnic assimilation (melting pot) story. Hayden White[24] argues that all historical writing may be located in one of four master narratives or "modes of emplotment" (romantic, tragic, comic, and satirical). Perhaps. On a more substantive level, however, there are culturally grounded narrative forms that impose plot on particular stories if they are judged to be instances of the form. Common, appealing, or powerful narrative forms can absorb particular stories, obscure their individuality, and subsume them as instances of something they may or may not be. The United States recently appeared to suffer a rash of racially motivated church burnings, a repetition of sad chapters in the American past treated in the Jim Crow narrative. On closer examination, however, the church burnings were found to be less than epidemic, common to white and black churches alike, as often the work of deranged parishioners black and white as that of skinheads. These facts had little effect on the reaction of national alarm propagated by the media, Congress, and the president, whose interests were served by denouncing the outrage. The "familiar story" of racial injustice provided a narrative form capable of assimilating particular instances to one interpretation and mobilizing political action.[25]

There are, of course, events that do not depend for their existence and perseverance on particular narratives. *Events,* historical facts, have no autonomous (objective) epistemological status but acquire their credibility from social consensus fashioned by time, negotiation, and corroboration. Native Americans *did* die in epidemic numbers as a result of the initial introduction of European pathogens, mistreatment by military and missionary personnel, and U.S. Cavalry massacres. In Monterey, there *were* poor squatters forced to struggle with engrossing landlords just as there *were* property interests with decisive political power to monopolize wealth. History is more than narrative, even if it is socially constructed in a series of imperfect interpretations. Indeed, historical fact, like scientific fact, rests in the end on a consensus reached in a normative social process.[26]

One important implication of the distinction between narratives and events is that narratives are frequently disputed in the form of countermemories based on alternatively experienced events. *Countermemories* are beliefs that challenge and subvert narrative interpretations without necessarily producing a fully formed narrative of their own.[27] The story of Serra's bones in Native American oral tradition is a countermemory to the missionary narrative. So is La Pérouse's comparison of the missions with Caribbean slave plantations or McWilliams's with Nazi concentration camps. Countermemories may inspire or inform oppositional narratives, though they need not in order to play a vital role in history. *Silences* are cases of the effective suppression of countermemories by dominant narratives—the Native American experience until recently, the lives of women under Mexican rule or of Chinese when nativism pervaded California society.

Long a subject of historical reflection, collective memory has lately become a fertile field of social research and theoretical debate. *Collective memory* refers to the process in which societies and communities represent their past, portray the experience of the group, produce an account of past events that shape the present. Despite the renewed popularity of this work, however, historians and social scientists are deeply divided on the question of how collective memories are produced and sustained. For the sake of clarity, two influential interpretations summarize the debate.

The first school of thought reflects the familiar notion that the victors in society's wars and social struggles write the history—"write" it in a variety of texts (monuments, museums, architecture, books) that celebrate their interests and support their continuing domination. This theory of *cultural hegemony* derives from the political philosophy of Antonio Gramsci and its development by the school of British cultural studies headed by Raymond Williams.[28] They argue that the same interests in society that monopolize wealth, power, and the means of industrial production also control the means of cultural production and use them to legitimate the prevailing order. One powerful way to accomplish that end is to control the process of collective memory, to sustain a version of history that shows that the status quo is the proud accomplishment of progressive developments in the past. In the nuanced interpretation of Raymond Williams, hegemony is achieved by tradition, "the most evident expression of the dominant and hegemonic pressures . . . ; indeed it is the most powerful practical means of incorporation. . . . [It is] not just 'a tradition' but a *selective tradition:* an intentional selective version of a shaping past and a pre-shaped present, which is then powerfully operative in the process of social and cultural definition."[29]

Cultural hegemony has demonstrated its ability to illuminate the construction of collective memory in a number of historical studies. Trouillot shows how the first major social revolution in the Americas, carried out by blacks in Haiti, was silenced in subsequent Western history, made a nonevent through the selective use of archival and narrative power. A social revolution by former slaves against their European colonial masters was "unthinkable" to those who controlled the production of history.[30]

The anthropologist W. Lloyd Warner studied historical symbols in a New England community dominated by Yankee business interests as those were expressed in the town's tercentennial celebration. The commemorative parade stressed the town's vaunted puritan heritage, its connections to the republic's founding fathers, and its peaceful progress— while silencing the role of Indian wars, unscrupulous merchants, and political bosses. The historical event was in fact an exercise in legitimation of the local elite who sponsored the production; "if they were to retain their own legitimacy it was mandatory for them to trace their ancestry to the very beginnings[;] . . . for the maintenance of their position it was necessary to invent new myths and new expressive rituals to hold the power of the ancestors."[31] There are striking parallels between Trouillot's silenced revolution and Warner's commemorative celebration and Monterey's Californio revolution in 1836 and the Street of History parade in 1938. Warner summarizes the process of constructing collective memory in words that capture these and doubtless many other cases.

> They were saying not only what history is objectively, but what they now *wished* it all were and what they wished it were not. They ignored this or that difficult period of time or unpleasant occurrence or embarrassing group of men and women; they left out awkward political passions; they selected small items out of large time contexts, seizing them to express today's values. Thus, at times they denied or contradicted the larger flow of history and the intentions of yesterday's understanding, often repudiating beliefs and values that were once sanctioned and honored.[32]

The second interpretation of history production relies on the notion of *social memory,* the argument that social groups form distinct memories through the agency of social class, ethnic, gender, educational, occupational, and generational experiences. Collective memory is less a matter of imposed ruling ideas than a plurality of mental worlds that may exist in conflict with or insularity from competing ideas. The French sociologist Maurice Halbwachs coined the term "collective memory," which he understood as prior to and the source of individual memories. Group memories are selective readings of historical fact that change as groups themselves are reconstituted over time. "History is neither the whole nor even all the remains of the past. In addition to written history, there is a living history that perpetuates and renews itself through time and permits the recovery of many old currents that have seemingly disappeared. . . . Groups that develop the reigning conceptions and mentality of a society during a certain period fade away in time, making room for others, who in turn command the sway of custom and fashion opinion from new models."[33]

Distinct social memories are demonstrated in studies by James Fentress and Chris Wickham, who compare the different "grammars" in which experience is recalled by peasants, working-class groups, women, and national communities. Among other engaging illustrations, they show how a myth of Sicilian national identity based on the Mafia was created by groups, including police, who were otherwise at a loss to explain and solve certain kinds of crime.[34] An extraordinary study of collective memory by Yael Zerubavel deals with the construction of a Jewish national tradition based on selective, mythologized, and politically charged interpretations of Israeli history. The Halbwachian influence on Zerubavel's

39.   Chinese Grave. This gravesite in a far corner of the Catholic cemetery
marks the important Chinese presence in Monterey. The Chinese characters
on the left refer to the Confucian admonition that one "revere ancestors as if
they were still alive," and above the oven doors they read "Stove of collected
treasures." This stove probably served as a crematorium of funerary objects,
including money and model figures of valuable possessions that the deceased
would need in the next world. In Chinese culture the stove served as the family
hearth and was attended by a household god. (Photo by the author)

study is clear where she discusses the connections between childhood
socialization (in schoolbooks and outings) and myths of Israeli state origins, as well as more recent mellowing of Zionist positions with the
progress of peace in the Middle East.

> Israeli culture today encompasses a greater diversity of commemorative nar-
> ratives that offer different interpretations of the past. These multiple texts may
> at times coexist without apparent tension; at other times they become sub-
> jects of intense debate. The growing diversity within the society and the in-
> creased pressures from within and without have challenged the hegemony of
> the commemorations that crystallized during the prestate and early-state pe-
> riods and gave rise to multiple commemorative texts.[35]

Once again, there are impressive convergences between the theory of social memory and the experience of history production in Monterey. So-

cial groups, from Indian neophytes to Sicilian fishermen and cannery workers, constructed very different accounts of their historical experiences at different times, just as missionaries and soldiers, or squatters and landlords, did concerning their contemporaneous experiences. Like the growing diversity of Israeli narratives, moreover, Monterey has enjoyed a recent democratization of historical claimants. In a general way, the interpretations of both cultural hegemony and social memory fit the evidence from Monterey.

In more exacting ways, however, the results of this study call for new interpretations that build on earlier traditions, criticize, and move forward. The idea of cultural hegemony and a dominant narrative never really worked in California (giving one pause about other cases in which cultural resistance has not been explored). Even in periods characterized by a dominant narrative, such as after the American conquest of 1846, countermemories (and more often competing narratives) existed. Groups struggled for a voice in the official transcript, an entry in the public record, sometimes subverting "archival power" and leaving their own documents to future narrators. If the motive (according to Williams), or the function (Warner), of cultural hegemony is social control, moreover, the dominant narratives failed. They failed to engender conformity, co-opt dissent, or fool anyone. As E. P. Thompson remarked in a similar context, "[P]eople are not as stupid as some structuralist philosophers suppose them to be. . . . If the law is evidently partial and unjust, then it will mask nothing, legitimize nothing, contribute nothing to any class's hegemony."[36]

The theory of social memory poses complementary problems, particularly the idea that independent narratives are as common as distinct sites of group consciousness. Social memory helps to explain the diversity and change of collective memories but neglects their generality, interrelation, and coercive capacity. It ignores, in short, the role of power—"the many ways in which the production of historical narratives involves the uneven contribution of competing groups and individuals who have unequal access to the means for such production," as Trouillot says.[37]

Although these are important criticisms in the two interpretations of how history is constructed, they are not the core of the problem. Missing in these structuralist explanations are grounded accounts of how historical actors and narrators actually behave, how they interact in real situations. Alternatively, I propose a theory of social memory based on collective action. This study demonstrates that the production and maintenance of historical narratives is a contested, chancy, changing process. Narratives have pragmatic origins. They are produced by groups with an agenda. Public history is constructed, not, in the main, for the purposes of posterity or objectivity, but for the aims of present action (conquest, social reform, building, political reorganization, economic transformation). Narratives make claims for the virtues of their individual and institutional authors, often as counterpoint to rival claimants. They characterize the past in certain ways for the purpose of shaping the future. The ability of narratives to effect change depends in the first instance on their institutional power; whether they are produced by a powerful church, conquering state, fledgling town, or contending voluntary associations. Whatever their origins, the effects of historical narratives depend on history itself, on the interplay of actors, social circumstances, and situational contingencies.

In collective action theory, public history is at once heritage and rhetoric. It must be understood as a set of claims made by particular groups within a community, although typically expressed on behalf of the community as a whole, claims about what "our" history signifies. Public history is self-congratulatory, even in those instances in which it endeavors to right a past wrong. Typically it lauds features of the past in the context of an unfolding present and directs present action toward a desired future. Narratives that serve such strategic purposes are necessarily facile; they are selective, often credible, and sometimes pure invention. Monterey's public history includes a variety of narratives ranging from relatively perceptive accounts of local society (e.g., Richard Henry Dana's version of the Yankee narrative) to elaborate myths (e.g., the Spanish romance).

California history bears instructive parallels to the development of historical myth in Europe. Edward Peters argues that a relatively benign practice of the Latin Catholic church for defense of the faith against heretics, maintained through investigations derived from Roman law and called inquisitions, was mythologized over time in politically motivated accounts of a draconian *Spanish* Inquisition.[38] In fact, inquisitions evolved over centuries and in common practice were penitential public ceremonies designed to reaffirm popular devotion. The church, like states of the time, attempted to regulate religious conformity and discipline prodigals. Yet the inquisitions (of Rome, Venice, and Portugal, as well as Spain) were typically underfinanced, poorly staffed, and irresolute. Investigations might exonerate the subject, and the usual result was reconciliation of church and penitent. In other cases, punishments varied and, in the rare instance of torture or execution, the state carried out the sentence. European states routinely used such means for punishing civil offenses. Certainly there were instances of barbarous acts by inquisitions, but these were exceptional and often associated with complicating political circumstances. The myth of the Inquisition can be traced to the late sixteenth century when Spain's international dominance was challenged by emerging rival states, the Netherlands Revolt, the rise of confessional sects, and new civil rights in Protestant countries. The Inquisition was metaphorized to stand for Spain's alleged arbitrary power and suppression of civil liberties, themes rehearsed in prolific works of history, art, and literature. Condemnations of subsequent witch trials and anticommunist crusades achieved their purpose by drawing analogies to the mythical Inquisition.

The important parallel between socially constructed history in Europe and Monterey lies partly in the power of myth to become heritage, but equally in the social process in which stories are elaborated over generations of collective action. California's Spanish romance narrative, which begins in the colonial period and survives to the present in successively revised forms, demonstrates processes similar to those operating in the myth of the Spanish Inquisition.

An analogous, and confirming, case of this collective action process is the more recent history of commemoration of the Vietnam War. Robin Wagner-Pacifici and Barry Schwartz studied the stages in which the Vietnam Veterans Memorial evolved; how its development confronted the problems of commemorating an ambiguous chapter in American history (an unpopular war that nevertheless extracted commendable sacrifices), reconciled diverse interests participating in the process, and in the end produced a popular shrine capable of many interpretations. Echoing discoveries in the Monterey case, the authors note, "These processes were, in their substance, interactive: moral entrepreneurs interacting with their constituencies and with political and cultural authorities; politicians interacting with their colleagues[;] . . . veterans interacting with their memories[;] . . . artists interacting with political guidelines[;] . . . visitors interacting with the wall. The key to the Memorial's multifold meaning lies in this interaction web."[39] An interpretation of socially constructed history centered on collective action captures the dynamics of the process while incorporating the constraining situational influences of state and economy.

NARRATIVE AND COLLECTIVE ACTION IN MONTEREY

Schematic representations of complex processes are risky but useful. Table 5 offers a summary of Monterey's historical periods and their diverse representations of collective memory. Recalling earlier chapters, the Spanish colonial period produced two competing narratives based on experiences of the church and the military respectively. The Franciscan story initiated by Palóu had far greater influence owing to its institutional sponsorship and appealing narrative form. In addition to the oppositional narrative of military and civil authorities, moreover, the colonial period witnessed countermemories in the critiques of European expeditionary observers such as La Pérouse and Vancouver. The Indian voice was effectively silenced, Indians constituting part of the natural background, except in palimpsest documents where they show through as recalcitrant problems of labor and discipline.

During the period of Mexican rule, the dominant narratives change, revise, invert. Society is in transition, Mexico's control of the strategic colony is on the wane, and, as a result, its public history is unattended, unsponsored, of use to no one save the endangered Californios who record their discontents. A new and influential Yankee narrative is being produced at the hands of commercial adventurers like Richard Henry Dana and Alexander Forbes. With secularization, the missionaries are reduced to recusants harboring their own countermemories. Indians remained silenced along with subservient segments of the Hispanic population such as women—with the rare exception of someone like Guadalupe Castillo who refused to be bullied by the governor.

The force of American conquest effectively supplanted competing narrative accounts in the latter half of the nineteenth century. Indeed, it was only during this period that a single hegemonic cultural history prevailed. Although prominent Californios like Mariano Vallejo spoke of and recorded their countermemories, they accepted the wisdom of joining the new order. They, too, believed in American progress. As wealth and political power were redistributed, however, the ranks of silenced voices grew to include newly differentiated paisanos, imported Chinese workers, squatters, and diminished numbers of deracinated, intermarried Indians.

As a narrative form, the dominant story of American progress also occluded important events of the late nineteenth century. Notably, the dramatic story of David Jacks, his monopolization of the land market, decisive control of local politics until the town rebellion of the 1880s, and founding of a real estate empire that continues to the present—all were suppressed, if not silenced, in historical narratives. Engrossing property tycoons, exploited squatters, evicting landlords, threats of violence, the whole underside of uneven frontier development did not fit

TABLE 5
HISTORICAL PERIODS AND NARRATIVES

	Spanish Colonial 1770–1821	Mexican Territory 1821–1846	American Settlement 1846–1900	Industrial Community 1900–1950	Contemporary Society 1950–Present
Narratives	Missionary Colonial State	Yankee Californio	American Progress	Working Class Spanish Romance	Heritage Environmental
Countermemories	European liberalism	Missionary	Californio	Paisano, conservationist	Native American
Silenced groups	Indians	Indians, women	Indians, paisanos, squatters, Chinese	Asians	——
Key social pattern	Competing colonial institutions	Political transition, incorporation	New social order classes	Competing social	Plural Society

the narrative of American progress. Jacks, who owned the town and sat at the center of its commercial life for sixty years, is remembered only in Jacks Peak Park, overlooking the bay (and even then most people think it is some anonymous Jack's peak). The etymology of Monterey Jack cheese is news to many. But fellow Scotsman Robert Louis Stevenson, who spent three months in Monterey mostly bedridden with asthma, vies with Father Serra and Mayor Walter Colton for the honor of first citizen. If patterns of social and political inequality effectively silence portions of the historical record, narrative forms equally censor the unpleasant, uncomplimentary, or ill-fitting memory. And the reason, again, lies in the collective action frame of public history. No one wanted to celebrate or emulate the miserly life of David Jacks—at least not in public.

Monterey's industrial era witnesses a dramatic change in collective memory, a return to more typical competing narratives and a complete inversion of earlier patterns. With the rise of industry, a new working class, the depression, and the interventionist New Deal state, the working-class narrative assumes prominence. It competes with the Spanish romance recently revived by civic associations and property interests, but in the crunch of important political choices, working-class interests prevail. Monterey is the toiling sardine capital of the world, not California's first capital or the site of a world-famous luxury hotel. The town stinks, and the fact is celebrated in poetry. But all is not well in this tough industrial city. Countermemories of state biologists warn about depletion of the fishery and Steinbeck's stories of the underclass suggest that poverty survived. A variety of Asian immigrant workers filled the gap left by Chinese exclusion and suffered in silence.

The contemporary period brings something new. Popular groups are still key actors in society and in narrative but now as ethnic groups that disaggregate and reconfigure social class experience. A new environmental narrative emerges with social movements and political programs at the national and local levels. The environmental narrative also reorganizes events of the past, discovering ecological awareness among Native Americans, poets, and town planners. The times are more egalitarian, at least in the public arena of historical claimants. No story is truly silenced, although some command more attention than others. And relatively powerless groups such as Native Americans do, with help, significantly alter the social construction of history. Historical memory and environmental protection, moreover, have become *self-conscious strategies* of civic action and interest group politics. New property developments include a history center, or boast measures to protect the environment. Commemorative events and heritage festivals crowd the calendar.

Looking across the periods, several summary points emerge. Multiple historical narratives are the rule, sometimes as oppositional positions and other times in complementary relation. Countermemories and silenced voices are regularly present until recently, when most, if not all, groups are at least heard. Once silenced stories may later become important narratives. History making has been democratized. Some narratives transcend periods, although they undergo important revisions over time. The story of early California is the best example: beginning in the oppositional narratives of church and state, modifying in the Californio story, sinking into the shadows of countermemory, and forcibly reappearing in the sentimentalized but powerful Spanish romance.

A serendipitous result of the historical chapters shows that claims about collective memory are most vigorous during periods of social and physical reorganization—conquest, economic transition, and reconstruction of the material landscape. They are urged on the public when the United States occupies and annexes California as an explanation for those events. They appear in the hiatus between Monterey's life as an elite "watering hole" and its industrial boom to provide an account of how it became a working-class town. These transitions were accompanied by spatial alternations of the city's boundaries, architecture, and relation to the natural landscape, the sea. The tumbledown colonial landscape was upgraded to accommodate briefly the state capital. Monterey underwent a series of urban renewal episodes beginning with the eradication of blight (poor people) in the 1890s and continuing in thoroughgoing slum (small business) clearance under federal urban renewal in the 1960s and 1970s. These were critical moments for local government and civic associations that, as interested actors in the commercial process, assigned themselves the task of redefining the community and its history; the responsibility for deciding what should be preserved and what should go in order best to reflect the town's historical character.

Waxing and waning collective memories move in tandem with changing social circumstances. One of the most influential of these is commercial development. The "mission revival" movement that began in the late nineteenth century and crested in the 1920s and 1930s was driven by economic engines: real estate development, tourism, town business, railroads and automobile clubs, related preservationist societies. The point can be overemphasized, but only with great effort. There are, of course, other initiatives that shape the social construction of public history. Among them earlier chapters have identified institutional (e.g., church, military) chronicles, political programs (New Deal programs, urban renewal), civic associations (MHAA), and social movements (environmentalism, civil rights). If these circumstances help to prompt the construction of public history narratives, it is in the process of collective action that forces, institutions, agendas, and actors meet, interact, and produce changes subject to all manner of contingencies.

Finally, narratives can acquire a power of their own and, in reflexive fashion, shape the very history they chronicle. Although St. Patrick's Day as a civil holiday and occasion for parades is a tradition invented in American cities, an influx of free-spending, heritage-seeking tourists to Dublin every March 17 has caused city officials to create a popular festival nominally honoring the Irish saint and infusing public history with new meaning.

The phenomenon is universal. In his great novel *One Hundred Years of Solitude,* the Colombian writer Gabriel García Márquez described a fateful 1928 strike at United Fruit Company banana plantations on the Caribbean coast. Although army suppression of the strike cost the lives of three to five people, García Márquez wrote that three thousand were killed because numbers that would "fill a whole railway" were necessary for "the dimension of the book."[40] What was poetic license for the novelist, however, soon became historical fact as Colombian history books began to adopt not only García Márquez's description of events but also his casualty figures, thus transforming knowledge of the events themselves. Similarly, in *The Pioneers,* James Fenimore Cooper portrays upstate New York during the revolutionary period, where his father was a promoter and developer, as a maturing frontier where unscrupulous land deals and Indian property claims were unknown. Alan Taylor shows that Cooper the son rewrote history, sanitized his father's story, and

> crafted a reassuring past intended to secure the Republic's future stability. He understood that people sought the future based upon a collective identity derived from narratives that made sense of the past; histories shaped the trajectory of the nation's future. People live out the stories they tell one another. By narrating the memory of their revolution and frontier expansion in conservative terms, they would make a conservative republic governed by a meritocracy of wealth and gentility.[41]

The history-making power of certain powerful narratives is a recurrent fact in Monterey. Palóu's *Life* of Serra is the essential source for hundreds of biographies and mission histories that followed. Yet the *Life* is a poetic work lodged firmly in the genre of church hagiography—and a good read brimming with firsthand description of Indians, soldiers, and colonial life. But its narrative emplotment is a single-minded testament to Serra's Christian virtue. Dana's *Two Years Before the Mast* is a literary memoir of adventure on the high seas, trading in exotic ports, and the customs of their native inhabitants. It is a narrative plotted on the premises of Yankee self-confidence, superiority, and manifest destiny. Yet the poetic narratives of Palóu and Dana are read as history, employed as factual sources in subsequent texts. The melding of narrative and history is demonstrated best in Steinbeck's memorable stories of Monterey's common folk. Tortilla Flat is sought out by residents and visitors. Cannery Row is redeveloped, scraps of it preserved, ironically, by trying to remain "true" to Steinbeck's description and characters. Steinbeck's creations are reinserted in the historical record; in standard texts concerning the fishing industry, but even in primary sources. A marvelously detailed memoir of the early days of Monterey's fishing industry describes the availability of paisano day labor at the boatyards, and recalls particularly "Pilon" (a character who came to life only with the 1935 publication of *Tortilla Flat*) as one of the regular day laborers in 1916 who worked for wine rather than wages.[42]

The point of these examples is neither to denigrate public history nor to fault the written record for fictional contamination. On the contrary, the argument here is precisely that narrative and history are confounded. Poetic form, narrative plot, and assiduous efforts to identify historical fact are all part of the process in which history is socially constructed. That is why collective memory must be understood as a process of interaction between narrative and history, the interplay of stories and events.

STORIES

The poem that begins Leslie Marmon Silko's novel *Ceremony* says stories "are all we have, you see, all we have to fight off illness and death." In her story, a World War II Native American veteran recovers his sanity by recovering his culture, by breaking free of the society that has stolen his wits and his history. The lesson is larger. History as a social process means, among other things, that it rewards people differentially—lionizes some, maligns others, forgets most. People nevertheless want to know their history, their root. The great opportunity presented to those who study collective memory and its social construction lies in recovering the peoples' history, and perhaps a bit of their sanity.

In this chronicle, we recover memories of Baltasar, the Rumsen village leader who worked at Serra's mission but rebelled against its oppressive control and returned home to his ailing wife. We meet the hacienda peons Jeronimo, Altarsiano, Proto, and Albaña who petitioned local authorities claiming that their "rights as Indians" were violated by one of the powerful Vallejo brothers. We hear Guadalupe Castillo protest Governor Alvarado's unfairness, calling his banishment order "despotic, tyrannical, unconstitutional"; accepting it for a time but insistently returning to her life in Monterey. Jonathan Douglas elbows his way into history by squatting on "government land claimed by David Jacks the robber of the widow [and] the orphan." Chinese workers in local hotels make their presence known in work stoppages and, perhaps, in protest arson (at least they leave a mystery buried in the archival record). Mrs. Garnet Sture, who was president of the Cannery Workers Union Local No. 20305, and Charlie Nonella, who organized for the insurgent CIO, return as the real people of Cannery Row. By analyzing the relation between history and narrative, we learn not only who these people were but also why their stories were neglected and how they can be restored in a better, if always imperfect, history.

On a recent spring evening, a troupe of youngsters turned out to redeem the mean streets of East Salinas. Their group, Barrios Unidos, devoted to prevention of violence and drug abuse, chose as the vehicle for peaceful demonstration a performance of Aztec dancing that was, they believed, "a spiritual and ancient ritual." Dressed in feathers, loincloths, and leggings hinting, perhaps, of Arapaho origin, the dancers moved rhythmically past neighborhood onlookers. In the Aztec dance tradition, they said, "every move means something." The purpose was to bring peace to warring gangs, "to bless the street." From the sidewalk a bemused teenager remarked, "It needs it."[43]

These young people are historical agents, civic actors endeavoring to fit collective memory to a desired future. Their resources are meager and their legacy malnourished. Their presumed Aztec heritage is of little relevance locally (nor is it especially estimable for that matter, given the Aztec penchant for imperial domination and human sacrifice). They are people who deserve rescue from the enormous condescension of history. Their stories have been lost. Yet these are Hispanic people living on ancestral land that was once used as the Spanish government's provisioning Rancho del Rey (the King's Ranch) and later incorporated during Mexican rule into the commercially profitable, ten-thousand-acre Rancho Sausal (Willow Grove Ranch) of Governor José Castro and merchant Augustín

Soberanes. They may possess Aztec heritage at some five-hundred-year remove, but they are much more recently an amalgam of native Ohlone, mestizo colonists, and Anglo settlers—leavened by Yaqui, Sonoran, and Okie immigrants. They are descendants of Californios; heirs to a society that rose in rebellion against Mexico, declared itself independent under Alvarado and Vallejo, and created a multicultural community in the schools of Hartnell and Colton. They are today's paisanos for whom historical narrative can be relevant and generous. They are people with a story in need of construction.

Notes

PREFACE

   1. Vlach 1993.
   2. Rolston 1992.
   3. Trouillot 1995: 2.
   4. McWilliams [1949] 1979.
   5. Starr 1985: 55.

2.   SPAIN'S FAR FRONTIER

   1. Tibesar 1955, 3:293–95; Hackel 1997.
   2. Tibesar 1955, 3:409.
   3. Milliken 1987.
   4. Milliken 1995; Cook 1943.
   5. Tibesar 1955, 2:105–7.
   6. Neve in Bielharz 1971: 154–57.
   7. Tibesar 1955, 3:367.
   8. Levy 1978; Chartkoff and Chartkoff 1984.
   9. Costello and Hornbeck 1989, 3:305.
   10. Rawls 1984; Margolin 1978.
   11. Priestley 1937: 64. See also Milliken 1995; Broadbent 1972; Levy 1978.
   12. Milliken 1990, 1993; Levy 1978; Hester 1978a, 1978b; Rawls 1984; Gutiérrez and Orsi 1997.
   13. Weber 1979; Boob 1962; Priestly 1916; Stein 1981; Bancroft 1884, vol. 1.
   14. Tibesar 1955, 1:177.
   15. Tibesar 1955, 1:145.
   16. Brandes 1970: 99.
   17. Tibesar 1955, 2:113.

18. Temple 1906.
19. Periquez in Tibesar 1955, 1:402.
20. Temple 1906: 35, 45.
21. Tibesar 1955, 2:107; Bancroft 1884, 1:639.
22. González 1997; Tibesar 1955.
23. Tibesar 1955, 1:143–45.
24. James 1913: 171–72, 186.
25. Guest 1985.
26. Tibesar 1955, 1:151.
27. Walker, Lambert, and DeNiro 1989.
28. Tibesar 1955, 1:265. Emphasis in original.
29. Tibesar 1995, 1:267.
30. Cullerton 1950: 105; Hackel 1997.
31. Tibesar 1955, 2:141.
32. Tibesar 1955, 2:139.
33. Kenneally 1965, 2:199.
34. Walker, Lambert, and DeNiro 1989; Jackson and Castillo 1995; Kenneally 1965, 2:203; Hackel 1997.
35. Guest 1983: 53.
36. Tibesar 1955, 1:145.
37. James 1913: 242.
38. Milliken 1995.
39. Cullerton 1950: 48.
40. Tibesar 1955, 2:141.
41. Cullerton 1950: 104.
42. Cullerton 1950: 129.
43. Hackel 1997.
44. Milliken 1995: 69–70.
45. Bancroft 1884, vols. 1, 2; Jackson and Castillo 1995; Heizer and Whipple 1951.
46. Castañeda 1990.
47. Archibald 1978; Hackel 1997.
48. Kenneally 1965, 2:373–74.
49. Kenneally 1965, 2:214–15.
50. Hackel 1994: 122 ff.
51. Cullerton 1950: 123; Kenneally 1965, 2:213.
52. Kenneally 1965, 2:207.
53. Cook 1943: 145–53; Engelhardt 1934: 123–29.
54. Schuyler 1978; Hoover 1989.
55. Bancroft 1884, 1:395; Milliken 1995: 73, 98.
56. Neve in Bielharz 1971: 159–60.
57. Bancroft 1884, 1:683; Cullerton 1950: 143; Engelhardt 1934; Hackel 1994.
58. Cook 1943; Jackson and Castillo 1995.
59. Archibald 1978: 153.
60. Cullerton 1950: 106; Hackel 1997.
61. Kenneally 1965, 2:212.

50. Mexican Archives, Monterey County Historical Society, 3:943–50.

51. Mexican Archives, Monterey County Historical Society, 10:1483.

52. Hutchinson 1978: 36, 28.

53. Hutchinson 1978: 93, 96.

54. Forbes 1839: 145–147, 82, 89.

55. Bancroft 1884, 4:152.

56. Dana 1965: 64, 66.

57. Dana 1965: 64–65, 137.

58. Shapiro 1961.

59. Starr 1973: 41.

60. DeVoto 1942; Johannsen 1985.

4. AMERICAN PROPERTY

1. David Jacks Collection, Stanford University Libraries Special Collections, Correspondence, Box 2.

2. Bancroft 1886, 5:235–37.

3. Bancroft 1888, 6:529–81; Royce 1886; Robinson 1948; Gates 1991; Perez 1996.

4. Royce 1886: 487; Bancroft 1888, 6:576, emphasis added; Rolle 1963; Pitt 1966.

5. Gates 1971: 404–5, 421; Pisani 1994.

6. Gates 1971.

7. Gates 1971: 410.

8. Pisani 1994: 305.

9. Colton 1860: 17.

10. Colton 1860: 19–20, 45, 68–69, 84.

11. Colton 1860: 152, 67.

12. Colton 1860: 197, 112, 41.

13. City Records Project, Minutes of Decision Bodies, vol. 1 (Colton Hall, Monterey).

14. D.R. Ashley, Monterey Archives, Bancroft Library (1874).

15. City Records Project, Minutes of Decision Bodies, vol. 1, Colton Hall Museum, Monterey.

16. Roach to Board of Aldermen, 10 April 1850, Monterey Collection, Huntington Library.

17. D.R. Ashley, Monterey Archives, Bancroft Library (1874).

18. Bestor 1945.

19. City Records Project, Minutes of Decision Bodies, vol. 1 (Colton Hall, Monterey).

20. *Monterey Peninsula Herald,* 18 January 1963.

21. David Jacks Collection, Stanford University Libraries Special Collections, Correspondence, Box 3; *Monterey Sentinel,* 28 July 1855.

22. Assessment Roll of the Taxable Property in Monterey County, A.D. 1854. Monterey County Historical Society, Salinas. Summary of 1851 Monterey County Tax Assessments in Elliot and Moore, 1881, pp. 104–5.

23. Tenth U.S. Census of Population, 1880 (published); Seventh U.S. Census of Population, Monterey County, California 1850 (manuscript).

24. *Monterey Californian*, 12 August 1879 and 21 February 1880; *Monterey Weekly Herald*, 11 March 1876.

25. *Monterey Sentinel*, 11 October 1855.

26. Bancroft 1888, 6:206; Guinn 1910, 2:288–90.

27. Stevenson 1892: 94–97.

28. Stevenson 1892: 94, 99.

29. *Monterey Gazette*, 28 November 1867.

30. Jail Register Monterey County (1850–72), Colton Hall Museum, Monterey.

31. *Monterey Sentinel*, 3 May and 10 May 1856; *Monterey Gazette*, 19 May 1865.

32. *Monterey Gazette*, 5 October 1866; Jail Register Monterey County (1850–72), Colton Hall Museum, Monterey.

33. *Monterey Gazette*, 12 October 1966.

34. *Monterey Gazette*, 12 June 1967.

35. *Monterey Gazette*, 13 May 1969.

36. Hobsbawm 1981.

37. *Monterey Gazette*, 4 March 1969.

38. *Monterey Weekly Herald*, 12 February 1876.

39. *Monterey Weekly Herald*, 30 May 1874.

40. Shumate 1983: 44.

41. *Monterey Weekly Herald*, 20 March 1875; Sánchez 1995: 293.

42. Bestor 1945; Stone 1989.

43. Gould 1992; Stone 1989.

44. Bestor 1945: 13–14; *Journal of the Senate of the State of California* 1856: 595.

45. *Monterey Sentinel*, 30 June 1855.

46. David Jacks Collection, Stanford University Libraries Special Collections, Correspondence, Box 1.

47. *Monterey Sentinel*, 19 April 1856.

48. Jacks Collection, Huntington Library, Legal Papers, Box 20.

49. Jacks Collection, Huntington Library, Legal Papers, Boxes 20 and 22.

50. *Monterey Californian*, 24 July 1880.

51. *Monterey Cypress*, 18 July 1891.

52. *Monterey Sentinel*, 14 July 1855.

53. *Monterey Gazette*, 25 March 1864; *Monterey Californian*, 24 February 1878; *Salinas Weekly Index*, 17 June 1880; Fisher 1940; Bakken 1985.

54. *David Jacks v. Carlos Baldez et al.*, California Supreme Court, 2 April 1891.

55. *Monterey Californian*, 18 November 1879; *Monterey Californian*, 29 September 1887; *Jacks v. Buell*, California Supreme Court, 21 May 1873.

56. *Monterey Weekly Herald*, 22 May 1875; Jail Register Monterey County (1850–72), Colton Hall Museum, Monterey.

57. Jacks to Hartman, 6 December 1866, Jacks Collection, Huntington Library, Correspondence, Box 1.

58. Ashley to Cole, 8 August 1866, David Jacks Collection, Stanford University Libraries Special Collections, Correspondence, Box 2.

59. Jacks to Ashley, 13 March 1868, and Ashley to Jacks, 8 July 1868, David Jacks Collection, Stanford University Libraries Special Collections, Correspondence, Box 2.

60. Jacks to Alonzo, 30 October 1866, and Alonzo to Jacks, 6 November 1866, David Jacks Collection, Stanford University Libraries Special Collections, Correspondence, Box 2.

61. Jacks to Stuart, 29 December 1868, David Jacks Collection, Stanford University Libraries Special Collections, Correspondence, Box 2.

62. Stuart to Jacks, 29 November 1869, Jacks Collection, Huntington Library, Correspondence, Box 1.

63. Unruh to Jacks, 27 June 1878, Jacks Collection, Huntington Library, Correspondence, Box 2.

64. Whitworth to Jacks, 4 March 1878, Jacks Collection, Huntington Library, Correspondence, Box 2.

65. Douglas to Sanborn, 10 February 1880, Jacks Collection, Huntington Library, Correspondence, Box 3.

66. Bowen to Jacks, 28 July and 7 August 1880, Jacks Collection, Huntington Library, Correspondence, Box 3.

67. Whitworth to Jacks, 24 November and 25 November 1880, Jacks Collection, Huntington Library, Correspondence, Box 3.

68. Douglas to Jacks, 2 July 1881, Jacks Collection, Huntington Library, Correspondence, Box 3.

69. *Hand Book of Monterey and Vicinity,* 1875; *Monterey Weekly Herald,* 10 October 1874.

70. *Monterey Cypress,* 8 May and 25 December 1897, 5 November 1998.

71. *Monterey Cypress,* 29 April 1899; Henneken to Jacks, 2 October 1902, Jacks Collection, Huntington Library, Correspondence, Shannon binder, 1902.

72. *The People v. K. M. Henneken,* Testimony and Proceedings, Justice Court at Salinas, December 1902, Jacks Collection, Huntington Library, Legal Papers, Box 24.

73. Hansen to Jacks, 16 February and 19 March 1879, Jacks Collection, Huntington Library, Correspondence, Box 3.

74. *Monterey Sentinel,* 23 June 1855, 29 March 1856.

75. *Monterey Sentinel,* 10 October 1855; Lydon 1985: 156.

76. *Monterey Weekly Herald,* 24 October 1874, 11 November 1875, 25 December 1875.

77. *Monterey Californian,* 20 September 1979.

78. *Monterey Californian,* 11 February and 4 February 1879.

79. *Monterey Sentinel,* 13 October 1855, 26 January 1856.

80. *Monterey Gazette,* 20 May 1869, 12 June and 26 June 1867.

81. Saxton 1971.

82. *Monterey Californian,* 29 January and 5 March 1878.

83. *Monterey Californian,* 18 February and 28 October 1879.

84. *Monterey Californian,* 11 March 1879.

85. *Monterey Californian,* 18 March and 1 July 1879; Lydon 1985.

86. McElroy to Jacks, 27 May 1880, Jacks Collection, Huntington Library, Correspondence, Box 3.

87. E.g., *Monterey Weekly Herald,* 8 January 1876; *Monterey Californian,* 27 March and 12 June 1880; *Monterey Cypress,* 4 August 1994.

88. *Monterey Cypress,* 20 August and 7 September 1889, 17 May 1990, 1 April 1993.

89. Stevenson 1905: 91–92.

90. *Monterey Weekly Herald,* 1 August 1874.

91. *Monterey Gazette,* 17 March 1865, 24 June 1864; *Monterey Weekly Herald,* 18 July and 24 October 1874.

92. *Hand Book of Monterey and Vicinity,* 1875: 50–54.

93. *Monterey Weekly Herald,* 12 December 1875, 8 January 1876.

94. Petition to Lovett, David Jacks Collection, Stanford University Libraries Special Collections, Correspondence, Box 2.

95. *Monterey Californian,* 26 February and 5 March 1878.

96. *Monterey Californian,* 18 November 1879; Lydon, 1985.

97. *Salinas Weekly Index,* 20 May 1880.

98. *Monterey Californian,* 16 December 1879.

99. *Monterey Californian,* 15 May 1880.

100. *Monterey Californian,* 15 May 1880.

101. *Monterey Cypress,* January–June 1889.

102. *Monterey Cypress,* 23 March 1889.

103. *Monterey Cypress,* 8 June 1889.

104. *Monterey Cypress,* 6 April 1889.

105. *Monterey Cypress,* 6 September 1890; Gilliam 1992.

106. *Monterey Cypress,* 29 June, 20 August, 7 September 1889.

107. *Monterey Cypress,* 17 May 1890, 1 April 1993.

108. *Monterey Cypress,* 30 March 1889, 18 July 1991, 23 October 1997, 22 July 1998.

109. Tuthill 1866.

110. Caughey 1946; Clark 1973; Etulain 1991.

111. Bancroft 1988.

112. *Monterey Herald,* 29 May 1875.

113. *Monterey Californian,* 11 November 1879, 10 June 1880.

114. *Monterey Cypress,* 6 June 1891.

115. *Monterey Cypress,* 14 March, 9 May, and 11 July 1996.

116. Kirker 1960: 16.

117. McClure 1976; Starr 1973.

118. Atherton 1932: 189.

119. Atherton 1932: 168.

120. Atherton, 1932:168

121. Starr 1973: 346.

122. *Monterey Californian,* 14 August 1880.

123. *Monterey Cypress,* 18 May 1901.

124. *People v. E. T. M. Simmons,* 13 June 1887, Monterey County Historical Society, Salinas; *Salinas Weekly Index,* 23 June and 30 June 1887.

125. *Monterey Argus,* 13 November 1886.

126. *Monterey Cypress,* 21 September 1889.

127. *Monterey Argus,* 10 July 1886.

128. Sánchez 1995.

5.   INDUSTRY AND COMMUNITY

1. *Monterey American,* 5 December 1917.

2. Colletto 1960.

3. *Monterey Daily Herald,* 7 October 1926.

4. *Monterey Daily Herald,* 8 October 1926.

5. *Monterey Daily Herald,* 25 and 26 October 1928.

6. *Monterey Daily Herald,* 14 October 1929.

7. *The Monterey Trader,* 25 August 1933.

8. *Monterey Daily Herald,* 6 February 1934.

9. *Monterey Daily Herald,* 15 March 1937.

10. *Monterey New Era,* 25 May 1904.

11. *Monterey New Era,* 23 March 1904.

12. Yamada 1995; Lydon 1997.

13. *Monterey New Era,* 16 March 1904.

14. *Monterey New Era,* 21 December 1904.

15. *Monterey New Era,* 14 June 1905.

16. Lydon 1985.

17. *Monterey New Era,* 29 November 1905.

18. *Monterey New Era,* 14 February 1906.

19. *Salinas Daily Index,* 17 May 1906.

20. Lydon 1985.

21. *Salinas Daily Index,* 18 and 21 March 1906; Lydon 1985.

22. Lydon 1985; *Salinas Daily Index,* 23 May 1906.

23. Pacific Improvement Company records, Special Collections, Stanford University Library.

24. *Monterey New Era,* 3 February 1904.

25. *Monterey Daily Cypress,* 12 February 1907.

26. *Monterey Daily Cypress,* 24 January 1907.

27. *Monterey Daily Cypress,* 14 January 1908.

28. Gilliam and Gilliam 1992.

29. *Monterey Daily Cypress,* 10 October 1907.

30. Pacific Improvement Company records, Special Collections, Stanford University Library.

31. *Monterey Herald,* 11 April 1999 and records of Stewart Title of California, Monterey.

32. Steinbeck 1935: 2.

33. Ariss 1988; Clark 1991.

34. *Monterey Daily Cypress,* 25 March 1908.

35. *Monterey Daily Cypress,* 27 August 1908.

36. *Monterey Daily Cypress,* 30 July and 6 August 1907.

37. *Monterey Daily Cypress,* 1 March 1907.

38. *Monterey Daily Cypress,* 17 July 1907.

39. *Monterey Daily Cypress,* 6 August 1907.

40. *Monterey Daily Cypress,* 5 March 1909.

41. Typed draft, Pacific Improvement Company records, Special Collections, Stanford University Library.

42. *Monterey Daily Cypress,* 29 January 1909.

43. *Monterey Daily Cypress,* 20 May 1911.

44. Hull England and Stavanger, Norway ranked ahead of Monterey in tonnage of processed fish. *Monterey Peninsula Herald,* 25 March 1938.

45. The city of Monterey had a population of 9,141 in 1930 and 10,084 in 1940. At peak season roughly 30 percent of the entire population was employed in the industry and in support services such as rooming houses, restaurants and bars, equipment and repair businesses, and transportation. *United States Census of Population,* 1930, 1940.

46. *WPA Guide* 1989: 69.

47. A few Asian women and at least one African-American man worked directly in fishing.

48. *The History of Portola* n.d.

49. Steinbeck 1945: 1–2.

50. Steinbeck and Wallsten 1975: 273.

51. Mangelsdorf 1986; Lydon 1997.

52. *Monterey New Era,* 15 June 1904.

53. McEvoy 1986: 96.

54. McEvoy 1986: 113.

55. Rosenberg 1961; Mangelsdorf 1986; McEvoy 1986.

56. *Monterey Daily Cypress,* 11 August 1909.

57. Friday 1992.

58. *Monterey Peninsula Herald,* 23 February 1940.

59. *Fish Bulletin* 1946.

60. Scofield 1929; Phillips 1930; Rosenberg 1961.

61. *Monterey Peninsula Herald,* 28 February 1941.

62. Rosenberg 1961: 141.

63. McKibben 1991: 16.

64. Ruiz 1987.

65. Monterey Fishermen's Historical Association 1995.

66. Lautaret 1990: 15.

67. *Monterey Peninsula Herald,* 27 February 1942, 7 March 1947, 2 April 1948.

68. Sutherland 1941.

69. *Monterey Peninsula Herald,* 2 April 1948.

70. "Fishing and Canning Industry in Monterey," Records of the Seafarer's International Union, Monterey History and Art Association, Stanton Center, Monterey, n.d.

71. Official Report of Proceedings before the Tenth Regional War Labor Board in the matter of Monterey Fish Processors Association and Seafarers' International Union of North America, Fish Cannery Workers Union of the Pacific of Monterey (AFL), San Francisco, August 1943. National Archives Regional Branch, San Bruno, California.

72. Dawley 1976; Katznelson 1986.

73. Yancey, Erickson, and Juliani 1976.

74. *WPA Guide* 1941: 67.

75. Lydon 1985: 381.

76. Cinel 1982: 197.

77. Cinel 1982: 221.

78. Cutino 1995: 100.

79. Russo, cited in McKibben 1998: 44.

80. McKibben 1998: 44.

81. McKibben 1998: 56.

82. *Monterey Peninsula Herald,* 23 February 1940.

83. Steinbeck 1941: 24–25.

84. Rosenberg 1961.

85. *Monterey Daily Cypress,* 26 July 1920.

86. *Monterey Daily Cypress,* 30 July 1920.

87. *Monterey Daily Cypress,* 27 July 1920.

88. *Monterey Daily Cypress,* 2 September 1920.

89. *Monterey Daily Cypress,* 1 September 1920.

90. Cinel 1982: 219.

91. Ferrante Family History, n.d.

92. Mangelsdorf 1986: 55.

93. Mangelsdorf 1986: 88.

94. Rosenberg 1961: 127.

95. *Monterey Peninsula Herald,* 19 July 1926.

96. *Monterey Peninsula Herald,* 7 August 1926.

97. McEvoy 1986: 10.

98. McEvoy 1986: 181.

99. *Monterey Peninsula Herald,* 22 and 28 January 1937.

100. McKibben 1991: 16.

101. Kinney and Lonero 1987: 12.

102. Mangelsdorf 1986: 117.

103. *Monterey Peninsula Herald,* 17 July 1937.

104. *Monterey Peninsula Herald,* 8 and 26 June 1938.

105. *Monterey Peninsula Herald,* 27 December 1938.

106. *Monterey Peninsula Herald,* 10 March 1939.

107. *Monterey Peninsula Herald,* 24 February 1939.

108. Pagliarulo 1968; Temple 1980; Morgado 1987.

109. *Peninsula Daily Herald,* 12 July 1924.

110. *Peninsula Daily Herald,* 11 October 1924.

111. *Peninsula Daily Herald,* 11 October 1924.

112. *Peninsula Daily Herald,* 13 October 1924.

113. Ford 1926: xi.

114. Ford 1926: 99, 102, 111, 226–27.

115. *Monterey Peninsula Herald,* 20 January 1931.

116. Annual Reports, Records, Monterey History and Art Association.

117. Minutes of the Board of Directors, 1935, Records, Monterey History and Art Association.

118. Powers to McGinley, Parish records, Box 461.10, Monterey Diocese Archival Center.

119. *Fray Junipero Serra,* File Box "Serra Cause: Miscellaneous Serrana," Santa Barbara Mission Archive.

120. *Monterey Peninsula Herald,* 25 August 1934.

121. *Monterey Peninsula Herald,* 25 August 1934.

122. *Monterey Peninsula Herald,* 25 August 1934.

123. *Monterey Peninsula Herald,* 24 and 25 August 1934; Parish records, Box 461.10, Monterey Diocese Archival Center.

124. Powers 1934: 68, 94, 176, 179.

125. Bartlett 1933.

126. Fisher 1940.

127. Sandos 1988, 1989a, 1989b.

128. Bolton 1917, 1921: 279, 282.

129. *WPA Guide* 1941: 64.

130. *Monterey New Era,* 28 March 1906.

131. *Monterey Peninsula Herald,* 11–14 May 1938.

132. Ariss 1988.

133. *Monterey Peninsula Herald,* 17 February 1937.

134. *Monterey Peninsula Herald,* 15 March and 15 April 1937.

135. *Monterey Peninsula Herald,* 17 September 1937.

136. Ariss 1988: 3.

137. *Monterey Peninsula Herald,* 22 March 1939.

138. *Monterey Peninsula Herald,* 25 March 1939.

139. *Monterey Peninsula Herald,* 5 May 1939.

140. *Monterey Peninsula Herald,* 21 March 1938.

141. Benson 1984.

142. *Monterey Peninsula Herald,* 18 January 1938.

143. "Material Dealing with the Planning Progress toward the Preservation of Historic Monterey, California," State Division of Parks, 1939, Monterey Public Library; *Monterey Peninsula Herald,* 16 and 18 July 1938.

144. *Monterey Peninsula Herald,* 21 September 1937, 2 February 1938.

145. *Monterey Peninsula Herald,* 18 December and 31 March 1938.

146. Fox 1990.

147. *Monterey Peninsula Herald,* 23 April, 27 April, 11 May 1945.

6.   THE HISTORICAL PRESENT

1. *Monterey City Herald,* February 21, 1999.

2. *Monterey Peninsula Herald,* 4 January 1958.

3. *Monterey Peninsula Herald,* 14 July 1960.

4. *Monterey Peninsula Herald,* 28 June 1960.

5. *Monterey Peninsula Herald,* 22 April 1958.

6. *Monterey Peninsula Herald,* 13 April 1961; *San Francisco Call-Bulletin,* 27 July 1961.

7. *Monterey Peninsula Herald,* 24 March 1961, 18 April 1961.

8. *Monterey Peninsula Herald,* 13 June 1961, 15 June 1961, 2 August 1961, 7 August 1961, 24 August 1961.

9. *Monterey Peninsula Herald,* 6 October 1961, 17 February 1962.

10. *Monterey Peninsula Herald,* 15 April 1964.

11. *Monterey Peninsula Herald,* 4 February 1964.

12. *Monterey Peninsula Herald,* 28 January 1966, 2 February 1966, 14 February 1966.

13. *Monterey Peninsula Herald,* 26 March 1971, 7 April 1971, 25 May 1971, 16 September 1971, 13 April 1972.

14. *Monterey Peninsula Herald,* 13 July 1973, 12 August 1977.

15. Healy et al. 1978; Sabatier and Mazmanian 1983.

16. Adams 1973.

17. Fischer 1985.

18. *Monterey Peninsula Herald,* 1 August 1980, 4 October 1984, 14 October 1984.

19. *San Jose Mercury News,* 9 June 1998.

20. *Rancho San Carlos Update,* November 1995.

21. Fitzpatrick 1996.

22. *Monterey Peninsula Herald,* 28 May 1999.

23. *Monterey Peninsula Herald,* 15 January 1999, 17 May 1999; *Pebble Beach Scoreboard,* January 1999.

24. *Monterey Peninsula Herald,* 22 May 1999.

25. *Monterey Peninsula Herald,* 11 June 1999.

26. Breschini and Haversat 1989.

27. Breschini 1992.

28. *Monterey Peninsula Herald,* 8 August 1993.

29. *Monterey Peninsula Herald,* 8 August 1992, 10 September 1992; *Californian,* 22 August 1992; *Carmel Valley Sun,* 6 August 1992, 1 October 1992.

30. Gordon 1977: 1.

31. Henson and Usner 1993.

32. Gilliam and Gilliam 1992: 6.

33. Hobbs 1990.

34. Brower 1965.

35. Lydon 1985.

36. Lydon 1997.

37. Yamada 1995.

38. Cutino 1995; McKibben 1998.

39. Margolin 1978; Costa 1987; Castañeda 1990; Hackel 1994.

40. Fink 1982; Abrahamson 1990.

41. *Monterey Peninsula Herald,* 26 February 1957.

42. Norkunas 1993.

43. Person 1972; Reinstedt 1978; Mangelsdorf 1986; Hemp 1986; Larsh 1995.

44. *Monterey Peninsula Herald,* 8 March 1957.
45. Norkunas 1993: 63.
46. Steinbeck and Wallsten 1975: 467, 279, 281.
47. Steinbeck 1935: 39–41.

7. CONCLUSION: ACTION, NARRATIVE, HISTORY

1. Critser 1985.
2. *Los Angeles Times,* 27 March 1986.
3. *Serra: American Founding Father,* 1987.
4. *The Serra Report,* 1987.
5. Sandos 1989a, 1989b.
6. *Los Angeles Times,* 24 and 28 November 1986.
7. Costa and Costa 1987: 1–3.
8. Sandos 1988.
9. *Los Angeles Times,* 26 September 1988.
10. *Monterey Herald,* 26 September 1988.
11. McWilliams 1946: 29.
12. Engelhardt 1909.
13. Lummis to Engelhardt, 1 April 1909, Santa Barbara Mission Archives, Serrana, vol. 1.
14. Lummis to Engelhardt, 14 May 1909, Santa Barbara Mission Archives, Serrana, vol. 1.
15. Sandos 1989: 314a.
16. Fisher-Geiger correspondence, February–March 1948, Santa Barbara Mission Archives, Serrana, vol. 1.
17. Fisher-Geiger correspondence, February–March 1949, Santa Barbara Mission Archives, Serrana, vol. 1.
18. Abrahamson 1989: 11.
19. Ortiz 1999.
20. Trouillot 1995: 2–3, 22.
21. Becker 1958: 61.
22. Guillermoprieto 1990: 49.
23. White 1987: ix.
24. White 1973.
25. Kelly 1999.
26. Kuhn 1959; Latour 1987.
27. Here I follow the spirit of Foucault's (1977) use of countermemory while benefiting more from Zerubavel's (1995) somewhat different usage.
28. Gramsci 1971; Williams 1977.
29. Williams 1977: 115.
30. Trouillot 1995.
31. Warner 1959: 164.
32. Warner 1959: 110. Emphasis in original.
33. Halbwachs 1980: 65.
34. Fentress and Wickham 1992.
35. Zerubavel 1995: 235.

36. Thompson 1975: 263.
37. Trouillot 1995: xix.
38. Peters 1988.
39. Wagner-Pacifici and Schwartz 1991: 416.
40. García Marquez, cited in Posada-Carbo 1998: 395.
41. Taylor 1995: 423.
42. Colletto 1960: 14.
43. *Monterey Herald,* 18 April 1998.

Bibliography

Abrahamson, Eric.
   1989.   *Historic Monterey: California's Forgotten First Capital.* Monterey: California Department of Parks and Recreation.
Adams, Janet.
   1973.   "Proposition 20—A Citizens' Campaign." *Syracuse Law Review* 24:3 (Summer): 1019–46.
Alvarado, Juan Bautista.
   1876.   *Historia de California.* Bancroft Library, University of California, Berkeley.
Archibald, Robert.
   1978.   *The Economic Aspects of the California Missions.* Washington, D.C.: Academy of American Franciscan History.
Ariss, Bruce.
   1988.   *Inside Cannery Row.* Monterey: Lexikos.
Ashley, D.R., Monterey Archives, Bancroft Library, University of California, Berkeley.
Assessment Roll of Taxable Property in Monterey County.
   1854.   Monterey County Historical Society. Salinas, California.
Atherton, Gertrude.
   1890.   *Los Cerritos: A Romance of Modern Times.* New York: Lovell.
   1893.   *The Doomswoman.* New York: Stokes.
   1932.   *Adventures of a Novelist.* New York: Lightfoot.
Bakken, Gordon Morris.
   1985.   *The Development of Law in Frontier California: Civil Law and Society, 1850–1890.* Westport, Conn.: Greenwood Press.
Bancroft, Hubert Howe.
   1884–90.   *History of California.* 7 vols. San Francisco: History Company Publishers.

1886.   *Pioneer Register.* San Francisco: History Company Publishers.
1888.   *California Pastoral, 1769–1888.* San Francisco: History Company
             Publishers.
Bartlett, Virginia Stivers.
    1933.   *Mistress of Monterey.* Indianapolis: Bobbs-Merrill.
Becker, Carl L.
    1958.   "What Are Historical Facts." Pp. 41–64 in Phil L. Snyder, ed.,
             *Detachment and the Writing of History: Essays and Letters of
             Carl Becker.* Ithaca: Cornell University Press.
Benson, Jackson J.
    1984.   *The True Adventures of John Steinbeck, Writer.* New York: Penguin.
Bestor, Arthur Eugene, Jr.
    1945.   *David Jacks of Monterey, and Lee L. Jacks His Daughter.* Stan-
             ford: Stanford University Press.
Bielharz, Edwin A.
    1971.   *Felipe de Neve: First Governor of California.* San Francisco: Cali-
             fornia Historical Society.
Bolton, Herbert E.
    1917.   "The Mission as a Frontier Institution in the Spanish-American
             Colonies." *American Historical Review* 23:1 (October): 42–61.
    1921.   *The Spanish Borderlands: A Chronicle of Old Florida and the
             Southwest.* New Haven: Yale University Press.
Boob, Bernard E.
    1962.   *The Viceregency of Antonio María Bucareli in New Spain,
             1771–1779.* Austin: University of Texas Press.
Bowman, J. N.
    1961.   "Libraries in Provincial California." *Historical Society of South-
             ern California Quarterly* 43: 426–39.
Brandes, Ray.
    1970.   *The Costansó Narrative of the Portolá Expedition.* Newhall,
             Calif.: Hogarth Press.
Breschini, Gary S.
    1992.   *Archaeological Studies at Rancho San Carlos, Carmel Valley,
             Monterey, California.* Archives of California Prehistory, 36. Sali-
             nas, Calif.: Coyote Press.
Breschini, Gary S., and Trudy Haversat.
    1989.   *Archaeological Excavations at CA-MNT-108, at Fisherman's
             Wharf, Monterey, Monterey County, California.* Archives of Cali-
             fornia Prehistory, 29. Salinas, Calif.: Coyote Press.
Broadbent, Sylvia M.
    1972.   "The Rumsen of Monterey, an Ethnography from Historical
             Sources." *Contributions of the University of California Archae-
             ological Research Facility,* no. 14 (January): 45–93.
Brower, David.
    1965.   *Not Man Apart: Photographs of the Big Sur Coast, Lines from
             Robinson Jeffers.* San Francisco: Sierra Club.

Carroll, Lewis.
   1960.   *Through the Looking-Glass*. New York: Signet Classics.
Castañeda, Antonia I.
   1990.   "Presadarias y Popladoras: Spanish-Mexican Women in Frontier Monterey, Alta California, 1770–1821." Ph.D. dissertation, University of California, Berkeley.
   1997.   "Engendering the History of Alta California, 1769–1848: Gender, Sexuality, and the Family." Pp. 230–59 in Ramón A. Gutiérrez and Richard J. Orsi, eds., *Contested Eden: California before the Gold Rush*. Berkeley: University of California Press.
Caughey, John Walton.
   1946.   *Hubert Howe Bancroft: Historian of the West*. Berkeley: University of California Press.
Chartkoff, Joseph L., and Kerry Kona Chartkoff.
   1984.   *The Archaeology of California*. Stanford: Stanford University Press.
Cinel, Dino.
   1982.   *From Italy to San Francisco: The Immigrant Experience*. Stanford: Stanford University Press.
City Records Project. Colton Hall Museum, Monterey, California.
Clark, Donald Thomas.
   1991.   *Monterey County Place Names: A Geographical Dictionary*. Carmel Valley, Calif.: Kestrel Press.
Clark, Harry.
   1973.   *A Venture in History: The Production, Publication, and Sale of the Works of Hubert Howe Bancroft*. Berkeley: University of California Press.
Colletto, Sol.
   1960.   "A Fisherman's Story." Manuscript. Monterey History and Art Association, Stanton Center, Monterey.
Colton, Walter.
   1860.   *Three Years in California*. New York: Evans.
Cook, S. F.
   1943.   *The Conflict between the California Indian and White Civilization, III: The American Invasion*. University of California Publications: Ibero-Americana 23. Berkeley: University of California Press.
Cooper Ledger Book. Cooper-Molera Papers. Bancroft Library, University of California, Berkeley.
Costa, Rupert, and Jeannette Henry Costa.
   1987.   *The Missions of California: A Legacy of Genocide*. San Francisco: Indian Historian Press.
Costello, Julia G., and David Hornbeck.
   1989.   "Alta California: An Overview." Pp. 303–31 in David Hurst Thomas, ed., *Columbian Consequences*. Vol. 1. Washington, D.C.: Smithsonian Institution Press.

Coulter, Edith.
    1941.   *An Account of a Visit to California, 1826–17*. San Francisco: Grabhorn Press.
Cowan, Robert G.
    1977.   *Ranchos of California*. Los Angeles: Historical Society of Southern California.
Critser, Greg.
    1985.   "The Million-Dollar Canonization." *California Magazine* 10:3 (August): 88–119.
Croce, Benedetto.
    1941.   *History as the Story of Liberty*. London: G. Allen and Unwin.
Cullerton, James.
    1950.   *Indians and Pioneers of Old Monterey*. Fresno, Calif.: Academy of California Church History.
Cutino, Peter J.
    1995.   *Monterey—A View from Garlic Hill*. Pacific Grove, Calif.: Boxwood Press.
Cutter, Donald C.
    1960.   *Malaspina in California*. San Francisco: J. Howell.
    1990.   *California in 1792: A Spanish Naval Visit*. Norman: University of Oklahoma Press.
Dakin, Susanna Bryant.
    1949.   *The Lives of William Hartnell*. Stanford: Stanford University Press.
Dallas, Sherman F.
    1955.   "The Hide and Tallow Trade in Alta California, 1822–1846." Ph.D. dissertation, Indiana University.
Dana, Richard Henry.
    [1840] 1965. *Two Years Before the Mast*. New York: Airmont.
Dawley, Alan.
    1976.   *Class and Community: The Industrial Revolution in Lynn*. Cambridge, Mass.: Harvard University Press.
DeVoto, Bernard.
    1942.   *The Year of Decision, 1846*. Boston: Houghton Mifflin.
Duhart-Cilly, August Bernard.
    [1830] 1997. *A Voyage: To California, the Sandwich Islands and Around the World in the Years 1826–1827*. Translated and edited by August Frugé and Neal Harlow. San Francisco: Book Club of California.
Elliot and Moore.
    1881.   *History of Monterey County*. San Francisco: Elliot and Moore Publishers.
Engelhardt, Zephyrin.
    1909.   *The Holy Man of Santa Clara*. San Francisco: James H. Barry.
    [1934] 1973. *Mission San Carlos Borromeo*. Ramona, Calif.: Ballena Press.
Etulain, Richard W.
    1991.   *Writing Western History: Essays on Major Western Historians*. Albuquerque: University of New Mexico Press.

Fentress, James, and Chris Wickham.
    1992.   *Social Memory.* Oxford: Blackwell.
Ferrante Family History.
    N.d.   Monterey Fishermen's Historical Association.
Fink, Augusta.
    1982.   *Monterey County: The Dramatic Story of Its Past.* Santa Cruz, Calif.: Western Tanager Press.
Fischer, Michael L.
    1985.   "California's Coastal Program, Larger-than-Local Interests Built into Local Plans." *Journal of the American Planning Association* 51:3 (Summer): 312–21.
Fish Bulletin.
    1946.   "The Commercial Fish Catch of California for the Years 1943 and 1944." No. 63, State of California, Division of Fish and Game.
Fisher, Anne B.
    1940.   *Cathedral in the Sun.* New York: Carlyle House.
Fitzpatrick, Elayne Wareing.
    1996.   "Stevenson Cabin to Be Saved." *Monterey Peninsula Herald, Alta Vista Magazine,* 29 September.
Forbes, Alexander.
    1839.   *California: A History of Upper and Lower California from Their First Discovery to the Present Time, Comprising an Account of the Climate, Soil, Natural Productions, Agriculture, Commerce, &c. A Full View of the Missionary Establishments and Condition of the Free and Domesticated Indians. With an Appendix Relating to Stein Navigation in the Pacific.* London: Smith, Elder, and Company.
Ford, Tirey L.
    1926.   *Dawn and the Dons: The Romance of Monterey.* San Francisco: A. M. Robertson.
Foucault, Michel.
    1977.   *Language, Counter-Memory, Practice: Selected Essays and Interviews.* Ithaca: Cornell University Press.
Fox, Stephen.
    1990.   *The Unknown Internment: An Oral History of the Relocation of Italian Americans during World War II.* Boston: Twayne.
Francis, Jesse Davies.
    1976.   *An Economic History of Mexican California, 1822–1846.* New York: Arno Press.
Friday, Chris.
    1992.   *Organizing Asian American Labor: The Pacific Coast Canned-Salmon Industry, 1870–1942.* Philadelphia: Temple University Press.
Gates, Paul.
    1971.   "The California Land Act of 1851." *California Historical Quarterly* 50 (December): 395–430.

1991.   *Land and Law in California: Essays on Land Politics.* Ames: Iowa State University Press.

Geiger, Maynard J.

1955.   Foreword to Maynard J. Geiger, *Palóu's Life of Fray Junípero Serra.* Washington, D.C.: Academy of American Franciscan History.

Gilliam, Harold, and Ann Gilliam.

1992.   *Creating Carmel: The Enduring Vision.* Salt Lake City: Peregrine Smith Books.

González, Michael J.

1997.   "The Child of the Wilderness Weeps for the Father of Our Country: The Indian and the Politics of Church and State in Provincial California." *California History* 76 (Summer–Fall): 147–72.

Gordon, Burton L.

1977.   *Monterey Bay Area: Natural History and Cultural Imprints.* Pacific Grove, Calif.: Boxwood Press.

Gould, Sondra L.

1992.   "State Legislative Power and Municipal Trusts." Pp. 244–46 in John W. Johnson, ed., *Historic U.S. Court Cases, 1690–1990: An Encyclopedia.* New York: Garland.

Gramsci, Antonio.

1971.   *Selections from the Prison Notebooks.* New York: International Publishers.

Guest, Francis F.

1978.   "Mission Colonization and Political Control in Spanish California." *Journal of San Diego History* 24 (Winter 1978): 97–116.

1983.   "Cultural Perspectives on California Mission Life." *Southern California Quarterly* 65 (Spring): 1–65.

1985.   "New Look at California's Missions." Pp. 77–88 in Francis J. Weber, ed., *Some Reminiscences about Fray Junipero Serra.* Los Angeles: California Catholic Council.

Guillermoprieto, Alma.

1990.   *Samba.* New York: Vintage.

Guinn, James Miller.

1910.   *Historical and Biographical Record of Monterey and San Benito Counties.* Los Angeles: Historic Record Company.

Gutiérrez, Ramón A., and Richard J. Orsi, eds.

1997.   *Contested Eden: California before the Gold Rush.* Berkeley: University of California Press.

Haas, Lisbeth.

1995.   *Conquests and Historical Identities in California, 1769–1936.* Berkeley: University of California Press.

N.d.   "What Did Freedom Mean? The Indian Voice in California's Emancipation Process." Unpublished paper.

Hackel, Steven William.
  1994.   "Indian-Spanish Relations in Alta California: Mission San Carlos
            Borromeo, 1770–1833." Ph.D. dissertation, Cornell University.
  1997.   "Land, Labor, and Production: The Colonial Economy of Span-
            ish and Mexican California." Pp. 111–46 in Ramón A. Gutiér-
            rez and Richard J. Orsi, eds., *Contested Eden: California before
            the Gold Rush*. Berkeley: University of California Press.
Halbwachs, Maurice.
  1980.   *The Collective Memory.* New York: Harper.
Hammond, George P.
  1951.   *The Larkin Papers.* Vol. 1. Berkeley: University of California Press.
Hand Book of Monterey and Vicinity.
  1875.   Monterey: Curtis and Walton.
Hartnell, William.
  1839.   "Diario, Informe, y Borradores de Correspondencia." Bancroft
            Library, University of California, Berkeley.
Healy, Robert G., et al.
  1978.   *Protecting the Golden Shore: Lessons from the California Coastal
            Commission.* Washington, D.C.: Conservation Foundation.
Heizer, Robert F.
  1978.   *The Handbook of North American Indians.* Vol. 8, *California.*
            Washington, D.C.: Smithsonian Institution Press.
Heizer, Robert F., and M. A. Whipple.
  1951.   *The California Indians: A Source Book.* Berkeley: University of
            California Press.
Hemp, Michael Kenneth.
  1986.   *Cannery Row: The History of Old Ocean Avenue.* Pacific Grove,
            Calif.: History Company Publishers.
Henson, Paul, and Donald J. Usner.
  1993.   *The Natural History of Big Sur.* Berkeley: University of Califor-
            nia Press.
Hester, Thomas Roy.
  1978a.   "Esselen." Pp. 496–99 in Robert F. Heizer, ed., *The Handbook
            of North American Indians,* vol. 8, *California.* Washington,
            D.C.: Smithsonian Institution Press.
  1978b.   "Salinan." Pp. 500–503 in Robert F. Heizer, ed., *The Handbook
            of North American Indians,* vol. 8, *California.* Washington,
            D.C.: Smithsonian Institution Press.
History of Portola.
  N.d.   Monterey, Calif.: K. Hovden.
Hobbs, Fredric.
  1990.   *The Spirit of the Monterey Coast.* Palo Alto, Calif.: Tioga.
Hobsbawm, Eric.
  1981.   *Bandits.* Rev. ed. New York: Pantheon.
Hoover, Robert L.
  1989.   "Spanish-Native Interaction and Acculturation in the Alta Cali-

fornia Missions." Pp. 395–406 in David Hurst Thomas, ed., *Columbian Consequences*, vol. 1. Washington, D.C.: Smithsonian Institution Press.

Hurtado, Albert L.
1999.   *Intimate Frontiers: Sex, Gender, and Culture in Old California*. Albuquerque: University of New Mexico Press.

Hutchinson, C. Alan.
1969.   *Frontier Settlement in Mexican California: The Híjar-Padrés Colony, and Its Origins, 1769–1835*. New Haven: Yale University Press.
1978.   *Manifesto to the Mexican Republic*. Berkeley: University of California Press.

Jacks Collection. Huntington Library, San Marino, California.

Jacks, David, Collection. Stanford University Libraries, Special Collections.

Jackson, Robert H., and Edward Castillo.
1995.   *Indians, Franciscans, and Spanish Colonization: The Impact of the Mission System on California Indians*. Albuquerque: University of New Mexico Press.

Jail Register, Monterey County.
1850–72.   Colton Hall Museum, Monterey, California.

James, George Wharton.
1913.   *Francisco Palóu's Life and Apostolic Labors of the Venerable Father Junípero Serra Founder of the Franciscan Missions of California*. Pasadena, Calif.: James.

Johannsen, Robert W.
1985.   *To the Halls of the Montezumas: The Mexican War and the American Imagination*. New York: Oxford University Press.

Journal of the Senate of the State of California (Seventh Session).
1856.   Sacramento: James Allen, State Printer.

Joyce, James.
[1922] 1986. *Ulysses*. New York: Vintage Books.

Katznelson, Ira.
1986.   "Working-Class Formation: Constructing Cases and Comparisons." Pp. 3–41 in Ira Katznelson and Aristide R. Zolberg, eds., *Working-Class Formation: Nineteenth-Century Patterns in Western Europe and the United States*. Princeton: Princeton University Press.

Kelly, Michael.
1999.   "Playing with Fire." *New Yorker,* 15 July.

Kenneally, Finbar.
1965.   *Writings of Fermín Francisco de Lasuén*. 2 vols. Washington, D.C.: Academy of American Franciscan History.

Kinney, James, and Kathy Lonero.
1987.   "Down on the Row." *Weekly Herald Magazine* (April 26): 12.

Kirker, Harold.
1960.   *California's Architectural Frontier: Style and Tradition in the Nineteenth Century*. San Marino, Calif.: The Huntington Library.

Kuhn, Thomas S.
  1959. *The Structure of Scientific Revolutions*. Chicago: University of Chicago Press.
Kundera, Milan.
  1994. *The Book of Laughter and Forgetting*. New York: Harper Perennial.
Lamb, W. Kaye.
  1984. *George Vancouver, a Voyage of Discovery to the North Pacific and Round the World, 1791–1795*. 3 vols. London: Hakluyt Society.
Langum, David J.
  1987. *Law and Community on the Mexican California Frontier: Anglo-American Expatriates and the Clash of Legal Traditions, 1821–1846*. Norman: University of Oklahoma Press.
Larsh, Ed B.
  1995. *Doc's Lab: Myth and Legends from Cannery Row*. Monterey: PBL Press.
Latour, Bruno.
  1987. *Science in Action*. Cambridge, Mass.: Harvard University Press.
Lautaret, Mavis.
  1990. "Out of the Office, Into the Muck." *Monterey Peninsula Herald, Alta Vista Magazine*, February 10.
Levy, Richard.
  1978. "Costanoan." Pp. 485–95 in Robert F. Heizer, ed., *The Handbook of North American Indians*, vol. 8, *California*. Washington, D.C.: Smithsonian Institution Press.
Lydon, Sandy.
  1985. *Chinese Gold: The Chinese in the Monterey Bay Region*. Capitola, Calif.: Capitola Book Company.
  1997. *The Japanese in the Monterey Bay Region: A Brief History*. Capitola, Calif.: Capitola Book Company.
Mangelsdorf, Tom.
  1986. *A History of Steinbeck's Cannery Row*. Santa Cruz, Calif.: Western Tanager Press.
Margolin, Malcolm.
  1978. *The Ohlone Way: Indian Life in the San Francisco–Monterey Bay Area*. Berkeley, Calif.: Heyday Books.
  1989. *Monterey in 1786: The Journals of Jean François de La Pérouse*. Berkeley, Calif.: Heyday Books.
Mason, William Marvin.
  1998. *The Census of 1790: A Demographic History of Colonial California*. Menlo Park, Calif.: Ballena Press.
McClure, Charlotte S.
  1976. *Gertrude Atherton*. Boise, Idaho: Boise State University.
McEvoy, Arthur F.
  1986. *The Fisherman's Problem: Ecology and Law in the California Fisheries, 1850–1980*. Cambridge, Mass.: Cambridge University Press.

McKibben, Carol.
    1991.   "Women of the Canneries." *Monterey Peninsula Herald, Alta Vista Magazine,* February 10.
    1998.   "Of All the Gifts You Gave Me, the Most Important One Is I Belong. The Italians: Gender, Class and Community in Monterey, 1880–1998." Manuscript.
McWilliams, Carey.
    [1946] 1973. *Southern California: An Island on the Land.* Salt Lake City: Peregrine Books.
    [1949] 1979. *California: The Great Exception.* Salt Lake City: Peregrine Books.
Mexican Archives.
    1835–1846. Monterey County Historical Society, Monterey, California.
Milliken, Randall.
    1987.   *Ethnohistory of the Rumsen.* Papers in Northern California Anthropology, no. 2. Salinas, Calif.: Coyote Press.
    1990.   *Ethnogeography and Ethnohistory of the Big Sur District, California State Park System during the 1770–1810 Time Period.* Salinas, Calif.: Coyote Press.
    1995.   *A Time of Little Choice: The Disintegration of Tribal Culture in the San Francisco Bay Area, 1769–1810.* Menlo Park, Calif.: Ballena Press.
Monterey Archives (of D. R. Ashley).
    1874.   Bancroft Library, University of California, Berkeley.
Monterey Collection. Huntington Library, San Marino, California.
Monterey Fishermen's Historical Association.
    1995.   Oral Histories. Monterey, California.
Morgado, Martin J.
    1987.   *Junípero Serra's Legacy.* Pacific Grove, Calif.: Mount Carmel.
Norkunas, Martha K.
    1993.   *The Politics of Public Memory: Tourism, History, and Ethnicity in Monterey, California.* Albany: State University of New York Press.
Northrup, Marie E.
    1976.   *Spanish-Mexican Families of Early California: 1769–1850.* Vol. 1. New Orleans: Polyanthos.
Ogden, Adele.
    1927.   "Hides and Tallow: McCulloch, Hartnell and Company, 1822–1828." *California Historical Quarterly* 6: 254–64.
    1941.   *The California Sea Otter Trade, 1784–1848.* Berkeley: University of California Press.
Ortiz, Beverly R.
    1999.   "Honoring the Dead and the Living." *News from Native California* 12:4 (Summer): 22–24.
Pacific Improvement Company Records. Special Collections, Stanford University Libraries.
Padrón General.
    1836.   Census of Monterey. Bancroft Library, University of California, Berkeley.

Pagliarulo, Sister Marie Celeste.
    1968.   "The Restoration of Mission San Carlos Borromeo, Carmel, California, 1931–1967." M.A. thesis, University of San Francisco.
Perez, Crisostomo N.
    1996.   *Land Grants in California.* Rancho Cordova, Calif.: Landmark Enterprises.
Person, Richard.
    1972.   *History of Cannery Row.* Monterey: Department of City Planning, City of Monterey.
Peters, Edward.
    1988.   *Inquisition.* New York: Free Press.
Phillips, George Harwood.
    1975.   *Chiefs and Challengers: Indian Resistance and Cooperation in Southern California.* Berkeley: University of California Press.
    1993.   *Indians and Intruders in Central California, 1769–1849.* Norman: University of Oklahoma Press.
Phillips, J. B.
    1930.   "Success of the Purse Seine Boat in the Fishery at Monterey, California." *Fish Bulletin* 23 (April): 5–27. State of California, Division of Fish and Game.
Pisani, Donald J.
    1994.   "Squatter Law in California, 1850–1885." *Western Historical Quarterly* 25 (Autumn): 277–308.
Pitt, Leonard.
    1966.   *The Decline of the Californios: A Social History of the Spanish-Speaking Californians, 1846–1890.* Berkeley: University of California Press.
Posada-Carbo, Eduardo.
    1998.   "Fiction as History: The Bananeras and Gabriel García Márquez's 'One Hundred Years of Solitude.'" *Journal of Latin American Studies* 30:2 (May): 395.
Powers, Laura Bride.
    1934.   *Old Monterey: California's Adobe Capital.* San Francisco: San Carlos Press.
Pratt, Mary Louise.
    1992.   *Imperial Eyes: Travel Writing and Transculturation.* London: Routledge.
Priestley, Herbert Ingram.
    1916.   *José de Gálvez, Visitor-General of New Spain (1765–1771).* University of California Publications in History 5. Berkeley: University of California Press.
    1937.   *A Historical, Political, and Natural Description of California by Pedro Fages, Soldier of Spain.* Berkeley: University of California Press.
Rawls, James.
    1984.   *Indians of California: The Changing Image.* Norman: University of Oklahoma Press.

Reinstedt, Randall A.
    1978.   *Where Have All the Sardines Gone: A Pictorial History of Stein-
               beck's Cannery Row.* Carmel, Calif.: Ghost Town Publications.
Reséndez, Andrés.
    1999.   "National Identity on a Shifting Border: Texas and New Mex-
               ico in the Age of Transition, 1821–1848." *Journal of American
               History* 86:2 (September): 668–88.
Robinson, Alfred.
    1947.   *Life in California: A Historical Account of the Origin, Customs,
               and Traditions of the Indians of Alta-California.* Oakland, Calif.:
               Biobooks.
Robinson, W. W.
    1948.   *Land in California.* Berkeley: University of California Press.
Rolle, Andrew.
    1963.   *California: A History.* New York: Crowell.
Rolston, Bill.
    1992.   *Drawing Support: Murals in the North of Ireland.* Belfast: Be-
               yond the Pale Publications.
Rosenberg, Earl H.
    1961.   "A History of the Fishing and Canning Industries in Monterey,
               California." M.A. thesis, University of Nevada, Reno.
Royce, Josiah.
    1886.   *California, from the Conquest to the Second Vigilance Commit-
               tee in San Francisco: A Study of American Character.* Boston:
               Houghton Mifflin.
Ruiz, Vicki L.
    1987.   *Cannery Women, Cannery Lives: Mexican Women, Unionization,
               and the California Food Processing Industry, 1930–1950.* Albu-
               querque: University of New Mexico Press.
Sabatier, Paul A., and Daniel A. Mazmanian.
    1983.   *Can Regulation Work? The Implementation of the 1972 Cali-
               fornia Coastal Initiative.* New York: Plenum Press.
Sánchez, Rosaura.
    1995.   *Telling Identities: The Californio testimonios.* Minneapolis: Uni-
               versity of Minnesota Press.
Sandos, James A.
    1988.   "Junípero Serra's Canonization and the Historical Record."
               American Historical Review 93 (December): 1253–69.
    1989a.   "Junípero Serra, Canonization, and the California Indian Con-
               troversy." *Journal of Religious History* 15 (June): 311–29.
    1989b.   "Junípero Serra and California History." *Californians* 7:2 (March-
               August): 18–25.
Saxton, Alexander.
    1971.   *The Indispensable Enemy: Labor and the Anti-Chinese Move-
               ment in California.* Berkeley: University of California Press.
Schuyler, Robert L.
    1978.   "Indian-Euro-American Interaction: Archaeological Evidence

from Non-Indian Sites." Pp. 69–79 in Robert F. Heizer, ed., *The Handbook of North American Indians,* vol. 8, *California.* Washington, D.C.: Smithsonian Institution Press.

Scofield, W. L.
1929.	"Sardine Fishing Methods at Monterey, California." *Fish Bulletin* 19 (March): 5–61. State of California, Division of Fish and Game.

Serra: American Founding Father.
1987.	Los Angeles: Franciscan Communications.

The Serra Report.
1987.	Monterey: Monterey Diocese.

Shapiro, Samuel.
1961.	*Richard Henry Dana, Jr., 1815–1882.* East Lansing: Michigan State University Press.

Shumate, Albert.
1983.	*Boyhood Days: Ygnacio Villegas' Reminiscences of California in the 1850s.* San Francisco: California Historical Society.

Starr, Kevin.
1973.	*Americans and the California Dream, 1850–1915.* New York: Oxford University Press.
1985.	*Inventing the Dream: California through the Progressive Era.* New York: Oxford University Press.

Stein, Stanley J.
1981.	"Bureaucracy and Business in the Spanish Empire, 1759–1804: Failure of a Bourbon Reform in Mexico and Peru." *Hispanic American Historical Review* 61: 2–28.

Steinbeck, John.
1935.	*Tortilla Flat.* New York: Viking/Penguin.
1941.	*The Log of the Sea of Cortez.* New York: Viking/Penguin.
1945.	*Cannery Row.* New York: Viking/Bantam.

Steinbeck, Elaine, and Robert Wallsten.
1975.	*Steinbeck: A Life in Letters.* New York: Viking/Penguin.

Stevenson, Robert Louis.
1905.	*Across the Plains, 1883–1894.* New York: Scribners.

Stone, Virginia W.
1989.	"Who Was the Real David Jacks?" *Noticias del Puerto de Monterey* (Monterey History and Art Association) 40 (March): 3–13.

Sutherland, Arthur T.
1941.	"Earnings and Hours in Pacific Coast Fish Canneries." *Bulletin of the Women's Bureau,* no. 186. Department of Labor. Washington, D.C.: U.S. Government Printing Office.

Taylor, Alan.
1995.	*William Cooper's Town: Power and Persuasion on the Frontier of the Early American Republic.* New York: Knopf.

Temple, Sydney.
1980.	*The Carmel Mission.* Santa Cruz, Calif.: Western Tanager Press.

Temple, Thomas Workman.
1906.	"The Stormy Catalan, Don Pedro Fages, as Seen Through the Eyes

of Mariano Carrillo." *Historical Society of Southern California* 15: 28–50.

Thompson, E. P.
1966. *The Making of the English Working Class.* New York: Vintage.
1975. *Whigs and Hunters: The Origins of the Black Act.* New York: Pantheon.
1993. *Customs in Common.* New York: New Press.

Tibesar, Antonine.
1955. *Writings of Junípero Serra.* 4 vols. Washington, D.C.: Academy of American Franciscan History.

Trevor-Roper, Hugh.
1983. "The Invention of Tradition: The Highland Tradition of Scotland." Pp. 15–41 in Eric Hobsbawm and Terrance Ranger, eds., *The Invention of Tradition.* Cambridge, Mass.: Cambridge University Press.

Trouillot, Michel-Rolph.
1995. *Silencing the Past: Power and the Production of History.* Boston: Beacon Press.

Tuthill, Franklin.
1866. *The History of California.* San Francisco: Bancroft.

Underhill, Reuben L.
1939. *From Cowhides to Golden Fleece.* Stanford: Stanford University Press.

United States Census of Population.
1850, 1880, Washington, D.C.: U.S. Government Printing Office.
1900, 1930.

Vlach, John Michael.
1993. *Back of the Big House: The Architecture of Plantation Slavery.* Chapel Hill: University of North Carolina Press.

Wagner-Pacifici, Robin, and Barry Schwartz.
1991. "The Vietnam Veterans Memorial: Commemorating a Difficult Past." *American Journal of Sociology* 97:2 (September): 376–420.

Walker, Phillip L., Patricia Lambert, and Michael J. DeNiro.
1989. "The Effects of European Contact on the Health of Alta California Indians." Pp. 349–64 in David Hurst Thomas, ed., *Columbian Consequences,* vol. 1. Washington, D.C.: Smithsonian Institution Press.

Warner, W. Lloyd.
1959. *The Living and the Dead: A Study of the Symbolic Life of Americans.* Yankee City Series, vol. 5. New Haven: Yale University Press.

Weber, David J.
1979. *New Spain's Far Northern Frontier: Essays on Spain in the American West, 1540–1821.* Albuquerque: University of New Mexico Press.
1982. *The Mexican Frontier, 1821–1846: The American Southwest under Mexico.* Albuquerque: University of New Mexico Press.

White, Hayden.

   1973.   *Metahistory: The Historical Imagination in Nineteenth-Century Europe.* Baltimore: Johns Hopkins University Press.

   1987.   *The Content of the Form: Narrative Discourse and Historical Representation.* Baltimore: Johns Hopkins University Press.

Wilde, Oscar.

   1894.   *Intentions.* New York: Dodd, Mead.

Williams, Raymond.

   1977.   *Marxism and Literature.* Oxford: Oxford University Press.

Woolfenden, John, and Amelie Elkinton.

   1983.   *Cooper: Juan Bautista Rogers Cooper, Sea Captain, Adventurer, Ranchero, and Early California Pioneer, 1791–1872.* Pacific Grove, Calif.: Boxwood Press.

WPA Guide to the Monterey Peninsula.

   1989.   Tucson: University of Arizona Press. Originally published in 1941 by the Writers' Program of the Works Progress Administration of Northern California.

Yamada, David.

   1995.   *The Japanese of Monterey Peninsula: Their History and Legacy, 1895–1995.* Monterey: Monterey Peninsula Japanese American Citizens League.

Yancey, William L., Eugene P. Erickson, and Richard N. Juliani.

   1976.   "Emergent Ethnicity: A Review and Reformulation." *American Journal of Sociology* 41(3): 391–40.

Zerubavel, Yael.

   1995.   *Recovered Roots: Collective Memory and the Making of Israeli National Tradition.* Chicago: University of Chicago Press.

Index